Other books by Frank Moore:
*Art of a Shaman*
*Cherotic Magic*
*Chapped Lap*
*Frankly Speaking: A Collection of Essays, Writings and Rants*
*Skin Passion*

*Deep Conversations In The Shaman's Den, Volume I*
by Frank Moore
© Inter-Relations 2015
All rights reserved.

ISBN-13: 978-1511691451
ISBN-10: 151169145X

Cover illustration and book design by Michael LaBash.
Opening page art: Frank Moore's business card by Michael LaBash

Inter-Relations
PO Box 1931
Eagle, ID 83616

Printed by CreateSpace, An Amazon.com Company.

# DEEP CONVERSATIONS IN THE SHAMAN'S DEN

## VOLUME I

# FRANK MOORE

*Frank Moore's letter board (video capture)*

# Preface

In 1998, Frank Moore was surfing the internet looking for an erotic webcam and discovered ARTelevision.com, where three artists, Art, Mimi and Sus were exploring using the webcam as a new performance art form. Frank sent them an email and began an email conversation with Art, who was already aware of Frank's work. In one of Art's emails he mentioned that he was a DJ for an online radio station called FAKE Radio. Frank told Art that he always wanted to be a DJ and Art granted his wish by putting Frank in contact with the creators of the station. Thus was born *Frank Moore's Shaman's Den* which streamed for two plus hours almost every Sunday evening for 14 years.

The Shaman's Den aired on FAKE Radio for just a few months before Frank created his own station, Love Underground Vision Radio (LUVeR). In 2000, the Shaman's Den began streaming as video and Frank changed the name of the station to Love Underground Visionary Revolution (LUVeR) to reflect that.

For the first few Shaman's Den shows, Frank mostly played music and read some of his writings. But soon Frank started inviting people to be guests on the show. These included friends, poets, artists, writers, politicians, musicians, and even entire bands.

Frank was born with cerebral palsy and was spastic. He could utter sounds but not words and communicated by pointing to letters and words on a wooden board strapped to his wheelchair. During each show, Linda (Mac), Frank's lover and partner in crime for 38 years, would sit next to Frank and read his board for the listeners. Mikee (Michael LaBash) was Frank's "tech guy"; he made sure everything ran smoothly. Erika (Shaver-Nelson), whose name appears in a couple of these interviews, is one of Frank's students.

Here is how Frank described the show:

> *"The Shaman's Den will arouse, inspire, move, threaten you, not with sound bites, but with a two hour (usually longer) feast of live streaming video show. You might get an in-studio concert of bands from around the world ... or poetry reading ... or an in-depth conversation about politics, art, music, and LIFE with extremely dangerous people! But then you may see beautiful women naked dancing erotically. You never know, because you are in THE SHAMAN'S DEN with Frank Moore."*

Unfortunately, in most cases, the only photos of these shows are low resolution video captures from the tapes of the Shaman's Den shows, so the quality of the photos in this book are not as good as we would like.

In this, Volume 1, we are just skimming the surface of a deep well of great conversations. There are more volumes to come. Enjoy!

In Freedom,
Linda Mac and Michael LaBash

# Table of Contents

# Paul Krassner

## Conversation Between Two Muckrakers

Recorded April 30, 1994, Berkeley, California

..................................................................................................

"Basically he's one of the Counter culture's mothers ... And one of my heroes since high school when I got into trouble for getting *The Realist*, his no-bars satire zine." – Frank Moore

Paul Krassner's *The Realist* was first published in 1958. Paul went on to be a member of Ken Kesey's Merry Pranksters, and then co-founded the Yippies with Abbie Hoffman and Jerry Rubin. He has been a subversive cultural satirist since the 1950s, wearing many hats ... journalist, author, interviewer, comedian, editor, and joyous muckraker. Like Frank, his work has often blurred the lines between audience and performer, reader and subject.

This interview came out of a short meeting at La Peña in Berkeley, where Frank approached Paul and talked with him after Paul's stand-up performance. During the course of this conversation, Frank showed Paul his zine, *The Cherotic (r)Evolutionary* and asked Paul if he could interview him for it. Paul came over to the house, the two of them together for two hours in Frank's living room with an audio recorder.

Although this conversation was not officially a Shaman's Den show, we have included it in this book as the first step in the evolution of *Frank Moore's Shaman's Den*.

Frank wrote about this interview, "I'm a very lucky guy to be able to spend time with one of my heroes ... who else has dropped acid with Groucho?" He interviewed Paul again six years later, for the Shaman's Den. They corresponded over the years. And when Frank ran for President in 2008, Paul was one of the first to endorse his candidacy.

Frank: "Will you endorse me, bless me, or whatever one does in this situation?"
Paul: "Sure, why not ..."
Frank: "... I smell the vapors of success! Of course, you'll be my security advisor!"

..................................................................................................

**Paul:** Ready when you are coach.

**Frank:** Why have not you gotten big?

**Paul:** (laughs) Well, big is relative. Sometimes people hear my name and they think I'm Paul Kantner from the Jefferson Airplane. And I wonder the same thing myself sometimes. I performed last week and somebody called me an unacknowledged Robin Williams. But I think it's, you know, on one hand it's because I haven't compromised ... and on the other hand it's because I'm lazy.

**Frank:** Me too!

**Paul:** Welcome to the club.

**Frank**: But I have worked hard not to get big.

**Paul**: Well, (laughs) I could handle getting big because I would like to reach a lot of people, but ... and it could happen. I'm ready to sell out. But I wouldn't sell out, they would buy in.

**Frank**: (laughs) Don't you reach a lot of p ...?

**Paul**: P ...? Do I reach a lot of p (laughs) or people? Yeah, well when *The Realist* was a magazine, it reached a hundred thousand people, and a million pass on ... now it's only a newsletter, it reaches 5,000 people and maybe several thousand pass on readership, and then with my book, it sold 15,000 copies and we published in paperback more. So, I think that I'll probably reach more people when I'm dead. (laughs)

**Frank**: Always.

**Paul**: Oh yeah ... it's probably true of Abbie Hoffman and Richard Nixon.

(both laugh)

**Frank**: Why did Abbie (Hoffman) kill himself?

**Paul**: Abbie was clinical manic/depressive ... and he had injured his foot and was in a lot of pain and he was separated from his girlfriend, and he wanted to start a school for organizing but he didn't have the money and so ... I would like for him to have stayed alive, but nobody can judge the level of anybody else's pain, so I guess that was his final act of power to get rid of his pain, physical and emotional and you know it made me sad and angry but it was his choice.

**Frank**: How did you start the Yippies?

**Paul**: We wanted to protest the war in Vietnam and the Yippies was just a name I made up to describe this phenomenon that already existed, it was the hippies and the political activists and at first they thought they were adversaries and the hippies thought that the political activists were just playing the game of the administration and the political activists thought the hippies were dropping out and not being responsible. But then they realized, ah, that if a hippie was smoking a marijuana joint in the park, that was a political act of defying an unjust law. And the hippies saw that the political activists by protesting the war had the same value system and so they began to affect each other. So the political activists started to smoke dope and let their hair grow long and wear tie-dyed shirts and the hippies, instead of just staying in the park, went to anti-war rallies and civil rights demonstrations. So it was happening already ... and sometimes you have to just give a name to something that's already going.

**Frank**: Yes.

**Paul**: Oh, you agree ... that was easy ... I agree with your agreement.

**Frank**: I always i n v e n t ...

**Paul**: Wait, what word am I dealing with here ...? Oh, invent ... yeah.

**Frank**: ... words.

**Paul**: The other word I invented was "soft-core" pornography because the Supreme Court

*Frank Moore and Paul Krassner. Photo by Linda Mac.*

said that hard-core pornography wasn't protected by the First Amendment. And so soft-core pornography meant, you know, they use it in TV commercials ... that's soft-core pornography ... it gives a man a soft-on. What words have you invented?

**Frank:** When I and Linda were in Annie Sprinkle's video on orgasm, she wanted us to do safe sex. (both laugh) But we have been in a relationship for 20 years.

**Paul:** Well, that's about as safe as you can get.

(both laugh)

**Frank:** Exactly. That was what I told Annie. But, (both laugh) she wanted to be politically correct.

**Paul:** (laughs) So some people fake orgasms, you'd have to fake safe sex.

**Frank:** Finally she said we could do soft-core.

(both laugh)

**Paul:** She stole my word.

**Frank:** What is that? (laughs)

**Paul:** Soft-core ... ?

**Frank:** But, we agreed.

(both laugh)

**Paul:** Well that was very agreeable of you ... anything to help out Annie. That's why we were late, we were having dinner with her (Annie) ... and you know, she likes to talk while she's eating.

**Frank:** I just did a review of her show.

**Paul:** Oh yeah? I assume you liked it.

**Frank:** The show, yes. Her (Annie), yes. But, the goddess, no.

**Paul:** That's very interesting, because, she talked about the goddess today and I thought a female god is just as unlikely as a male god. Excellent.

**Frank:** Exactly.

**Paul:** Oh, I'm glad you thought that, because I thought that today, and it's nice to have consensus on reality.

**Frank:** We all have both in us.

**Paul:** Oh, so you objected to her just doing only the female goddess?

**Frank:** The gender.

**Paul:** Well, you know, Robert Anton Wilson once wrote in *The Realist* that if people continue to refer to god as "he" then they should think of a giant penis in the sky.

**Frank:** So, now it is a cunt ...

**Paul:** (laughs)

**Frank:** ... in the sky.

**Paul:** That's right and that's why when we hear thunder it's just cock and cunt fucking in the sky ... that's what thunder is ... and lightning.

**Frank:** Annie is not a s e p e r i s ...

**Paul:** What word am I on ... wait, start again ... Annie is not a ...

**Frank:** Separatist.

**Paul:** Oh, no but she has great cleavage ... that's pretty separate.

**Frank:** But the separatists are using her ...

**Paul:** The separatists are using her? Oh, the separatists are using her ... yeah, you can't control what people do with what you put out. You know, if we didn't get misunderstood, you and me and her, we wouldn't be doing our job right. The separatists are using her ... for what?

**Frank:** To justify their trip.

**Paul:** Right. It's always that way. Everybody has their own agenda and it's true, it's true ... and they'll use us too. But that's OK. It's better than not being used at all.

**Frank:** Don't you build in bombs?

**Paul:** Don't I build in bombs? (laughs) Well, in a way. (both laugh) In a way ... don't I build in bombs? Yeah, to fool them. To fool them? Yes, it's like magic, sometimes, to divert their attention ... if that's what you mean? Or, it's like a lawyer will give seven objections when he only wants one or two, so he builds in a few bombs, if that's what you mean? And if I write something for a magazine, I may put something that I know they'll take out and they'll leave something else in. So if that's what you mean by a bomb, yes, I build them in.

(Frank laughs)

**Frank:** Me too.

**Paul:** Yes, we're the secret bombers.

**Frank:** Are people more serious now?

**Paul:** Some of them are, some of them aren't. I think they both happen at once ... and it's not separate either, it's two sides of the same coin, you know, serious and frivolous. And I think what people get serious about are their own hang-ups.

**Frank:** Maybe I mean fragile.

**Paul:** Oh, more fragile. In a way yeah, because of diseases and because of gangs, you know, fragile because ... it's like what kids in the ghetto have in common with kids in Bosnia at the age of 14 ... they are already planning their funerals. So, that is fragility at it's most heightened state. Yeah, because the quality of life is fragile, so people are more fragile. Yeah, that's an accurate word for it.

**Frank:** When I was growing up, I was dumb. I did not know I could not do things so I did them.

**Paul:** Oh, (laughs) yeah, me too. Right, and then they told you you couldn't do it, but it was too late, 'cause you already did.

**Frank:** But, now people think they cannot and they blame whatever.

**Paul:** They blame whatever? Well, yeah, that's the trend now, blame. That's one of the biggest things is blame. People blame their astrology chart ... people blame their childhood ... and the ultimate is people blame the victim ... it's the victim's fault for getting in my way.

**Frank:** So how can you do satire?

**Paul:** Well, you just report what's happening, and they think you're making it up. I have an article in the new *Realist* on a support group for people who drink their own urine. It's a real group! But people think I made it up. (both laugh) But it doesn't make any difference because it gets in their consciousness.

**Frank:** That was one of the things I loved about *The Realist*.

**Paul:** Me too.

**Frank:** You cannot tell what is real. (laughs)

**Paul:** I know, sometimes I don't even know myself. Sometimes I'm not even sure if the page numbers are real. (laughs)

**Frank:** My dad got pissed at the LBJ ...

**Paul:** LBJ! (laughs)

**Frank:** ... fucking.

(both laugh)

**Paul:** Oh, well, a lot of people got pissed off at that. You know now Frank, that was in 1967, so this is ... '67 ... '77 ... '87 ... twenty what years ... 27 years and people still come up to me and tell me how that blew their minds. So, yeah, I can understand why he would get pissed, you know, it's no surprise.

**Frank:** And my mom thought it was real! (laughs)

**Paul:** Well, it was real. How do you know? A lot of people thought it was real. Sometimes only for five minutes, but that was good enough for me. (laughs) Because they thought Lyndon Johnson was OK for dropping napalm but they thought he was crazy when they read that, and that was the point ... so your mother was in good company. A lot of people thought it was real. But that meant that she thought that LBJ was capable of it.

**Frank:** And he was!

**Paul:** Oh, and he was capable of it ... yes, yes. (laughs)

**Frank:** I like playing with reality.

**Paul:** How do you play with reality? I mean, I do too, but everybody has their own way.

**Frank:** One trick is to say, "But, I may be lying."

**Paul:** I know, do you know the average person lies 25 times a day. But that includes the times we lie to ourselves.

(both laugh)

**Frank:** I do 48-hour performances ...

**Paul:** Forty-eight hours? Well, that's more than I do. If I do an hour and a half I'm satisfied. (laughs)

**Frank:** ... where I mix realities up.

**Paul:** Oh, yeah, well, look, if reality mixes us up, then it's only fair that we mix reality up ... tit for tat. (laughs)

**Frank:** Like Andy ...

**Paul:** Warhol?

**Frank:** ... Kaufman.

**Paul:** Oh, Andy Kaufman? Oh, the comedian? Oh, yeah, yeah ... he did that good. I remember him. He was just on the edge ... you know, you just watch it to see is he really going to go on with this? Yeah, he played with reality ... I like that.

**Frank:** And you were never quite sure.

**Paul:** It's true ... it's true ... he was on the edge ... he was on the edge. He may still be alive, that may be his ultimate playing with reality.

**Frank:** (laughs) That is what *The Realist* did.

**Paul:** Yeah, that was the purpose to find the left and right lobes of the brain and get between.

**Frank:** How did you get there?

**Paul:** Well, I started at *Mad Magazine*. My jacket has Alfred E. Neuman on the back ... "What, me worry?" But that was for teenagers and there was nothing for adults and I wanted something for me, 'cause I figured I wasn't the only one ... I wasn't the only Martian on the block. And so it was kind of to find who else was out there. So we could have our own Martian tribe. So, I was working for Lyle Stuart who had a newspaper called *The Independent* and it was anti-censorship. And so when I started *The Realist* it was a combination of the satire from *Mad* and the anti-censorship from *The Independent*.

**Frank:** But in *Mad* you knew it was not real.

**Paul:** Well, that's true, but I took it a step further because I also published serious stuff and if I labeled it, like *Playboy* labels something: satire, article, fiction ... And I wanted the readers to decide for themselves. I didn't want to take away the pleasure from them. Or I didn't want to take away the confusion from them either. (laughs)

**Frank:** Exactly.

**Paul:** Exactly. I know this board already now ... I can do it with my eyes closed. So, you didn't tell me a word that you invented.

**Frank:** Eroplay.

**Paul:** Eroplay? Oh, like erotic play. I like that, that's good ... OK. Well see, that will be in the dictionary some day ... after we're dead.

**Frank:** People are using it.

**Paul:** For what?

**Frank:** In their language.

**Paul:** Language? Eroplay?

**Frank:** It amazes me ...

**Paul:** Oh, yeah. I know.

**Frank:** ... how fast.

**Paul:** It's true. 'Cause everything is accelerating now. In the '60s when the word "black" replaced the "negro", they didn't do it right away. But now, when "african american" replaced "black", they did it quicker, 'cause everything's accelerating ... including "soft-core" and "eroplay".

(both laugh)

**Frank:** How did you get to edit Lenny ...

**Paul:** ... Lenny Bruce's book? Well, *Playboy Magazine* serialized it and they knew that Lenny and I knew each other and he was writing it but ... they needed somebody to help structure it and to draw him out ... get questions answered. And so they asked me. And I jumped at the chance, because he was a rare individual and influenced comedians today who don't even know they were influenced by him. And he was attacked for the language he used, but he was really attacked because he used organized religion as a target. And that was really why they went after him.

**Frank:** Who ...

**Paul:** ... Lenny Bruce we're talking about ... oh ...

**Frank:** ... but, who went after him?

**Paul:** Well, the police ... if the police would go after him in San Francisco, then the police in Los Angeles would say we got to go after him, then the police in Chicago say well we got to go after him. Especially in Chicago where the church was big. When he was on trial in Chicago it was Ash Wednesday, and all the jurors and the judge and the prosecutor had the ash on their forehead there. It was very spooky.

**Frank:** I am playing dumb ...

**Paul:** Oh, well, I am dumb. I am playing dumb ... OK ... devil's advocate.

**Frank:** ... because lots of people don't know.

**Paul:** Oh, yeah, of course, that's right. OK, well, when you play dumb, you're playing with reality again.

(both laugh)

**Frank:** They think he self-destructed.

**Paul:** Yeah, a lot of his friends thought that at the time. But, you know, it's just a matter of opinion. I think to be consistent with your principles is not self-destructive, but a lot of people thought he should compromise. And that would have been self-destructive.

**Frank:** They say he was not funny any more.

**Paul:** He got serious, but ... when I first interviewed Lenny I asked him, "What's the role of a comedian?" And he said, "To get a laugh every 15 to 25 seconds." But then later on, when he was reading from court transcripts and police records ... and I said to him, "Lenny, you're not getting a laugh every 15 to 25 seconds." (both laugh) And he said, "Yes, but I'm changing." And I said, "What do you mean?" He said, "Well, I'm not a comedian, I'm Lenny Bruce." So he knew that he had become a symbol of free speech. He was still funny, but he didn't get a laugh every 15 to 25 seconds. He was funny sardonic.

**Frank:** It is like when Mort (Sahl) went after JFK's killers.

**Paul:** That's true, yeah, he dropped out, Mort Sahl dropped out and worked for Jim Garrison as a researcher. And he wasn't funny then. And there were times when I got heavy into conspiracy and the readers would complain. And I said, "Sometimes you have to earn the right to be funny."

(both laugh)

**Frank:** Who is doing that today?

**Paul:** You mean besides me? (laughs)

**Frank:** And me!

(both laugh)

**Paul:** Just us. Nobody else. No, there's a few, there's a few ... there's a comedian named Jimmy Tingle who's good. There's Elayne Boosler, who's good. There's a few. But most of them talk about their first date or TV commercials or airplane food. They're like clones on a conveyor belt in a factory, most comedians. But there are a few good ones.

**Frank:** How about the black?

**Paul:** Yeah, there's a few. There's a guy named Franklyn Ajaye who's excellent. Who else ... ? A lot of the black comedians are very raunchy. But who else is good that I've seen ... ? Richard Pryor is kind of sick. Dick Gregory is making diet powder. (laughs) There are some new black comedians, but I think that Franklyn Ajaye and Paul Mooney are two of the best. I haven't seen them all. They have them on *HBO Def Comedy Jam*, but they do such raunchy material that it makes me blush. (both laugh) And I support their right to do it, but sometimes you wonder if they don't have a larger vocabulary.

**Frank:** If they have a big picture ...

**Paul:** But they want to be successful, and so they don't always have the big picture. A few of them do, but they're afraid their audience ... they make a separation ... once again separation ... they make a separation between them and the audience. Whereas you and I don't. You know, we respect the audience, that they either get us or they don't.

**Frank:** That is what is wrong with Dennis Miller.

**Paul:** Dennis Miller? That's a good point because he likes to show off his references ... but he's better than a lot of others. He's OK ... he could be better but ...

**Frank:** But he is all over the place.

**Paul:** Yeah, I know, but so is pollution. (both laugh)

**Frank:** I mean in his act.

**Paul:** Oh yeah, yeah, because he'll pull out a reference from a TV show from 1940, and then from a musical group from 1990 ... yeah, but he means well ... but then so did Hitler.

**Frank:** That is what is scary.

**Paul:** Yeah, I know, but what would we do if we didn't have something to be scared about.

**Frank:** People who mean well can do more harm.

**Paul:** Oh yeah. Wasn't that a Barbra Streisand song ... "People who mean well can do more harm ... " (both laugh) Yeah, it's true, it's true, because they're self-righteous about it and they think that they're on a mission from god.

**Frank:** And people feel they are honest.

**Paul:** Yeah, well, that's what I said before ... that in the 25 lies a day that we tell, a lot of them are to ourselves. Because if you want to deceive other people, you have to deceive yourself first. That's a prerequisite.

**Frank:** How about Bill Maher?

**Paul:** Oh, Bill Maher. I like him. I was on his show, *Politically Incorrect*. And he's an ex-Catholic who took acid. (Frank laughs) And so, he had Tim Leary on ... he has people on that other people don't. He's good. He's nice and irreverent. He's wrong on some positions, but, that's only because I disagree with him.

**Frank:** Yes, but he has a big picture.

**Paul:** Yeah, he does, he does. Do you watch his show ... do you get cable?

**Frank:** Yes.

**Paul:** Yeah, he has several writers but ... he's excellent. I've seen him do reports for Jay Leno from events. And he's very irreverent and very smart. He doesn't talk down to the listeners. Yeah, he's good ... I forgot to mention him. He's good.

**Frank:** What would you like to do that you have not done?

**Paul:** That I have not done? (both laugh) It's a big question. OK ... write a novel. Fuck three girls at once. And be young again. Oh, I've done that already ... cancel that one. (Frank laughs) Have unlimited power. (laughs)

**Frank:** For what?

**Paul:** Just for the hell of it. You mean, the power? Oh, to make miracles. Somebody just asked Ram Dass what he thinks is the most important question of the twenty-first century. And he thought, and he thought, and he thought for a long while, then he said, "How can we get rid of greed?" So if I had unlimited power, I would just say, "Greed is out and compassion is in!" And then I'd get some fudge.

(both laugh)

**Frank:** One time I took my students to a drug conference and when I walked into the lobby Leary ran up and hugged me.

**Paul:** Yeah, that was one of the things about the '60s, that men could hug other men. Before that it was considered homosexual, instead of just love.

**Frank:** And then Dass ...

**Paul:** Ram Dass? Oh well, he had an extra hug.

**Frank:** ... hugged me. And (laughs) then the widow of Huxley ...

**Paul:** Huxley ... oh, Laura Huxley ... she's still around.

**Frank:** (laughs) ... hugged me.

**Paul:** It was a regular hug fest. A lot of hugging.

**Frank:** And during the intermission I was flapping my arms ...

**Paul:** (laughs) Arms? (claps and laughs)

**Frank:** ... and Leary started flapping his.

(both laugh)

**Paul:** Him too! (laughs) Yeah, that's good. He's a good mirror.

**Frank:** Was I on drugs or what?

**Paul:** Maybe, maybe not. Only you know for sure.

**Frank:** How could I tell? Your test did not work!

**Paul:** Well, it must have worked, if you thought you were dreaming ... if you were flapping your arms. (Frank laughs) At that point it doesn't make any difference. Reality was playing

11

with you again. (Frank laughs) But in order to flap his arms he had to stop hugging you.

**Frank:** The two groupies did not know what was going on. (laughs)

**Paul:** I know, it's a secret language. When I performed at an island off Canada where I did the flapping my arms thing. And for two weeks after that everybody on the island was flapping their arms. It was good. I added that to the language. But nonverbal language.

**Frank:** What should I ask? (laughs)

**Paul:** Let me think. Am I optimistic or pessimistic?

**Frank:** OK. Or a realist.

**Paul:** Realist? Well, because I'm a realist, I'm optimistic on Monday, Wednesday and Friday; I'm pessimistic on Tuesday, Thursday and Saturday, and Sunday I rest ... my case.

**Frank:** A realist is an idealist.

**Paul:** I know, but don't tell anybody!

**Frank:** Skeptic ...

**Paul:** Yeah, I'm a professional skeptic. I wish I could get paid to be a skeptic, 'cause that's what I do. (laughs)

**Frank:** Don't you?

**Paul:** What, get paid for being a skeptic? That's true I do, yeah. See how quickly my wish came true. (laughs)

**Frank:** I do. (laughs)

**Paul:** Get paid for being a skeptic? Welcome to the club. (laughs)

**Frank:** People think cynical is the same.

**Paul:** No. No. 'Cause a cynic is negative and a skeptic searches for the truth. It's a big difference.

**Frank:** Cynicism is a illness.

**Paul:** Right. And a cynic thinks there's no cure for this. (both laugh) Yeah, it's too bad but ... you know, people get their identity from any number of things, and some people get their identity from being cynical. And they go to a party and they're cynical. And then their personality freezes that way. Our mothers were right.

**Frank:** Is that what happened in the '80s?

**Paul:** Is that what happened in the '80s? Yeah, yeah, people ... yeah ... it was a combination of greed and cynicism and selfishness. It's all the same. Yeah, money became more important than people. But a lot of those same people now are getting more socially conscious. You know, some of the baby boomers had babies themselves, and when they saw hypodermic needles washing in from the ocean, they thought they better do something about it. So I think some of the greed has changed to social consciousness. But that may just be wishful thinking.

**Frank:** No.

**Paul:** No? It's not wishful thinking?

**Frank:** Because the people who come to my performances have changed.

**Paul:** Have changed? How have they changed?

**Frank:** Like in the '70s they had dreams about freedom. They wanted it. They may not have thought it was possible ...

**Paul:** Yeah, well, but, you know, it always starts with a dream.

**Frank:** In the '80s (laughs) they had not dreams and did not want it and why was I forcing them. (laughs)

**Paul:** (laughs) I give up. Why?

**Frank:** In the '90s they have not dreams, but when they find it, they want it.

**Paul:** Well, that's a hopeful sign. At least they think it's possible. Even if they stumble on it. When I travel around I meet a lot of young people who are the way we were in the '60s. Except they have less innocence. We were innocent.

**Frank:** What do you think of zines?

**Paul:** They're like the underground press was in the '60s. Because now there are the alternative papers but they're like a farm team for the mainstream. So they want to get discovered. In the '60s the underground press, like the zines now, were a form of personal revolution as opposed to the alternative papers, which are just a good career move.

**Frank:** (laughs) In a way you are the root.

**Paul:** Oh, in a way, but I had my roots ... it keeps going back ... to the cave people. (both laugh) When they were writing on the cave walls, there was somebody who was writing on a rock in the field. And that was the first underground paper.

**Frank:** I always get the criticism I am old-fashioned.

**Paul:** Old-fashioned? You old-fashioned?

**Frank:** They say I do '60s art. (laughs)

**Paul:** Well, so what? If you like it ... you have to do what comes from your insides.

**Frank:** I say I am more old-fashioned. I do cave (art).

(both laugh)

**Paul:** That's real old-fashioned (claps and laughs). That's right. Pre ... even before the caveman ... when you were a fish. (both laugh) Yes, right. I guess I'm old-fashioned too, then. Oh, our time has gone.

**Frank:** When did art become fashion?

**Paul:** Oh, well, you know, Abbie Hoffman said fashion is fascism. So, whenever people buy something, if they spend money on it, they think it must be art. 'Cause they don't want to waste their money. But, you know, art is ... true art is self-expression and that's very often out of fashion. And when we get in fashion, we better start worrying.

**Frank:** I have been doing what I am doing for 25 years.

**Paul:** How will you know when you're finished?

(both laugh)

**Frank:** Sometimes it is in fashion. Sometimes it is not.

**Paul:** Monday, Wednesday and Friday ... Tuesday, Thursday and Saturday ... !

**Frank:** I do the same thing. (laughs)

**Paul:** You don't change?

**Frank:** It evolves.

**Paul:** That's right.

**Frank:** But, they think I don't change.

**Paul:** Well, fuck 'em! That's what I say. Fuck 'em if they can't take a change.

**Frank:** And when I am in fashion, I have to work hard to not get big.

**Paul:** That's where we started.

(both laugh)

**Frank:** You always have inspired me.

**Paul:** Well, I'll tell you Frank, it's a two-way street 'cause you inspire me. So, let's continue to inspire each other.

**Frank:** How?

**Paul:** How? Because you work hard ... and you say what you mean ... and you communicate. It's difficult to communicate and you do it. And that's the most important thing ... that's what life is about is communication. And I respect it a lot. So, what else is there to do in life but communicate. You know, and you do it with passion and honesty. So that's inspiring.

**Frank:** That is a great end.

**Paul:** Better than death. (both laugh) Very nice interview. Excellent. I had a good time.

# Stephen Emanuel

Recorded February 25, 2007 on luver.com

.......................................................................................................................

As Steve wrote when Frank passed away, "I first met Frank way back in 1968 on the quad at the campus of Cal State San Bernardino … I was the young hippie riding a skateboard to class and he was, Frank … in the chair with his pointer and board. We instantly connected and soon were stirring up controversy and trouble in that little pond."

Steve is now a registered nurse in Oregon. He is also a musician and has played bass with Les Gendarmes du Swing, the Wild Whiskey Boys, The Primal Music Syndicate, Mescal Martini, the DadoSa Band, Jazzmind and many others. He played upright bass with Frank and with Frank's Cherotic All-Star Band a number of times after catching up with Frank again in 2006, including several performances in Los Angeles when Frank toured there as part of his campaign for President. Steve gave a "fiery passionate introduction speech" for Frank at Il Corral, an underground music club in L.A.

This interview is a look into the history of the 1960s, 1970s, and beyond through Steve's and Frank's stories. At the same time, they share an alternate approach to life that endures, and talk about how the small acts we perform in our daily lives and relationships have deep and powerful effects.

.......................................................................................................................

**Frank:** I met this dude 40 years ago in San Bernardino, California. He was barefo …

**Linda:** He was barefoot.

**Frank:** On a s …

**Steve:** Skateboard …

**Frank:** Throwing a Frisbee. Playing a harmonica.

**Linda:** All at the same time. (laughs)

**Frank:** He turned into one of the most important people in my life. What does that say about my life? (laughter) Steve Emanuel!

**Linda:** Take it, Steve!

**Steve:** It's always an honor to be in the presence of Frank, to be perfectly frank, which is something it is impossible for me to be, but anyways. Yeah, Frank and I go back quite a ways and we've had some rather amazing and unusual experiences together which we will probably speak about in a little bit.

**Frank:** He is (Frank sounds) taller than …

**Linda:** Taller than you! That's not talk show etiquette … the host is taller than the guest. (laughing)

**Steve:** Well, I've never been much for etiquette! (laughing)

**Frank:** Do you remember the first time you saw me?

**Steve:** Oh yeah, man, Cal State, San Bernardino. (Frank sounds) That was just a small campus, there really wasn't much to it at that point.

**Frank:** And a new campus.

**Steve:** And a new campus too, and so ... It was only the second year the thing had been there. There weren't even any dorms or anything. So, everybody had to live off campus, which was kind of fun, actually. It was better that way. 'Cause there was this funky neighborhood mostly near by and ... which was a real mixed up neighborhood, that's where we met our mutual friend, Louise, she had this hippie commune down the street from where I lived and so ...

**Frank:** Really, it was before I met Louise.

**Steve:** Yeah, right, well I introduced you to Louise 'cause I found Frank on campus and gravitated towards him 'cause he was about the most interesting thing on that campus, you know. There were some pretty girls, I will admit (laughs).

**Frank:** Why was ...

**Linda:** Frank interesting?

**Steve:** Well, look at him ... he's interesting (laughter) period. What the heck, plus I rapidly found out he's a rather outrageous character and you know, that's the part that I liked the best, was the fact that he's just, you know, out there! And I being somewhat out there at the time myself, you know, it was a logical association, shall we say, it fell together pretty easily, and, um ... it was a neat time, you know. It was 1968, things were kind of really hopping, you know in terms of the changes that were happening to the way people thought about things especially in the college situation where people's ... You know, it was just a real new era. I mean, it didn't last very long, but it was a very new era while it lasted for those four or five years that it was like that. It was just really, you know, very expanding to the way people thought and felt, the way they acted. The kind of relationships they had with each other were ... a lot of it was really new ... much of it didn't last! Most people did not have the emotional equipment or the endurance or whatever, to really pull that off, you know. Every once in awhile I'll run into somebody who knew you back then and what happened to poor Frank (Linda laughs) ... well, I'll tell you, bro ... you know, he's not doing quite so bad as you might have expected (laughing).

You know at that time when I first met Frank and we were first palling around with each other, I don't know, it just, it seemed real natural ... you would be you, the way you are and I would be me, the way I was, you know, we're both kind of societal misfits, in our own peculiar way. Maybe I elected to be that way, but I really didn't have any choice either, you know what I mean. I was going to be like that. You know, you grow up like you're going to grow up. And you're raised the way you're raised and I grew up in a bohemian atmosphere. There was always all kinds of people throughout the households that I grew up in. Artists and musicians of all types, and races and ages and all that stuff.

*Frank Moore and Stephen Emanuel (video capture)*

(Frank sounds)

**Frank:** I grew up ...

**Linda:** Military dad, ex-Mormon mom ...

**Steve:** Yeah, right. He came out of this horribly repressive situation and then that caregiver you had back then was a mother fucker. (Frank sounds)

**Linda:** The guy who pulled the gun?

**Steve:** Yeah, right. So you know ...

**Frank:** I called the Black Panthers ...

**Linda:** When the guy pulled the gun.

**Steve:** It was funny, back then, because you know we had our little SDS chapter. They weren't even called the Black Panthers back then, you know, they'd kind of listen to you every once in a while.

**Frank:** They hid me for two days.

**Steve:** Yeah, I vaguely remember that whole situation. (Frank sounds)

**Frank:** And I talked to Moe (Frank sounds). I did not know him ...

**Linda:** Moe? You talked to him but you didn't know him.

**Frank:** But I said I need a place to go. He ...

**Linda:** He was a fellow student at the campus?

**Steve:** Yeah, right.

**Linda:** You didn't know him but you told him you needed a place to go. So, he set it up.

**Steve:** Yeah, right.

**Linda:** What did he set up?

**Frank:** A house and his two friends were my attendants.

**Linda:** So he set all that up. (Frank sounds)

**Steve:** Right.

**Linda:** And you knew Moe at that point (to Steve)?

**Steve:** Yeah, I knew Moe. Well, you know, it's a small college and ... less than a thousand people there.

**Frank:** In fact, you moved into the house.

**Steve:** Right. (Frank sounds)

**Linda:** But you guys already knew each other?

**Steve:** Yeah, right. (Frank sounds)

**Linda:** And you moved into the house through Frank?

**Steve:** Yeah, more or less, yeah (Frank sounds). I had a lot of households back then. (laughs) (Frank sounds)

**Frank:** You was the first who dared to help me drop acid.

(Steve laughs, Frank sounds)

**Steve:** I helped everybody drop acid (laughs) (all laugh). Yeah, you know, I wasn't scared, you know, I give a lot of people acid, and you know, I didn't see why Frank should be any different. (laughs)

**Frank:** People would give me pot ...

**Linda:** ... but they wouldn't give you acid.

**Steve:** Yeah, they wouldn't give him acid. You know, I don't know, LSD was always and probably still is my favorite mind-altering substance and, um ... I was into it back then. I thought it was good for people. I realized it wasn't good for everybody, OK. But for people that I felt had a strong inner character, it was quite a transformative kind of experience. I think more than anything else it really changed people's minds about what was going on at the time. It was like a shortcut to figuring out that there was a whole different way of perceiving things. And that there was a whole other realm of consciousness beyond ordinary thought and there was a whole different way to interplay with your senses beyond just the usual way you did it. You know. In my personal life, it completely changed the way I looked at things and it affects me today. Not that I have flashbacks all the time ... I wish ... it'd be nice ... it's just a fundamental shift in attitude that happened when at certain significant experiences that I had under psychedelic drugs that really made me lose the distance and separation that I had between my self and the world and myself and other people and kind of ... that has really endured. The fact that it's all one cosmic world and one cosmic cosmos and that our ... what was funny is there's some books now, written by physicists that explore the relationships between ultimate physics and (Frank sounds) transcendental meditation kind of things ... and also, I had this book ... well, the preface is this, you know, one of the first times I took LSD was at this outdoor concert, one of the first big outdoor concerts in the L.A. area. I whacked down some LSD with this friend of mine and we got this revelation about how it really is, how this whole thing works. And it was this whole reality comb theory of existence. We had this comb that funneled down, like all the possibilities and then there was like, your little brain down here that filtered it into this line that was hooked to the reality of the world. Well, a few years ago I found this book on Tai Chi that's actually a really gnarly, very extremely sophisticated book on Tai Chi, and here's this same damn diagram in that book. Basically explaining the same thing from a 2,500-year-old Chinese idea. Which then indicates to me, well then, my idea was not just a psychedelic flash. (Frank sounds) It was actually tapping into a certain version of reality that is shared by a bunch of people. That is a legitimate way to look at things. I mean, obviously, we create this entire reality with our brains. Our brains are completely responsible for all this stuff. You know what I mean? Well, you say, when I die does it all go away? Well for me it does, but still, every single person creates the universe by the act of being here and thinking and experiencing it makes it be what it is. And, if we ... if our senses were tuned slightly differently, it'd be a completely different universe, you know. Which would get to be real interesting with people like synesthesia. People that see, read everything in colors. All the letters have colors, every time they read them. Or when they hear music, it always comes out in colors in their mind. And that one note will have the same color every time for that particular person. Well, on psychedelics you'd experience that every once in a while, you know for two hours or three hours or something like this. Some people have that permanently.

**Frank:** Especially hiking on someone's shoulders through the woods at Big Bear ...

**Steve:** Oh, Big Bear?

**Frank:** In the winter on acid.

(laughter)

**Linda:** Which was your experience!

(all laugh)

**Frank:** Or trying to eat dinner ...

**Linda:** Oh, with your mom feeding you? At the dinner table with your mom and dad and brother (Steve laughs) ... on acid.

**Steve:** Yeah, I remember one time I had to paint my mother's kitchen on acid. (laughter) I forgot I committed myself to that one. I painted her kitchen electric yellow. (all laugh) It was interesting.

**Frank:** Hey, so what is wrong with that ...

**Linda:** Electric yellow? The same colors we painted ...

**Steve:** Electric yellow is fine. It's just when you open up a can and look at it when you're tripping. I'd taken an extra large dose that day 'cause I was going down (unidentified play) to go play. The amazing part is that she never really figured it out. (laughs) I'm a pretty good painter, even when I'm stoned.

(Frank sounds)

**Frank:** So, what are other things about what we did?

**Steve:** Well, other things about what we did. Well, of course I always loved the time we went up to Lama Foundation. That was a gas. Lama Foundation is this place up near Taos, New Mexico. Extremely gorgeous up there. And it's a retreat place. A spiritual retreat. Baba Ram Dass was one of the original founders of this place.

**Frank:** On a st ...

**Steve:** Side of a big old mountain, man, I'm telling you, it's steep up there, OK. And you drive up there on this long, windy, dirt road. Taos is down here on the plains and huge mountains that are up behind it, and it's absolutely gorgeous and Lama's Mountain is a little bit north and west of Taos. The actual foundation up there is probably about 9,000 feet where it sits. And Taos is like 7,000. So, you climbed up this funky old dirt road and you finally get back and there's the parking lot. Well, the Lama Foundation is way up here (gesturing). And it's just a dirt trail (sounds and laughing). And I get Frank in his wheelchair and we roll on up, you know. What the hell. We're there to have fun. (laughing) I think it was Chögyam Trungpa that was doing the lecture that day. That Tibetan guy who ...

**Linda:** Yeah.

**Frank:** Up was o ...

**Steve:** Up was OK, yes, going up was OK! (all laughing) Then we went up there and we heard this lecture, and it was really fun. Very interesting, this guy Chögyam Trungpa. That was who it was, wasn't it. (Frank sounds) Yeah. Chögyam Trungpa was one of the first Tibetan lamas who really brought a lot of Tibetan Buddhism to the West in a very deliberate manner. I mean, he came here. It was so funny. We go up to see this guy ... and everybody's like ... oh, the holy man is going to come out ... and everybody's expecting some guy in some lemon saffron robes. He comes out he looks just like a Navajo. He's got a cowboy hat on, he's got cowboy boots on. He's got a quart of Miller's. (all laughing) (Steve makes a can popping sound) He opens up the Miller's chug chug and then proceeds to give this really wonderful spiritual discourse, right.

**Frank:** Every holy man you've ever met was a dirty old man.

**Steve:** Well, you know, come on, you're coming from the highlands of Tibet, then you come here and there's all these cute little California girls, (laughing) come on. That's why I've decided, you know, once I get finished doing all this work, I'm going to start a new religion and it'll appeal to college girls, I'm sure! (laughing)

**Frank:** Hey, I ...

**Linda:** Frank did start a religion!

**Steve:** Well, I'll be a high priest or something. Anyway! I'll be a priest that's high. Anyway. So, we're up there and we watch this whole thing and it's very nice in this absolutely lovely place, like I say. Then we decide to come back down. And of course, me being in the sort of hell raiser category decided that, well, Frank doesn't ever get to do anything fun, everybody treats Frank nice and never like risks his life in anything interesting, so I just hop on the back of the wheelchair (Linda says, ooooohhhh!) and we go down the trail. (laughing) Well, we rapidly pick up a lot of speed. And when we hit that third boulder, I guess it was, man, we wiped out good, man. (laughing) Bent his chair beyond recognition. We both went ass over tea kettle down the hill. (Steve makes crashing sounds) I mean, his wheelchair was totally bent. They had to give you a whole new wheelchair, right? (laughing)

**Frank:** Not for eight ...

**Linda:** Weeks?

**Steve:** Oh yeah, that's right. It took eight weeks to get the ...

**Frank:** Whole months ...

**Linda:** Eight whole months! You were without a chair?

**Steve:** Scott fixed it together, man. A Scottish guy we used to call Scott. I think he was the one that pounded that thing back together if I don't miss my guess. (laughing)

**Frank:** Tell Steve about Ram Dass.

**Linda:** Oh, when we met him. We went to ... there was a thing about psychedelics at a big hotel here, the Claremont. (Frank sounds) This was in the late '80s. And it was Leary and Ram Dass and ... oh man, there was a bunch of them.

**Frank:** L ...

**Linda:** The widow of Huxley.

**Steve:** Huxley's widow. Laura Huxley or whatever her name is.

**Linda:** Yeah, and um .. So you want to talk about Ram Dass in particular? Well first of all, we go into this hotel, and Leary spots us and comes running up to us. There were at the time ... Frank brought all of his students. It was kind of a class project. (Steve laughs, Frank sounds) It was Frank and I, and Mikee was there, Alexi, and maybe 2 or 3 other people, so there was a bunch of us. And we were looking the way we look now. But he ... we've never met him before ... he spots us and comes running up to us like we were his long lost friends, hugging everybody, hi, it's so great to see you and stuff. And it's like, whoa, it's starting to have that kind of "acidy" feeling. (Steve laughs) And it just kept happening. Ram Dass did the same thing. Came up to us like old lost friends. Huxley did the same thing. It was all scattered throughout the night.

**Frank:** Then ...

**Linda:** Oh, you and Leary? And then, Frank and Leary were playing. There was like an intermission and we were just cruising around the halls, and he was sitting there with these two young, very earnest guys and they were hanging on his every word. (Steve laughs) And we're wheeling by and as Frank wheels up next to him Frank is flailing his arms around, and Leary, boom, picks up on it right away and in the middle of talking to these guys he ...

**Steve:** Starts to moving around ... (laughing)

**Linda:** Starts moving his arms around. And so there the two of them are, doing this little dance together, and the two earnest ones are looking like they're trying to figure out what's going on. (Steve laughing)

**Steve:** That's like those Zen stories of this guy who goes to visit the master, and the master's out in the middle of the forest and he's raking leaves in the middle of the wild forest. And the guy is like, let me take that rake from you. He's raking away industriously and suddenly realizes what the fuck am I doing? Can you imagine, what are you doing? Raking leaves in the forest. Why are you raking leaves in the forest? I know why I was doing it, but why are you doing it? (laughing) Similar kind of moment for those guys.

**Frank:** You dropped me off at the community in Massachusetts? Oh no, at Louise's ... at the crash pad in Santa Fe.

**Steve:** Oh yeah!

**Linda:** Tell about that?

**Steve:** You mean the old crisis center thing?

**Frank:** Yes. You left.

**Linda:** You dropped Frank off and left.

**Steve:** I had to go down to Albuquerque or some place. I can't remember.

**Frank:** Back to San Bernardino.

**Steve:** Oh, I had to go back to San Berdoo. We took you out here and stuff you there. I remember that. Once again, it was under the whole idea of, Frank never gets to do anything. So, let's get him out to do something, you know. So a bunch of us got together and dragged his funky ass out here. That was an epic little voyage in that Nissan Centro or whatever the hell it was. With Marty, remember Marty? A young guy named Marty.

**Frank:** Yes.

**Steve:** Yeah, he drove all the way. (Steve laughing)

**Linda:** Frank tells the story of about how he was at the crisis center, 'cause Louise was supposed to come out shortly, but it took her a whole lot longer.

**Steve:** It took her a whole lot longer (laughing) yeah, yeah, yeah.

**Linda:** So he was there with no money or anything.

**Steve:** Oh, yeah.

**Linda:** Hoping that every morning there'd be somebody that would feed him and dress him and stuff. (Steve laughing)

**Steve:** Well that made you develop your skills better now, didn't it? (Frank sounds)

**Frank:** It took you a while to move out to Santa Fe.

**Steve:** Yeah, what hung me up that time ... I went back and forth between Berdoo and Santa Fe so many times, man. I know that road completely. I could drive it with my eyes closed backwards, I'll tell you! We thought nothing of commuting back and forth.

(Frank sounds)

**Frank:** We again lived together ...

**Linda:** ... in Santa Fe ...

**Steve:** Yeah, we had several pads in Santa Fe actually. Our mutual friend, Louise, was kind of at the center of a lot of those pads. And she became a very important caregiver, and her whole ... she had a whole family, kids and all that kind of stuff ... it was a natural thing. I'd known Louise for a really long ... you know, I met her when I first moved to San Bernardino. Like I said, there was this community close by there, Muscoy. And just about everybody in the world lived in Muscoy. Man, you had bikers living next to evangelical Christians. Some people actually had money there. Most people were pretty poor. And she had this commune down the block and that's where the whole connection to Santa Fe came in. Because some of those people started drifting up to Santa Fe and then dragged us all out there eventually, basically. So we had quite a few households out there. And then I drifted down to college in Albuquerque.

(Frank sounds)

**Frank:** I went to Massachusetts.

**Steve:** Right. And that was an amazing little thing right there because ... we were hanging out at this crisis center ... I worked there and Frank hung out there. And we were all sort of involved in this thing. It was the first crisis center in Santa Fe. So Frank used to hang out there, and people would come by, and it was kind of like a place that people traveling through would kind of tend to breeze through to see what was going on. There were posters up about what was going on around town, etc. So, you met these people that came through from this commune in Massachusetts. There was some guy that was the head dude and a big house, you know, the whole nine yards back East, you know. (Frank sounds) So, Frank says to them, I'll come out and visit!

**Frank:** Three ...

*Stephen Emanuel (video capture)*

**Linda:** 300, there were 300 people.

**Steve:** Yeah.

**Frank:** Not to visit ...

**Linda:** You said you wanted to move there. (Frank sounds)

**Steve:** Yeah, right. You had me put up a card on the ride board: I need a ride to Massachusetts. (laughing) Whatever, Frank, you know. (laughing) So you know, I put up a card: I need a ride to Massachusetts. And then these two kids come and give him a ride! (Frank sounds) What they're like 16 and 17, a brother and sister!

**Frank:** B ...

**Linda:** Yeah, a brother and sister.

**Steve:** A brother and sister! And, well, ...

(Frank starts spelling ... d ...)

**Steve:** This is how you do it, you know ... this is all the equipment and you're going to have to like do it all, you know! How did they do? (Frank sounds)

(Frank makes sounds)

**Linda:** They were alright.

**Steve:** They were alright, yeah! They were OK! I had a feeling. They seemed like good kids, you know.

**Frank:** But they ...

**Linda:** Just dropped him at the community, and left ...

**Steve:** Yeah, 3 in the morning or something like that, right?

**Frank:** No, after ...

**Linda:** In the afternoon?

**Frank:** But I ...

**Linda:** He beat the people there that he had met, so no one knew that he was coming.

**Steve:** Right! Yeah, so here he just shows up. Here's this guy sitting out there in a wheelchair in front of the place, right: Hi, I'm moving here! (laughs)

**Frank:** People ...

**Linda:** ... freaked out.

**Steve:** Well geez, I know (laughing) like I say, most people just don't have the emotional equipment to handle this kind of thing. (laughing)

**Frank:** But the ...

**Linda:** ... leader of the group?

**Frank:** Walked by ...

**Linda:** ... walked by, as they were freaking out and trying to figure out what to do with you.

**Frank:** And said, "He stays!" (Frank screams, Linda laughs)

**Steve:** That's what I'm saying, you develop skills after a while. (Frank sounds, laughing) Yeah, so that's how Frank got out of Santa Fe for a while. It's pretty funny. Then we got a phone call that he had gotten married. We were like, OK ... we gotta meet this girl (laughing).

**Frank:** That is the 3 a.m ...

**Linda:** That's the 3 a.m. call.

**Steve:** Oh yeah, right. (laughing)

**Frank:** We (Frank sounds) tried San Francisco ...

**Linda:** You and Debbie tried to move to San Francisco.

**Frank:** Moe gave us some money ...

**Linda:** So that you could get a place. (Frank sounds)

**Frank:** But we were kicked out of four places in four days, four nights.

**Steve:** That gets a little boring.

**Frank:** (Frank sounds) This was before …

**Linda:** … disabled rights.

**Steve:** Yeah, well, had a lot of work to do back then.

(Frank sounds)

**Frank:** So I took a bus to …

**Linda:** … to Albuqu … to Santa Fe. (Frank sounds) And that was the 3 a.m. call?

**Frank:** And Belle was just driving by.

**Steve:** Oh, Belle Carpenter. Belle Carpenter was a friend that we had out there. She was actually a somewhat wealthy woman. A just absolutely lovely, gracious creature. I mean, if there ever was a woman to be named Belle, she was it. And she was even from the South. And she was just absolutely wonderful, compassionate, gorgeous human being. (Frank sounds) And you know, she just showed up right at the right time, you know. (Frank sounds) I loved Belle, she was wonderful.

**Frank:** And called Louise. (Frank sounds)

**Steve:** Right. (Frank sounds)

**Frank:** Guess who is in town? (laughing)

**Steve:** Who is back in town! (laughing)

**Linda:** That's when you found out that Frank was married?

**Steve:** No, we got a phone call right after he got married. And we were just going like, whoa, we got to see this girl. And then he shows up and like, wow … alrighty Frank! (Frank sounds) So then we all kind of regathered the entourage together for awhile. (laughing) (Frank sounds)

**Frank:** Stayed with you.

**Linda:** You and Debbie stayed with Steve.

**Steve:** Yeah, I was down at my place in Albuquerque, right? Yeah. I had kind of gone back to college. I was going to college at the University of New Mexico. I had a pad down there. So, it was like, come on down baby! And that's where those first workshops started developing. I actually went to some of those. (Frank sounds) Did I go to the first one … was I in the first one? (Frank sounds)

**Frank:** Yes.

**Steve:** I thought so! (laughs)

**Frank:** Not the workshop, but the all-night performance.

**Steve:** Yeah, yeah. (Frank sounds) I remember that quite well! (Frank laughing and sounds) (Steve laughing)

**Steve:** The foundation for what's happening these days, right?

(Frank sounds)

**Linda:** Yes.

**Frank:** Is it not amazing how it developed?

**Steve:** It is amazing how it develops. The music sure is a good part of it. I like that part! And a … yeah, it's a neat thing and yeah, it was pretty much part of the times, too, back when those types of performance things at that point … certainly nobody was doing it in Albuquerque, you know, besides (laughs) … But you know …

**Frank:** Hey, I tried to in S-a …

**Steve:** Oh, in Santa Fe.

**Frank:** San Bernardino.

**Steve:** Oh, in San Bernardino, yeah, right, well ah. (laughs) Never … what was that girl's name you painted that night? Jackie, yeah right, Jackie. He painted her. (laughs)

**Frank:** I saw her …

**Steve:** You saw Jackie?

**Linda:** Oh, was she the one that Louise didn't … oh no, that's a different one.

**Frank:** I saw her 15 …

**Linda:** 15 years ago.

**Steve:** Yeah. She was kind of …

**Frank:** O …

**Linda:** Old. She seemed old.

**Steve:** Well, I'm not surprised. She was a lovely young thing back then, but I think she had a serious bi-polar disorder, or something like that. She was actually kind of unhinged. She was probably one of those people that psychedelic drugs were not too good for.

**Frank:** How could you tell … ?

**Steve:** How could I tell?

**Frank:** … back then …

**Linda:** Who was unhinged and who wasn't? (laughs)

**Steve:** (laughing, and Frank sounds) It's kind of a relative thing but … (all laugh and Frank sounds) that was one of the things about hippies man, like hippies didn't care if you were unhinged. I had so many unhinged people around in my life, I swear to God …

**Frank:** Exactly. It is only in the last twenty years … (Frank sounds)

**Linda:** That what? (Frank sounds) Unhinged is a negative?

**Steve:** Oh, yeah, right (laughs) I don't know, I still like being unhinged myself, but …

**Linda:** He means in the big picture.

**Steve:** There was a short period of time, like I say, when there was sort of a fringy thing, especially out here on the west coast where, you know, people accepted people for being almost anything, or any kind of way, you know. And the fact you were basically bi-polar and psychotic could be sort of charming for a while, but then, you know, then when people seriously started disfunctioning that's when you decided, yeah, well … I mean, I've sent at least three people to the psych hospitals out of my households. It's like, you know, when they start doing really self-destructive things, or just really acting completely, you know, wrong, then you got to do something. Anyway, she struck me as somebody … I knew that she had some real personality frailties, shall we say, and just didn't, you know, she was care-worn, shall we say …

**Frank:** Well, painting her whole …

**Steve:** Oh, her whole body, yeah …

**Frank:** Did not help …

**Steve:** Did not help, yeah. She kind of got a little funky after a while, 'cause you know, if you paint too much of a person's body, the skin can't breath, and they get kind of funky, so we had to take quick photographs and wash it off.

**Frank:** We did not (laughs) …

**Linda:** … know any of that at the time. What did you paint her with?

**Steve:** I think it was acrylics. (laughing)

**Linda:** It wasn't body paint!

**Frank:** That would do it!

**Steve:** That would do it, yeah! I can't take full responsibility for driving her nuts, but I'll take some. (laughing)

(Frank sounds)

**Steve:** You get better color out of acrylics, come on, man. (laughing)

**Frank:** I have done a lot of research on body …

**Steve:** Body paint.

**Linda:** Body paint. Well, because we've been painting bodies ever since, I guess. And have a lot of different kinds of … we found some good body paints.

**Steve:** There are kinder paints. Yeah, there are kinder paints. There are paints that do allow your pores to breath a little bit. There are many theatrical paints. The Star Wars guys, they get kind of gooped up. (laughs, Frank sounds)

**Frank:** What do you …

**Linda:** What do I want to know? Well, the part that I was most interested in is when you were talking about the context ... the time that you guys met each other. The way you said Frank seemed like an interesting character, and you were that way and that it was a time of possibilities ... I don't know, that sort of thing was of interest to me. Like maybe talking about the kinds of things that ... what it was like ... what you ...

**Steve:** Yeah, they study us in history class and it really cracks me up.

**Linda:** Yeah, (laughs) or maybe how it's different now than then.

**Frank:** This was San Bernardino.

**Linda:** Yes.

**Frank:** There was about 5 ... (Frank sounds)

**Linda:** 5,000? 500?

**Frank:** 50 radicals in ...

**Steve:** ... in the whole Tri-County area (Frank sounds). Yeah, it certainly was a hot bed of political tension, for sure. Yeah. Well, that's the other part of that time, too, is the political thing was somewhat similar to this time. But what was so fundamentally different about that time is we'd come from this whole point ... our society had come from this whole point of ... everybody was really trying to be pretty much the same, you know. The ideals of our parents were to get ahead, succeed, and they'd really done well with it, you know. And these guys came back from the war and they were just like really ready to forget all that misery and horrible shit they'd gone through. Raise some families. Make some money. And, by the way, we'll build this country great while we do it, you know. (Frank sounds) And, God bless their souls, in many ways that they did what they did, even though they totally fucked us later. (Frank giggles) It was ... there was a lot of that. Certainly the post-depression kind of mind-set that their parents had gone through and all that stuff, just made it very industrious, and that's why we created this giant prosperity, right? But, people had their minds very focused in on just that and there was no other real imagination. There was always the beatnik element and various jazz musicians and people like that...

**Frank:** On purpose ...

**Linda:** On purpose.

**Steve:** Yeah, people kept themselves locked in on purpose, is that what you're saying? Yeah, because that's how ... they created the system, like corporate America ... it works because everybody thinks the same (Frank sounds), you know. And if you're really an individual in that, you screw the whole thing up and they throw you out. That's why I never lasted very long working for a hospital. I'm too individual and iconoclastic to stay in a big institution. So anyways, my little point being that when we became more or less of age, you know, like late teenagers, the Vietnam war was beginning to go sour, and people were beginning to take psychedelic drugs. And all of a sudden there was this whole idea that you didn't have to do what your daddy did. You could actually do something completely different. In fact, you could entertain a fantasy of just not even being part of this society at all. You could drop out and live in a tepee up in Taos, New Mexico and eat peyote and roll around in the dirt. And you could do that for years at an end, and actually travel all over the country and just do that. You know, rather than going and getting a job, finishing your education and getting a job, (clapping to make his points) getting a car, getting married and having ten kids. You could just ... explore things in just an open manner, and there was no fixed agenda, there was no idea exactly about what you were doing except that you were going to go have some fun, you know. And a lot of people wanted to just go have some fun. It wasn't like all that many people, but it was a significant amount. (Frank sounds)

**Linda:** But, that period ... that feeling of all possibilities, that's what's not now ...

**Steve:** All of a sudden that opened up. We had opened it up in a very short amount of time, in other words, you know, between '66 and '69, this thing just exploded. Especially up here in the Bay Area, and, all of a sudden everybody's going, God, you're my brother, we can ... together we can bring peace to the world, we can feed the hungry, we can do all this stuff. And people were really excited about it, because they never even really thought about it. Their parents hadn't even ... I mean, always somebody has, you know. But as a movement it didn't really ... it wasn't like that. And it was a marvelously completely anarchistically non-structured movement, you know. But at the same time a whole political agenda was beginning to emerge. The whole thing about the war and corporate institutions and how the world was getting poisoned by the policies and the mind-sets of the people that were running these corporations began to really sink in. Not only was it because of people's awareness but also science was beginning to catch up to that. Science was beginning to realize, hey, there's cadmium in the water and all the fish are going belly up! And that science had not really happened that much before. You see, I also studied science, that's what I studied when I went to college. I ended up with a degree in biochemistry (Frank sounds). I think about things scientifically and that ...

**Frank:** Which is news ...

**Linda:** News to you? (laughs, Frank sounds) Frank didn't know that!

**Steve:** Yeah, well that's what I ended up with at the university ... I went to U.N.M. (University of New Mexico) to study art and music, OK, and I ended up with a degree in biochemistry. Go figure! Anyway, yeah, so. The political thing started to come in and a lot of people got politically active. I mean, this horrible war was happening. We had the awareness that you didn't have to go to war. You could burn your draft card. Hey buddy we burned ...

**Linda:** You guys did that!

**Steve:** We burned our draft cards. Went and hassled the Marines and ...

**Frank:** I got other guys to burn theirs too ...

**Linda:** With you.

**Steve:** Yeah. Here we are out in this little funky little campus, in the middle of nowhere. Redneck filled to the max. And we're still up there burning our cards. You know, we had our little SDS group. And we had a little political thing. They even tried to infiltrate us. It was hysterical. You know, there's five of us, you know. And some other guy comes and he's like (Linda laughing) hey, what's happening? You going to bomb the world? Yeah man, we're going for it, yeah.

**Frank:** They tapped ...

**Linda:** Tapped your phones?

**Steve:** Yeah, I know, it's just like, you guys ... and you know, that's one thing that's funny, actually, it's funny, sad. These days they're going right back to that. They want to tap everybody's phone, you know. And the thing is is that, what we talked about is it's just stupid, you know, there's really nothing there and yet, that's part of the dichotomy that started happening then. A small amount of people that think in a very holistic way. They thought the world is all one thing. The people are all one people, and that you could create some sort of harmony within that situation. It's not an old concept, but it was new to have it as a primary focus for your life ... for Americans at least, OK. And that's what most people could not maintain ... was that truly holistic attitude. (Frank sounds) It stayed ... a lot of the people ended up having, maybe not even through a choice of their own, had to leave it behind. Because they ended up getting jobs in corporate America, and threw the surfboard into the garage. And now, drive a car, and run around and go ... man, we had some fun back then, but boy, I'll tell you, my kids are going to college. So, you know, it's easy and that's what happened is that ... to the movement in general. You get co-opted by economic pressures and the force of, you know, the actual force of civilization.

**Frank:** Louise linked us to an extended family of changers that go way back.

**Linda:** Changers? An extended family of changers. (Frank sounds)

**Steve:** Yeah, Father George, remember him ... he was our ... the local priest. (Frank sounds) (Steve laughs) Of course, he was a gay priest ... he picked on guys, not boys. (laughing)

**Frank:** Don't tell the women who gave him money that ...

**Linda:** That he was gay!

(Steve laughs)

**Steve:** Yeah, he was a handsome devil. (laughing) (Frank sounds)

**Linda:** Do I have anything else I want to know? Nothing's coming to me. Mikee ... Erika?

**Mikee:** You could tell the story of the Marines, because people may not have heard that one. That's a good one.

**Steve:** Yeah, that was back in San Bernardino, back on campus there, and the Marine recruiters were there ... had their little place on campus, so then of course, I had to wheel Frank in there. He says, I want to sign up! And they're like, yeah, right! And the guy was getting all insulted, huffy.

**Frank:** I (Frank sounds) want to do my part! (Frank screams)

(laughing)

**Steve:** Yeah, that was funny. (Linda laughing) This guy was just having such a hard time with the whole process! (Frank screaming and laughing. Linda laughing) Talking to Frank is like

... you know, talking to Frank! And he just, you know, this guy was just not ready for this yet at all.

**Frank:** Don't you want me?

**Steve:** Yeah, and he's just (makes sounds). (laughing) So finally this guy just like spits out, but what can you do?!

**Linda:** That's what the guy said to Frank?

**Steve:** Yeah, what can you do? You know.

**Frank:** I can ...

**Linda:** (laughing) Push the button.

**Steve:** Push the button. (laughing) The guy just like ... ah, get out of here. (laughing) He didn't like that one at all. And of course, laughing hysterically.

**Linda:** You're just standing there ... you're making him spell Frank out and everything?

**Steve:** Oh yeah, make it as hard as possible! (laughing)

**Frank:** I ran for president ...

**Steve:** Of the college? Yeah. What I liked was like, Frank would be sitting there and a sorority girl kind of girl, she would come and she'd be like, oh poor Frank, and she'd feel obliged to sit and chat and he'd just get his hand ... (gestures) (laughing, Steve makes a screeching sound) she can't slap him, it was great.

**Linda:** You're watching all this?

**Steve:** I'm rolling on the floor, laughing is what I'm doing. (laughs)

**Linda:** So, tell us more of what you thought of Frank.

**Steve:** Well you know, I've always ... I thought Frank was just a thoroughly interesting character. I started talking to him and I realized he had a real great wit, you know, he was really humorous and I like humorous people. Also, he was genuinely searching. He had some really burning questions in his mind about what it was and what it wasn't and why it is and why it wasn't. I guess that's one of the things that most attracted me to you (Frank sound) was the fact that you just really really wanted to know, you know. And it was really ... and had this real hunger for experience of all kinds. That's why I took him out and crashed and burned him on the side of the mountain. (laughing) Come on, man, you want to try something? I did this all the time, but, you know, you might as well too, just to see what it's like. And so, I got interested in that project, you know. So that's why I psychedelicized him and things like that. The other thing I like about Frank was that here's this guy with disabilities and what not and he just didn't make a big deal out of it, you know. What it taught me was, you are who you are and what you got is what you got. We used to boogie to the song, one thing you can't hide is when you're crippled inside. You know what I mean? It's like OK, look at you now. And, our mutual friend, Jackie, say twenty years ago she looked old. Well, she was crippled inside and I knew it back then. I could just tell, this poor girl ... and I'm sure she looks old

*Frank Moore and Stephen Emanuel (video capture)*

'cause she's care-worn. She just worried herself ... she probably worried herself to death by now. Some people just got worry in the brain, it's a biochemical abnormality or something. And you're like Alfred E. Neuman, what me worry?! What the hell, you know. (laughing)

**Frank:** Why?

**Steve:** Why? Yeah, I'll tell you what. Very little I find important enough to really get worried about. (laughing)

**Frank:** Hey, it is fun!

**Steve:** Fun is what it's all about. And that's the thing, I think a lot of people, and certainly our parents didn't have enough fun. And I think a lot of kids these days aren't having enough fun. The kind of fun they're having is really limited.

**Frank:** Did you read about Ramen?

**Linda:** Oh, did you read the thing Frank sent out about what happened ...

**Steve:** (laughing) Oh yeah ...

**Linda:** About those kids running home to their parents ...

**Steve:** Yeah, well, that's what I mean, you know. OK. These kids have spent ... they're like what 18 ...

**Linda:** Well, the one kid was a senior in high school, the others were like in their early twenties!

(Frank sounds)

**Steve:** OK, but, still, so alright …

**Linda:** They're not that young!

**Steve:** They're not that young, but still, the world they've grown up in … what they've seen … they probably watched on television, twenty thousand people get shot with hand guns. But on television they probably … maybe they saw Janet Jackson's breast, OK? But, it's so funny that our culture is so obsessed with sex and violence, (Frank sounds) but violence anybody can see. But sex is something is that just … and nudity … a naked breast! Oh my God! When you girls walk down the street with your shirt off, cars crash into each other, because everybody is like, oh my God, there's tits on the street (laughing) … to me, it's just like … I like to read anthropology. I was staying at my aunt's house and she's got this marvelous library full of all kinds of real books. And I've been reading about these people in the Amazon, a tribe in the Amazon, from anthropologists they are seeing these people in the '20s and '30s. So these are unspoiled natives, they haven't been co-opted by civilization… these are the first white cats to see these people. Their take on sexuality and their take on how kids experience sexuality … this one tribe, you know (Frank sounds), if a kid by age fourteen, if a young man by fourteen hasn't bonked somebody yet he is just ruthlessly teased by his father and his uncles and everybody else and all the other girls and everybody else. Like, come on! They live in one hut, and they sleep in the same hammocks and the kids are used to their parents making love all the time. Or they'll be walking through the forest and there is Uncle Joe doing his third wife, you know. (laughing) They do it underneath the trees because (Frank sounds) they feel that if you have sex underneath the fruit trees the fruit's better, you know? (Frank sounds, laughing)

**Linda:** Wow.

**Steve:** Our society is like … you look at advertising … There's three quarters of a tit everywhere but you can't see that nipple, by God, and if you do, you better run out the door and go tell mommy because that's bad for you.

**Frank:** And no one asked, why?

**Linda:** No one asked why … why we were doing what we were doing … ? No …

**Frank:** None asked why …

**Linda:** Oh, in our culture? (Frank sounds)

**Frank:** A …

**Linda:** You can't see a nipple? (Frank sounds) Nobody asks why, everybody just accepts that.

**Steve:** Right, nobody asks why, everybody just accepts it. If you go to, like Europe or Sweden or southern France, all women sunbathe without their tops on. It's no big deal. Guys don't stub their toes walking down the sand just because some broad shows her breast (laughing) … never happened to me.

**Linda:** So people don't even question that. Everybody just accepts that that's the way it is.

**Steve:** Yeah, that's what I'm saying. The American culture is so funny that way. Because we're so obsessed with sex and yet, if the real thing comes along, most people cannot handle that. Especially in the wrong context, you know. In a theater, a lot of people just can't handle it!

**Frank:** They ran ...

**Linda:** Yeah, they ran, literally, they literally ran, literally run. (laughing) (Frank sounds)

**Steve:** And if you're Ozzy Osbourne and you're biting the head off a bat on stage, they probably would have stayed.

**Linda:** Right, yeah, that's right. (Frank sounds)

**Steve:** So, it's just like, OK!

**Frank:** I never got the lines ...

**Linda:** You never got the lines, between what's OK and what's not OK. (Frank sounds)

**Steve:** Yeah, well I never got the lines either. And what was fun about back then (Frank sounds) ... I don't want to wax nostalgic or anything but ... (laughing) ... the lines were a lot looser. The lines were a lot further apart. People for a brief period were very experimental with their sexuality and relationships and you could just boff somebody in a night, just be friends the next day, and a bowl of granola ... and maybe you see them again a few weeks later, maybe you boff them again or not, but it was a free and easy kind of thing. And there was not a big, heavy, emotional overlay to a lot of the sexuality. But like I say, most people just couldn't maintain that kind of sense of freedom and got locked into thinking ... you start having kids and you need a job and lalala ... and it wears people down. And most people, fundamentally weren't that changed. (Frank sounds) They really went back to what they'd known before. Then there's the lunatic fringe of us that still seem to like ... fringe around ... (laughing)

**Linda:** That kept going from there.

**Steve:** Yeah, right. I think of myself, you know, OK, well what am I like now? Am I much different than that? Well, OK, I work harder now. I got a steadier job. But, it's the same kind of job (laughs). And I basically feel the same way about things. OK, I got a steady girlfriend, and I don't boff every girl I meet, but I might still want to, you know. (laughing) (Frank sounds) But, intrinsically I feel that people should be open and I feel that people should embrace different kinds of expressions of sexuality and different ways of living. And I think, up here in Berkeley you guys got a nice little bubble going here and you can do all kinds of things in Bezerkeley that you can't do in Ohio.

**Frank:** Not really.

**Linda:** I mean it's conservative here too, compared to what it used to be.

**Steve:** Yeah, I know, but still ...

**Linda:** He's comparing it to other places ... (Frank sounds)

**Steve:** Like, I mean there's a lot of openly lesbian couples, or openly gay couples, that live and own homes and have jobs and pick each other up and have their kids and take them to school and all that kind of stuff (Frank sounds, Linda saying "yeah") and they're not getting beat up on the way. You try that in Laramie, Wyoming and it just doesn't quite play as well.

**Linda:** Right, right … (Frank sounds)

**Steve:** Despite *Brokeback Mountain*.

(laughing)

**Linda:** What? Well, I guess there were things that popped into my head. The idea of the freedom and the possibilities and stuff and, oh fear! That was the word that popped into my head! 'Cause it seems like there's a lot of fear now (Frank sounds) and that was something that was not there.

**Steve:** Well, OK, yeah, the fear thing …

**Frank:** Like I could hitchhike across …

**Linda:** … the country.

**Steve:** Yeah, people were certainly … there was a lot more trust and there was more opportunities to trust and people got away with it a lot more. And you could trust people and they usually didn't fuck you over so much.

**Linda:** Right.

**Steve:** And, certainly, I hitchhiked up and down this coast and all over the place all the time …

**Linda:** I did too, by myself, all the time.

**Steve:** Most of it was a really, really wonderful experience. Certainly society these days is … the increasing polarization that's happened now in these thirty, forty years, and the huge gap that's now stretched between the rich and poor. And the incredible difference of what's real opportunity and what isn't. The desperation that has become standard for so many people, has just changed that whole equation completely. And when I look at … I hang out with a lot of young people in their twenties and thirties … are some of the people I hang around the most these days (Frank sounds) and they didn't get to have this kind of fun. Many of them are really, really, very nice sweet people with their heads screwed on really nicely. And the college kids, college kids will always be college kids, thank God. (laughing) But, they never got to have the innocence and love and peace and freedom situation that we had there for four or five years, where everything was just like, wow, it's so nice!

(Frank sounds)

**Linda:** Yeah, OK, so … it's time for the jam!

**Frank:** We could do this again sometime.

**Steve:** Yeah, I think so. I'm interested in it. And I'm going to be a grandpa in like August. And I think about grandkids and the kind of world that they're coming up in. It's up to us to try and make it nice, you know. (Frank sounds) Forces of evil, the Axis of Evil are working overtime, but the thing is the microcosms that we create is what really makes it all happen.

**Linda:** Absolutely.

**Steve:** Everything reflects out of that. And if you got enough little tiny groovy bubbles, they get to be bigger and bigger groovy bubbles.

**Frank:** Yes, that is how we see it.

**Linda:** That's totally how we see it. We have to live the kind of life that we want things to be and that's affecting everything else.

**Frank:** Piss and jam! (laughing)

**Linda:** OK, don't go anywhere! We're going to piss and jam! (laughing)

# Louise Scott

November 15, 1998 on fakeradio.com

......................................................................................................

Frank called this interview, "a deep conversation with a wise woman, a cultural pioneer, a midwife, an international bag lady …"

Frank always said that Louise was "to blame" for his life … he also wrote that "thanks to the gentle guidance by Louise Scott, I started to see my body as a tool." This interview reveals the depth of that friendship of 45 years, starting from the very first time they saw each other at an all-night party of folk singers in 1968 San Bernardino. But it also dives deep into Louise's down-to-earth wisdom from her profoundly rich and full life, with glimpses into just a sampling of the many chapters of this life. With joy and compassion, weaving through the beatniks of 1950s San Francisco, hanging out with satirist/author Mort Sahl when he first performed in L.A., starting communes and cultural centers through the 1960s and 1970s, traveling the world, being a midwife and working in hospice, and living outside of the borders and limits of society as a way of life … Louise is a model of this freedom, and has always been a mother and a friend, not just to Frank, but to people in general.

......................................................................................................

**Frank:** I know there are a lot of people, all over, in all lines of work, who wish I was not in the world.

**Louise:** They wish you weren't in the world?!? Good God, Frank.

**Frank:** Well, we have someone here who they can blame for that. (all laughing) If it was not for her, I might not be here.

**Louise:** Well, you know Frank, if it wasn't for you I might not be here either. (Frank sounds)

**Frank:** And there are a lot of people who … (Frank screeching, Louise laughing)

**Louise:** Watch out, watch out, watch out.

**Frank:** Who would blame me for that too. (all laughing) This is Louise Scott.

**Linda:** What? You want me to sum up? Oh!

**Louise:** Careful, careful there!

**Linda:** I'll say what I know and you can correct me. I am going to attempt to tell a brief story of how Frank and Louise hooked up.

**Frank:** And you can stop me …

**Linda:** Yeah, you can fill in …

**Louise:** I can correct you or I can … OK …

**Linda:** Yeah, and fill stuff in …

**Lousie:** And I'm sure Frank will have a few little …

**Linda:** Frank was living at home with his mother and brother. (Frank sounds) I guess, in San Bernardino County.

**Louise:** Right.

**Linda:** He had made an attempt to leave home at one point, by getting an attendant who turned out to be drunk (Frank sounds) who pulled a gun on him, so now he's back living with his mom, aware of the fact that if he doesn't get out of the house soon, he could turn into the crip son who stays with his mom his whole life, so he was feeling like something had to give. He was toward the end of his college years. Louise was the cool, hippy lady that lived in town with … on kind of a little farm or something? Or some piece of land or something?

**Louise:** I had an acre there with a lot of out-buildings and whatnot … and my previous husband and I made a swimming pool and we made a sweat and we were really into it. We were supporting ourselves doing landscaping.

**Frank:** What is a sweat?

**Louise:** A hot steam bath, so we could get in there and get real hot then jump into the cold water, then get back out and whatnot. And, the first time I remember seeing Frank was at Sally … what was her name, a folk singer … we were all at this house, and here's Frank, my God, here's Frank. And, I, I, I … I watched him watching people. And I felt like he saw so much more than other people saw. And I felt a little uncomfortable about it, of course. (Frank low sounds) And that was initially … and then I was off, after that, off with the hippies. When I came back I got in it with Frank.

**Frank:** We did not talk at that time …

**Louise:** No, no, no. But I watched. And he was watching. And then, that was before I went off with all the hippies, right? (Frank sounds) And then I was up here at Haight Ashbury and Nevada City. And I left that and went back to San Bernardino and that's when we really connected.

**Frank:** While you were gone, some of my friends from college moved in …

**Linda:** To her house?

**Louise:** Oh, those guys! (Frank screeches) (everyone laughs) Oh, OK. Well anyway then, when I go back, is when I really got involved with Frank. (Frank sounds) He would be by, and, with friends of his and whatnot. And in the meantime then, shortly after that, I moved to Santa Fe, when the big exodus to the country was happening. And I was back trying to sell that piece of property. Want the story about I was crying? (Frank sounds) I had been very sick and I was in the bedroom crying one day because I was losing my hair. And I heard someone was there and I walk in the kitchen and here is Frank. (makes sounds mimicking Frank's sounds) You know, full of joy and all that! And I just … that was when I really felt a real breakthrough with Frank. And like, at that time I said, oh my God man, I'm out there crying about my vanity, you know, and I felt really bad about it. How could I be so vain, you know? And a day or two later, he brought me this beautiful painting that he had done of this

Louise Scott, Frank Moore and Linda Mac. Photo by Michael LaBash.

head. (Frank sounds) And he said this is vanity. All golden curls and earrings and lipstick and this and that. He said, vanity is very beautiful. And then in talking about Santa Fe, he said, oh I wish I could go there. I said, you want to come live with us? (all laughing) (Louise mimics Frank's sounds) Yeah. And so, we moved all to Santa Fe with me and my kids. (Frank screeching)

**Frank:** No!

**Louise:** No?

**Frank:** But I went before you got there.

**Louise:** Oh yeah! A friend, Steve, took him in the car. And then I came with all this furniture and stuff. Maybe I get it wrong, Frank! (Frank sounds) You know!

**Frank:** You said (Linda giggling) it would be two weeks. (Frank screeches)

**Louise:** How long was it?

**Frank:** Two months. (laughing)

**Louise:** Was it that long? In the meantime, he was at a place called The Center. That was set up at that time, the late 1960s right? Very late '60s, early '70s ...

**Frank:** Early '70s.

**Louise:** Every dissident in the United States was on the road. (Frank sounds) Going right through Santa Fe. The word was out there was free land. And this friend of ours who had become a Catholic priest at the time, Father George ...

**Frank:** I first saw him when he was MC'ing for Lee Michaels.

**Linda:** Was this in San Bernardino? (Frank sounds) That's the first time you ever saw Father George.

**Louise:** I don't remember Lee Michaels. I mean, I don't remember that. But that was away from me. I mean, it wasn't connected with me particularly.

**Linda:** Yes. (Frank sounds)

**Louise:** So Frank is here, right in the middle of all these people, going all over the world, (Frank sounds) doing just dandy!

**Frank:** My first real time on my own. (Frank laughing)

**Louise:** On his own, right.

**Linda:** So you should describe where, what, like, what it was. I don't think we've told anybody.

**Louise:** We called it The Center. And it was an old nursing home that we rented. It was huge. It had a commercial kitchen and all of that.

**Linda:** And it was you and George that started it?

**Louise:** That got this started ... plus some other people. I mean, you know there were ... it was really a joint effort, communal effort.

**Linda:** Yeah.

**Louise:** But, there was one guy in Santa Fe who volunteered to come and help everybody fix their broken down cars. (Frank sounds) And we had the Chicano Center that were a lot of the Chicano people. It was kind of the first integration there actually, between gringos and Chicanos ... happened through there. Oh, everything happened through there (Frank sounds) really ...

**Linda:** It was like a crash pad, where people could stay ...

**Louise:** It was like a crash pad ... people could stay. And we got people to donate produce ... everybody kind of cooked and contributed and whatnot. And this got going there. And then I arrived, and then Frank lived with me and my kids because they threw Father George in jail for running a disorderly house or something. (Frank laughs) I don't remember what they got him on. But I'm real grateful this happened. Because the amount of pressure that took off of Santa Fe that summer, God knows what would have happened. (Frank sounds) You know, I mean, kids were making love in the plaza, right? And they're getting thrown in jail. (Frank sounds) It was ... it was heavy. There was too much, all of a sudden, happened to Santa Fe. You know, we liberated hippies go there (Frank sounds) without our brassieres and that was totally outside of that culture at that time, and there was a huge clash that this prevented. (Frank sounds)

**Frank:** In fact, they bombed The Center.

**Louise:** Yeah, I wasn't there when that happened. I was still going back and forth trying to sell this house in San Bernardino. See Frank was there. Steve got him there. Then I got there and we got a house rented and we got the other situation together. But most of the ... initial work at The Center, I was involved in. But that was before Frank.

**Linda:** Yeah.

**Louise:** So when Frank got there ... I don't know why I was that long getting there, Frank. I was on my way. (laughing)

**Linda:** He said you had to settle things with the selling of the house?

**Louise:** Yeah, I never got the house sold. (Frank screeches) I probably rented it out again. There were problems. Government FHA loans and stuff. So I didn't sell it at that time. But Frank was ... you know, he was in his glory after being pretty much isolated. Although he'd been going to college. But, I mean, I'm sure he was just having a ball there. (Frank sounds) You know, it was good for him.

**Linda:** Yeah.

**Louise:** And then he lived with me and my children. And we were still very much a part of this alternate society. And fully a part of ... remember the night in the tepee? The peyote meeting. (Frank sounds) We dug a hole in the ground so Frank could be propped up. (Linda laughs) You know, because there's no ... everybody's on the floor, on the ground in the tepee. And you know, Frank was always ready for anything. Whatever it is, he wants to try it! He wants to do it!

**Linda:** Yeah.

**Louise:** So, there was a lot of that type of (Frank sounds) ... whatever everybody else was doing. Which, it started in San Bernardino. You better believe he wants to get in the sweat and get in the pool. (Frank sounds) You know, tough buzzard. (Frank laughing)

**Linda:** Yeah, yeah. (laughing)

**Louise:** So, ask me something. Ask me.

**Linda:** So did you live with Louise for about a year? (Frank sounds) You guys lived in the same ... yeah, OK ...

**Louise:** And then, I was real upset. Some people he had met invited him to go back east to a commune. And I was real worried because his care, as you guys know, can be really kind of heavy. I was real ... you know, I was real concerned about this. Frank never acts from fear!

**Linda:** Right. (Frank sounds)

**Louise:** You know, he goes for it, he goes for the love and forget the fear. But my fears, you know. I got this maternal kind of thing going about it. And he wrote them a long letter and they wrote back and said, come on! We put him in the car and off he went, you know! (laughing)

**Frank:** But I beat them to ...

**Linda:** The community? The people who you had met, who invited you to go ... you got a separate ride from them and then you got there before they got there.

**Frank:** So no one …

**Linda:** … knew who you were when you got dropped off by your ride.

**Louise:** Oh really, I didn't know that! Oh God! (all laughing)

**Linda:** So this person drops Frank off and is ready to pull away and they're going, oh, wait a minute …

**Louise:** Yeah! I don't know. Frank was going! It was more or less a domestic scene. There was a lot going on in the household, but it wasn't … the best Frank had been The Center, then to go to this commune, because of course, his desire to communicate, you know, was so strong. You know, forever. (Frank sounds) So he was really going for any of these opportunities where he could get out in the world and really communicate.

**Linda:** Yeah. (Frank sounds)

**Louise:** So, here you are!

**Frank:** Then a year later you get a call.

**Louise:** Oh yeah, my God, I get a phone call from a mutual friend. I forget who it was now. But, she said, I thought I saw Frank on the corner.

**Frank:** Belle.

**Louise:** Was it Belle?

**Linda:** Yes.

**Louise:** She called and it's like, I saw Frank on the street. Are you sure it was Frank? (all laughing) How ridiculous! And then, of course, he shows up with Debbie at that time.

**Linda:** Yes.

**Louise:** And you know, here they were again. Obviously doing just dandy. And he wasn't as wobbly anymore either. (Frank screeches) He'd really …

**Frank:** Sex will do that!

**Louise:** Yeah, will do marvels! (all laughing) The first time they're there I go in and he's alone on the toilet! My God, I'm scared to death! (Frank sounds) Ahhh, Frank! No problem. I mean, he was on the toilet, you know. (Frank giggles) (all laugh)

**Frank:** Was you … you think your nude pictures are embarrassing? They (screeches!) …

**Linda:** We're always taking photos of Frank on the toilet! (Frank keeps screeching) I could do a toilet series of Frank from over the years, for the last 25 years (laughs) … on the toilet.

**Louise:** This one house we rented … the first house I got after I got there was kind of out in the country. And it was lovely. But, it was difficult like to … I didn't want to leave Frank home alone much. And I was driving this big old one ton truck. So, to get him into town, I had to put him in the back of this truck. And going up the hill, the first time, I hear … (imitates Frank's sounds) (Frank also makes the sounds along with Louise) I go back there and he's slipping out (laughing) ... it's like, what the hell ... Frank sliding back (laughing) yeah, yeah, I almost lost him! And anyway, so then I moved into town. And it was a small place, but it was in what they call compounds. Which would be like a bunch of little apartments all around together. And very interesting people living there too. Real alternate society type thing. (Frank sounds) The toilet! The floor was ... remember the floor around it was all kind of rotted out and to get his chair over it and not have Frank go through the floor with the wheels of the chair. And, my God, there was so many people there sometimes. It was ... had a kitchen, and two rooms and a little bathroom. (Frank sounds) And when we didn't have company and there were only like five of us, six of us or seven of us there, it was like we were home alone or something. (Frank sounds) But that was good too because then there were neighbors there too that were in and out and you could communicate with. And that worked out real well. (Frank sounds) We moved several times, didn't we Frank? My God! (Frank sounds) All the stuff.

**Frank:** I wrote for the ...

**Linda:** The underground paper?

**Louise:** There was an underground paper, a newspaper. Northern New Mexico was really getting organized in those days. They had free medical and free boxes. (Frank sounds) You know, a lot of stuff was going on good.

**Frank:** Godfrey ...

**Louise:** Yeah, Godfrey (Reggio) was involved. He had this Chicano group and we did a rent strike.

(Frank sounds)

**Linda:** Tell people who Godrey is, he's saying.

**Louise:** He was a director who eventually became a director of a film called *Koyaanisqatsi*. They had a Philip Glass score. It was very much an anti-technology film. It's about ... oh my God, how long along now? (Frank sounds) It was very avant garde and it's a filmmaker's film and now it's kind of a classic, a cult film all over the world, with groups of people and whatnot.

**Linda:** Yeah. (Frank sounds)

**Louise:** It had a tremendous influence on the film industry, hopefully, people's minds.

**Frank:** But then he ...

**Louise:** He had a Chicano group there.

**Frank:** But the same guys who (Frank sounds) b ...

**Louise:** ... before were at The Center. Yeah, well, there was a whole history. He had been a monk at the college of Santa Fe and had organized ... I guess back even early '60s or before the whole hippie era happened ... a youth group of Chicano kids. And then Godfrey became involved registering voters in the south. And became excommunicated as a result of his political action. And was actually with a group called the Weathermen in Chicago, which were pretty heavy duty revolutionaries. (Frank sounds)

**Linda:** Right!

**Louise:** He came back to Santa Fe then and with these kids that he had in a youth group, formed this La Gente de La Raza, the people of the race. And the only thing that remains in Santa Fe from that now is the clinic. He brought doctors there. The whole thing was really going ... they got bombed. That was way before he made the film. (Frank sounds)

**Frank:** I rode with them when they foll ...

**Linda:** Followed?

**Louise:** Followed in the cop cars! Well, they did a thing, they got all connected on the police band. Is that what you're talking about? (Frank sounds)

**Linda:** Yes.

**Louise:** Well, they would interpret a call to the police from the Chicano neighborhood. And they'd get out there and have it solved before the cops got in there. The guys from La Gente, would get out there. And the cops would get there and there was no problem. (Frank sounds) Godfrey knew all of these people. And then they got bombed there. You know. (Frank sounds) It was pretty heavy duty around Santa Fe when Frank and I were there. Now it's yuppieville. It's like adobe Disneyland, but ...

**Frank:** We did a rent ...

**Louise:** Yeah, we did a rent strike there too. We marched around the plaza. Where I moved from the country, into this compound, they had evicted Chicano families who'd been there for like twenty years, because they could get more money, because we hippies were there. (Frank sounds) So, you know, we found this out. And of course all the hippies are taking out false ceilings, and exposing the brick work and making beehive fireplaces. Really tripping the places out. And of course, we all got rent increases. (Frank sounds) And we did this rent strike with them. And at one time with the La Raza people, Godfrey and these guys, we did the fiesta, which was in the old Santa Fe style where each compound would open up their doors for ... and invite open house for other people. (Frank sounds) And that was really gratifying, because all we hippies had our doors open and we cooked beans. (Frank sounds) And we had all this ready. And it was a real ... we even did this thing with a greased pig. (Frank sounds) Except that the hippies couldn't handle catching the pig and we had to sit and call the pig. (laughing) You know, we didn't want anything too rough in there. And, that was a really good thing. Good fun, I mean! There was a really good spirit then, in northern New Mexico, at that time. There were free stores. And we got the first food co-ops going. The first free school was there.

**Frank:** What ...

**Linda:** What is a free store?

**Louise:** Yeah, it was where everybody put things. You put things you don't need and you take out what you do. And then we got bulk grains, rather than paying Kellogg prices on things. (Frank sounds)

**Linda:** Yes.

**Louise:** You know, kind of like what the food ... what were food co-ops, which are now taken over, of course, by the corporations. (Frank sounds)

**Linda:** Right, yeah.

**Louise:** And the prices are way up. And the first free school in the country was in Santa Fe. (Frank sounds) Where there was a parent involvement and the type of people you really wanted raising your children. You know, the best people, as far as I was concerned. So, you know, we were happy to be a contributing part of that. (Frank sounds)

**Frank:** How did you get from a wife to a ... (Frank sounds)

**Louise:** From a wife?

**Linda:** From being a wife to what you became, I guess? (laughing)

(Frank sounds)

**Louise:** Frank, you know, I think maybe it was those toad stools, when I was a little girl. (All laughing) I mean, maybe, I don't know. There was no real change. You know, there never was any real change. I mean I was very much a juvenile delinquent, if you want to call it that. When I was really quite young I liked college boys. But I liked the college boys who were into the early Charlie Parker. You know, the first jazz at the philharmonic. I was kind of born avant garde. And when I was a kid babysitting, and I would say, I'm not doing this one!

**Frank:** When was that?

**Linda:** When were you born?

**Louise:** I was born in 1933. But it was in the late '40s when I was a teenager. I was all over the place. And I hated school, of course. (Frank sounds throughout this) But I was really into reading. I mean, I read Spinoza because I had a boyfriend who was a philosophy major. I can't say I understood much of it, but those interests were there. You know, real early on. (Frank sounds) Then I went through a whole series of marriages and divorces. I never should have married anyone! But, of course, one did marry then, you know. There were no alternatives. You know, the great American dream, which I had never ... when I was babysitting with kids I'd say, my God, I'm not doing this (Frank sounds), you know. And, so, my kids went through a whole lot with me through all these changes of course. But they always knew they were loved. (Frank sounds) You know.

**Frank:** Were you a b-e-a ...

**Louise:** A beatnik. Well, in the beatnik time, before Kerouac came out with his book, I was living at Jason Deli City College and I met a group of people that lived up by the Hollywood Bowl in Pinehurst. And they were ... I really liked this group of people. They were really ... Mort Sahl was one of them. Really intellectual, political people. And I was fascinated. And through Mort Sahl coming up. His first big thing was at the hungry i, of course.

**Linda:** Yes. (Frank sounds)

**Louise:** And so I was really like a little groupie really with it. (Frank sounds) My friend, Hank read poetry and he was a jazz drummer you know, when poetry and jazz was happening and all that. Then I was just, really I was on record, I was just taking all of this in. I liked it. And then, of course, Kerouac's book got popular and, you know, here we go, you know. (Frank sounds throughout) All of a sudden it's beatniks and this and that and the bus tours come through North Beach, like they did later through the Haight. You know, the whole thing's over the minute it gets publicized, it's over with.

**Linda:** Yeah.

**Louise:** You know, everybody says they're a beatnik, or everybody says they're a hippy. Without any idea of what starts these movements. These are organic things that grow, usually from a small group of committed people. And then by the time it hits the press, you know, forget it, baby! You know, it's what's next? Do you want me to say more about this?

**Linda:** Yeah.

**Louise:** You're looking at me ...

(laughing)

**Linda:** Yeah, he wants to hear more ...

**Louise:** Hear more about it.

**Linda:** That hungry i period and ... Is that what you want? (Frank sounds) Yeah.

**Frank:** Because Mort Sahl is one of my ...

**Louise:** I mean, but I wasn't ... you know, I was no contributor to anything during this. I had two kids already. (Frank sounds) And I'm working a job. It was through friends of mine who were involved that I had, you know, some sort of involvement. It was exciting to me. But I don't really have too much to say about that, Frank. It was such a nice time too. I mean, Sunday afternoons we used to go, what was it called, the Purple Onion, or someplace where you went downstairs and they had classical music and wine and then poetry and jazz was happening. And I went there last week because my friend, Carlene ... (Frank giggles) There's the hungry i and there's City Lights Books and there was Vesuvio which I remembered, you know, but, I was so young! (Frank sounds) You know, I was so young, I didn't know what was happening. It just was fun.

**Frank:** When did you know ...

**Linda:** What was happening?

**Louise:** (laughing) I still don't know what's happening! (all laughing) What's happening? I don't know what's happening! (Frank screeching) You know, things interest you, they get sparkly. And I've usually been pretty much interested in what was on the crest of the wave. (Frank sounds) You know, that's what's interesting. Instead of the same old thing over and over again. Or putting a patch on it. Let's have something new! Let's have some new ideas. Let's try other things. Because, I wish I had some new ideas now. I wish somebody had some new ideas, 'cause I think it's a mess! And I'm really glad I'm living in Mexico. (Frank sounds)

And I'm in culture shock being back in this country every time. It's hard on your nervous system. And I'm finding everybody's on Prozac. (Frank sounds) And they don't change the stress situations. They sell Prozac, you know and then they ... no marijuana, because there's no profit in that one. You know, let's have these tranquilizers and don't change things, you know.

(Frank sounds)

**Louise:** So, what do you want me to rant and rave about next?! (all laughing)

**Frank:** I am lazy. I just am sitting back ...

**Louise:** You're just sitting back and seeing what I'll do, right?

(All laughing)

**Louise:** If you don't give me something to do, what will I do? (laughing) Well ...

**Frank:** How did you meet Father George?

**Louise:** Aaaahhhh, OK. Boy, that's a story! (Frank sounds) The very early hippie thing was just happening ... it was about 1964, 1965 ... I'm not too good on years. And I moved into L.A. because I was sewing to support my ... by now I have four children, three girls and my son. And I was sewing stuff, so I moved into L.A. and opened a shop. Right when the whole thing's starting to happen. People were ... the first LSD was happening. People were buying trip clothes. Guys from groups were coming in. It was really an interesting time. And, for New Years Eve, I went to a KPFK New Years Eve party with the boys in the band. And there was this man there that I kept watching. I was fascinated by him. And I did something that was very unusual for me. Before we left with the band, I wrote my name and phone number on a piece of paper. (Frank screeches!) And I went up to this man ...

**Frank:** That was ...

**Linda:** (laughing) Was not unusual?! (laughing)

**Louise:** No, no, no, come on, no, no! (Frank screeching and Linda and Frank laughing continues) I hadn't done that one. You know, I might have given him the eye or something. It wasn't that kind of thing. It was not that kind of a thing. (Linda and Frank continue laughing) I was just ... I knew this person ... it sounds silly to say it, of course, but I knew this person had some information for me that was important. It wasn't my usual jazz, Frank!

(Frank screeches, Linda laughs)

**Louise:** I gave it to him and I said, I feel that you have something for me, and I would like to hear from you. And he phoned me and that was Will, who was a filmmaker who was filming the very earliest commune in the L.A. area, Strawberry Fields. A guy named Gridley Wright had it out in the Malibu country. (Frank sounds) Which, of course, burnt down like most of the hippie things.

**Frank:** I am trying to get a copy of ...

**Louise:** Of Will's film!

**Linda:** Yeah.

**Louise:** Well, I'll see what I can do about it. (Frank sounds) I don't know where one is. It was called *Infinity Equals One*. (Frank sounds) And, he has all this great footage of the really early thing that happened with this whole movement from the beginning. But anyway, he had gotten in touch with me. He called me. And ah, I said ... Gridley Wright's thing out there with this first commune, anybody could go out there, but the whole thing was, you had to let it all hang out, you had to be open. (Frank sounds) And here I am with this clothing shop and something looks like the devil on somebody, do I say it looks like the devil on them? No. That looks great, lady. (Frank sounds) Oh man, what a world if we could all just say it like we saw it! (Frank sounds) And I told Will, this man that I had given this paper to, I said, if I didn't have four kids I would do that. And he said, because you have four kids, you should do that. (Frank sounds) And we got together. The commune started in L.A. and we called ourselves the House of the Seventh Angel. Which is from Revelations when the last angel blows its trumpet. He says the time is now! (Frank sounds) And, of course, we believed the time was now! It's always now. And then we moved up into Nevada City and spent time also here on the Haight. We had an apartment here on the Haight. I spent most of my time in Nevada City during this time. I loved the Yuba River and (Frank sounds) my kids and all that. But I was in and out of here then. What was the question?

**Linda:** How you met Father George! (Frank sounds and giggles)

**Louise:** Oh, OK! When I first came up George had one of the early communes ... was up in the Santa Cruz mountains, up at Boulder Creek, called Holiday. I go there with my friend Elizabeth, who you know, Elizabeth Gips, from Santa Cruz. (Frank sounds) And ah, as we walked down, the group there's, ah ... I don't know who all, the Grateful Dead, I mean, all these guys, I mean, I don't know who was who, you know, all these great musicians are playing and I see this wild man out there with this bushy hair like people had then, dancing. I just jumped in and start dancing with him, (Frank sounds) you know. It was ... it was great. That's how I first met him. And then I became friends with him later. You know, that was just, kind of, how I met him. (Frank sounds) And then later on, through this whole communal thing that was happening, mainly around San Francisco, Berkeley, up in this area. When I took my kids and moved back to this place I had in San Bernardino, some of the people from this communal thing came there. And we lived extended family. And that was when I first became really involved with Frank.

**Frank:** What is that?

**Louise:** What is what?

**Frank:** E ...

**Linda:** Oh, what is an extended family? (Frank sounds)

**Louise:** Well, I was there with four children. George lived there. There were three or four other people. The house had all these kind of separate buildings around it that we had fixed up with stained glass and all this stuff. And instead of just living there myself with my children, or a marriage, it was ... everybody was living there. (Franks sounds) And we went through all sorts of stuff. We went through confrontation like you wouldn't believe it! And we all had so much buried anger, sometimes I thought we were going to tear each other to pieces! You know, when there would be conflict between two people in the house, we'd all get around the table (Frank sounds) and get it out. And work it out ... we all had our exit lines. That was one of the rules, you could leave. And mine was, "I don't see why we can't all get along". (Frank howls, Linda laughs) Everybody had their little line they would say when the pressure got on them too much. It was really worthwhile. It was really worthwhile. It was very painful to go through. Because we weren't used to that. You know, really, getting it out and saying it. People don't do that much. (Frank sounds)

**Frank:** I do.

**Louise:** You do! I know you do! And everybody tells you to shut up! (laughing)

**Frank:** No ...

**Linda:** No?

**Frank:** No. All my life ... (Frank sounds)

**Louise:** They've been telling you to shut up or you ...

**Frank:** Yes.

**Louise:** Yeah, of course, (Frank sounds) of course. You can say more by saying "eeehhhh", Frank, than most people can with a hundred pages. (Frank sounds)

**Frank:** They should say keep talking.

**Linda:** You think that might shut you up? (Frank sounds) If they told you to keep talking?

**Louise:** That that would shut me up?

**Linda:** No, that that might shut him up, he's saying. (Frank sounds)

**Louise:** Oh, well, I find now, really I don't feel that everybody has to understand me or I have to understand everybody. (Frank sounds) I think now you say your piece, and then let everybody kind of think whatever they want to think, is kind of how I relate. But I don't spend much time with people like that, you know, now, there's plenty of people you can be open with and you can say it like you feel it. But there sure wasn't when I was growing up. I mean, everything was artificial.

**Frank:** What changed that?

**Louise:** I really think the hippie thing changed that. You know, the beatnik thing was a thing of nihilism, iconoclasm ... we're breaking the old images. And I think that had to happen before there could be this surge of hope (Frank sounds) that the early hippie thing was. It was, I am you and you are we and we are all together. You know, and this whole vibration hit the planet at that time. LSD. The Beatles, for sure. And now it sells toothpaste! You know, we need something new. I wish something new would come up. And sometimes I'm concerned. I mean, I know some of the youth ... it has to be the youth. It's always the youth, you know, that do it. And I don't know...

**Frank:** We ...

**Linda:** The WE Fest. People like the people that put on that festival in North Carolina that we were telling you about.

**Louise:** Yeah, but I don't see that much of that. I see everybody trying to get a good job. To get a good ... your education is not for education, it's to get a job! You know, I see the vast majority of the kids are not rebelling.

**Frank:** F-a ...

**Linda:** FAKE Radio?

**Frank:** Has a chance to be that motivation.

**Louise:** Motivation! Well, see, you guys, I mean, I don't know about this. You know, I can't make any comment on this (Frank sounds) because I'm up in the mountains of Mexico now. You know, all this, all this internet and all this is ... I'm a virgin on it. (Frank giggles) I don't understand it. I hope there's hope for the world in all this. But it's not part of my reality. I mean, it is right now. (laughing) All the equipment lights blinking! But, I hope so, Frank (Frank sounds) because I don't know what ... if there's any hope if it isn't this. You know. (Frank sounds) You know, because you certainly don't on commercial radio or commercial TV or film or the news ... oh my God, you know. You don't hear any kind of real truth. It's all the commercial corporate slant, you know. But I guess with internet, people all over the world are saying what they see. (Frank sounds) Ah, for a long time when I was traveling, you know, around the world, I could see this network going on between people traveling on the cheap. Mainly students and people on sabbaticals, teachers and whatnot. And great communication that way. And it still happens on the beaches of Mexico. You know, there're people down from our country, of course. But a lot of people like from Scandinavia or France or Germany or whatnot. (Frank sounds) And they're ... that's a very free thing. Kind of like the street people thing was. Where people, you know, they'd get together and play music and ... are pretty open and pretty free, and very political as far as what they say. There's tremendous agreement. You know, with people all over the world but it doesn't get out to the voting majority, who are worried about our president's sexual perversions, or whatever they want to call it. You know, I mean, good God.

(Frank howls)

**Frank:** A boat sank under you ...

**Linda:** A boat sank, oh, when you were traveling.

**Louise:** Oh, when I was in Sumatra! You want me to tell the boat story? (Louise laughs)

**Linda:** Yes.

**Louise:** I was telling ...

**Frank:** You are the international bag ...

**Louise:** Bag lady. The international bag lady! (laughing) Yeah, after my kids were raised I took off to go see the world. And I was telling this story to someone and she said, gee, that was the perfect trip, she had Dengue fever and the boat sank on her. (laughing) But, you know.

I thought I had Indonesian well enough to get off the tourist path. And I didn't know "api" means "fire". (laughs) I'm in this little boat going down the Siak rivers in the morning. I'm in the front of the boat all night. I had first class, which meant you had about (gestures) this much on a board, and it was right behind where the engine heat ...

**Linda:** To sit?

**Louise:** Yeah, it was so hot I was terrified of being in that room with all these people. The Indonesian people stayed there because they had their things. I thought, if they rip me off, let them take it! And so, I slept above deck ... they had all these onions. I slept upstairs with all the onions, which was really just fine. And in the morning I'm in the front of the boat, I'm wondering if there might be alligators around or ... (Frank sounds) We're going through all these mangroves ... getting close to the mouth of the sea where the sea is ... everybody's going crazy. People are jumping overboard. (Frank sounds) People are screaming, they're grabbing their children, they're all rushing to the front of the boat. There were some Indonesian soldiers on board. They're shooting their guns up in the air, "Api! Api!" (laughing) A man I had met in Pekanbaru, an Indonesian man, spoke very limited English, but he spoke some English. And he had told me he would watch out for me because there really are pirates in that area. It really wasn't a safe trip. And he said, fire, can you swim? And I turned my head and that flame, (makes swishing sound) up it was going. And I didn't think about anybody or anything. I just dove overboard and swam rapidly away from the boat. (Frank sounds) Eventually, because the soldiers had been shooting their guns up in the air, because there were little tiny fishing villages along, so people came in their fishing boats. And here I am in the water. I mean, I'm thinking, what am I doing here? (laughing) You know. I could still see the cumulus clouds and the water. It was fine, really. And I could see the boat burning. (laughing) And, the few people ... Indonesian people don't swim. They use the water as their sanitation. They shit in the water. And in the ocean, there are sea snakes and things like that, so they're not swimmers. (Frank sounds) The few Indonesian people who could swim were getting people and getting them over to the mangrove trees where they could hold on. Well anyway, so, I'm out there treading water. And this boat comes, and this little tiny Indonesian man is trying to pull me up out of the water. Finally succeeded. I stepped over a dead woman. And, somebody was holding a little girl about three years old, upside down. And I took the child without any thought and I did artificial (makes blowing sounds), you know. And on about the third time I blew in her mouth, she (makes catching breath sounds), so I just sat with her, upside down, and eventually, we were all taken to this village. And there were dead bodies! There were about ... there were 169 people dead, drowned. Out of what I would assume were maybe 225 or 250 people. (Frank sounds) And, the Indonesians feel so totally different about death. I mean, I'm pretty good in any kind of an emergency, but after we're in this village, I can't ... the tears just kept coming. (Frank sounds) And the Indonesian people are making little fires and they're drying their things out. And they were so concerned, like ... was I hurt? Because their idea of death ... it's really a whole different ball game over there. And then, days later, the only other non-Indonesian on the boat was the black boy from Ghana who had been in a missionary school and had left with his bible to teach the ways of the Lord and he goes to Indonesia (laughing) ... and everybody's starving. The Indonesian people took him in and shared their rice. He didn't even know he was off a tourist path. (Frank sounds) You know, the *Lonely Planet* books and whatnot that help you get around the world (laughing)

... He didn't even know about those. And, everybody ... when the Indonesian people ... after this happened, people would see me and they'd give me what you call the bagus, you know, thumbs-up sign. You know, and they ... oh the sharing with some of those people, of the survivors. And it was days later, finally, Robert and I, eventually make it into Singapore. Now, it's a whole different trip there, than Indonesia. Singapore is ... must be the loveliest city in the world! We get off this boat. I still got pants on that I've been in the river with, right? And there's street lights, and sidewalks and it's neat and tidy, and ... we have no money, but I did have my money in traveler's checks in a belt. So the first thing is to change it. Robert and I are walking down the street one way. Coming toward us was a very small Indonesian-looking man and a black man. And as they came toward us I said, excuse me, do you speak English? They said, of course ... you know, I mean, it's bilingual, you know. (Frank sounds) Everybody else speaks English. What's your problem? It turned out Robert and the black guy were from the same tribe in Ghana! And these guys took us to a restaurant and fed us and got us a room. (Frank sounds) And, of course, I'd lost my address book. All my stuff had sunk with the boat! But I had a friend who had invited me to stay with her in Singapore, but I didn't have her address. But, I called my kids. And I had told them what the address was ... and next day this guy from Ghana was there, and he said, I'm at your disposal, however I can help you. So I ended up in Singapore, happily, with a guest room with my own bath! (Frank sounds) (laughing) Good Lord, what a trip! (laughing) But, as they say, it was successful. Dengue fever and a boat sinking was a good trip! And it was. (Frank sounds) You know, you don't want these things to happen and I'm really cowardly. I mean, I would never jump out of an airplane or ... (Frank sounds) I think people are crazy to hang glide. (Frank sounds) But, life does put you into these situations. (Frank sounds)

**Frank:** Just a chapter in your life.

**Louise:** Yeah. I must say, life is interesting. (Frank sounds) I get shy about talking about my life, you know, Frank. This is a little difficult for me. (Frank sounds) I have this happen sometimes. I go see friends who know a lot about me. And they've talked to me about me to friends of theirs. I can't say a word. I get real shy. (Frank sounds) So, you talk!

**Frank:** You came to New York City to ...

**Louise:** Oh right. To deliver Ki-lin and Koala. Yeah, I got all involved in the very early birth movement. The home birth movement.

**Frank:** Because the hospital would not let me ...

**Linda:** Oh, be there for the ...

**Frank:** Even on the floor!

**Linda:** Where the birth was going to take place.

(Frank sounds)

**Frank:** Because I was a crip. And I would freak ...

**Louise says in unison with Linda:** Freak them out! (Frank sounds)

**Frank:** ... the other mothers out. (Frank sounds)

**Louise:** Well, the other mothers were freaked out even before they even see you, Frank! They had those women … they wouldn't allow them out of caged beds, you know. I mean, it was just horrible what was happening with birth. So when the home birth movement got started, I couldn't not deliver babies. I would try to talk people out of it. I didn't really … after I had delivered two babies before I had really any medical training. Just because it was happening and I was a little bit older. My children were all born in a hospital and it was horrible. And ah, so, finally after two births, our doctor friend said, look, I'd better … there was a woman who was in Santa Barbara, when they were doing pepper gas on the students in those days … (Frank sounds) I forget what years those were. And I got training, and I still didn't think of myself as a midwife. But, people were having children at home, and would I come? And I wasn't going to pull on a breech. (Frank sounds) Right? That's Frank's story … I don't know how many people know that that's the story with Frank. He was a breech baby and the doctor pulled. Therefore, you know, his damage happened.

**Linda:** Wow.

**Louise:** And, I had delivered 29 babies, saying where's a doctor? When finally, Dick Moskowitz, you know, and the people started showing up. Who were into the home birth movement. And now there's loads of midwives. When I went back and delivered those babies in New York, Frank, I talked to the legal nurse midwives in New York. And they were saying, oh, I wish we/I could do births like that! Well, you could, (Frank sounds) except you could also … you also had your neck out to be prosecuted for practicing medicine without a license. (Frank sounds) Or in the case of a still birth, for murder. (Frank sounds) That's how it was. And it's not that way anymore. There's loads of good midwives in home birth.

**Linda:** So it wasn't legal at that point when you were doing it?

**Louise:** Oh no, no, no, no, no, no!

**Linda:** Wow.

**Louise:** Uh uh. The doctors didn't want to touch it because of insurance. Not because … I mean, it's safer. You're in your own bacterial field and I mean, it's just better, all the way around. But, no, no. So, people were just having babies at home with nobody! Ah, you know, that's how I really got into it. And after the first two births … I mean it was lovely. They were lovely. I mean, I didn't know what's going on. I just … it looked alright to me, you know so I was … (laughter) well, you know, really, I didn't really know. You know, it was happening, the baby was coming and …. Really, nobody needs to do anything, although births can become a medical problem. It's more apt to be a medical problem if they're in the hospital, that's for sure. And then the third … after I'd gotten this … I stayed with this doctor for a week in Santa Barbara. She taught me to suture on a pork roast. But, I really only had one episiotomy to do that was ever necessary. But, I got back to Santa Fe, and a friend of mine said, please my sister's going to have her second child at home. She hasn't seen a doctor. Refuses to! Would you come to the birth? (Frank sounds) So I met her and I said, yeah. But I did find one doctor who wouldn't do home birth, but he said he would examine her. So I made this appointment for her on Monday, Sunday night she has the baby. (Frank sounds) But then my friend, Cathy, her younger sister, had been at the birth. And then Cathy tells me that she is pregnant and would I deliver her baby. And that was the first one I didn't try to really talk out of it, because now, you know, I'm getting a feeling for what's the norm. I've had this training. I'm reading *Williams Obstetrics* ... scare anybody to death, reading that. (Frank sounds) You know, but ah, so, I'm real pleased and it was a real blessing to be with those births, and those babies.

**Frank:** But it was illegal.

**Louise:** Oh yeah, it was illegal! You better believe it was illegal! (Pause) Yeah, but, you know, there were cases where there was no one with any knowledge there at all. Like people will say, I wanted to have a home birth, but it's a good thing I didn't because the cord was around the baby's neck. Hey, bullshit! All you do is cut it. It's better to not cut it because the baby gets the extra blood ... it's no big thing! You know, ah, but there were cases where the father ... in one case the father freaked out, started pulling. People would freak out. The mother's uterus was inverted. She was dead on arrival. So, how was I not going to go? You know, I mean, you have to do the best you can ...

(Frank sounds)

**Linda:** Yes, yes.

**Louise:** And I was at the first nurse midwife, lay and nurse midwife meeting in El Paso. The midwife down there, boy, she was really something. People would come across the border from Mexico wanting their child to be born in this country. They'd come across when they were in labor and knock on her door. And she was delivering those babies.

**Linda:** Wow.

**Louise:** Most of my women, you know, I got them real early. Real early in their pregnancy. And I'd have a little lab work done, and the blood pressure and the urine. And I worked with doctors for backup, always! Or as soon as I found one, or knew what to have them do.

**Frank:** Doctors who were willing to risk ...

**Louise:** Well, no, no, no, no. Early on there wasn't any doctor who was willing to risk. (Frank sounds) There was a Seventh Day Adventist doctor in Santa Fe who, you know, I tried him. And I said, you know, what was happening, like when I say that I made an appointment for her on Monday. He agreed that he would check her out. (Frank sounds) But he wasn't going to have anything to do with the birth. I delivered 29 babies before any of these doctors, these young, beautiful doctors, showed up, who were into the home birth movement. And it was really nice working with them. You know, like many times, I would take a doctor's birth, or they would take mine, or we would go together, and you know, so then it wasn't any problem. (Frank sounds) But early on, I got this ... God bless this doctor who would get lab work done and do what he could, but he would not ... no, he wouldn't do home birth. And then I was delivering babies in Santa Barbara, and there was a doctor I got to do the lab work there, who really wanted to do home birth. But he wanted to take the hospital to the home. And that isn't what you want! (Frank and Linda sounds) If you got a problem, you want to get to the hospital, you know. And God bless those doctors, they're good in an emergency. I've watched them hold the baby's head just perfect on the monitor, while they set up and did a Caesarean. The thing about birth ... people think, oh the birth is the big thing. No, it's the labor, if it all goes well. When the labor doesn't go well, you go where they do emergency work. And they're good at it.

**Frank:** That is what happened with Jo.

**Louise:** Yeah, with Jo. She was slow labor, which is not really any problem, but all of a sudden her labor came on real fast. And when that happens you're apt to have a placenta that's separating. And you want to go to the hospital, which we did. And, I don't ... I think almost all the babies that were born in a hospital because it could have been a medical situation, probably would have been OK at home.

**Linda:** Yeah.

**Louise:** But, you know, why ... we're not playing games here. We've got a life here and if it becomes medical, you go to the hospital. And so, I felt that as long as there's a normal thing of birth, the woman doesn't need anybody around. She's going to have that baby just dandy! So that was mainly what I felt my role as a midwife was. Is if this is going to become a medical problem, if it goes away from the norm, they're good when it gets to that point.

**Frank:** Yes.

**Louise:** But they're not very good about keeping it away from that point. Or they weren't. I mean, I know it's all changed now too. Hospitals have birthing rooms today. It's a totally different situation today. (Frank sounds) And today any woman who really wants a home birth can have it, you know. And they don't keep them in caged things having to ... you know, it's just much more enlightened.

**Frank:** Funny, I videoed a birth ...

**Linda:** Oh, in a hospital? (Frank sounds) Right. This would have been like in the late '70s. Somebody was having a natural birth ...

**Louise:** A natural birth, but in a hospital.

**Linda:** But it was in a hospital so we were there with our video camera, videotaping the whole thing. So that's how far it came from ...

**Louise:** Yeah, yeah.

**Frank:** And the father ...

**Linda:** Oh, was a guy in a wheelchair. And there was no problem with him being in the room with his wife having the baby. (Frank sounds)

**Louise:** Yeah, you know, there are areas in the world that are getting much better.

**Linda:** Yeah, yeah. (Frank sounds)

**Louise:** But, I understand. I mean, I don't keep up with this now. I'm not delivering babies now. I was asked to deliver a baby in Mexico from some friends of mine. And, I didn't feel I should. You know, I don't know that normal sound of the heartbeat now. Or things like ... I miss the births. But, you know, I'm not doing it now, so. (Frank sounds) That was then. And after working with birth I had the blessing of working with hospice. Working on the other end when people are leaving. Home death.

**Frank:** What is that?

**Louise:** Well, that was for people who are terminally ill and who don't want to go to the hospital. They don't want to be on tubes. They want to just go in their bed peacefully, thank you. And that's really the way to go, you know. And I'm not afraid of dying. As a result of what the people taught me. It's just like ... it was the women who taught me about birth. Not the doctors. Not *Williams Obstetric*, it was the women. (Frank sounds) And the same thing with death. People say, well, they were in such pain. Well, they were in pain in the hospital. And I'm not ... you know, I can't speak for all of it because I don't know, maybe some home ... maybe some of them are better off in the hospital, I don't know. But I know, I know you extend life past what the person would do by keeping them alive longer. And it's just ... all these people suffering in hospitals long periods of time because they're so afraid to die, you know. (Frank sounds) And I have seen ... experiences I've had with death is it doesn't hurt. (Frank sounds) You know. I remember one woman, I'm rubbing her back and I realized she's not breathing any more. Marjorie! Where are you, Marjorie? (Frank sounds) (Linda laughing) You know, just nobody home anymore. You know, they're gone. And the body looks just fine. But, see, this is something else that ... we've lost our touch with birth and we've lost our touch with death. You know, we go to funerals. And people die in the hospital. It's away. You know, and of course, we're going for immortality in the body today! Which scares the bejesus out of me! What they're doing! With biogenetics and now they've got the stem ... cell stems, where they can create any organs. Are we going to quit having babies?! So everybody can just take up the space on earth. The old people! I mean, ah, oh man, it's really crazy! (Frank sounds) I mean, ah, don't believe that there aren't people being cloned today, man! If they can clone a sheep, don't you know, somebody's being cloned! And all these transplants ... we're supposed to be good people and donate our organs so somebody can live a few more years, I don't know. It's the wrong ... we're going down the wrong track on all that. (Frank sounds) If they can do it, they will do it. If they can do it, they are doing it. DNA characteristic traits. Who wants an aggressive child?! Nobody.

**Frank:** Who wants me?

**Louise:** I want you, Frank! (all laughing) I want you! They wouldn't have caught you, your birth defect! Your genes are probably just dandy! Probably the best genes going! (Frank sounds) But that's the truth. Who wants girls as opposed to boys!? Everybody wants a son, right? I mean ...

**Frank:** They don't realize that is what makes evolution happen.

**Louise:** Right. We don't know what's connected to what! (Frank sounds) We have no idea what's connected to what! And this bank of things ... I ... it's taken us billions of years to evolve to where we are and already the sperm pool is wrecked. They keep people alive that shouldn't. You know, immediately we do surgery. That's on the genetics on a lot of this stuff. Somebody's got something to say about it.

**Frank:** Heidi ...

**Linda:** Heidi [one of Frank's students - Ed.] does volunteer massage for hospice.

**Louise:** That's beautiful. Yeah. So she knows what ... how it is. And people work things out.

A lot of working with hospice where I felt I helped the most was the families. Because they would try to act like everything's going to be hunky dory because of their fears of death, their denial. And usually the people who are hospice patients accepted it, or they wouldn't ... they'd be in the hospital going through the numbers. One woman, I called her because it looked like her mother was going to go. And I thought she might want to come. She came and she went in the bedroom and I left to leave them time alone. She came out and she burst into tears in my arms. She said, oh, I was so afraid I would break down in there. I said, honey, you go in there and cry with your momma. You know, I mean, let's get real here. You know. And, or one woman ... Helen had a couple of days left to live, and her husband's trying to have her take one more bite of Jell-O, bless his heart. And she says to him, she says, don't blame me any more. You know, (Frank sounds) I mean, you see ...

**Frank:** Death is a part of life.

**Louise:** Yeah, yeah, (Frank sounds) it is and we're all going to make that big trip. We're all going to make that big trip. (Frank sounds) And nobody knows. Nobody knows what's on the other side.

**Frank:** It is healthy to die! (Frank sounds)

**Louise:** Yes, of course, (Frank sounds, laughing) of course, I mean, that's the play. We don't really know why we're here or where we're going or how we got here ...

**Frank:** But it is not "of course" in the ...

**Linda:** Oh, for the medical world ... you say, "of course" it's healthy to die, that's what you said, "of course". And Frank said it is not "of course" for the medical world.

**Louise:** Oh, no, no! And I understand that. When life is in your hands you want to do all you can to preserve it. I don't think we can blame the doctors on this. We can blame the pharmaceutical companies that pay to support the medical schools that train the doctors, you know. But, it's more of a spiritual level for each person, I think. I think unless you've ... I mean, accept death? I don't know. I must say it gives me a few shivers. You know, (laughs) what's it like when we're not here, you know. (all laughing) (Frank sounds) But, the process of dying. And I trust this that life is dandy (Frank sounds) whatever it is. And even if it's nothing! It's dandy.

**Frank:** I have always been curious about ...

**Louise:** About what is going to be ...

**Frank:** After death. (Frank sounds)

**Louise:** Yeah, I think we're all ... I think so, you know.

**Linda:** We're all curious.

**Louise:** Well, I mean, you know, it's a matter of faith. But you know, I really believe that we're not even here! I really got heavy in the *Course of Miracles*, right. This is all an illusion, gang! You know, we think we are here in this ego and that this is all there is to it. And I know that's not true. You know, and my personal feeling is probably after we die it's not much different.

*Frank Moore and Louise Scott. Photo by Linda Mac.*

You know what I mean? Wherever we are, we are. It's in our heads, where we are.

**Linda:** What? Let's see ... do you want me to see what's going on here? (Linda reads from the chat room) "The only unhealthy is fighting it."

**Louise:** Right!

**Linda continues reading from the chat room:** "The soul fragment we're given can't deal with death at first. Shock, it does not understand it, just like when you're born, existence is a shock."

**Louise:** Um, hummm.

**Linda continues reading from the chat room:** "It was just a part of perfection a split second ago. Love can be a shock to it too, but you're drawn to love, aren't you? It seems to be a need." This is all Cyberpup talking in the chat room.

**Frank:** Shock is the challenge. (Frank sounds)

**Louise:** Well, you know with birth ... you know, I've had babies come out ... of course, they come out nose down, and then they kind of turn towards their shoulders. And I've had babies before they were out even, their shoulders went out their heads had turned. And I swear, focus right in the eyeball. You know, this is a fallacy that babies don't see at birth! That's because they put the nitrates in their eyes. And the bright light, and all of that. (Frank sounds) And how do they know to look you right in the eye and focus? And then, I think of other things like, children love to be thrown in the air! Most children believe they can fly! You know, we have these angels that fly. I mean, there's a lot of stuff. And, you know, I've wondered with death, if somebody's on the other end, saying, oh, here she comes!

**Linda:** Catching you! (all laughing) Just like in birth!

**Louise:** You know! Somebody's commenting on that too.

**Linda:** OK. Let's see. (reading from the chat room:)"It seems to be a need. A part of what's missing ... "(laughs) OK, so he didn't realize we were reading everything he's saying out. (Frank sounds) He said, "Oh I didn't know that this was live! That we were going to be reading..." He didn't know we were going to be reading what he was typing.

**Louise:** What did he say?

**Linda:** (continues reading from the chat room) "What we know as our lives seems to be how we deal with it. The point in the middle."

**Louise:** Uh huh. That's all we can deal with.

**Frank:** The now. (Frank sounds)

**Louise:** The now! The rest is all a dream. If the past exists, where is it?! (Frank sounds) You know, where is it? Well, let's get (inaudible) (all laughing) (Frank sounds)

**Linda:** (continues reading from the chat room) "If you take one part of perfection away, all of a sudden it needs. Now you have action. It's not whole." (Frank sounds)

**Frank:** We are getting deep. (laughing)

**Louise:** Yeah, well, you know, we can go off in the clouds on it, you know. It's ... you know, actually, you guys, I'm falling asleep on you. (Frank sounds)

**Linda:** It's almost twelve o'clock! (Frank sounds) We've kept you almost two hours.

**Louise:** Yeah, I mean, really, it's been a long day.

**Linda:** Yeah. (Frank sounds)

**Louise:** So, may I leave, Frank? (laughing) (Frank sounds)

**Frank:** Yes.

**Louise:** Oh good. Good night. Time to bed. Good night Mikee. Good night Linda. That was so interesting you guys. I can't even believe this high tech world! (laughing) (Frank sounds)

# Dr. Richard Kerbavaz

## How to Reform the Health Care System

Recorded May 2, 2008 on luver.com

..........................................................................................................

"Kerbavaz is a rare guy! He knows practically everything, enjoys life/people, and is available!"
– Frank Moore

Frank first met Dr. Rich Kerbavaz when Frank was a patient at Rockridge Medical Group in the early 1980s. Twenty-five years later, they had become dear friends, Frank was running for president of the U.S., and Rich came over to discuss Frank's health care plan and to compare it with the plans of the "major" candidates.

Two years later, Frank went into the hospital for a routine operation, and instead spent six weeks in intensive care, and almost died. Rich Kerbavaz was there following Frank's care, and was his unfailing advocate. Frank said, after surviving this hospital experience, that if he did not have Rich, who was "willing to go against the prevailing expectations, it would have been much harder for me to beat the curse of their expectations, judgments, projections." This gives you an idea of who Rich Kerbavaz is.

With 30 years as a highly respected ENT doctor and surgeon, Rich knew the medical and medical insurance systems. In this interview Rich and Frank work together to develop an alternate, more humane model for health care in this country.

(Frank's complete presidential platform can be found in Appendix 1.)

..........................................................................................................

**Frank:** ... is what they don't want.

**Richard:** Ah, the bigger cross-sections kind of things.

**Linda:** Gathering together like that.

**Richard:** Yeah. I guess there is a certain amount of just resistance to having any kind of a gathering at this point.

**Linda:** Yes, it seems so.

**Frank:** Other than corporate-sponsored events.

**Richard:** Yeah. And that's OK. But if it doesn't have that kind of sponsorship and a narrow goal that they can justify somehow, they don't want it to happen. I think the fear is loss of control. And it's just sort of the issue of controlling a lot of actions and behaviors.

**Frank:** I think that they is a big part of why we don't have universal free health care.

**Richard:** Ah, what a segue! (laughing) Good point, good point.

**Frank:** The rich don't want to be in the same system as the rest.

**Linda:** As the unrich.

**Richard:** And there's just a lot of obstacles or things that keep getting thrown up that are just not really true, but are the way people believe or the way people react to things. It's really interesting in all the big surveys, if you just ask Democrats the question about some sort of health plan or national health plan, it's overwhelmingly popular. And if you ask Republicans the same questions, it's overwhelmingly negative. And if you phrase the exact same question the same way to two different groups it just is totally polarized. It's very interesting. At almost every level asking it, whether they're in favor of a plan or opposed to the plan or whether they think it would be good for them or good for the country ... there's all these different ... the same kind of a survey's been done a half a dozen times and each time they ask slightly different questions, and it still comes out a big divide right along party lines! And those who are not declared in either major party, it sort of splits 50/50. So it's interesting.

**Frank:** Why is that?

**Richard:** I think that it's just how people frame the internal discussion or the internal dialogue. They're using their political filters to look at a bigger issue. And so it's a threat in some way to the Republican party or to the Republican ... the people who support the Republican party. And so people who are either a little bit more liberal or more of a Democrat, more of a social Democrat or aren't really involved with any organized party, tend to be in favor of the universal health plan. And that's across the board, however you ask the question.

**Frank:** Like if the rich were in Medi-Cal, Medi-Cal would get better fast.

**Richard:** Yeah, it would. (laughing) It would make a big difference. Actually, the ones that you want to get in Medi-Cal are the politicians. (laughing)

**Frank:** Because they would not stand for it.

**Richard:** No, they wouldn't stand for those kinds of things. And clearly they would not be eager to keep doing all the cuts that they seem to keep doing now to the Medi-Cal program. Just every year, anytime there's any kind of a budget crunch, the first thing that goes is health care! The easy thing ... actually there was another survey not too long ago that, in California, people were more in favor of cutting health care than cutting K through 12 education. I'm not sure exactly how they asked the question, but there was more support in the budget crunch time of cutting health care than cutting educational expenses. Tough choice, but nobody was really eager to raise taxes.

**Frank:** (making sounds) It is not really a choice. We need both.

**Richard:** Yeah, right, right. And then the trick is coming up with some sort of a funding mechanism that's a little more fair across the board. Which is one of the things that's nice about some of the tax proposals that you put out there, is that it eliminates a lot of the very strange, skewed tax codes that we have now and tries to make it a little more fair to everybody.

**Frank:** And the 7 ...

**Linda:** The 75% tax over $1 million per individual and $5 million per corporation ...

*Frank Moore and Dr. Richard Kerbavaz (video capture)*

**Frank:** Would take the greed out of the picture.

**Richard:** Right, right. And that would be a very good thing to do as well. 'Cause clearly we've got an awful lot of issues at the very top. That most of the people who make that kind of money aren't paying taxes, at all! They manage to find shelters for everything. So where's the justice in that, where the bulk of the tax burden is being carried by the middle class.

**Frank:** But I get: that is discrimination.

**Linda:** That's what you get? Yeah, that's what people criticize: that he's discriminating with that.

**Richard:** Discriminating against the wealthy?!

**Linda:** Yes.

**Richard:** (laughter) Interesting concept.

**Linda:** And I'm sure it's not rich people saying that, either.

**Richard:** That's an interesting concept. That there are ... I guess there are enough people that aren't in that tax bracket or in that income bracket who want to be, but they view it as a threat to their dreams or their aspirations, somehow.

**Frank:** But they don't see box seats as discrimination.

**Richard:** That's an interesting point. (laughter) Well, you see, box seats are to give them something, and taxes takes something away.

**Frank:** And the rich need some perks (laughter) to be rich.

**Richard:** (laughing) That's true! Otherwise you stop being rich! It's terrible! It ruins the whole point! So maybe what you should do is just allow that for everybody who's in that tax bracket, that they get a box seat some place. (laughter)

**Frank:** And my policy on patents would help medicine.

**Richard:** Yeah, because it would eliminate a lot of the profit margins and in terms of the patents for like drugs and devices which creates a total monopoly on a lot of the product. That's actually an important way of cutting down costs. That if now suddenly there's not that big premium on all those products, they could be sold at a much more reasonable price, closer to the cost of production. And still allow a profit margin for the companies but not such an obscene profit margin.

**Frank:** Also royalties to the public on anything that is based on something that was developed in the universities.

**Richard:** It would give the public a return on the investment they've made in these universities so that the products can actually be back to the public domain.

**Frank:** Or by the government.

**Linda:** Or developed by the government.

**Richard:** Yeah. So if it's created by the government dime, why should some individual then be given the reward for that?

**Frank:** Yes. So that would be part of how we can fund the health care system.

**Richard:** Yeah. Health care and education. So we can have it all! Right. There's lots of places there where savings can be had and earning go plugged back into the public domain or the public good.

**Frank:** And medicine for the non-profitable diseases.

**Richard:** Yeah, and then you could treat things, so that if profit margin is not the only driving force, now there could be access to care for people who have things that don't happen to be fashionable or don't happen to have high profit margin. Thus, primary care. You know, all the things that don't have a big payoff immediately, but in terms of public good, make a huge difference. Things like immunization. Things like basic health care.

**Frank:** I just saw that smallpox is coming back because people don't get immunized because they don't trust it.

**Richard:** Yeah. And even measles. There was a thing in the paper I think today that measles is having a come back. This is the worst year for measles for years. It was just because people aren't getting immunized. Some of it is immigration, people weren't immunized where they were born. But a lot of it is people don't trust the vaccines. They're afraid of the potential side effects.

**Frank:** Autism.

**Richard:** Oh yeah, autism, yeah. And I'm not sure that that's as big of a risk as people are afraid of, but it's pretty scary for a parent thinking about it.

**Linda:** And that is one of the risks of some of the vaccines? And that's always been the case or is it more so now?

**Richard:** Nobody really understands it, which is the problem. It's just that it's scary. It's become ... it's easy to sort of demonize the industry because you don't trust the drug industry for anything else, why would you trust them for this? On the other hand, things like smallpox and measles still kill people. And the danger of not getting immunized ... when you look at all the old data, before there were these vaccines, a lot more people died from all these diseases. And there was a lot more disability and a lot more death absent the vaccine than there has been since the vaccine is around. Perhaps if we had a better system for taking care of kids who had autism there would be a lot less fear about having that be the outcome.

**Frank:** And if we took greed out ...

**Linda:** ... of the picture maybe people would be more inclined to trust the medical companies.

**Richard:** Yeah, and you can't really blame people for not trusting the drug companies because look at what they've brought us. And there have been a lot of wonderful drugs, but there have also been a lot of things that caused an awful lot of problems. And they've been sold equally with greed as the motive. It was all profit motive that drove the whole process. And now there's a lot of controversy about how some of the research was rigged.

**Frank:** Yes.

**Richard:** And how some of the FDA studies were not really being done with any kind of goal of finding truth but only promoting a drug. So, we've not done really well as a profession these days.

**Frank:** Science has been kidnapped by profits.

**Richard:** Yeah. Profits and politics. You know, it's scary when you look at how many even professional sort of public sector scientists feel like in the last seven years that they've been really limited in what they can do and told what to say. So the FDA, all of the big groups that are doing ... EPA ... all of the things that are trying to be good stewards have not been able to do their job in the last term, the last presidential cycle. So there's a lot of hope that some of the people who are in there who are trying to do a good job, will stick it out for a little bit longer in the hopes that the next administration, like yours, would maybe make the science part more of a priority and not the profit part.

**Frank:** Because science needs the freedom to explore.

**Richard:** And from that freedom and from that exploration new discoveries and new growth and new potential can happen.

**Frank:** Not to be funneled down to a search for what will make the most money.

**Richard:** Right! And I think that when you talk to people who are really scientists most of the time what they're really interested in is the quest, is the knowledge, is the exploration! That's what drives people in science. Not the profit motive. It happens somewhere else along the way where they ... the only way to get funding is to go through some company or go to create a product for a particular purpose. But I think that that would really generate a whole new enthusiasm in the sciences. Not just medicine, but all the sciences.

**Frank:** That is one thing that the guaranteed minimum wage ...

**Richard:** Because that also then frees up people, totally removes the profit motive and allows people to do what they love.

**Linda:** The guaranteed minimum income.

**Richard:** Because again, that just changes the whole complexity of how people work for a living or what they do. Also, just the issue of the guaranteed health care, because so many people now work, not even so much for the income as for the health care. They're just afraid not to have insurance. And if you take that out of the equation it makes a big difference in terms of freeing people up to make choices of where they live and how they live.

**Frank:** And even if you have medical insurance, it don't cover ...

**Richard:** Right. And then the other ... yeah, that's the other part of the question, the things that it chooses to exclude. Or if you have a condition which they choose not to provide insurance for, you can just be kind of aced out of the whole thing now.

**Frank:** And they pay only a percentage.

**Richard:** Right. And the co-pays, the deductibles, all the things that they don't pay for like eyeglasses or dental care. It's not that those things are not important, it's just that they managed to carve that out. Or hearing aids! Another one that most of the insurance plans don't pay a nickel toward hearing aids. And as you know, it makes a huge difference in quality of life. And it's just one of those things that the insurance industry has been allowed to not pay for.

**Frank:** Teeth are not a body part.

**Richard:** (laughing) Only until you need to take a bite out of something!

**Frank:** They don't pay for dental.

**Linda:** Medi-Cal? Medi-Cal pays for dental, but good luck finding a dentist!

**Richard:** Right, that's the trouble.

**Linda:** Frank has never used his Medi-Cal for dental.

**Richard:** Because there are very few dentists who take it at all. And most of the dentists I've talked to say that the rate, even before the current set of cuts are actually less than the cost of the materials. So not only is the labor free, they're actually subsidizing the materials as well.

**Frank:** For a medical system to work, all doctors have to take all patients.

**Richard:** Right. And there has to be a system in place where that can happen transparently so that there isn't suddenly these issues of who has what kind of insurance and has access to certain kinds of care. Because that's really the sort of de facto rationing that we have now. It's really not that health care isn't rationed, it's only rationed by who has money and who has insurance.

**Frank:** Michael Moore said if the insurance companies are a part of a medical ...

**Richard:** Are part of the medical health plan?

**Frank:** Yes. That plan is a con.

**Richard:** Right. You know, currently they just have basically the right to take as much out of the system as they can. And there have been all these different estimates about how much money we paid for insurance. Essentially it's at least 30% and probably a little more of all of the health care dollars goes strictly to the insurance companies, or go to the system that we create to pay for insurance. So there's the insurance companies themselves and their marketing, and the costs of all our offices dealing with all these different insurance companies. So right off the top you could probably save 30% by getting them out of the equation.

**Frank:** But neither Hillary Clinton nor Barack Obama will get the insurance companies out of the equation.

**Richard:** They pay an awful lot of money as fees to all these different people and they own all the lobbyists. And thus, they control huge parts of Congress. So it's going to be very difficult to get them out of the equation unless you have a major sort of a turn over as to how people think about insurance. There's already a lot of support in the public! The problem is actually convincing the politicians of that.

**Frank:** They would force people to get insurance.

**Richard:** So they're basically forcing everybody to subsidize the insurance companies to that however many billions of dollars they get. It's an interesting business model.

**Frank:** And just the big ...

**Richard:** ... big companies, because they're the ones who can compete. All the plans basically stack the decks in favor of the big insurance companies. And it's essentially a public subsidy. The other part, of course, is that they all would use tax dollars to buy insurance for the people who don't have the incomes to support it. So it's yet another way that the public is supporting the big companies.

**Frank:** Rather than directly pay.

**Richard:** Right, right. And it's for some reason more acceptable to pay the insurance companies than it is to just pay for health care. It's still a big government subsidy, it's still a big government system, it's still in lots of ways socialized medicine which is kind of a bugaboo. It's still money coming out of the public coffers to pay for health care but we get to pay more because we're paying the insurance companies to administer it for us. Instead of using an existing system to pay for it, like Medicare and all these other things that the government is already paying for. It's just an interesting model.

**Frank:** Doctors could be paid at a certain amount per patient.

**Richard:** Um-hum. And there are some systems that do that now in terms of the managed care where you get paid a certain amount per patient. Or there's models now where there's also ... you know, like the VA already exists where doctors are just paid a salary. The military system exists, where doctors are just paid a salary. So there are lots of ways in the existing system that you could do either a capitated model where you get paid so much per patient or continue like Medicare where you pay so much per service and just somehow control how the utilization works, like Medicare does. And Medicare already sort of controls how much we can charge for everything we do. And you still can do what you think is right for the patient. That's one model. Or you could have more of either capitations of paid per patient per month or just get paid a salary for what you do. And all those are already in existence.

**Frank:** A key would be the patient/doctor relationship as the base.

**Richard:** Right. Because ultimately that's where it happens. It's in the interaction between the doctor and the patient. And a lot of the other trappings that we put into the mix get in the way. And currently we're letting the insurance keep that relationship from being as effective as it can be.

**Frank:** The doctor and the patient decide what the patient needs.

**Richard:** Right. And that's the best solution, is to just have everything else pushed aside and really determine what the needs are. And figure that at an individual level where it's really between the doctor and the patient that that decision can happen. And that includes all the other kinds of ancillary services, like the dental stuff. That includes all the alternative things like acupuncture, Chinese herbs, which you guys have found very successful. And so those are all things that really should be accessible equally with everything else that's done.

**Frank:** And then patients could rate the ...

**Richard:** Rate the doctors? Yeah, see that would be great! (laughter) Another very interesting sort of way to turn things around a little bit. You know, if you could sort of have the salaries based on patient satisfaction or quality outcomes or all these other things that could be a very revolutionary way to model things!

**Frank:** So, there would be no pre-authorizations.

**Richard:** Right! Because if the decision is between the doctor and the patient you don't need to have the insurance company pre-authorizing things, if it's not an issue of what's going to get paid for, it's just an issue of what's the right decision is.

**Frank:** And then, if there is a question, then there could be a hearing.

**Richard:** A hearing or some sort of ... and the other thing that is I think really useful is a second opinion system whereby, if you're not sure, that you have a built-in opportunity to get a second opinion from somebody else. And either hearing ... the other way that they do sometimes with some of the managed care plans is they don't do pre-authorizations before the procedure, but they look at utilization patterns over time. And, so, if there's somebody who gets CAT Scans on everybody, that gets taken to some board or reviewed so you can actually look at it after the fact to just see how people are utilizing the system. And there may be a perfectly good reason, but you like to have somebody ask the question of why that's happening, why are these higher cost procedures being done.

**Frank:** Before HMOs, doctors sometimes had cozy ...

**Richard:** Oh, cozy relationships with some of these ... actually, yeah, there have been all sorts of situations where the doctors were investors in some CAT Scan or MRI machine or ... so there was essentially some profit margin in ordering these tests.

**Frank:** That was a part of why HMOs came in.

**Richard:** Yeah. Actually the other part that controlled a lot of that was one of our local congressmen, Pete Stark, who did a lot of work with sort of Medicare and health issues in general. And he's the one who created most of the laws about what you can and can't do. And tried to put a real division between investments and practice of medicine so there wasn't sort of a kick back thing. As a doctor you can't own an interest in the MRI scanners or the nursing homes or something else that would be a potential profit margin that would interfere with your judgment clinically.

**Frank:** Again my tax ...

**Linda:** ... tax plan would take care of some of that.

**Richard:** Right! Again, because it takes the greed issue out. Once you have less issue of the greed, it solves a lot of problems across the board.

**Frank:** And hospitals should never be for profit.

**Richard:** Right. Because again that's ... it's a built-in conflict of interests. Although again, the high tax on corporate profits over a certain amount also takes of care a lot of that problem.

**Frank:** Exactly.

**Richard:** So mainly this kind of eliminates the greed motive.

**Frank:** Again, before HMOs some hospitals kept patients in longer ...

**Linda:** ... than they needed to be.

**Richard:** Right. Well, both HMOs ... the part that's interesting, of course, is that what shifts when you have all these HMOs is now the only people left who are allowed to make the money are the insurance companies. Because you know all these other things have restricted profits and cut back on some of these means that they had of getting more income streams, but they've still granted more and more to the insurance companies. So it's actually an incredibly regulated industry, both the hospital level and individual practitioners, and yet the group that has the least regulation makes the most money, that's the insurance companies.

**Frank:** And is in control.

**Richard:** And is in control. And provides absolutely nothing of any value. (laughter) Because at least the hospitals and the doctors, they're all providing something that the people value. I don't know anybody who likes insurance. Nobody likes the insurance companies. Nobody really ... but we pay them tremendous amounts of money.

**Frank:** Now they kick people out of the hospital before they should leave.

**Richard:** Exactly. Because now there's more profit in getting people back out on the streets.

**Frank:** Joe.

**Linda:** Oh, our neighbor, he's in his 70s and he has cancer. And he's getting all these treatments, which are just killing him. They're really killing him. But, he'll end up in the hospital for something and they'll send him right back. The woman he's with, he's been with for thirty years or so, she's old too. So she's, why are you sending him home? She can't lift him, she can't get him on and off the toilet. So it's like they call us and Corey and Alexi go down and are picking him up off the floor all the time.

**Richard:** Oh man!

**Linda:** But, they won't keep him in the hospital long enough to get him so he can stand up.

**Richard:** And they're probably also not providing any kind of home support or any other resources that might actually help him be at home.

**Linda:** Oh no, nothing! A walker!

**Richard:** A walker. Yeah, that's a big help.

**Frank:** I invented a mop.

**Linda:** Oh, for Joe?

**Richard:** A mop?

**Linda:** Well, it's because ... he's still who he is. So when he washes his hands he gets water on the floor. He likes to clean it up.

**Richard:** (groans)

**Linda:** So he leans over to clean it up and he falls down and he can't get up. So then Corey and Alexi run down the street. So Frank said, make him something with like a mop, some kind of a stick ...

**Richard:** Brilliant!

**Linda:** ... that he can dry the floor with without bending down.

**Richard:** Yeah! That's brilliant! That's great. (laughing)

**Linda:** He's not going to stop trying.

**Richard:** Does it work for him?

**Linda:** I'm hoping that that's happened!

**Richard:** That's great.

**Frank:** That is what the ...

**Linda:** ... doctors or medical people should be doing, dealing with things on that level.

**Richard:** Right! That's really getting to where the rubber meets the road. That's quality of life on a daily basis.

**Linda:** Yeah. And they're totally on their own with all that stuff. Nobody's dealing with that. We're dealing with it.

**Richard:** Yeah. Well, it's good that you guys are able to, because you have a little sophistication with this stuff, and you actually can think about these kinds of things and make something work for him. But just think if he were really alone. If he didn't have the support of the neighborhood.

**Linda:** If Betty and Joe were alone, yeah, I don't know what they would do.

**Richard:** That would be a terrible thing.

**Frank:** They would be in a nursing home.

**Richard:** Yeah.

**Linda:** Not together either.

**Frank:** Not a retirement community ...

**Linda:** ... but a nursing home.

**Richard:** And then the challenge there, too, is in terms of getting it paid for. You know, that's another big problem for people where a lot of the insurance plans don't cover long-term care at all. And so people who need to get nursing home level care are basically using up their resources, whatever they have and then they're stuck. So it's really a challenge for getting people into long-term care as well. I think it's better in general to be in a supportive community instead of the nursing home.

**Frank:** Yes.

**Richard:** And to have the independence to be in their own home doing the things they love to do gives him a much better quality of life, as long as he's able to do that.

**Frank:** And it would create jobs.

**Richard:** Right. Right. And you have better quality of life and an opportunity for people who are currently under-employed to do something really very personally rewarding and something that's very personal in terms of just the contact with somebody. And that would be great. And most people, as we have an aging population, most people really fear the nursing home. That's not viewed as something that's life, that's considered to be sort of an early death. And this is really something that we should offer better alternatives to our seniors.

**Frank:** Six months is the average.

**Linda:** Of what, of how long people live, last in a nursing home?

**Richard:** Six months, yeah. It's clearly better to be able to age in place and to have a structure where that happens is really kind of rare.

**Frank:** And cheaper.

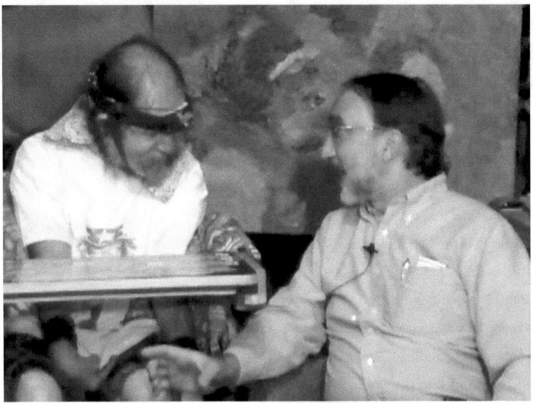

*Frank Moore and Dr. Richard Kerbavaz (video capture)*

**Richard:** It's more effective, it's more humane and it's ultimately cheaper than comparing its infrastructure.

**Frank:** Preventative medicine would cut costs.

**Richard:** Because clearly it's cheaper to treat something before it becomes a big expensive problem, as well as kinder to everybody involved.

**Frank:** Meals in schools would cut medical costs ...

**Linda:** ... if the meals in schools were healthy.

**Richard:** Cut medical costs and also improve kids' performance in schools and change the entire environment of the school. Because now the school becomes much more of a community. And it's also a useful model for communities that aren't terribly interested in education.

**Frank:** But now Oakland is raising the cost for lunch in school.

**Richard:** How much are they raising it to, do you know?

**Frank:** No.

**Richard:** And again, it seems crazy that of all places to raise the cost, the kids and the parents are not in a position to really argue with that.

**Frank:** It should be free!

**Richard:** It should be part of the education. Because it's important for the education to happen.

**Frank:** And a part of the health system.

**Richard:** Because clearly it's not strictly educational, it really is part of health, health and wellness. Maybe instead of a health system we should call it a wellness system, and try to get everybody really healthier, more well as we go along.

**Frank:** Yes.

**Richard:** The other kind of school thing that I thought was interesting are the efforts to try to have the kids more involved with growing food and having school gardens and projects that are part of that so that they're connected to what the product of the food is, and it's not just something that comes on a tray, but they understand some of where it came from. That's another way to give kids options to not only grow and encourage them to do other things. But to show them how they fit into the universe.

**Frank:** And arts and music.

**Richard:** Yeah. Again, those are all part of what it is to be human and should be part of what we all learn.

**Frank:** All make you more healthy.

**Richard:** Right. So the question is, what things are not part of the health care system? (laughing) We've sort of got everything rolled in there now, and it makes total sense.

**Frank:** Prisons should be ...

**Richard:** ... part of health care as well. (laughing) Wow.

**Frank:** And education ...

**Linda:** ... should be part of the health care system?

**Mikee:** Prisons should be part of the education and health care systems.

**Richard:** So do you separate those out or do you try to have them sort of rolled together to try to create more of a cohesive concept?

**Frank:** Maybe in some way.

**Richard:** Yeah. And it makes sense. Because you really want to integrate it. And you want to have education part of whatever prison system you have. And you want to have the health care supporting across all those boundaries. That would be good. It would be an interesting idea. How to try to get it all together. What you need is to find a health care and prison and education czar to run the whole thing together.

**Frank:** How?

**Richard:** How to run it all together? I don't know. That's going to be a challenge because you really need to have it working from a similar basic premise of the individual and so clearly you need to get the prisoners involved in figuring out what happens in the prison. How is

73

this going to work to support their needs too, as well as society's needs? The students to some degree have to be involved in the education. How is it going to support their needs? Just as we emphasize the doctor/patient relationship in the health care system, we need to come up with some similar way to empower everybody who's involved in the other systems so that it becomes part of the same thing.

**Frank:** Yes.

**Richard:** But it's a major paradigm shift in how we look at all these different things to now, instead of splitting them apart, try to bring them together again and put them under one kind of conceptual roof.

**Frank:** Rockridge was a model.

**Linda:** Rockridge was HealthAmerica, it turned into HealthAmerica, but originally was Rockridge.

**Richard:** Oh yeah! That's right. Which is where I met you first actually, yeah.

**Linda:** Yeah! A model of bringing all the different, at least within the medical system, together.

**Richard:** And they made a real effort to bring in the social works side and all the home services and all those things.

**Linda:** Yes.

**Richard:** There's another group in Oakland, On Lok, which is a seniors organization. Again, the idea of aging in place. Providing home services instead of having people go to a nursing home. So it's again, kind of along that way of trying to bring other players that are not usually thought of in the health care system into the arena where they're working together to make things happen.

**Linda:** That's like a private organization?

**Richard:** Yeah. It's a private organization. I'm not sure exactly how they're funded but I know that they do a certain amount of Medicare, HMO stuff and a lot of home health services, including things like vans to take people to appointments.

**Frank:** Where Erika works is a model but it is only for people who can afford it.

**Linda:** We always think if it was like that, if everybody, anybody could move into a place like that, when they got to the point where they couldn't live alone or didn't want to …

**Richard:** And when you look at the quality of life, all the things, the resources that they have compared to the average nursing home, it's completely different. And the level of support that really lets them be pretty independent within that construct.

**Frank:** And there is no reason why …

**Linda:** … everybody shouldn't be able to have that option.

**Richard:** Right. Right. And indeed there could be ways to try to convert some of the existing nursing homes into something that's more like that kind of a model. It should ultimately be less expensive. When you think about the level of support services and people that it takes to run a nursing home compared to what you guys have, you get by with a very small staff comparatively speaking to the number of people that live there.

**Frank:** And if we had home care it would not have to be isolated.

**Richard:** Right. And ideally you could have more like what you guys have in this neighborhood. Where you are all supporting your neighbors. And you can really build on the neighborhood model so that the community itself supports other members of the community. That's one of the nice things about this neighborhood, that you guys are an amazingly cohesive community, considering how diverse the population is.

**Linda:** Yeah.

**Frank:** And Rockridge worked except for Medi-Cal.

**Richard:** Yeah, that was the problem, I guess. That they somehow or another either weren't making enough money or the Medi-Cal system cut them out. Originally they were being supported to some extent through Medi-Cal and I think they just restructured what they were paying for.

**Frank:** Crack.

**Linda:** It was a crack? Crack down? Oh, the drug, crack?

**Richard:** Oh!

**Frank:** They took everybody, so when ...

**Linda:** ... crack cocaine started to be a big issue, they had a lot of patients ... and that was a problem?

**Richard:** It started to cost them too much money or they couldn't really provide care anymore.

**Frank:** And Medi-Cal would not cover it.

**Richard:** Ah! Yeah.

**Frank:** On the other side, the corporations saw it as a money-maker so they bought them up.

**Richard:** They bought them out and totally changed the mode.

**Linda:** Yeah.

**Frank:** Promising the doctors they would still be in control.

**Richard:** But they weren't!

**Linda:** But once they took over, then that wasn't true.

**Richard:** So all those people who were so invested in Rockridge were so disappointed when that happened. An awful lot of people had really ... were very idealistic and altruistic and made that thing work and they just really felt like they were being kicked/shoved out the door.

**Frank:** But the model worked.

**Richard:** The model worked. And the whole thing worked well enough that they became a target of the profit ... and the corporate people took it over.

**Frank:** Exactly.

**Richard:** The funny part was they took it over and then completely changed it, and all the things that made it work stopped working! (laughing) Odd choice!

**Frank:** And they did not get it.

**Richard:** Right, they didn't get it. And I don't know that they ever really figured out why it stopped working. (Frank sounds, laughing)

**Frank:** Rockridge was a community.

**Richard:** It was, it really was. It was a fun place to work for that reason. It was really a lot of fun working with all those people.

**Frank:** That proves it does work.

**Richard:** Right, it does work, it really does. And also it shows that the importance of that kind of a community feel from the provider's standpoint, it pays a dividend that you don't get in other ways. There's just a pleasure to that working environment, the support that lets you do things you probably wouldn't do otherwise.

**Frank:** Is a hospital like that?

**Richard:** Not really. Not now. I suppose it could be. But at this point, it really isn't quite that same sort of a community sort of feel. There are individuals you find that you really do work well with and work kind of as a team, but there's also a lot more sort of division of labor, things get sort of separated out more than they did at Rockridge. And it's also because it's not as primary care oriented where you're actually taking care of a full spectrum of things. You're taking care of people who are much sicker. And because of the issue of getting people in and out, there's much more fragmented care. So you deal with one episode in their life and then you may never see them again.

**Frank:** And your regular doctor don't ...

**Linda:** ... is not involved in the hospital aspect of your care?

**Richard:** No, very few doctors now do follow their own patients in the hospital. More and more they now have people who are so-called hospitalists, the people who actually work in the hospital and take care of the patients while they're in the hospital. And most of the time, the way it's set up is that the primary care doctor sort of turns their patient over to the hospitalist and then picks them back up again after they leave.

**Linda:** Is there communication at all while it's going on?

**Richard:** Very little. Very little. So it's almost now that the doctor comes and does a social call, to visit and see how their patients are doing, but they're not really involved in the day-to-day decision making.

**Linda:** Wow!

**Frank:** That is scary!

**Richard:** It is! It is! And it's neither ideal for the patient or the doctor. I don't think the doctors like it as well.

**Frank:** So, why have a doctor then?

**Richard:** Well, because 90% of your life you'll spend not in the hospital. And so you still need someone to help coordinate all those other things that happen in the rest of your life.

**Linda:** Because I think it was like, a lot of times we'll think, well it's good to have a doctor in case something really happens. Then you have somebody who knows you, but now it sounds like that's not what happens!

**Richard:** Not so much any more. And there are still some doctors who follow their patients through the hospital, but more and more the primary care doctors don't. And some of them don't even have privileges at the hospital. They take care of the patients only on the outside and then just turn them over when they get admitted.

**Frank:** Why is that?

**Richard:** I think part of it is that it's hard to run an office practice and then also go to the hospital and take care of the patients. So I think that there was sort of a financial push on a lot of the small practices especially to have somebody else who's available to do rounds and do all these other things. And from the hospital standpoint, it's easier if they have a group of people that work there and that they can sort of control a little bit. I think in terms of getting people in and out of the hospital. Somebody who's in the hospital all day to make sure the tests are done, and the results are back. And when the results are back, you move them on or you get the consultants. It's just a more corporate model or a more like a factory model as opposed to the sort of hands-on thing.

**Linda:** So that's somewhat recent that it's been like that?

**Richard:** That's been happening more and more over the last few years.

**Frank:** Would our taking greed out ...

**Linda:** ... address that?

**Richard:** I don't know. It probably ... it would I think in so far as it removes some of the pressure on the individual practices. But I think that if you didn't have the issue of the practices needing to see a certain number of people to make a living, to do all the things that are necessary, and you had a more close doctor/patient relationship I think both the doctors and the patients would prefer that the doctor who knows you be the one who takes care of you in the hospital.

**Frank:** And most people don't know that we have a crisis in how many doctors and nurses and hospitals there are.

**Richard:** Yeah. It's actually ... it is a greater problem all the time. And there are a lot fewer hospitals than there used to be, and a lot fewer hospital beds in the community. So that when there is a problem, or any kind of an epidemic or even just in the flu season, there aren't a lot of empty beds, so people end up waiting longer and longer to get in to the hospital or are not allowed to stay in the hospital. As soon as they start getting a little bit healthier they boot them out, because they need those beds for people sicker than they are.

**Frank:** And in the 1980s the HMOs did not think they needed that many doctors and nurses.

**Richard:** Yeah. It's interesting because just in the time that I've been practicing we've had that pendulum swing where for a while there was a big push to try to get more people through medical school and nursing school and more hospital beds and then the HMOs and all the other cutbacks came in and there were fewer and fewer nurses and doctors and hospital beds. And now they're trying to reverse it again. And especially in nursing there's an effort to build new nursing schools and they recognize that with an aging population we're going to need more and more health care, not less and less.

**Frank:** In fact, that would be a major hump we would have to deal with in the first years of a free universal health care.

**Richard:** Yeah. Another issue that sort of ties into that a little bit, that it should be addressed is that, at least in California, there's been these mandates that all the hospitals that are not seismically safe need to be rebuilt. And currently there's been no funding for any of that. So none of it's happening. So most of the hospitals in the immediate Bay Area are not really earthquake safe by the standards that the state has set. So there's going to be a huge need for new buildings, just physically new places for hospitals to be. And currently no one has quite the political wherewithal to make that happen.

**Frank:** Just to replace the existing buildings.

**Richard:** Just to replace the existing buildings. Like the whole thing with Children's Hospital. They had a bond issue to try to have funding tax-based, to try to build a new building for Children's Hospital, which failed. I guess people didn't really want to have more taxes. But the trouble is the building still needs to be replaced. And we still need to provide care for all the kids. And there is not currently a lot of support for raising taxes.

**Frank:** And we will need to train more doctors and nurses.

**Richard:** Right. I think that's going to be true over the next twenty years that we'll need to continue raising the numbers of people in training. Partly, I think, that there are people who would like to do it and we just have to create a system whereby that's ... that they're taken care of, that they're provided a good place to work. And I think that community issue of trying to build something that really offers sort of non-monetary rewards, but just the pleasure of doing that kind of work should get people involved.

**Frank:** And GP ...

**Richard:** General practitioners, GPs? Yeah! Because the more emphasis we put on primary care, the more GPs, nurse practitioners, primary care people we need to generate and train and have a system for them to work.

**Frank:** In the meantime, why not bring the military hospitals home?

**Richard:** Right! That's a good point! That saves a lot of money right there. And actually if you put all the military hospitals and nurses and doctors and put that whole system into place, that all already exists. Why not put it to good use? And actually, by the time you start eliminating some of the standing army, you'll have a lot of people who are currently under-employed.

**Frank:** And less crips.

**Richard:** Less crips? That's true. Because we're creating crips as fast as we can over there. (laughs) Very true! One more fringe benefit to the war plan.

**Frank:** And the VA could be for the general public.

**Richard:** Right! Because it's another federal system we already have in place, we've already paid for, the buildings are there, the people are employed. Just kind of broaden the mission and change exactly what they're doing. Because now, once you eliminate the issue of insurance versus non-insurance there's no reason why people couldn't choose what hospital they go to and doctors couldn't choose where they practice.

**Frank:** Yes. And the reason for the VA would not exist.

**Richard:** Right, right. So there would still be veterans for awhile, but we wouldn't be creating new ones quite so quickly.

**Frank:** But they would be covered by the universal health care.

**Richard:** Exactly!

**Linda:** So they wouldn't need special health care.

**Richard:** They would just be part of the health care system, as opposed to a separate system.

**Frank:** Yes. And that brings up why was the VA needed in the first place?

**Richard:** Well, because too many of the veterans were uninsured and they felt like that was an unacceptable alternative too! (laughs) So actually it was our ... one of the big pieces of our socialized health care system that we already have. So in that setting, the government already owns the buildings, employs all the people who work there and decides who gets care. So we already have socialized medicine, but only for certain people.

**Frank:** Why don't we ever hear this kind of discussion?

**Richard:** Well, you just have to look at the right places. It's out there. It's not new information. It's just that it's not something that people tend to talk about in that sort of way.

**Linda:** About what you just said about not hearing this kind of discussion? Yeah, it seems like that's a lot of ... that whole thing of this kind of thing not being available to people so it doesn't get their heads working in this way. That seems like a lot of ... that's part of the problem too.

**Richard:** And a lot of it is spin. Realistically, that so much of this is a politically driven process

*Dr. Richard Kerbavaz (video capture)*

that how you discuss things becomes how people perceive it. And as long as there's a push to demonize universal health care and calling socialized medicine as some sort of an evil thing when in fact we already have big chunks of our population under socialized medicine by any kind of standard. And the government already pays more than 60% of all the health care costs.

**Frank:** The VA is socialized medicine.

**Richard:** The VA is socialized medicine and the government completely controls the system. And yet people don't demonize the VA.

**Frank:** And the military is socialized.

**Richard:** And there's also the whole military health care system is strictly socialized, again like the VA. And the public health hospitals and all of the other government-run systems are already socialized health care.

**Frank:** In the past we thought the doctors were against ...

**Richard:** Against socialized medicine? But they manage to find lots of people to work in all of those hospitals! And they aren't opposed to that! Not everybody chooses to work at the VA, but they don't seem to have any trouble recruiting people. And the other part is some of these systems like Kaiser, in terms of the physicians, Kaiser is just a private version of socialized medicine, where there's an organization that controls the hospitals and controls the doctors and pays the nurses' salaries and structures the whole thing. The difference is that to get into it you have to buy in, usually by where you work and what your employer offers. But in terms of the actual structure of the system, it's really not that different. It's just who's paying the bill.

**Frank:** And the difference between my system and Kaiser is the doctor/patient relationship being the base.

**Richard:** Right. Right. And ultimately instead of having people get in by virtue of where they work, that they would have coverage based on being here. By where they live. Being a member of that community entitles you to access to care.

**Frank:** What do the other candidates' plans offer?

**Richard:** Well, interesting you asked that! (all laughing) I just happen to have ... so one of the things that I, just in preparation for this, I tried to do my homework. And this is actually a whole list that I got off the internet that talks about a sort of side-by-side comparison of John McCain, Hillary Clinton and Barack Obama, but somehow they left off the Frank Moore plan.

**Frank:** I will give my ...

**Linda:** Frank will fill in his section.

**Richard:** I think you should fill in your section, right. We'll start out: the stated goal. John McCain: provide access to affordable health care for all by paying only for quality health care, having insurance choices that are diverse and responsive to individual needs and encouraging personal responsibility. (Frank screeches, all laugh)

**Linda:** Whatever that means!

**Richard:** Hillary Clinton: affordable and high-quality universal coverage through a mix of private and public insurance. (Frank screeches) And then Barack Obama: affordable and high quality universal coverage through a mix of private and an expanded public insurance. And the Frank Moore plan ... ? Universal access to health care.

**Frank:** When they say affordable (giggling), watch out!

**Richard:** (all laughing) Right, good point!

**Frank:** I will push for free universal pre-natal to the grave health care.

**Richard:** Very good. So, the overall approach to expanding access to coverage. John McCain: remove the favorable tax treatment of employer-sponsored insurance and provide a tax credit to all individuals and families to increase incentives for insurance coverage. Promote insurance competition and contain costs through payment changes to providers, tort reform and other measures. Hillary Clinton: every American required to have coverage with income-related tax subsidies available to make coverage affordable. Private and public plan options would be available to individuals through a new health choices menu operated through the Federal Employee Health Benefits Program, FEHBP. Coverage through employers and public programs like Medicare continues. Barack Obama: require all children to have health insurance and employers to offer employee health benefits to contribute to the cost of new public program. Create a new public plan and expand Medicaid and SCHIP (which is the children's health plan). Create the National Health Insurance Exchange through which small businesses and individuals without access to other public programs or employer-based coverage could enroll in the new public plan or in approved private plans.

**Frank:** I will have free universal pre-natal to the grave health care. Everybody would be in the same system. Every doctor, nurse, hospital, alternative medicine will be in the same system. Preventative and nutrition will be important parts of the plan. I would pay for it by cutting the military and by cutting the pork and royalties for drugs and etc. that are based on research done by public universities and the government.

**Richard:** Very good.

**Linda:** We're going to get this transcribed!

**Richard:** Definitely! This is great! This is definitely relevant.

**Frank:** Why I am not in the debates.

**Richard:** That's right! There you go. (all laughing) Well, I think you can use all of this very well to your advantage.

**Frank:** I am right now! (all laughing)

**Richard:** Good! You are! (looking at the chart) Let's see what's another good one here ... here's the tax change, we already talked about that. Changes to private insurance although you're pretty much going to eliminate the private insurance issue, so that's not really relevant. And the cost containment, you talked about some of how that's going to work too. State flexibility. This is a national plan, this is not states' issues. It's all one thing for everyone.

**Linda:** (asks Frank) Is that right?

**Frank:** Yes.

**Linda:** Yes, it's a national plan.

**Richard:** And improving quality health system performance, that was the issue you talked about that's basically putting the primary relationship between the doctors and the patients is the major goal and the major tool for making quality happen.

**Linda:** Right.

**Frank:** Read their ... (Frank looks at the chart Richard is holding)

**Richard:** Oh! OK! For quality control. (Frank screeching)

**Linda:** To make you look good!

**Richard:** For quality control, this is the John McCain answer: to change provider payment to encourage coordinated care. That is pay a single bill for high-quality health care rather than individual services. Provide Medicare payments for diagnosis, prevention and care coordination and bar payments for preventable medical errors or mismanagement. Require transparency by providers with regard to medical outcomes, quality care, costs and prices. Establish national standards for measuring and recording treatments and outcomes. Promote deployment of Health Information Technology (HIT). Where cost effective, employ telemedicine and clinics in rural and under-served areas. And then the Clinton plan: provide federal recognition to physician-driven maintenance and certification programs that promote continued education about latest advances in care and procedures. (I'm not sure what that means.) Invest in independent public/private consensus-based organizations to certify performance for enhanced reimbursement, identify gaps in existing quality measures, set priorities for development of new quality measures, and disseminate cost effective protocols and treatments through a best practices institute. Fund improvement of web-based tools to provide consumers with user-friendly information on provider performance and development of tools to promote informed patient choice about treatment options. Incentivize quality through increased federal payments for excellence in care.

**Frank:** She is a lawyer.

**Richard:** Yeah. (laughing) Yeah, you can tell. (all laughing) Well, so is Barack Obama. Let's see what his says. Support an independent institute to guide comparative effectiveness reviews and in required reporting of preventable errors and other patient safety efforts. Reward provider performance through the national health insurance exchange and other public programs. Address health disparities, promote preventative care and chronic disease management and require quality and price transparency from providers and health plans. Require health plans to collect, analyze and report health care quality data for disparity populations and hold plans accountable.

**Frank:** The patient should know how much was charged.

**Richard:** Under these plans (gesturing to the charts)? Or under your plan?

**Linda:** Under your plan the patient should know how much was charged for the service?

**Richard:** Right. That seems a good way for patients to kind of control what's happening. To understand the costs and charges.

**Frank:** Like I get chux. I don't know how much ...

**Linda:** ... is being paid for that?

**Frank:** Or how often?

**Linda:** We're completely out of the loop with that. And we kind of get a sense that there might be stuff going on that maybe isn't honest?

**Richard:** Yeah.

**Linda:** But we're not in the loop at all.

**Richard:** Yeah. And it seems silly that in your own health care you can't actually figure out where the money goes. It's even worse actually at the hospital level because the bills are just incomprehensible. And there's just layer upon layer of charges for aspirin and anything that possibly gets used generates a charge, but by the time you've been in the hospital for a few days, it's just page after page after page of charges for things you don't even remember happening. So, it's a very strange system. And most of the time, since insurance picks it up, the patients either never see the bills or never actually look at it carefully enough to understand what it was that they were being charged for.

**Frank:** So they don't get outraged.

**Richard:** Outraged, right. Because they don't really see it. They're insulated from it. It's not real money.

**Linda:** I remember ... like when we go on the road, we rent a hospital bed and a commode. And there was one time when we went and we just really couldn't afford it so we asked the Regional Center if they would pay it. And I knew how much it all cost because we did it all the time. And I saw the bill. And I saw the same people that we were renting it from, when they knew that somebody else was paying it, they charged them way more money. I called them and I said that's not how much you charge us and they had to then charge the organization the same amount they charged us because ...

**Richard:** Oh, they did actually reverse it because you noticed!

**Linda:** Yeah! Because I talked to the organization too! I said that's not how much we pay for this. I know that and I have the bills to show them. And so they had to pay them what they were charging us. But it was like that was a case where we got to see how that worked. Whereas if we got a bill every month for the amount they're charging Medi-Cal for the stuff that Frank gets, we would be the quality control! Because we would say, wait, that's not right!

**Frank:** You don't have to pay ...

**Linda:** ... someone else to do that if you just kept it simple.

**Richard:** Right. Let the patient actually be their own kind of watchdog to make sure the system isn't being taken advantage of.

**Linda:** Because all of that just seems like it is way out there. And you kind of feel spaced out when you hear it. It's like, oh, OK. Whereas when Frank talks about stuff it's like right here. It's like, oh, right!

**Richard:** Yeah, and if you actually had that bill in front of you and you understand where the money is going you can actually make some real choices about where the health care dollar gets spent.

**Linda:** Yeah.

**Richard:** It's actually a very good quality control thing too, in terms of making sure that the costs are being contained.

**Frank:** And you respect the people by doing it that way.

**Richard:** Right. Right. Because it's a little patronizing, really, to say you don't need to worry about this. Don't worry your little head about this. But yeah, putting people back in charge of their own health care consumption.

**Frank:** We got a lot out.

**Linda:** During this show.

**Richard:** Yeah, I think so! That's good. Covered a lot of bases.

**Frank:** What else do they say?

**Richard:** Oh, on this thing (gestures to the chart)? I should have mentioned, actually, the source of this is from a survey or a project that was done by the Kaiser Family Foundation. So it's actually trying to be as impartial as possible. And they actually give links to all the different quotes from articles and from talks that the various public candidates have said. So that they actually vet pretty much what exactly they're promoting. So it's actually a fairly good, fairly objective and not particularly partial issue. So one of the things here: other investments. So again, this is the McCain one to start with: support federal research related science-based care and cure of chronic disease. Promote education of children about health, nutrition and exercise. Support public health initiatives to stem obesity and diabetes and deter smoking. (Frank giggles) So Hillary Clinton: provides federal funding to address nursing through new training and mentoring programs linking nursing education and quality to encourage diversity and cultural competency in health care workforce. Support initiatives to reduce health care disparities, including funding for more accurate data collection, development of quality measures target at reducing racial and ethnic disparities and prioritizing the development of medical homes designed to improve quality for minorities. And strengthen consumer protections for long-term care insurance. And then Barack Obama: expand funding to improve the primary care provider and public health practitioner workforce including loan repayments, improved reimbursement and training grants. Support preventative health strategies including initiatives in the workplace, schools and communities. Support strategies to improve the public health infrastructure and disaster preparedness at the state and local level.

**Frank:** Well free education would do more than any of that.

**Richard:** Right. Well, we've covered it pretty well. The rest of the page is more just the quotes. And then the issues here, they talk about all the premium subsidies to individuals, all related to the health care side, or health insurance side rather than the health care side. By eliminating the health insurance part you don't have to deal with who's paying what premiums. It all becomes a federal mandate or a federal funding program.

**Frank:** As a doctor would what they say make your job easier?

**Richard:** Somewhat in that if they could really come up with something that did provide more universal health care there would be fewer barriers to taking care of everybody. And that would be a good thing, a good outcome. My concern is that it's a really expensive way to do things.

**Frank:** Yes.

**Richard:** And basically you're just moving 30% of the health care dollar into the pockets of the insurance companies. That's not a good investment to my mind. I don't think that's where we should be putting our tax dollars. I'd rather have it go directly to taking care of people.

**Frank:** Yes. And take corporate control out.

**Linda:** And take corporate control out of the picture.

**Richard:** Yeah. And I think that the more you do that, the more you basically empower the individuals, the patients to help to figure out how they want their health care to look. What sorts of resources they want to use. Do they choose to go to an acupuncturist or somebody else? And I like the transparency where if you know what all the pieces of your health care cost, you can use that money the way you want it spent. And sort of see that it's actually going toward something productive.

**Frank:** And get paid at a reasonable rate.

**Richard:** Yeah. And I think that's again definable based on relative to other things and how things ... what do things cost? The tax structure takes a lot of the sort of the greed element or the need to be higher paid out of the equation. I think that would go a long way toward leveling the playing field.

**Frank:** So every doctor would see anyone.

**Richard:** Yeah. Or they could. And that basically I think that it's up to the patients to choose who they see. And that's going to be the tricky part, educating them about what the difference is, what different doctors do and what their style is like. But I think that that could ... you'd learn that as you came along.

**Frank:** Like now if I did not have you and John Good.

**Linda:** Frank's GP.

**Frank:** I would ...

**Linda:** You'd be out of luck! (all laugh)

**Richard:** That would be a challenge! That would be a challenge!

**Linda:** Yeah!

**Frank:** Because no ...

**Linda:** Nobody takes Medi-Cal anymore.

**Richard:** Right. Right. And they keep cutting reimbursement on Medi-Cal so it gets to be harder and harder to find people to take it.

**Frank:** Under my plan everyone is equal when they go to a doctor.

**Richard:** Yeah. And that would be a very powerful switch. That would be a very powerful switch. And you mentioned earlier, the thing about how to make things change would be to have all the rich people have Medi-Cal, and I said no, you really need all the politicians to have Medi-Cal. And so now you can actually level it in a better way, or more positive way, so that you can have a system where everyone really has equal access and has equal chances to get the care they need.

**Frank:** On the level that the Congress and the president now have!

**Richard:** Exactly! And that indeed would be a perfect system if everyone had equal access, everyone had the same insurance that the president had.

*Frank Moore and Dr. Richard Kerbavaz (video capture)*

**Frank:** So why are not Obama and Hillary talking like this?

**Richard:** Well, again, it's a matter of how much power and clout the insurance industry has. And how unwilling to rock the boat the other political candidates are. And you have no fear of rocking the boat. And I think that gives you a great deal of freedom to say these things.

**Frank:** Yes. Things like most doctors will not take Medi-Cal is hidden.

**Richard:** Yeah. Because unless you have Medi-Cal or know someone who has Medi-Cal you don't appreciate that that's an access disparity. And people who have insurance don't really think very much about people who don't have insurance and what the implications would be. But more and more people find themselves without insurance for at least part of every year. And I think what that ends up doing is giving a little bit more sensitivity to the issue to the people who are employed most of the time or have their coverage through work most of the time.

**Frank:** People say if you are rich or on Medi-Cal you are covered.

**Richard:** Hmmmm. That's interesting. Yeah, but Medi-Cal's not really covered in quite the same way. (laughter)

**Linda:** That's the point that people don't really know what it's like to be on Medi-Cal.

**Richard:** And even with insurance, there's getting to be more and more disparity between the insurance plans and how restrictive some are. And more and more doctors are not taking some of the insurance plans that are just too much trouble to be worth.

**Linda:** Like we had ... the thing that we have, Alameda Alliance, through being home care attendants, we had one eye coverage that was great. We kept going to our optometrist. It was covered. It was every two years, and that wasn't that great, but still we kept going to the same person. And then they switched it out and the only place that would take the new coverage is like a quickie place. It was horrifying. You'd go in and boom, boom, boom, boom. And it's like you see the eye doctor for like 10 minutes maybe. I'm used to a 45 minute eye exam. It was horrifying. It was all about product. You felt like they were trying to get you to buy the newest kind of thing in eyewear ... this is covered but, you really want this!

**Richard:** Yeah. For only so much more ...

**Linda:** Yeah, yeah. The optometrist was here on this part of the room, and then they were on the other part of the room. And they were clearly in control, the people selling the glasses.

**Richard:** The sales pitch was the biggest part of being there.

**Linda:** Yeah, yeah.

**Richard:** Right. Even people who have private insurance ... or some of these insurance plans, like United Health care is the biggest health insurance company in the country ... their recently retired CEO had to give back 400 million dollars of his severance package because it was shown it was one of those illegal post-dating or stock deals. But that was OK because he still took more than 400 million home. So this is where a lot of the profits from these insurance companies end up going, is to pay these guys off.

**Frank:** You can cover most Medi-Cal with their retirement packages.

**Richard:** Right. You could cover an awful lot of health care with that. Just by itself, taking some of those back would take care of some of those disparities.

**Frank:** Like Erika has a good job with health care but each year she pays more for less.

**Richard:** Just be grateful you didn't get sick, because then you might not be able to get any at all. (laughs) No, it's just a very strange system we have now.

**Frank:** And in Europe and Canada they ...

**Richard:** ... they have a different system again. Well, pretty much every other country has some sort of a universal health care system. We're really the only major industrialized country that doesn't have it. Each country has their own way of paying for it and some are more like true ... more like an insurance plan, more like Medicare, and some are more like ... the English model is more like the VA where the hospitals and doctors are all employed by the government. And then there's other models in other countries that are more like private insurance but sort of paid for by the government. So everyone else has come up with a way of doing that. Somehow we've never organized it in a single system, or had any kind of a comprehensive approach.

**Frank:** And our health system shows it.

**Richard:** Yeah, we pay more than any other country per capita and on an absolute dollar amount, and yet don't do that well in terms of infant survival or overall longevity. On most of the parameters we're way down into the middle of the pack, except in the one of cost. Because we currently are paying almost twice as much as the next vocal competition. It's just interesting how much we pay for how much less we get.

**Frank:** Why?

**Richard:** Why is that? Oh! Well, a whole bunch of reasons, but largely it's that so much of the money gets taken out of the system and put into other things. Like advertising. Like collecting health insurance premiums. And then we have a system where people who can't afford to get care delay care until it becomes a crisis. And then the most expensive and inefficient way to provide care is through a hospital emergency room. And for many people it's the only way they can get care at all. So we have a very silly system. It's not really thought-out or organized in a way to either save money or to really provide care to people. But it does provide a great deal of profit margin to large insurance companies and large drug companies.

**Frank:** Greed.

**Richard:** Greed. A lot of it comes down to greed. Because we pay more for drugs. We pay more for all these other things than every other country in the world. They all have some sort of organized buying plan. We choose not to put any restrictions on the profits that the drug companies can make in the name of trying to promote more research. But all the other countries with their health insurance plans have some sort of a savings plan built into it that limits how much the drug companies can profit. We've chosen not to do that.

**Frank:** Why?

**Richard:** Just like those insurance companies, they pay an awful lot of bills to the politicians.

**Linda:** But it's not ... I wonder why that's not the case in other countries.

**Richard:** Well, because once the government is in control and determines ... has to pay the bill ... once the government is picking up the tab, they're not willing to allow those insurance companies or those drug companies to make those profits anymore. So they're trying to capture back some of the profits as savings to the insurance plans. Since we don't have the government nominally in charge of all those things, we kind of don't notice how much money comes out and goes other places.

**Frank:** We should do this again before the election.

**Richard:** Not a bad idea. Not a bad idea.

**Linda:** Because the time is up and it feels like we're just really getting going here.

**Richard:** Yeah. Well, we covered a lot of ground. I think you got a good chance to kind of make your platform known.

**Frank:** A special.

**Linda:** This will also be a special, yes!

**Richard:** Good! (laughing)

**Linda:** And you are ... ?

**Richard:** Oh, I'm Rich Kerbavaz. (laughs) Ear, nose and throat doctor in Berkeley. And trying to take good care of Frank's ears for many years now.

**Frank:** And one of my electors.

**Richard:** That's right. I'm officially an elector for Frank Moore's campaign.

**Frank:** And I need more ...

**Richard:** ... more electors.

**Linda:** Frank needs a total of 55 electors.

**Richard:** Yeah. And having done it, it's very easy. All you need to do is find someone to notarize your signature, get the form, and it's very simple.

**Linda:** You can get all of that off our website.

**Richard:** It's all on the website.

**Linda:** frankmooreforpresident08.com.

**Frank:** Or email.

**Linda:** Email Frank. fmoore@eroplay.com. That's it? Alright!

**Richard:** Alright! That's good.

# David Johnson & Elder Freeman

Recorded April 22, 2001 on luver.com

David Johnson was one of the San Quentin Six, a group of inmates at San Quentin prison accused of an escape attempt in 1971 that led to a riot on the cell block. Their 16-month trial was called "The Longest Trial" by *Time* magazine. David was convicted on one count of assault.

Elder Freeman, whose real name is Ronald Freeman, was a Catholic priest in the African Orthodox Church. He was also one of the founding members of the L.A. Black Panther Party for Self-Defense. He was in the leadership of the Southern California chapter of the party, and one of the leaders in the underground part of the Black Panther Party, which came to be known as the Black Liberation Party.

Frank first learned of David and Elder through a political prisoners conference that he had sent his crew to videotape to broadcast on LUVeR.

Elder Freeman passed away October 8, 2014.

**Frank:** Revolution has to be cheap.

**Linda:** The revolution has to be cheap!

**David:** Yeah, yeah, we don't have a lot of funds. We're all poor. (laughter, Frank sounds) We used to have a saying, back in the day: "Revolution is hazardous to your health and you don't get paid."

**Frank:** They got the money, we got the people.

**David:** The people. That's true. But we need more hearts and minds.

**Frank:** How do we get them?

**David:** Gotta start here. Starts with education. People have to understand there's another side to the story.

**Frank:** To what?

**Linda:** Another side to the story to what?

**David:** The story that they put out there.

**Elder:** You know, to get people to get involved and change, sometimes what causes it is the conditions, so that means that the system is setting it up for itself, for its own destruction, by what they're doing. By them opposing what's right. For them not treating people humane and not being ... well ... have no regards for the land, the water, the air ... human beings' medical care, feeding people. When they know they got the technology to resolve a lot of the problems that's going on in the world, and they take and they use this and they capitalize on it and they only use certain resources, as long as it's beneficial to a certain segment of people, the people that's in power. So, it's like, even when you're studying Marx and all the different struggles, and even before Marx, when people's conditions, the French Revolution, the American Revolution, the conditions got to where the people felt it was beyond ... the burden was too great for them to bear anymore, they rebelled against it. And that's what's happening like now. Even with the thing in Quebec. It's like, we've got to have safeguards on the world as far as ... for life to even go on! With the things that they're planning, they planning for everything to come to an end. So somebody got to say something! And it's a cause for the young people, the young people! We was young once. (Frank sounds)

**David:** The burden is on them.

**Elder:** They have to get involved, they have to take the front, and we have to support them in everything that they do that's right. If they're doing the right thing, if it calls for civil disobedience then you got every right to rebel against that and be disobedient to that law or rule.

**David:** It's in the constitution! If you want to go by that!

**Elder:** Right. You got societies where people ... what was good a long time ago, they find out that they have to change it because it didn't fit, it was old, like spitting on the sidewalk when the sidewalks were made out of wood. You had to change the law. So when times change, things have to change. So situations and dealing with like the drug problem that they got in the United States, the way they're dealing with it, they can't ... they don't want to for some reason recognize that they is wrong. That approach they took was incorrect and they have to re-change and revitalize it.

**Frank:** They are making money, so they don't want the change.

**David:** It's true. You know, you used to say one of the things of paramount importance, particularly as a revolutionary, is to safeguard the environment. Because if we don't safeguard the environment ... you see, the environment can exist without us, but we can't exist without the environment. (Frank sounds) And if we don't defend the environment as revolutionaries, then there's going to be no political landscape for us to wage political battles that we have to wage in order to honor human rights, human dignity. I got a thing about laws. And, I was taught this: all laws are not moral laws or just. At one time it was legal to have slaves. That's morally wrong. No human being has a right to subjugate another human being. And that's part of what we struggle about today. We don't have the right to determine our own destiny. We don't have the right to determine what happens to our community. And every community should have that right. And that's what we struggle for. The right to determine our own destinies.

**Frank:** In fact, they are taking our rights away fast.

**David:** That's true. That's true. And people have to understand that. Because a lot of our rights are being legislated away.

**Elder:** With the prison system, the way ... the whole operation, what they're doing to them with the prisons ... how they are building more prisons, they then turn it into ... it's big business. Instead of putting money in the communities where the majority of the prisoners are coming

*Frank Moore and David Johnson (video capture)*

from, and setting up programs in those communities. The Department of Corrections, when you first come in there, when they give you orientation, the first thing they tell you is that we do not rehabilitate. So their whole thing about being rehabilitated, they say, find you a program and don't cause us much ... as little trouble as you can, the less time you do. Other than that, they're just warehousing, that's all they do. Rehabilitation is a myth!

**David:** And that follows what comrade George Jackson said, about prisons being the chief repressive institutions in this society. Rather than address issues, this society would rather build more prisons. Prisons serve to repress revolution, particularly in this society.

**Frank:** They take would-be revolutionaries out of society.

**David:** That's true, that's true. And that's one of the battles that we're engaged in because the prison system in this country ... there are people in there who become conscious of why they got in prison. And like one of my mentors, comrade George Jackson said, that now that we're in these institutions, one of the things that is of chief importance is transforming the criminal mentality to a revolutionary mentality. So, that when we leave these institutions, we can go back into our communities and be an asset rather than a predator. And that's dangerous (Frank sounds) in terms of how the system looks at it. Because the more chaos and confusion that they can create, the more confused the people will be. And I look at myself as being a revolutionary. And I've faced death. Because, like I say, George says, once you say you commit yourself to revolution you become a criminal. Because in this society being a revolutionary is criminal. (Frank sounds) So that's why they said, we don't have any political prisoners in this society, because it's criminal. And that's accepted throughout the world. This is one of the countries that has an abundance of political prisoners, but by the standards that they have set, they can go to the United Nations and say, we have no political prisoners. Because a revolutionary in their eyes is considered a criminal. As opposed to a humanitarian, someone who's interested in the well-being of all people in this society.

**Frank:** And it is not just the prison but the institutions for crips and the schools, etc.

**Linda:** Well, like with the institutions for crips, Frank has said, a lot of the people in institutions for crips are a lot less disabled than Frank is. (Frank sounds) And yet ... like, Frank made a movie about a guy, who he plays, that gets the girl, and when he showed it at the Cerebral Palsy Center, these are kind of like inmates. These are adults that aren't allowed to go out on dates. Everybody stood up and started cheering! (Frank sounds) And they had a little revolution on their hand. They were saying, they won't let me date, I don't care if I get hurt! They say, oh you're going to get hurt. I don't care! (Frank sounds) And the teacher got real excited and said, Frank we want you back. And then we get a phone call saying it's been canceled. The head of the center said they don't want Frank back, they don't want him showing any of his movies. You know, they have this whole set-up. Nobody wants to lose their job and get all these people out having a life!

**David:** Right, right. See 'cause he's interested in changing the human condition. And they want to keep the human condition ... I mean, most of these institutions drug them. Even in prisons! Rather than deal with people's feelings. They'd rather give them drugs and numb them. They don't want you to feel. We live in a drug culture. You turn on the TV, pain is an indicator that there's something wrong. They don't want you to experience pain. They want us to mask pain, they want us to cover it up.

**Frank:** Pain is fuel.

**David:** For change!

**Frank:** Yes. (Frank sounds) (laughter)

**David:** But, see, they don't want us to deal with that. Like I said, we live in a ... every pain that you have, if you turn on the television, you can find an ad where they're going to tell you, you got a pain here, take this pill. You can't sleep, take this pill! Rather than really what is the source or the cause? Let's eliminate that. And if you don't feel your pain, you can't alleviate the pain.

**Frank:** Change the society that ...

**David:** Exactly.

**Frank:** ... caused the pain.

**David:** We're working on it! We're working on it. (laughter)

**Elder:** Yeah, well, that's the whole thing we have to point out, like with the prison systems and the things that society ... like the prison systems, showing that, if you want to curtail that, you have to deal with what the root of the problem is supposed to be. And that's supposed to be in the community, then you need to go to the community to start working to solve that problem. But that's not what they're concerned ... they're not concerned about changing or making the living condition better for everybody and giving everybody ... putting everybody on an equal footing and making it a better society in the world for everybody. That's not what they're concerned about. (Frank sounds) They're concerned about keeping the status quo. Being able to, for some reason, for some reason, to exploit, and for some reason to suck as much as they can out of everybody else from the world. And accumulate all this for ... more than they can spend, more than their families can spend, more than whole generations can spend. They want just to have control. You know that thing about power, absolute power corrupts, these are a bunch of corrupt people and they don't need to be in the positions of power. And that's dealing with education, with the schools, with housing, with employment, with the water, with the air, with the electricity. All these houses need to have solar energy panels on top of them, but they've made it ...

**Linda:** When we tried ... well, we thought, let's do that, let's start using solar power. (Frank sounds) So we made a bunch of phone calls, got all of this stuff to read and then we called the company and they said it would cost $55,000 ... (Frank sounds)

**Elder:** They got it priced out ...

**Linda:** You have to be rich! We were willing to borrow money, but $55,000!?

**David:** One of the things is, you're changing the world view. Did you ever read a book by Stanley Elkin called *Entropy*, where he talks about the patterns of energy consumption? And recycling. For a long time, big cars were the thing. And when you had Volkswagens coming into this country, a lot of the major auto workers didn't realize, or didn't pay attention to the trend at that time. So, because they were used to building big cars that consumed mass amounts of fuel, and produce all kinds of waste by-products. OK, you have to condition people to change. For solar energy to really take hold, then our energy consumption patterns of consuming fossil fuels has to change. There are some changes, and you can see it in the market with a lot of these hybrid cars. But, in order for us to be successful, the whole of society has to shift their way of thinking about the patterns of energy consumption that exist. And major energy companies are not interested in that because they're trafficking and dealing with fossil fuels.

**Frank:** They have the monopoly.

**David:** Exactly. And we're trying to break that monopoly through our actions, by educating people. Even when we get out there in the streets to protest, we're letting them know that we are tired of what they're doing.

**Frank:** The business school teaches that 80% of the people don't ...

**Linda:** Yeah, 80% of the people don't ...

**Frank:** ... matter.

**Linda:** 80% of your customers don't matter, so, it's only 20% of the customers where you're going to make your money.

**David:** So we're just expendable.

**Linda:** So, they just focus on that 20%, and forget about the rest of them.

**Frank:** Hence the prison!

**Linda:** Hence the prison system, that's the 80%.

**David:** Yeah, another thing about that is ... you know people don't realize that it is in the best interest of society that those institutions be more humane. Because those people have to come back out into society. If you set up an institution that creates monsters, which these prison systems do, that's not in the best interest of society.

**Frank:** I am much cheaper ...

**Linda:** Oh, than if you were institutionalized. The amount of money it costs for Frank to live is a lot less than if he was in an institution.

**David:** Right, yeah.

**Linda:** Yet, they would rather have him in an institution. (Frank sounds)

**David:** Right, right. Right. Right.

**Elder:** Well, you know, another thing about the whole medical system that they got even for what's going on in the streets, but also what's going on inside the prison, which is ... I don't see it really no different in the reflection on a lot of the medical institutions that they have all around the country, as far as people when you start getting AIDS, how the medical care that elderly people would receive, why I'm saying that in prison is because a lot of our friends are becoming the elderly in the prisons, and they're getting terrible medical care ... no medical care, missing medicine, no treatment. Some people they need to be on dialysis machines. They're not going to get that. They're going to die! Yeah, they're not going to put nobody on no dialysis machine. They're not going to take you out and get you no cancer therapy. You're not going to get no radiation treatments. No, no, no, no, no, no, no. Sugar diabetes, you get your medicine today, you might have an attack at one o'clock at night, you're ain't getting nothing.

**Frank:** And why are sick people in prison in the first place?

**Linda:** If they're sick, what can they do?!

**Elder:** Nothing!

**Linda:** Why don't they just let them out?

**David:** No, that would be too humane! One of the things ...

**Elder:** That would make too much sense! (laughter)

**David:** One of the things that we deal with is, in the '60s, in the '70s, a lot of people who stood up and identified themselves as revolutionaries and took a stand against the institutions in this country, some were framed up by COINTELPRO and other intelligence agencies in this country, and sent to prison! We have a lot of soldiers in prison who are doing twenty-five to life, who are sick, because as the result of government frame-ups. We went to New York for a conference, Critical Resistance conference ... was it last month? In March, the first part of

*Elder Freeman (video capture)*

March. And one of the things that we did is that is we went to visit this brother who's a part of the BLA, Bashir Hamid, who's in an institution in New York, Auburn institution.

**Frank:** What is the BLA?

**David:** Black Liberation Army. Which was an underground ... well, why don't you explain? (laughter)

**Elder:** The Black Liberation Army was ... the underground ... part of it was the underground part of the Black Panther Party, and various individuals throughout the black community all across the country. It wasn't all just Panthers, but ... a Panther couldn't belong to any other organization other than the Black Liberation Army, which was the military wing of the Black Panther Party. Which everybody in it wasn't in the Black Panther Party. So, we have people that was dedicated to the struggle of changing the conditions of the black community by whatever means was necessary for them to do that. Some people went as far as to even go as to take like a ... I don't know if most people know about it, but it's like a Mau Mau oath, when the Mau Maus in Kenya ... they had an oath when if things didn't go like they were supposed to, and then the people that committed themselves, then do like they committed themselves to do ... that this oath should kill them. In other words, whatever you're doing to liberate your people, you know, you're dedicating your life and everything else to the struggle of your people. So the Black Liberation Army was composed of people, young people, basically black people that was dedicated to ...

**David:** Overthrowing the government! (Frank sounds)

**Elder:** Liberating the conditions of their community. In other words, to change the politics of the community. To change the whole dynamics of how the police operated, the landlords, the businesses, everything. Like David said earlier, our right to self-determination, was one of the key ... is the number one point on the Black Panther Ten-Point Program. That's the first one! We want the power to determine the destiny of our own black community. And a lot of people were dedicated to that liberation.

**David:** Also, in response to a lot of brutality and violence that was inflicted upon the black community by various police agencies. I mean, the Black Liberation Army grew out of the systematic assassination and violence of various police agencies, and one of the things that comes through is the government shifts its responsibility in its role in trying to undermine any type of organization or institution that advocates a change in the status quo is considered a threat. And a lot of ... you look back at the history of this country and a lot of the officers of the Black Panther Party were subject to massive police assaults ... for no reason! They would fabricate reasons to justify armed assaults on the Black Panthers!

**Frank:** In the '60s we thought our phones were tapped. People said ... (Frank sounds)

**Linda:** ... they were being paranoid!

**David:** Yeah, well, <u>they</u> admit that they did that!

**Frank:** Yes.

**David:** They engaged in a lot of criminal activities. None of them have ever been brought to answer to those charges.

**Elder:** You know we talk about it now, before, a lot of times, people said, we didn't talk about ... we done made up our minds, the ones from the East Coast and even us on the West Coast ... we done made up our minds, that we didn't recognize this vacuum that had existed for awhile within the struggle and we're not ... all of us are not dead yet. We're dying, and so we're saying this is going to be our last ditch effort! We're going to step back up. We're not scared of whatever the system going to do. Whatever they going to do, just bring it on. 'Cause the way we look at it, according to how Mao said, whatever they do to us, we got to turn that around and make it work for our benefit and not for them. So if they attack us, we got to make whatever attack that they do to us, work for the total liberation of all the people. 'Cause I want to point out something else about that, about the black liberation ... it wasn't, just because we was fighting within the black community, we saw the significance of our struggle that we was waging in relationship to the broader picture of the world. And we look at it, if we can get some justice in the black community inside the United States, that can have an effect on how all the rest of the people are going to be treated around the world. So we looked at our struggle in a world perspective. But we also had conditions that we had to deal with on a daily basis. Our black youth was being gunned down in the street. And it just was a point to where we had decided that we wasn't going to go on no more like this. If we going to just be dying down in the streets, there's going to have to be some consequences. And that's when ... you can say like what happened with the liberation, the Black Liberation Movement in the United States, it was like in its infancy, it was like in the mother's womb, like maybe you would say three months pregnant. It wasn't ready to be born! It had a lot more developing to do before it comes out. But the system recognizing how dangerous this birth would be, did everything that they did to cause it to be a miscarriage. So it was a miscarriage. But it didn't upset the whole ... the Mother Earth and the whole order of things to where's it can't come forth and be born again. There's not ... it's still fertile!

**Linda:** Yes!

**David:** See one of the things that takes place that bothers us is a lot of people trying to write the history of the '60s and the '70s. (Frank sounds) And what happens is, they tend to de-emphasize and minimize what our struggle was about. Our struggle was legitimate and genuine!

**Frank:** They make the '60s wimpy. (Frank sounds)

**David:** And that's an uphill battle, because see, one of the things ... you de-emphasize the importance and the significance of people's contributions. Just like the war in Vietnam. People protested the war in Vietnam. Years later, even these generals were saying, that was wrong! We knew back then.

**Frank:** Even McNamara!

**David:** Oh yeah, yeah. Exactly! (Frank sounds)

**Frank:** Where was he in the '60s?

**David:** Making money! Now, he's made his money (Frank sounds) his conscience is bothering him and he can say that!

(Frank laughing)

**David:** A lot of things are wrong. The Agent Orange. They use the Agent Orange to defoliate and kill all the vegetation in Vietnam. The environment hasn't recovered from that! Neither has the soldiers that they sent over there that they exposed those chemicals to. You know they are off-spraying ... their families are still suffering. Without compensation.

**Frank:** They are doing the same thing now ...

**David:** Exactly!

**Frank:** ... in Columbia.

**David:** Yeah, exactly. Exactly. They want to use those defoliants over there. They want to destroy the environment.

**Frank:** People think the Panthers were just about black.

**Elder:** Yeah, yeah, but that's no longer ... that's like Kathleen (Cleaver) had her International Panther Festival and it's going to have films that deals with our struggle from the international perspective. She was out here a few weeks ago and she was ... it was at a ... during women's month, and her and an Asian, Hispanic, and Indian women, they was all on the panel and they all talked about how (Frank sounds) the times and the whole situation, how everybody was together on things. How all the different groups of people was working together.

**David:** See the Panthers was concerned about the conditions in the black community. But at the same time, we also understood and recognized the international nature of this struggle.

**Elder:** What they was doing to the Panthers, they wasn't just doing to the Panthers! They was doing it to everybody else around the world! (laughing)

**David:** Yeah.

**Elder:** Yeah. It wasn't just the black community, it was the Indians, Hispanics, the Whites ...

**David:** We understood that.

**Frank:** They are not racists. They fuck everybody.

(laughter)

**Elder and David:** Yeah.

**David:** Yeah, they do.

**Elder:** But I wouldn't say they ain't racists!

**David:** They are racists!

**Elder:** I wouldn't throw that scenario in there, because ...

**David:** Racism is a means of control!

**Frank:** Yes!

**Elder:** You have a lot of the right wing, they have a tendency, even though they don't talk about it as publicly as much as they should, but the right wing in this country and around the world, like even they got in Germany, and France and England, the United States ... the right wing is a dangerous ... they are a dangerous group. And they got money.

**David:** They inflict a lot of hardship and pain on people of color. But if you're poor white, you're going to feel that pain too. (Frank sounds) But, racism is a tool. Because as long as they can keep division among people, then the longer they're able to maintain control.

**Frank:** I call it fragmentation.

**Elder and David:** Right, right. Yeah. Right.

**David:** As long as they keep us divided. And that became very clear in the '60s with COINTELPRO how they were able to create divisions among a lot of organizations that were pushing for change. And the tricks that they used then, we have to learn from. Because it is inevitable, if we are going to be successful in changing this society ...

**Frank:** Like what?

**Elder:** Oh, I can give you a good one! The Black Panther Party, we was having a breakfast at ... like we had the breakfast program in different cities all over the country ... we had a breakfast program in San Diego. We was having it at this Catholic church. Now, one of the rules that we did was, we didn't go into no facility. And many facility that we was using, we left it cleaner than it was before we came in. So, it wasn't we was having any problem with the facility (Frank sounds), or our care of the facility 'cause it was in better shape when the people came in for the church, it was cleaner than when they left it! So, it wasn't any problem with that. So what the FBI did was, they sent a letter to the diocese, to the archbishops of the Catholic church, saying that this priest was conspiring and was allowing criminal elements from the community to be in this church. What happened was, one night the police had the place kind of surrounded, so we just stayed in there. The priest say, don't leave. So, the next you know, then they send a letter to the congregation and this was all FBI, the whole thing was to get us out of that breakfast program. This is the kind of thing that they did. And they did it ... now the purpose of that was to alienate us from the community, and so they was ... to divide the community.

**Frank:** Isn't it amazing that free breakfast is more dangerous than guns. (Frank sounds)

**David:** Yes! 'Cause, see, one of the things that the government did, the party started the free breakfast programs and it's one of the programs that the government stole! The government started doing ... if you notice, even, there's some semblance of it left today where they used to give people, families vouchers so the kids could come and get meals. But if it hadn't been for the efforts of the party and people who were concerned about ... and we're talking about feeding children! If it hadn't been for that effort, the government wouldn't have ... and you can look at it as part ... as an attempt to neutralize the party! Oh, well, we'll adopt one of their programs, right, and put it into play, and put the emphasis on us! But had not the party did that, the government would have never instituted any program that fed hungry children going to school!

**Frank:** So that they then were in control.

**David:** Exactly!

**Elder:** Well, you know, that part, one advised about the breakfast program, and he was in some of the other programs that we started, was ... is that some of the things we was doing was pointing out the contradiction! Like at that time we were saying, and it was true, that hungry kids, kids going to school, and they going to school hungry, and it had been proven that kids that had a breakfast, and had something to eat, and the difference between the kids that didn't have anything to eat, their learning skills and ability was higher. So we are saying, as far as the government we are pointing out this contradiction about how inadequate the government was with dealing with the children of this country, how inadequate they were in dealing with that. So, we started a breakfast program. And we did a sickle cell anemia with the free clinic and everything. And the government started instituting ... we called ... we made, I guess, by our efforts, with the free sickle cell anemia testing, the government ended up spending and putting millions and millions of dollars into sickle cell anemia program which has benefited millions of people. You know, so, all of our actions, we can't say it was in vain, but they were designed to point out the contradiction. And show the inadequacies of the system in that what they wasn't doing, what they should be doing! And building more prisons is not what they should be doing!

**Frank:** But the media focuses on guns! (Frank sounds)

**David:** Yeah.

*David Johnson (video capture)*

**Elder:** Yeah, well (laughing) Malcolm, see Malcolm, I mean, when everything that's around you ... no matter what you want to say, we are a products of our environment. If guns are ... if every time we get confronted with things, these guns! For us, our psychic number one thing that we see is we have to arm ourselves in order to get any kind of respect, to get any kind of dignity, we have to arm ourselves. That got, in the black community, we could say, it got out of control. And that could be to a number of factors. Is that the system with them introducing a lot of cheap drugs into the community and introducing a lot of guns into the community, nobody was there to direct or give any kind of direction. We had a leaderless community. And the drugs was the leader. And the guns was for anybody who wants to take charge, you just had to fire a gun!

**David:** One of the things, you talk about guns, when the Panthers marched on Sacramento, they marched onto Sacramento, they were armed! They were armed, and had guns because, what they was trying to show was, at that time they were trying to pass a legislation which took away your right to bear arms. Now, there's nothing ... and I'm an advocate of armed self-defense because in a lot of instances when they had them armed assaults on various Black Panther headquarters, if people hadn't been armed, a lot of lives might have been lost. Because they would have been the only ones with guns assaulting various Panther offices! And they were engaged in assassinations! They assassinated people! Malcolm X got assassinated. Martin Luther King got assassinated.

**Elder:** Fred Hampton.

**David:** They were engaged in political assassinations!

**Elder:** They killed all them people down there down in western Oakland!

**David:** Waco.

**Elder:** Waco, Indians.

**David:** Any kind of dissent in this country, whether you agree with their politics or not, any kind of dissent against this government. Historically ... if you examine history, any kind of dissent in this country, the government has met with armed assaults! It is the government who institutes armed actions against people! Kent State! You can't forget Kent State! And then there's a black institution, a black college when they went in and killed up a lot of people! People don't remember. You remember Kent State.

**Elder:** And the Indians on their own land!

**David:** Yeah!

**Frank:** And no one was punished in any of those cases! (Frank screams)

**David:** Right! Leonard Peltier, a Native American who stood up to defend the rights of his people, he's in prison now! He is the victim of government-sanctioned repression. And that's the way the government deals with ... we are the advocates of peace! If a peaceful transition can occur in this society where everybody's interest is served, then we're all for it. But the government is not going to allow a peaceful transformation to take place. I mean why do you need a National Guard armed with automatic assault rifles? A National Guard is supposed to be for national things! Who are they going to use those assault rifles against? People! Us!

**Frank:** In Europe, the cops are not armed.

**David:** Yeah, I know, there's a lot of countries like that. But we're the only country where we have SWAT teams where, of course, there again those SWAT teams were designed to use against people! If this wasn't such a violent society we wouldn't need a SWAT team!

**Frank:** And SWAT teams are only a recent invention.

**David:** Yeah, true, true, that's true. (Frank screams) It's a product of the '60s. Geared toward repressing dissent.

**Elder:** So, we go back to when I mentioned Malcolm. Malcolm X is like, Malcolm was saying, he say, by any means necessary. But he also say, if the Ku Klux Klan, and the White Citizen's Counsel and the Minute Men, and everybody else turn in their gun, I'll turn in my gun! I'll go for it, if everybody else go for it! But until then (laughing) ...

**David:** Don't talk to me about peace!

**Elder:** Until then, until then ... and they got tanks now!

**Frank:** I knew about the government was behind the drugs, but I did not know they were behind the guns.

**Elder and David:** Yeah, yeah.

**Elder:** Yeah, they got some reports out of the whole thing about in L.A. where they left a train car, a railroad car parked down by the black community ... (Frank sounds) They left it ... this was years ago, they left it and it was full of guns. And they let them steal the guns. (Frank sounds) That was deliberate.

**David:** Then it had defective ammunition! The government was the problem in a lot of ...

**Elder:** You know the government is involved with a lot of ... with the Ku Klux Klan. They have this thing now where one out of every three of them is a FBI agent! (laughing)

**Frank:** How did you get into the Panthers?

**Elder:** It was basically looking at ... after I was in Los Angeles after they had the '65 rebellion in L.A. and I wanted to see some things change, as far as with the community, but I didn't exactly know how to go or where to place ... and the NAACP, the Urban League, none of them had that kind of track. It just didn't seem like they were addressing the issues seriously enough for me, but the Panther party ...

**Frank:** Liberals!

**Elder:** Right. The Panther party, when they came out, that was something more I could identify with. That these were some young men and they was my age. I was 21, 22, 23. They was my age, and they were sincere about wanting to see about some changing of the conditions in the community. What made me get involved was a lot to deal with the police brutality and the poverty that I seen with young adults starting off with their families and people living in the projects, and how hard of a life that they was having and knowing that if the system was rearranged, all of their needs, this here could be addressed. And I seen the police as a major factor in holding us at bay! And so it just came by them being the first line of defense, it seemed it was the first ones that had to be dealt with. And we had a whole program to deal with that too! Community control of the police! Where it would be the people in the community ... and we wanted the police to live within the community that they patrolled! So we wanted the police to be one with the community, not an occupying army! Just coming in and putting in eight hours and then going back out to the suburbs and coming down there and policing for eight hours, that's like ... remind me very similar to the old movies you see with the Indians and the forts that they had ... they put the fort there and then the soldiers come in (laughing) and then they just control that and then they let those soldiers go out and they bring some more soldiers in. I mean this was how the police, and they was treating us bad! And they still do some of the same things. Although I'm older and got this grey hair, but I see them still doing the same things that when I was 18 and 19, 17, 16, 15 ... when I was a young man, I see them doing the same thing that they're doing to our young people today.

**David:** Because the police brutality is a relatively new phenomena.

**Elder:** They harass, they direct everything at them, then they say, yeah, these kids are the cause of it, but there's nothing in the community for them. They don't have no job programs, no training programs. And the ones that they do are far and in between. There needs to be more. That's what I'm saying, they need to put programs down in the community and train people, instead of building all of these prisons! And then put IBM ... they going to close Silicon Valley down and they going to open it up in the California State Department of Correction and they going to have all them people inside them prisons ...

**David:** Slave labor!

**Elder:** Making them computer chips. I mean, it's in the making! It's on paper! They are formulating the plan as we speaking! This is going to be reality. (Frank sounds) And they want to put our kids in there!

**Frank:** The dot com-ers don't get that.

**David:** They will! (laughter) They're starting to feel it now!

**Frank:** I have a friend who thinks of himself as a liberal.

**David:** Liberals are dangerous.

**Frank:** He believes the media. He ...

**Linda:** Yeah, he has given us money to support LUVeR and yet he doesn't want to hear, he doesn't want to listen to it, he doesn't want to know anything about the content of it, and when he does, it upsets him and he thinks it's all a bunch of bullshit!

**David:** He doesn't want to deal with reality. There's a great segment of this society that's in denial about the horrendous conditions that exist here. Homelessness ... it's a crime!

**Elder:** It's all across the country.

**David:** It's criminal to be homeless! They've criminalized people who are suffering!

**Frank:** It is a crime to feed the homeless.

**David:** Yes, it is! You know, they ... (Frank screaming) It should be a crime to be homeless in this country! Not homelessness is a crime! But the government should be looked at as criminals for allowing that to exist in this country!

**Elder:** Yeah, and everybody should have a place to stay.

**David:** Not the people who are homeless as criminal, but the government should be looked at as criminals for allowing these conditions to exist!

**Elder:** Basic human rights, food, clothing and shelter and everything you study and everything in society, this is basically what our whole struggle has been about. We've been struggling with the environment. When you say man was here in his primitive stage, he's been struggling to create an environment where he could feed, clothe and shelter himself! We've been constantly in a development to do that. We done build all these buildings, and build all this ... this has all been in dealing with feeding, clothing and housing ourself. But at the same time, we done became such a society that we can allow a certain segment of us to still go hungry and still be without the basic necessities of life! That's criminal! That's criminal! And any government or any people that fails to address that, they're criminal! But they're turning around and charge the people with being criminal for not being sufficient, productive within society when they know in society they only creates so many jobs, they got so many people living here, somebody ain't going to work! (laughing)

**Frank:** Try closing the institutions and giving people attendants.

**Linda:** That would be a way.

**Frank:** That is jobs!

**Linda:** All the people that were the attendants would be working and making money,

**Frank:** We need more teachers, nurses, doctors! That is jobs!

**Elder:** Right, yeah. That's ... about the institutions ... I think what has to happen with the institutions, I wouldn't say closing them all down, I would say they would have to be reorganized and restructured. One of the things that I see that's wrong with a lot of the ... with hospitals and medical facilities is they have a lot of bureaucracy, they're a lot of top heavy! They need to have more dealing with the services, as far as servicing people. And in America, they are too bureaucratic! There's too much at the top, and not that much services being provided. There needs to be more services being provided to the people. And it should be free! And it shouldn't be something that people would have to pay for. Like they do in Cuba! You know, certain things, people should be ... it should be free! Medical care, housing, then you would have some way to provide, to sustain yourself, to be able to make a living, to be able to care for yourself. That should be something everybody should be able to ... there should be no problem! People shouldn't have to ... you know when they're out for a job, you got two thousand people standing around a building for thirty jobs! You know, I mean, there's that many people that are unemployed!? It should be to where's, yeah, there shouldn't be no problem about people being able to find work!

**Frank:** Buses should be free.

**Elder:** Right, right, right.

**David:** You pay taxes! See, the whole problem is the emphasis is on making money. In this country, the emphasis is on making money, it's not geared towards dealing with humanity. And that's a big problem.

**Frank:** On making as much money as possible.

**David:** Yeah, yeah. And the whole thing with the distribution of ... it isn't like ... this is one of the most productive countries in the world! Nobody should be hungry in this society. We have the highest technology. So nobody should suffer from a medical illness unless the diseases are untreatable. And in a lot of instances they don't want to spend the money to develop the medicines to treat those diseases. Now if it makes money, just like recently, South Africa has a big problem with AIDS. (Frank sounds) They just recently said, OK, well, we're not going to charge South Africa, we're going to allow them to try to find cheap ...

**Frank:** That smells ...

**Linda:** There's something that smells. When we were reading about that, it seemed like there was something going on behind the scenes.

**David:** Well, there's always that! But the point is that for a long time they fought, resisted ... because South Africa wanted to develop their own, find alternatives to these different

*Linda Mac and Frank Moore (video capture)*

medicines. Because, you know, AIDS is in epidemic proportions over there! And these chemical companies are blocking them from trying to find a way to get the medications to treat the problems! Maybe they found, like you say, there's something behind it! I mean we don't know what goes on in these boardrooms of the board of directors of these chemical plants! They could be making deals, OK we're going to let you do this and we're going to make so much money, and don't go in this area ... we don't know! Because they're never above-board in their dealings with us or in revealing to the public their intentions. A lot of the institutions in this society have noble considerations, but if the people who run those institutions have ulterior motives, then those institutions are not going to serve those noble purposes. 'Cause a hospital, if the intentions of the people who control the hospital is to turn them into a chamber of horrors, then that's what will happen. The people that run these institutions, it's what their motivations are.

**Frank:** What they want is to make everything private. (Frank sounds)

**Linda:** Right, to turn all the public utilities into private, privately owned companies.

**David:** Well, you see that ain't working. They talking about PG&E going bankrupt. (laughing) We're going to suffer for that one, you know. Poor people aren't going to be able to pay their utility bills!

**Frank:** Hospitals, mail, water.

**Linda:** Oh, the hospitals, mail, water ... they're talking about making all of those private. (Frank sounds) So, that they make it so that it is not affordable to even have water.

**Frank:** It is called serfdom.

**Elder:** That's just like we saying, you talk about the human rights, food and shelter. I mean, everybody got a right to air, water. (Frank sounds)

**Linda:** You didn't think you had to mention them! (laughter)

**Elder:** Yeah! Who's got the right to impose on the air that everybody ... impose on the water? I mean, the water, it was here! That's why life ... without it we're going to all die!

**David:** They're essential to our survival.

**Elder:** That's like sacred. That's like something you don't ... you don't mess with the water and the air! But they're doing it! And they know what they're doing.

**Frank:** Yes!

**Elder:** 'Cause they have the technology! They know what they doing! So you have to look at it as far as these people are evil! (Frank sounds) For no matter how much money they making ... I'm saying they making more than any of them can spend, so ... for them to have that kind of greed, and to realize what they doing is going to have irreversible effects on the planet! While we still got a chance. We still got a chance! Some things we can reverse a lot of the processes. But if we don't hurry up, and do something about it, some of this stuff is going to be irreversible! Because we see how it's killing certain species, animals and plants. And they're disappearing. And we know that when those little frogs and little animals start disappearing, that we aren't far along up on the chain before everything is going to be gone!

**David:** Yeah, nobody should have the right to pollute our water, pollute our air. I mean, that's a gift to us from a higher person, a higher being! (Frank sounds) Our environment was created for us by who, whether it evolved or however, it was created by a higher being! However you look at it! That environment was created for us, for our existence, and for someone to come in and pollute it, contaminate it, they don't have that right!

**Elder:** Intentionally!

**David:** They don't have that right. And we shouldn't allow it to continue. Just like they have no right to control our destiny!

**Frank:** Are you hopeful?

**David:** Oh, yeah! I'm very optimistic that, (Frank sounds) because, you know, I'm very optimistic, you have to be! (Frank sounds) Because hope, without hope, what do you have? (Frank sounds)

**Elder:** They say right shall overcome. That right will overtake wrong! The right, the true!

**Frank:** Our fuel ... hope.

**David:** Yes! Without hope you have nothing. (Frank sounds) You have to be optimistic that ... that's what makes a revolutionary. Being hopeful and optimistic that we can create a new society, a new woman, a new man. And really understand the gifts that we have as human beings. And appreciate each other (Frank sounds) no matter what our cultural or ethnic differences. Diversity is the key to our continued existence!

**Frank:** Yes! Yes!

**David:** Both in culture and environmentally! Diversity enriches us as a people!

**Frank:** It was what evolution is all about!

**David:** Agree!

**Frank:** They don't get that.

**David:** They don't! (Frank sounds) It is on us to push it across.

**Frank:** Read "Mutation is Evolution".

**Linda:** Frank wants me to read one of his poems. It is called, "Mutation is Evolution". (Frank sounds)

**David:** Mutate or die!

**Linda:** Yes. (Frank sounds)

**Frank:** Would you read it?

**Linda:** Frank is asking if you would read it. OK, I'll find it!

(sounds of locating the poem!)

**David:** I'll read some and Elder ...

**Elder:** No, no, no. My reading is bad. Don't get me started, we'd be all night! (laughter)

**David:** (reads Frank's poem, "Mutation is Evolution")

### Mutation is Evolution

Frank Moore

Friday, April 23, 1999


You foolish idiot!

You want to make

Everything,

Everyone

Normal!

You want to cure

Prevent

All crips,

Freaks,

Crazies,

Oddballs,

Slow ones,

Misfits,

Bums,

Artists,

Poets,

And all other impractical

        Different looking

        Strange mutations


You fool!


How to condemn the human species

To extinction!


Look...

The game of evolution is

Change by experimentation.


We freaks are the experimenters


The name of the game

        Is flexibly adapting

      Coping

        Leaping

          Risking into the unknown newness

      Of uncontrolled future

We crips,

We misfits have always been the adapters,

The leapers

Hell,

I'm not wasting my time

Talking to you about magic and such

Just about evolution

Well,

If you don't need us crips,

Us misfits

If you don't need us no more...

Our advice is

Don't breathe deep

In your air-tight coffin

Of normalcy

And move very slowly

Very carefully

In your thin-skinned world

Of ever increasing fragility

Oh yeah...

Good luck!

(all laughing)

**David:** Yeah, yeah, good luck! (Frank sounds)

**Elder:** That's saying a lot! That's saying a lot! What that just brings to mind is how imperfect of a society we live in and then they try to portray it as being some perfect kind of thing, which is the farthest thing from reality. (Frank sounds) It doesn't exist! Because they talk about what's supposed to be, I'm coming to find when they talk about the normal family, and they talk about this dysfunctional family. I'm finding out that 90% of the families are dysfunctional families! (laughing) There's only a small percentage of what they consider normal! (laughing) The rest of us is dysfunctional! (all laughing)

**David:** The norm is supposed to be the nuclear family and as time goes on, it's revealed that what they call the norm is the most dysfunctional! (Frank sounds)

**Frank:** The nuclear family is a recent invention.

**David:** Yeah, that's what I'm saying!

**Frank:** And it don't work! (laughter)

**David:** That's what I'm saying. What they call the norm, in this society they finding out is the most dysfunctional!

**Elder:** Right, right. Everybody else is become crazy, that's what's normal! (laughing)

**Linda:** Right.

**David:** It's all relative.

**Elder:** Well, you know, extended families, you know, people ...

**David:** The global village.

**Elder:** Going outside of just the nucleus of their family is how it functions (Frank sounds). That's really what is normal! That's the normal function of how society should function.

**Frank:** Yes!

**Elder:** And this unitarian, individual is an American ...

**Frank:** That is human.

**Elder:** Right, right.

**David:** We live in groups. But we've created ... it's like ... I read a book years ago by this right-winger. It's called, *Time, The Unprofitable Vice For Americans In Troubled Times*, and one of the things that this guy said was the more civilized we become, the more destructive we are. And then he looked at our waste. The more civilized we become, the more toxic ... and, you look at it! Our waste products are highly toxic now. In other societies, agrarian societies, most of your waste can be composted and put back into the ground and recycled! Now, we got these dumps and once we dispose of this waste, you can't even live there! Because all the chemicals and the toxins that we're putting into our environment!

**Frank:** And they never put that in the rich neighborhoods.

**David:** No, they don't! (Frank sounds)

**Elder:** That's like up here, Richmond. People out there still getting sick and they're still claiming that they're not making nobody sick, but, you know, the people are sick!

**David:** Ain't far from here!

**Elder:** Right.

**David:** The wind can blow all of that over here!

**Frank:** On luver.org we have a piece on the chemical ...

**Mikee:** The one about the real energy crisis? It has all the quotes and the history and looking back in the different points in history and examples of all of the things that have been knowingly done.

**Linda:** (to Frank) Is that the one you're talking about? Yes.

**Frank:** And it outlines their different raps.

**Linda:** The chemical companies' different raps? (Frank sounds) No.

**Frank:** First, it is absolutely safe.

**David:** Yeah.

**Frank:** Then ... (Frank sounds)

**Linda:** They admit a little bit more each step of the way, over the years, as they have to, as things are revealed. And it goes through a history of that starting back in the '40s.

**Elder:** Right, right.

**Frank:** Well, it is minor. (Frank sounds)

**Linda:** The negative effects are minor. (Frank sounds)

**David:** Hence, your poem, mutate!

**Frank:** It don't hurt people! Then, well, it is dangerous, but it is there. It is too late! (Frank sounds)

**David:** Yeah!

**Elder:** There are some things that we can reverse. We can just close and parse. We got the technology, we done created all of that. There has to be some kind of way we can use the technology. I know one thing about those toxic things is that they generate this gas. Now how much they can be able to recycle or use that to some kind ... for some use to where's it won't be more harmful than it already is. And they say it's going to take ... I don't know how long it's going to take for that stuff to decompose itself. They got this radiation stuff, they don't know whether ... they dropping it in the ocean. Yeah, that's strange. They putting the radiation in these containers that can only last for 100 or 200 years. (Frank sounds) But the radiation inside the container lasts for 5,000 years, so the radiation gonna outlast the container! So therefore, when it comes out in the ocean, what is it going to do to all of the stuff 200 to 300 years down the road?! They got to take all that stuff back out the water.

**David:** We don't live that long, so we're just dumping it on the next generation!

**Frank:** But they don't care about 10 years from now.

**Elder:** Right. But that's the whole thing about while we've been developing ourselves from our

*David Johnson and Elder Freeman (video capture)*

lower level, dealing with from gathering food. And we've been trying to create a society that was going to address our needs. What they doing, is they making it so ... I mean from one generation to the next ... so, we're setting things so our children don't have to go through as hard as we did. We plant the crops, we learn how to feed them. Put food up for the winter. We teach this to our children, so they can make it, so it won't be as hard on them. So they can teach their children, so they won't have a hard a life as we had! Now here we are, that's not what's going on! They're not preparing for the future generations! They have no concern for what our children going to have to go through and live in this society! That's criminal!

**David:** The stress levels of our children is, like I said, as we move through this, with all this technology ... this technology has done nothing but increase the stress levels on our children! Our suicide rates are high! Not too long ago they had ... what did they called us in the '60s? The flower children, at least we had a definition! Flower children! Now, what is it? Generation X! What is Generation X? At least we could say, oh, OK, they were flower children, they were interested in flowers. What is Generation X into? You can't even tell by its designation! X!

**Frank:** That is old-fashioned. Generation X is. You must have blinked.

**Linda:** Oh, what is it now? (laughter)

**David:** Oh, we missed it huh?!

**Linda:** (laughing) You must have blinked! Now there's some other thing, but we don't know what it is! (laughter)

**David:** Each generation has to have a sense of purpose! And they're destroying that!

**Frank:** I think it is the WTO Generation. I think the kids are getting wiser again.

**David:** I hope so!

**Elder:** You probably can tell better about these youngsters with their music, 'cause in their music there's a couple things going on. A lot of us, I guess you could say the black parents, don't like a lot of the music that they hear coming from their own kids. (Frank sounds) But, there's the thing that I say about that is, this is a reflection of their discontent! Of how they're seeing things going down! David, he's more in touch with them. He knows a lot of these young people that's into this rap music, personally. And you know how they be feeling about a lot of ... how they see society, the way it's going.

**David:** It's like us, and we tell a lot of these youngsters that we talk to today, yet, when we stepped up to the plate and decided that this society needed to be changed, we were their age, you know, we were like in our teens, early teens, when we were looking for a better way of life! When we started protesting the draft and being sent to fight a war that we weren't in agreement with. We took stands then. It's incumbent upon them, I can't re-emphasize this enough, it is incumbent on the youth of today to stand up for their rights! They have our support. Because they are the ones that are most affected by what is going on today. I mean, you know, we're older. We don't have that many more years to live. (Frank sounds) Considering the average life span, what, 70? And then being that we're people of color, it's less than that! It's 70 if you got some kind of money where you can get the medical attention that can prolong your life. But like we say, we got a lot of soldiers from the '60s who made commitments then, gave their life for the struggle to change the society, who are languishing in these prisons! And we don't have much time left. So, they have to deal with the reality that exists today. And they have to set upon the task of creating a future that's going to be bright and filled with hope.

**Elder:** The young people that was in Quebec. They was young.

**David:** Yeah, yeah. It's incumbent upon them to step to the plate.

**Frank:** Are they? (Frank sounds)

**David:** I see a tide rising.

**Frank:** How?

**Elder:** We were at the Critical Resistance.

**David:** Yeah. We were at a conference where young people were dealing with the questions of education, schools and not jails!

**Elder:** The prison industrial complex.

**Frank:** Real school! (Frank screaming)

**David:** Yeah, I think that's what they're concerned with. They're concerned with getting real knowledge, real education, instead of being programmed to become another cog in the machine. But there again, it is incumbent upon them to raise their voices about what

115

curriculums are being taught in these institutions. We fought for black studies. We fought for a lot of classes that deal with like humanistic psychology, where you deal with the whole human being as opposed to just looking at clinical psychology. I mean, shifts in our ways of looking at things.

**Frank:** Black studies for everyone. (Frank sounds)

**David:** I think we all need to be sensitive to, like I said, our diversity. Various cultures of the world. The world is filled with a lot of cultures. On some levels we appreciate them. On other levels we don't. Music, art, inventions. All people on this planet have contributed to culture. And culture is a way of making sense of your reality. (Frank sounds) Religion, spiritual stuff, politics, technology.

**Elder:** Social behavior.

**David:** Social behavior. Culture is very important to us. We don't appreciate it. Like I said, our cultural diversity.

**Elder:** You know, that's just like in some schools they teach now when you had that whole thing, where you have Black History month, then you have Hispanic holidays, you have the Chinese new year. Those, I guess you could say, kind of like when I was growing up it wasn't too much of all of that being taught. It was more basic European history, European culture. Now they're showing that in this society that we live in, you have to teach them the ethnic diversity of this society in order for everybody really to get along. You got to understand, it would be wrong for me to go, because some people they eat burritos and tacos all the time, for me to say because they're not eating collard greens and chitlins, that something's wrong with them! (laughter) Or vice versa, for them to set up a certain kind of attitude because of me just because of our cultural differences.

**David:** Ethnic differences have always existed throughout history, but I think that the advent of racism we see the devalueization of people's culture.

**Frank:** When we travel, we miss the diversity of this area.

**Linda:** We went up to Portland and Seattle and it seemed like everybody was white! (Frank sounds) And it was scary. (Frank sounds) And we come back here, and it's like, everybody is here.

**David:** Yeah.

**Frank:** Like eating white bread. (Frank screams)

**Elder:** (laughing) Oh, man!

**David:** Leached all the nutrients out of the grain!

**Linda:** That's right. (Frank sounds) (laughter)

**Linda:** We think we went the whole week without seeing anybody but a white person when we were in Seattle! (laughter, Frank sounds)

**David:** I've been up to Oregon, but I usually try to go … when I've gone up there, it's been to look at the diversity of the natural environment. I spend more time not so much in the urban areas, but in the natural environment.

**Frank:** Like, integration is not for the black people. It is how I want to live. (Frank sounds)

**Elder:** Yeah. I think everybody should have that right to ... if you want to live with the diversity like Oakland, like Berkeley and San Francisco, you should have the right to live there. And if you choose to where you want to live in an environment like you're saying, you went to Seattle and you didn't see anybody ... you should have that right to want to live in that too. But it shouldn't be to where because you choose to ... if black people chose to live down south, and white folks chose to live up north, and other ones decided they wanted to live in between or in either one, it shouldn't be to where you shouldn't have that right to do that!

**David:** See, here's the deal. Without the institution of racism, integration wouldn't even be something to consider.

**Elder:** Right.

**David:** Because ... and if you look at it, integration is only a phenomena that takes place here in this country. Because if you go to other parts of the world, you can travel in those environments, without problems, if you honor and respect the people of those areas. But because we have so many problems, we had so many problems. Even now, they tell you as Americans traveling, don't go to this part of the world, because what happened, then it went over to that world, that part of the world ... messed it up. So those people have an attitude to anybody going over there! And you haven't done anything to those people! They say, oh, you better not travel over here! Don't travel over here! It's getting to the point where you ain't going to be ... if we allow them to go to other parts of the world and ravish it like they do, we, as citizens of this society, won't be able to go nowhere because everybody going to be mad at us! They're going to think we're the ones responsible for all the hardships that's being inflicted on them. And they don't understand that we're victims like them!

**Elder:** We're victims too! (laughing)

**Frank:** Fragmentation.

**Linda:** That's fragmentation? (Frank sounds) Breaking ... all the different countries looking at each like that.

**David:** Artificial boundaries.

**Frank:** They talk about free trade, how about free movement? (Frank sounds)

**David:** Free movement, yeah. Trade has always been ... people have always traded. And there is nothing wrong ... they say fair exchange is no robbery. But exploitation, when this capitalist, imperialist system introduced exploitation into the equation, it means somebody gonna get fucked! (laughing) And more than likely, it ain't them! (Frank sounds)

**Frank:** The corporations can move all over the world.

**David:** It's called globalization.

**Frank:** But, people need passports.

**David:** Yeah.

**Elder:** Right, right. (Frank screams) Like it's the whole thing, you got to be able to go ... we've got to have ID here, if we want to go anywhere, but to be able to move freely around the world, yeah, that's a whole other, that's another one there. (laughing)

**David:** When convicts say, why do I need ID to get ID! (laughter)

**Frank:** If we could move, travel freely, they could not do the shell games that they do. (Frank sounds)

**David:** Yeah.

**Elder:** Well, that's the whole thing. They got everything under control. They're controlling the media, they're controlling all of the major transportation and all of those factories, it's under their control. So as far as people being able to travel freely around the world, to deal with different issues, they got it on a financial level. They're making it just about impossible ... like we want to go to Cuba in November, but it's making it real difficult for us to go down there, and meet with the Cuban people and meet with people on the international level to try to see if we can get some things resolved in the United States. That's not economically or politically or socially working in the United States' best interest, so they gonna do everything to make that as difficult for us to do that. And the main way they're doing that is finance!

**David:** Let me elaborate on the thing you said about Cuba. See, in November they're talking about having a conference on political prisoners and prisoners of war in Cuba to discuss the issue of political prisoners and who is a political prisoner and who is not. Basically it's ... like I say, we're dealing with a unique phenomena in this country in terms of political prisoners and prisoners of war. And some delineation has to be made on that, and some of the definitions have to be expanded because it has to be more inclusive. This country denies that it has any political prisoners. So, our interest, like I said, we got a lot of comrades who are prisoners of war, political prisoners, who are languishing in these prisons in America, that people don't even know about. Our commitment to them and to struggle is to make the world knowledgeable of these people who made great sacrifices in the interest of trying to build a better society and who became victims of these various police agency COINTELPRO, all of these charges brought against them that they used to justify imprisonment of these people.

**Elder:** And some of that is to try to bring some closure too, as far as in the United States, these people have been in prison for over twenty years. It's time to bring some closure. Even on the international level, to where's these people, even for whatever, in other countries when they held people for political beliefs around the world, they done let a lot of them go after ten or fifteen years. These people done been in jail for over twenty years, and what got them in prison was their political beliefs and the activities inside the United States, whether instituted or framed up by the police, or the police was the ones that set the plan in motion, like the murdering of Fred Hampton and everything. In order to justify that, they're saying they had warrants, but they also had ... they had these warrants, they had the police inside to create the situation for the warrant to be issued. So, government conspiracies, all of these things, it needs to all come to a closure. It needs to be finished. And as far as how this government, that has something to do with changing the government in itself. For the people to come to a realization they don't need this prison-industrial complex, they don't need the government to be moving in this military manner that it does. And in order to create jobs and an economy for people inside the United States, there's another way we can go now with all this technology, we don't have to have, we don't have to use these primitive methods. We don't even need this outdated 17th century, 15th century judicial system. This parliamentary procedure process that they're going through with all this crap that you got to go through, four to six years of legal learning. All of this legal language, and all of this terminology on an outdated, outmoded system. We're in the twenty-first century, and we're using a judicial system that's five, six hundred years old! It don't make no sense!

**David:** You know, we used to have a saying, going back to what you were saying, what do you do, we used to have a saying, heavy is the task of the liberator, but heavier are the chains of containment and yoke of oppression. So the task that we have in educating people in this society, in moving the people to action, is a heavy task. Because we don't have the resources at our disposal as the government.

**Elder:** What you're all doing here.

**David:** Yeah. Another thing is, in Vietnam, the people of Vietnam, the will of the people in Vietnam, demonstrates that the will of the people is greater and stronger than any forms of technology or military might that you have. (Frank sounds) Revolutions throughout the world demonstrate that the will of the people will always prevail, but moving people to exert themselves and exert their will is another task.

**Frank:** That is what LUVeR is here for.

**David:** I hear that. That's why we're here!

**Elder:** Right, right, right. You have to have these lines of communication, education, because the people have to be motivated to realize that they can do something about their situation. I think a lot of people may have a different attitude towards the electoral process, voting in this country, after this last presidential election. And realizing ...

**David:** The next one will be different, that's for sure! (Frank sounds)

**Elder:** ... that there's maybe ... people didn't realize because you say everybody's vote counts. So, that election right kind of showed that voting does make, can make a difference in things. So, I don't know ...

**David:** Either positive or negative, 'cause some people's vote, they show, you're vote don't count!

**Elder:** ... how it's going to go in the future, as far as changing things on a local level, because I see a lot of things that people can do with their vote on the local and state level more so than they can on a federal level. On a federal level they can have more to do so with electing state representatives and things that represent people on a federal level. But I see if we do a lot of things locally, and people are generated in this area, and I'm hoping that this election will show them that they can do something to make a change.

*Elder Freeman (video capture)*

**David:** Well, I look at it like this. As long as rich people control the electoral process, poor people ain't going to get nowhere. Because it's rich people and money that's dictating the flow and direction of the process.

**Frank:** When we webcast the Political Prisoners Conference on LUVeR, we were blown out by the love and the positivity of the people that had been in prison. That is the exact opposite of the media image. And by showing that love, it is very dangerous to the system.

**Elder and David:** Yeah, yeah, yeah.

**David:** Well, you said it, it is the task of the liberating. We're optimistic here that we can win this war.

**Elder:** Yeah.

**David:** On all levels. Like I said, we fight for the hearts and minds of our people and for people to get in touch with their humanity and understand the relationship to other people, and their relationship to the environment, it's all one.

**Elder:** I've been involved in the struggle for over thirty years, and the struggle I've been involved in has been a struggle of love, although there's been a lot of pain and a lot of suffering. But I got involved in this because I've got a love and a concern and I care about people. And that's why I got involved. And if it meant that I had to sacrifice a lot of my own individual things for the sake of the whole, I'm willing to make that sacrifice, and been making that sacrifice. So, and it's out of love, because the struggle is about love! It's because we care. Because we don't want to see people just gunned down in the street. Because we don't want to see drugs and people's lives are …

**David:** Homeless and starving.

**Elder:** … and homeless and the whole … and every dime they get they spending it on drugs and they're not doing nothing for their family and everything is a disgrace. It's out of love and concern and care that you don't want to see that going on.

**David:** Like Che said, the revolutionary started by great feelings of love.

**Elder:** And I'm glad you saw that love because everybody think that everybody that's been in prison, or come from prison, is that they're cold-blooded, heartless (Frank sounds) …

**Linda:** Bitter, hateful.

**Elder:** Yeah, we're far from that. We show a lot more humane treatment towards other people maybe because of our being confined and isolated. And that's another bad thing that they're doing now, with those Pelican Bays, the way they're building these new prisons where they're putting you in 24-hour, seven-days-a-week total isolation. Where you don't ever come in contact with another human being. It is inhumane, it's inhuman, because we are social creatures! And when we can't come in contact, in touch with … and you do this to somebody over a period of years, that person's mentality … when you let him come out, he's not … he can't function in this society because he had no preparation to do it! He's going to be an animal! They dehumanize you! They make you to where you become inhuman. And they got these prisons in … they got one in Pelican Bay, they're building another one in other states. They done built these underground, maximum security prisons which is total isolation. So, therefore, they're taking a part of our society, and these people don't stay in there forever. They let them out. They release them from there. No medical treatment. No adjustment to coming back into society, anything! They give you $200 and let you go. Now, what do you think that person is coming back to! So, just being human!

**Frank:** It is like a sci-fi movie.

**David:** Yeah, only it's real. It ain't a movie.

**Elder:** Yeah. (laughs)

**David:** Like I say, we live in a society, it's like what Gil Scott Heron used to say, we live in a lot of civilizations. And the violences we are subjected to, most people look at violence in its physical form, but the media subjects us to a lot of psychological violence and spiritual violence. Which in a lot of instances, the psychological violence can have far greater impact on the society than the physical violence because people are still left here, scarred, broken and … but the reality is there are a lot of people who have lost hope! One of the challenges that faces people who are concerned with creating the new man and the new woman is to spread the word, there is hope! That we can create a brighter future. And that's one thing … all it requires is for us to exert our will and be in touch with our humanity because if your objective and goal is to be a good human being, then your politics will be good, your spirituality will be good, and your physical deeds will be good. And that's what we struggle for! And I think

121

I'm going to close with that!

**Linda:** Amen!

**Frank:** By the way, who are you?

**Linda:** We never told people who you are!

**David:** My name is David Johnson. And I was one of the San Quentin Six. A lot of my ... what makes me the person I am is I came in contact with a brother in prison who was a great revolutionary and spearheaded the prison movement in California, George Jackson.

**Frank:** We need to have you back to talk about that.

**David:** OK.

**Linda:** And who are you? (laughter)

**Elder:** OK, usually, it takes a minute for this! My name is Ronald Freeman, but a lot of people they call me Elder Freeman, because I'm a priest, a Catholic priest, in the African Orthodox Church. (Frank giggles) I'm one of the founding members of the L.A. Black Panther Party for Self-Defense. When the party was started back in 1960 ... well, it came to L.A. in the end of '67, so I say the beginning of 1968 is when the L.A. Black Panther Party started in Los Angeles, and I was there from the beginning.

**David:** Also survived some of those shoot-outs down there when the police were attacking.

**Elder:** Yeah. Well you know, I'm one of the people, I was in the leadership of the Southern California chapter of the party, so when, Geronimo [ji-Jaga Pratt - Ed.] was somebody that I knew, when he came. So what happened to him, happened to me, it happened to other people. It just so happened that the cases that they had on me, it didn't work. And I beat the cases. I didn't have to end up spending all that time. They got me for awhile! I put in about eight.

**David:** Eight years.

**Elder:** So, that's who I am. I'm from the underground part of the Black Panthers, I was part of the political part of the party and I also was one of the leaders in the underground part of the Black Panther Party, which came to be known as the Black Liberation Party.

(Frank sounds)

**Linda:** So, we got to have them both back, huh?! (laughter)

**Frank:** LUVeR is a great con ...

**Linda:** To get together with people like you guys.

**Elder:** Alright, alright! I'm hoping I'll get good results back, feedback from this. It will be interested in what you all are doing here, because it's good! It's underground love! When I heard underground love (laughter), it's like, alright now, we're going to share some love here! The righteous truth!

**Linda:** Yeah. Who is next week? There is no Shaman's Den. It is the People's Park thing. Frank is reading one of his poems at the People's Park Anniversary.

**David:** We were just up there right before we came down here! We were up at the park and we were talking about the struggle, looking at the trees and all that, what a struggle it was to just to keep the park!

**Linda:** Yes. So, there's no Shaman's Den next week. And the week after that, Mary Israel is scheduled. She's talking about the work she is doing in Columbia.

**Frank:** She is in Columbia now.

**Linda:** Yes, so she'll come back and talk about that. That's May 6.

**David:** We can come on your station again and get the people to send us some funds so that we can get to Cuba! We're poor!

**Frank:** Hey, we need money too! (laughter)

**Elder:** Tell the truth!

**David:** Being a revolutionary is hazardous to your health and you don't get paid!

**Linda:** That's right!

**Frank:** It is cheap, but not free. (laughter)

# Sasha Cagen (& Michael)

Recorded March 18, 2012 on luver.com

........................................................................................................

Sasha Cagen is a writer, coach and community builder and the founder of the Quirkyalone movement. She is the author of the books, *Quirkyalone: A Manifesto for Uncompromising Romantics* and *To-Do List: From Buying Milk to Finding a Soul Mate, What Our Lists Reveal About Us*. She writes a blog on the *Huffington Post* and has appeared on CNN, the BBC and NPR.

Sasha attended Frank's performance, *The Uncomfortable Zones of Fun* in December 2011 and published a long review of the performance on her *Huffington Post* blog. Frank invited Sasha to be a guest on the Shaman's Den after reading her review.

........................................................................................................

**Linda:** ... and then Frank always says they complain ... (Frank sounds) And they say you know I can't get connected with people, and they blame it on their disability. And Frank says, hey, turn the letter board around, make it easier for people to talk with you. (Frank sounds)

**Michael:** Cool.

**Frank:** Reach out. But they want to blame the ...

**Linda:** Disability for all of their problems.

**Michael:** It hasn't stopped you. (laughs)

**Frank:** How did you get started ...

**Linda:** In your work? How did you get started in your work?

**Sasha:** I started writing ... oh, is there more?

**Linda:** I think so ...

**Frank:** Or in your ...

**Linda:** In your play? (Sasha laughs)

**Frank:** Life ... ?

**Linda:** Or how did you get started in your life?

**Sasha:** (giggles) ... Hmmm, now I don't know how to answer ... (giggles) How did I get started in my life ... maybe I should answer that one ... that seems interesting.

**Frank:** Yes.

**Sasha:** Well you know, it's funny, I was talking to my mother a few months ago about some early ... some childhood things and she said to me ... she was kind of questioning my interpretation of my childhood or something ... and she said, well, you were just always this kid who like always wanted to go and explore and meet people and when you were two and

124

people would come over, when they were leaving you would be sad and want to go with them and see what was going on. So it was actually really interesting to hear that. (Frank sounds) And I think that's true. That I am just very curious.

**Frank:** Like me.

**Sasha:** Yeah, probably.

(Frank sounds)

**Linda:** You want to hear more? Tell us more!

**Sasha:** (giggle) ... Wasn't that enough? (laughing)

**Frank:** I am not CNN.

**Linda:** He's not CNN (laughter) ... You can give longer answers.

**Sasha:** I know ... I've got my talking points ummm, ummmm, so then how did I get started in my life ... well, I went to nursery school, made some friends, then I went to kindergarten and um ... Yeah, I think that I just always had a ... I grew up in Rhode Island which is a very quirky interesting state ... I think it really kind of shaped me but at the same time I really wanted to leave it.

**Frank:** And you made a career out of "quirky".

**Sasha:** Yeah, I think so (laughter) and I am getting more explicit about it ... I think I am going to become more explicit about that 'cause I have been kind of not totally owning it.

**Frank:** How?

**Sasha:** I don't know yet, but I think it's going to be like the centerpieces, because I really am really interested in individuality and acceptance and celebration of individuality and I think that underlies all of my work ... and I'm actually working with a coach now to help me see that ... because there are certain parts I haven't ... I haven't made it coherent yet, but that is the center of it all.

**Frank:** What is quirky?

**Sasha:** Um ... it is unintentional difference. So it is basically being yourself in a way that is not ... it's not like trying to be quirky. For an example, I think quirky is hip right now and there was a Saturday Night Live sketch that was like Zooey Deschanel and other quirky characters in pop culture that have this kind of hip aesthetic and that's not quirky at all. Like that's totally commercial and predictable. So quirky is ... the example that I used in that *Quirkyalone* book was like it's a cowlick ... it's like your hair sticking up ... and it's uncontrollable ... you work with it, you don't hide it. You go with it.

**Frank:** And play with it.

**Sasha:** Yeah, right, if you can. Like first you have to accept it and be good with it. That's the first step. And then yeah, play with it ... it's more fun.

**Frank:** Why would not you accept it?

*Frank Moore and Sasha Cagen (video capture)*

**Sasha:** Why would you not accept it? Because it's not acceptable. It's not how you are supposed to look, behave or be. Or because it takes courage to accept your quirkiness.

**Frank:** But, if you are quirky, you don't have a choice. (Frank sounds)

**Sasha:** Um ... Well, you do have a choice. I mean you can camouflage it and blend in ... if you are self-identified quirky then you have made the choice to embrace your quirkiness. But everyone is potentially quirky ... I mean we all are, right? So that really is the difference between quirky people and non-quirky people ... the non-quirky people are hiding it.

**Frank:** Art and science are full of ...

**Linda:** Quirky people. (Frank sounds)

**Sasha:** Yeah, that is true. Yeah. (Frank sounds)

**Frank:** I just read ...

**Linda:** Which one are you thinking of, the science one? (Linda to Mikee) What's the name of that book we just finished reading about the science dude?

**Mikee:** Feynman, Richard Feynman.

**Linda:** Richard Feynman, it was a biography of him.

**Mikee:** Autobiography.

**Frank:** How he is quirky. (Frank sounds)

**Sasha:** Michael's read it.

**Michael:** I read it ... he is amazing. When he was studying physics, instead of reading the books, he did every experiment in history to understand on his own terms, so that by the time he became a scientist, he couldn't ... no one actually understood the ideas he had because he started all of them from scratch. He's really funny too. He is an awesome guy.

(Frank sounds)

**Frank:** He can pick locks.

**Linda:** Oh, pick locks? There was that whole thing where he got into picking locks.

**Michael:** For the challenge? (Frank sounds)

**Linda:** It was really safes. He knew how to pick most of the safes in the building that he was in at one point ... he kind of prided himself in that.

**Michael:** I should learn that skill ...

**Frank:** And the Manhat ...

**Mikee:** Manhattan project ...

**Linda:** Oh, the Manhattan Project, that was the organization where he picked all of the locks.

**Michael:** Oh, that is a great place to do it ... (laughs) Well, you know if you are going to go, go big, I guess. He was a more original thinker than almost anyone else around him and I never understood if it was just who he was or if that is what he learned to be. I keep reading those books, because I never get tired of them.

**Frank:** What was it called?

**Linda:** The actual book? Do you remember the title of the book, Mikee? He'll look it up.

**Frank:** You Must Be Kidding.

**Linda:** Oh, that was the name of it.

**Michael:** Yeah, *You Must Be Kidding, Mr. Feynman.* (all laugh) Good choice. Do you read a lot of physics books?

**Linda:** We read a lot of books. Frank has read a lot of physics books over the years.

**Sasha:** Do you all read books together?

**Linda:** Frank gets the talking books from the Library of Congress, it is a free service, so he can pick the books online, then we download them and put them on a little stick and they send us the machine to listen to them on. We always have two books going. We have one we read during the day and one we read late at night when we are getting ready for bed. It's really fun. We do a lot of reading.

**Frank:** After ten years at least of not reading.

**Linda:** Right, any books at all. (Frank sounds)

**Linda:** Well, it is because we started the radio station and we had that on all of the time, so we just stopped reading. Before that we had books going all of the time. And then we started again about a year and a half ago or so.

**Michael:** Have you read *Quirkyalone*?

**Linda:** No, we haven't read Sasha's book. Is it on talking book?

**Sasha:** I don't know. Anything is possible.

**Frank:** So, how did you discover the power of being quirky?

**Sasha:** Ha! That is a good question. (Frank sounds)

**Frank:** I am not Anderson Cooper.

**Sasha:** (laughing) Absolutely not. Totally different way of length and speed and, yeah ... he is much more combative. (laughing) Um, the power of quirky. I feel like I am still discovering the power of quirky. How did I discover the power of being quirky? (Frank sounds) It's like weird to say "power" and "quirky" together because they are not words that you would normally associate with each other because quirky is so sort of soft ... (Frank sounds)

**Frank:** The force of quirky.

**Sasha:** The force of quirky? Well, in a sense it's like being a writer and having an individual vision and like something that, um ... it comes down to wanting to offer something new, which in itself is probably going to be quirky at this point, because almost everything has been done or written about, so in that sense ... and I think that the internet ... I've been thinking about this quite a lot ... the internet makes it even more important to be quirky, or just to be different, because it's just a complete inundation of stuff, right? So it's having a distinctive point of view that people really want to read is the only thing that will make it important. And the power of quirky ... I feel like it should be something that's personal, the power of quirky, and ... I am trying to think about a moment in my life that I really felt that. 'Cause like quirkyalone, it's like "quirky" and "alone" that is a very ... it's about being quirky, but it's about a very particular experience of being alone in a social setting where you're supposed to be with a date. Right, so that whole book is about that project. So there are moments like that that I could identify. "Quirky" ... it is such a good question. I want to give you a good answer ... that is why I have to let it come to me. Yeah ...

**Frank:** On the surface it appears that you and I are opposites.

**Sasha:** (laughs) In what sense?

**Frank:** I am about tribal and community and melting ...

**Sasha:** Ummmm.

**Frank:** And your book is titled ...

**Sasha:** *Quirkyalone.* Yeah. Well, yes, on the surface that could seem true and then there's a bunch of layers under that ... 'cause there's the Quirkyalone movement, right? So there is a tribal component. But, I personally only organize one gathering a year, that's Quirkyalone Day, when people come together. And I could organize a lot more, it's just that I never really wanted to. And quirkyalone, it's like, the point of that word is to give people a reference point to collect and to feel more normal, in a sense, and to have a sense of community. But it's very conceptual. And people have met their best friends through Quirkyalone, especially through the online forums there are people who have met each other and they travel to hang out with each other and they like become really close. Umm, so there is that. But you're right, that it's not about melting. And I'm thinking about doing a book in the future that would be *Quirkytogether*, which is like the natural follow up. That's been like ten years in coming, right? And it would be very much concerned with like how do you melt but still be yourself. Or like melt, but not melt?

**Frank:** Ask ...

**Linda:** Him? Michael? Ask Michael that question.

**Sasha:** How do you melt, but not melt? (laughs)

**Frank:** That is quantum physics.

(Michael laughs)

**Michael:** Yeah, seem to be in both states at the same time. I don't know, I mean, that's ... you know better than I do.

**Sasha:** Why?

**Michael:** I love the concept ... I mean, I don't know it, I don't know it in your experience ... I'd love to know how those things merged.

**Sasha:** Melting but not melting?

**Michael:** Yeah.

**Sasha:** (sighs) I mean, that's the jumping off point for the whole book, so I'm giving myself like a whole research experience to understand it better. So, it's like, when I think about this topic, like I ... people have been asking me to do this for years, right ... 'cause it's like really natural, and I didn't feel ready to do it. Almost 'cause I wanted to have the perfect experience of it before I felt ready, but I haven't, and I've gotten to this point where like OK I think, the way for me to understand this is to take this on in my life and in writing and talking to people and ...

**Frank:** Is there such a thing as a perfect experience?

**Sasha:** Yeah, exactly that's probably the block.

**Frank:** Of anything ...

(all laugh)

**Sasha:** Yeah, exactly, (laughs) right, which would be a classic quirkyalone mistake, yeah.

(all laughing)

**Frank:** Really, that is what both of us are rebelling against.

**Sasha:** Ummm ... yeah, you're right ... yeah ... no, absolutely ... that's quirky.

**Frank:** The couple ...

**Linda:** The couple, the date.

(all laugh)

**Frank:** The "mister right".

**Michael:** (giggles) What do you replace it with?

**Frank:** (making sounds throughout this) I replace it with tribe and intimacy. And I think you replace it with the person is all fulfilled in his self.

(silence)

**Sasha:** I'm considering ... (laughs) (Frank sounds) umm ... (silence) I don't have the philosophy that all man or any man or woman is an island, so no, in that respect, no, and there's a significant part of my writing that's about friendship in that book, so it's the idea of significant others, instead of just having one partner, that you have many people in your life that are very close ... and it's not a formal tribe, but you know, it could be, depending on how ... whether all those friends are in one circle. So there can be a quasi-tribal nature, but I don't think, most people don't have tribes, it just doesn't work that way for most people.

**Michael:** 49ers?

**Sasha:** Have a tribe?

**Frank:** And now it's more ...

**Linda:** ... common ... we're finding it's more ... is that what you mean, it's more common?

**Frank:** That is very recent historically.

**Linda:** Historically? It's very recent historically that people didn't exist in a tribal reality, tribal situation? (Frank sounds)

**Michael:** Sports, I still don't understand sports ... I can't think of a more tribal thing that I've ever seen in my entire life ... because people ... you're thinking different tribes ... but everyone finds that thing, that has a flag, has something that represents them and they identify with it. It can be almost anything. But is that the kind of tribal or ....

**Linda:** (to Frank) That is not what you're talking about ...

**Frank:** People used to live in groups. Big families.

**Sasha:** Uh huh. Yeah, it's a very lonely society that we have, the way our society is structured, it's very individualistic to the extreme. For example, like being a mother is like a real uphill battle in our culture. I remember reading an essay by a woman who was Indian. She wanted to go and be back with the Indian family because she would get more support and she would be able to work and not be totally consumed all the time with taking care of her child.

**Frank:** We ...

**Linda:** (Frank sounds throughout this) We raised two boys, and there were five to six people that were the adults and then the two kids and it was a very sane way to raise kids, because the kids were discouraged to identify more with the biological parent. I mean, you know, it was OK, everybody knew, it wasn't like a secret or anything, but they ... we all raised them and they had to deal with all of us responsibly. So, we held them responsible and it was a ... it seemed like a very sane way to do it. There wasn't all of that craziness that happens ... I hear people talking about that, I think, oh, we never went through that ... we never went through that ... and I realize it was because there was like five or six of us, so it was all very integrated.

**Frank:** They could not play ...

**Linda:** Play us against each other ... the way sometimes, if you have two parents ... that didn't work.

(laughter) (Frank sounds)

**Sasha:** So it was two kids, and five adults, and you all cohabited ... Wow!

**Linda:** Yeah, the five adults were the parents, they thought of us all as parents.

**Sasha:** Was it mom 1, mom 2 ... or what were the names?

**Linda:** No, we all called each other by our real names, sure, yeah. But when they had like Mother's Day projects, they'd make something for all three moms, or dads for all three dads, but they didn't call us mom or dad, we all called each other by our regular names.

**Sasha:** Uh huh, wow, how old are the kids now?

**Linda:** They were born in 1975, so however old that makes them ...

**Sasha:** Yeah, it's about my age, yeah ...

**Linda:** Oh!

(all laugh)

**Frank:** (Frank sounds) But the couple is not ... it don't work.

**Linda:** The couple don't work. (Frank sounds)

**Sasha:** You're definitive? You think absolutely a couple doesn't work.

**Frank:** As a concept.

**Linda:** It doesn't work.

**Frank:** It isolates. And what is wrong with you that you are not married? (Frank sounds)

**Linda:** What's wrong with you that you're not married? (Frank sounds)

(silence)

**Sasha:** Uh huh ... so, is that a question?

**Linda:** No, I think he is saying that ... almost like it is an under-implication. It's like, the couple is supposed to work, that is supposed to be the model ... that is the thing that you are going for (though most people aren't doing it) ... and if you're not, then what's wrong with you ... it is like there is something lacking with you.

**Sasha:** Right, yeah, that is still basically the dominant idea ... it's changing though. A friend of mine is a sociologist at NYU and he just released a book called *Going Solo*. It's gotten a ton of attention and it is about the phenomenon of people living alone. And a lot of the book contradicts the stereotypes of what it is to either live alone or be single and basically finds that people who live alone are more involved with their community and likely to volunteer and basically be involved with others. Exactly what you said ... they're more forced to get out there than when you're in a couple and you live together, it can be more isolating or hermitic, but it doesn't have to be ... I mean not all couples are like that.

**Frank:** No. One is ... it is not the number ...

**Linda:** ... two people, if it's one person, two people ... however many people ... That's not the issue? (Frank sounds)

**Frank:** If you are enough ...

**Linda:** If you are enough, then it doesn't matter what the number is, if you are enough.

**Sasha:** Alone, you mean, or as one person?

**Frank:** Or 2 people, or 3 people ...

(sounds of understanding from all)

**Frank:** But they push that you are not enough. That your mate is not enough.

**Sasha:** Uh huh. So no one is enough.

(Frank sounds affirmation)

**Frank:** Exactly.

**Linda:** Yeah, no one is enough.

(sounds of understanding)

**Sasha:** Right.

**Frank:** So, you keep looking ...

**Sasha:** Uh huh. Yeah, I think the like "what is enough" thing is a fundamental question always, just for people. And another thing I do is I coach people, a life coach, and I find when I coach people it is often a core issue that comes up is this issue of "what is enough?" Whether it is talking about work or relationships or anything ... it is like this core dissatisfaction of "what is enough?" So it permeates. Whether you're single, whether you're with someone, any situation. (Frank sounds) Which I'm sure is particular to our culture. It is so strong in people.

**Frank:** How about when you get old?

**Sasha:** Hmmm. Who me?

**Frank:** People.

**Sasha:** People?

**Frank:** People. How about that?

**Sasha:** In terms of community and being single or being with a partner or family and all of that ...

**Frank:** All of those things ...

**Sasha:** Yeah, it's a huge issue. In fact, my friend Eric, who wrote that book, wrote about me and my family because I had an issue like that come up. Actually, the conversation comes full circle because I have this aunt who is like the definition of quirkiness ... no one could be more quirky than she is. Like, the most beautiful amazing spirit, actress ... she was a casting director in Hollywood, but really an actress at the core. She would have been here doing this interview ... she was like very counter-cultural. And she had a partner for 25 years, but they broke up, he wasn't there for her when she had another health crisis. And then she got brain cancer. So basically ... she had a ton of friends, she had a tribe, but it was more of a casual tribe, which is what most people have ... most people don't live together in a tribe. And in the end, the tribe couldn't cut it, for meeting her needs. Because the needs for someone who is in that situation are totally consuming. So my sister and I were commuting to L.A. to take care of her, which was not sustainable. And then she went and lived with my family in Rhode Island. But when it came up for me, it was quite scary ... what if I am ... she also didn't have any children ... like what if I'm at that age or at any age and get ill and don't have kids ... or a partner ... or even a partner ... like when you're in that situation you realize it is a tribe ... it is way more than one person can handle, way more ... so I think it's a big question ... for not only people who are single, or people who are in relationships, like the whole country, because people are living longer, but yet they need a lot of help to live and that situation they may be in.

**Frank:** For Betty ...

**Linda:** Betty is our neighbor. We might have even mentioned her at the performance, she is in her mid-80s ... she's a church-going lady. And when we first moved into this neighborhood in 1995, she was that much younger, and she was the one that just welcomed us. She used to knock on the door with cookies. She lived with Joe, they never had been married, but they had been together for decades. So, we got very close, in a neighborly way. She knew all about what we did. Even though she went to church every Sunday, she had no problem with the nudity, the eroticism, the art ... she just loved our spirit. (Frank sounds throughout)

**Frank:** They ...

**Linda:** We would video the performances and they would watch it. They would say, do we get the tape? (all laugh) Then the two of them would sit there and watch the performance tape, and they loved it! So, when Joe got sick with cancer, we just ended up being the ones. They didn't have any kids together, and so we were the ones that were with her for Joe being sick, 'cause she couldn't really take care of him, 'cause she was old herself. So, we were there and once Joe passed away, we just stayed. She lives on the corner in a little corner apartment. We have a house down the street that we built for Frank's students, so there's Corey, Alexi and Erika live there. Alexi makes everybody dinner. Betty is included in that. Erika goes down and has dinner with Betty every night and they watch her cable TV.

**Sasha:** So sweet. (Frank sounds)

**Linda:** And Erika bathes her and takes care of all of that. Corey and Alexi are also very actively involved. We're all involved. We're the ones who get her to the doctors, we take care of everything, the less she is able to do herself.

**Sasha:** Uh huh.

**Linda:** Yeah, we often think, somebody like Betty, at this point, would be in a nursing home, if she wasn't involved in this kind of a tribal situation. And there is no money involved in any of it. You know, she pays for her own food and she pays any expenses that are part of hers, but she is not paying us to do anything. It is just what we are doing.

**Sasha:** Right.

**Linda:** And, we think about that. If it wasn't ... what would somebody like that do in that situation. It is such a serious quality of life disparity. She is happy. She is having fun. We decorate her house for Christmas. We decorate her house for Halloween ... it is all in fun.

**Sasha:** Yeah ...

**Linda:** And it wouldn't be that way ...

**Sasha:** Yeah, it's really beautiful that you have that kind of community-based street where people know each other, and that you ...

**Linda:** Well, it's really just us ... (all laugh) ... it is not the street.

**Sasha:** You happen to live on the same street.

**Linda:** We created this.

**Sasha:** You created it.

**Linda:** Yeah. We created this. Betty started it and we responded to it and ... (Frank sounds)

**Sasha:** And initially it was her openness and welcoming and ...

**Linda:** Absolutely.

**Sasha:** The general feeling I get when I think about this question and hear people's stories when you are outside of a traditional family structure, it is about how much you've given to others, how much will come back to you when you're in that place of need. It's not like you could calculate about it, I'm sure she wasn't thinking, well, let me embrace this weird tribe of sex whatever ... to you know ...

**Linda:** No ...

**Sasha:** It's that spirit ...

**Frank:** But, it is obvious it is because she had always been open to people.

*Frank Moore, Sasha Cagen and Michael (video capture)*

**Sasha:** Uh huh. Yeah, and there's a lot of rewards to reaching out to people. You know, it can be so easy to stay within your own comfort zone, in your own bubble, but you get a lot of rewards from reaching out.

(Frank sounds)

**Frank:** Hence the title ...

**Linda:** Oh, of the performance series: *The Uncomfortable Zones of Fun.*

(all laugh)

**Sasha:** Because you get more by making yourself uncomfortable?

(Frank sounds)

**Linda:** I think you had said something like there are rewards, but you have to push yourself, or something like that ...

**Sasha:** Yeah, absolutely ...

**Linda:** So Frank is just saying like it's not like it is the easiest path or the most comfortable path, but there are more rewards ... by pushing ...

**Sasha:** I agree. That's why I'm here today ... because I think, yeah, this is a little edgy for me, but that's the way I live my life then, if you say no to interesting things then interesting things won't happen.

(Frank sounds)

**Linda:** Yes.

**Frank:** People don't get that.

**Linda:** The relationship of how that works.

**Sasha:** Yeah, I know. It seems really natural to me. But, I think that people don't get that, it's true.

**Frank:** In physics, there is no dividing line.

(all laugh)

**Michael:** Between matter and energy or between comfortable and uncomfortable (giggles)?

(all laugh)

**Frank:** Etc. ... And between two objects.

**Michael:** Yeah, it's funny, we're always looking for the grand unified theory of everything in our personal life, in the real world, but, I don't know, do you think a lot of our dissatisfaction is the separation, I think, not just between people, but in ourselves, between how we really feel and how we act ... all of those things, so ... Yeah, it's actually a really good metaphor when you think about it. I don't know how to bring them together ... ummmm, I haven't figured out physics, but ...

**Frank:** Because each needs the other to be what it is?

**Linda:** You're not sure how to put it. That's the thing of there's no dividing line ... as if there's like this and this ... there is no dividing line because this needs this to be, so there really isn't a division between the two because they need each other to exist and yet we experience things as divided.

**Sasha:** Hmmmm.

**Michael:** Like you said we almost need them to be quirky, to have the difference, so we notice it, right, and we feel the need to be different then ...

**Sasha:** Hmmmmm.

**Michael:** But how deep is that, I don't know?

**Sasha:** Hmmmmm. I mean, I guess you're talking about a binary opposition in a way not being real.

**Frank:** Yes.

**Linda:** And then you can apply that to anything, I think that is what Frank is saying.

(Frank sounds)

**Sasha:** It's a mind fuck ... like, when I think about ... I'm just thinking of things in my head

... because I constantly have that, you know ... like ... this way of thinking about it, that way of thinking about it ... I'm always doing that.

**Frank:** I wrote a book ...

**Linda:** Oh, *Cherotic Magic*, right, about all of that sort of thing. About energy and how all of that works and how it applies to relationships and how it applies to how life works ... this happens if you do this and ....

**Sasha:** So what's the bottom-line advice?

(all laugh)

**Linda:** Sum up the book ... (laughs)

**Sasha:** Tell me how to run my life!

**Frank:** Be responsible.

**Linda:** Be responsible.

**Sasha:** In what way?

**Linda:** In every way. (Frank sounds)

**Sasha:** But you could be responsible and still be gripped by binary opposition.

**Frank:** I am not. (all laugh)

**Sasha:** Doesn't it mean to allow for every possibility? Or what does it really mean? Or not choose? Not decide what's real, or what's right or wrong?

**Linda:** Well, there's a couple of things ... Frank is definitely someone I would say allows for all possibilities ... more than anybody I've ever met. He sees possibilities where I don't even notice them until he points them out. He is very aware of possibilities, but in terms of responsibility, Frank, I would say that I've never seen Frank behave as if something happened to him.

**Sasha:** Oh, personal responsibility ...

**Linda:** Right! Not in that kind of EST way.

**Frank:** Not being a victim ...

**Linda:** But in a real way. Of like taking ... having a certain way of approaching everything that happens as if it matters. (Frank sounds) Because Frank lives as if everything matters a lot, and yet, there's a certain kind of "this" (gestures) about that.

**Sasha:** Right, that's the play part, the mattering and it's play. Right. Have you read the book *The Infinite Game*?

(Frank sounds)

**Linda:** I don't recognize that ...

**Sasha:** You should read it. It's about life as a game. In a way it's like the sort of philosophy in the book is very ... anti-binary, like mind fuck kind of way. Just the way it's written and it's

137

very expensive mentally. I think it probably sums up the way you guys operate in some way.

**Frank:** Do you want to ask me any questions?

**Sasha:** Yeah, well I'm very curious about the community you have, including the raising of children and like who is in it and how did it get started, what are the principles ... like the whole shebang.

**Frank:** Ask questions ...

**Linda:** Specific questions.

**Sasha:** OK. When did this community begin?

(Frank giggle sounds)

**Linda:** Well, I would say there's a couple of things. When there's that and there's this, right ...

**Frank:** I have lived communally since ... the early '70s.

**Sasha:** Hmmmm ... where did you find each other?

**Linda:** Frank and I?

**Sasha:** And the community.

**Linda:** Oh, the whole bunch? (Frank sounds)

**Frank:** Which time?

(all laugh)

**Linda:** Try to narrow it down ...

**Sasha:** The first time.

**Frank:** Like maybe Louise ...

**Linda:** ... would be the beginning of that story. Louise ... when Frank was in college in San Bernardino, and living at home ... there was a woman that was older than the college-aged people ... the hippy woman ... that had some land with a pool ... and the hip college students hung out at her place. So, Frank hung out there, and made an impression on Louise ... and at one point ... well she would say stuff like ...

**Frank:** I kept trying to move out ...

**Linda:** He kept trying ... Frank saw that if he didn't get out of his home with his parents during his college years, it would be much harder when he was finished college, because this was a place where he had access to people. So he had tried unsuccessfully a couple of times to move out.

**Frank:** San Bernardino ...

**Linda:** ... was not a happening place, so it wasn't that easy to get something going.

**Sasha:** Uh huh.

**Linda:** So one time at Louise's she made some comment about that she was moving to Santa Fe, and Frank said, boy, I wish I could go to Santa Fe. And she said, well just come with me. And that was pretty much it, so he said OK. She said it would take her a couple weeks to settle with the house. But he just wanted to go, so he hitchhiked to Santa Fe, thinking that she'd be right behind him, with no money ... he didn't tell anybody. Because he knew if he told his parents they would try to stop him.

**Sasha:** And were you in a wheelchair then?

**Linda:** He's been like this since birth. He was born with cerebral palsy.

**Sasha:** So you hitchhiked in a wheelchair?

**Linda:** Yeah.

**Sasha:** Wow.

**Linda:** But he knew ... this was it, you know, he really had nothing to lose.

**Sasha:** Well this is the kind of responsibility you were talking about.

**Frank:** Really, one of my ...

**Linda:** Oh, was that the one that Steve ... oh, ok, this is not the hitchhike part, this is where Steve ... he got somebody to drive him there, right ... and he hitchhiked later.

**Frank:** And ...

**Linda:** Right ... dropped you off, right ... at a crash pad in Santa Fe. So Steve drove him to Santa Fe and dropped him off and then went back to San Bernardino. Frank didn't have any money or anything. So, he's at this crash pad where he has to depend on other people to get him on the toilet, to get him up, to feed him, to dress him ...

**Sasha:** Yeah, that's what I'm wondering about. Like were you afraid that there wouldn't be people to meet your needs?

**Frank:** No. I trust.

**Sasha:** Trust, yeah.

**Michael:** Do you ever get afraid of anything after doing that? What else could be there ...

**Frank:** Exactly. (all laugh)

**Sasha:** Right.

**Michael:** It's all downhill from here. That's a great way to do it.

**Sasha:** Yeah.

**Frank:** I met the guy who ran the place in San Bernardino ...

**Linda:** When you were in San Bernardino, you met the guy who ran the crash pad.

**Frank:** But he was not the one every day ...

**Linda:** He wasn't the everyday guy. So, once you got there it wasn't like he was there, but you didn't know that, I guess ... did you know that? ... And you went anyway.

**Michael:** Did Louise come?

**Linda:** It took her months.

**Sasha:** Wow.

**Linda:** Two months? Yeah.

**Sasha:** Huh, so you were hanging out at the crash pad for two months waiting for her. And took the chance ...

**Frank:** And visiting communes ... in New Mexico.

**Sasha:** During that two months?

(Frank sounds)

**Linda:** Uh huh.

**Sasha:** (laughs)

**Frank:** Then ...

**Linda:** ... Louise came. And you lived in a communal situation there. Louise had kids from various relationships and then she had other people that were friends so they all lived together and took care of each other and ... you were there for like nine months? Almost a year ... something like that. And the way you tell the story is that he could have just stayed there and been comfortable, but he felt like it wasn't the way to go ... that he had to push himself. And he met a couple that were driving through Santa Fe on their way back to a community that they lived in in Massachusetts.

**Sasha:** Huh. So it wasn't enough to stay there.

**Frank:** Not ...

**Linda:** ... on their way back ... on their way there? They were somehow associated with it ... and they told you about it ... and based on that meeting you decided to move to that community.

(Frank sounds)

**Sasha:** In Massachusetts.

**Linda:** Yes.

**Frank:** So I hitchhiked.

**Linda:** That's when he hitchhiked.

**Sasha:** Wow. How long did you have to wait typically for a ride?

**Frank:** No, I put a sign up ...

**Linda:** And you found somebody ...

**Frank:** In a record store.

**Linda:** That you needed a ride. And somebody said they'd give you a ride to Massachusetts.

**Sasha:** Oh, all the way ... one ride.

**Linda:** But they just dropped him off. So there he is just getting dropped at this place. And the couple that he had met weren't there. So nobody even knew who Frank was, or that he was coming, or anything.

**Frank:** And they freaked out.

(all laugh)

**Frank:** But I had nowhere to go so they had to deal with me.

**Sasha:** Uh huh. It was a couple or ... a family or ... ?

**Linda:** It was hundreds of people, it was a commune

**Sasha:** Oh, it was a commune. What town?

**Linda:** Frank, I never can remember ...

**Frank:** Warwick.

**Frank:** Northfield.

**Sasha:** In Western Mass.?

**Linda:** Yes, is that right, in Western Mass.? Yes.

**Sasha:** Huh, yeah, there would be more hippies in Western Mass.

**Linda:** So what happened was the leader of the community ... he was an ex-Hell's Angel guy, very charismatic ... came out and looked at Frank and told them that to take care of Frank is to be in his good graces. So he gave them the word ... (Frank sounds)

**Michael:** So you guys never met ... ?

**Linda:** No, no, he just looked at Frank ... (all laugh)

**Frank:** I was him, so ...

**Linda:** Oh, that's what he said to them, "Frank is me."

**Sasha:** Hmmm, no separation.

(Frank sounds)

**Linda:** And so you moved in and you lived there for a year?

(Frank sounds)

**Frank:** They were a cult.

**Linda:** Well, they were into channeling and so everything was about what you channeled, and Frank's feeling was that people weren't paying attention to each other, they were only paying attention to the channel, but they weren't really relating to each other, and so he would tell them that, but nobody listened.

**Frank:** They talked about past lives.

**Linda:** It was all about that sort of thing.

**Sasha:** Well, it is interesting, because I looked at your Wikipedia page and I noticed that they said, "has been edited by members of Frank Moore's sex cult", right? So I'm sure that ... I'm just guessing that if it's on Wikipedia, that that gets said about your group. So, I am wondering, number one, what do you say in response? And number two, what's your definition of a cult, versus a community ... how do you think about that yourself and respond to people?

**Frank:** Hey, the USA ...

**Linda:** The United States ...

**Frank:** Was founded by cults. (Frank laughs)

**Sasha:** Which ones ... with the religions, you mean ...?

**Frank:** A lot of cults ... (Frank sounds)

**Linda:** Well, I think there was a point, maybe in the '70s around the Jim Jones time, where that came up more often with the press. Where we would run up against that, where people would want to do stories on what we were doing, as a cult. But, we really don't run into that anymore.

**Sasha:** I was surprised when I read that because ... I don't know, it was surprising to me, and it was actually in the style of Wikipedia that I hadn't seen before. Because it wasn't even italicized, it was just in the text.

**Linda:** I don't even know what that is. We don't know what that is. This is the first time it has even come up in twenty years, you know, it just doesn't come up anymore. Because most of the people ... we've been doing stuff for so many decades, there's like bulk, so it seems kind of "surfacy".

**Sasha:** Uh huh.

(Frank sounds)

**Linda:** So you were there for almost a year, or about a year ... oh, so what happened was that nobody paid any attention to Frank telling them that they should focus on being on the earth and not past lives and spirit guides, and nobody paid any attention, so he channeled a spirit that told them the same thing.

(all laugh)

**Linda:** And then they all listened! They would sit around and wait for the spirit to come through to tell them how they should relate to each other.

**Frank:** Flexible.

(all laugh)

**Linda:** Whatever you needed to do.

**Sasha:** And how did you communicate it?

**Frank:** I ty ...

**Linda:** He would type it.

**Sasha:** OK, so the channeling came through typing ... would someone else type it then? Or, how did it work?

**Linda:** No, Frank typed it. He has a pointer ... that's how he uses the computer ... He has a stick ...

**Sasha:** Oh, great, that is a separate question ... I am really curious about all the prolificness and how it works.

**Linda:** The laser is recent, within the last several years. That's what Frank used through most of his life.

**Sasha:** To type ... ?

**Linda:** And to use on the board here, he used to ...

**Sasha:** So, it's like boing, boing, boing ...

**Linda:** Just push, yeah, and then on the computer he uses that ... when he used a typewriter he would use that.

**Sasha:** So, when you write, you are actually writing yourself with no intermediary.

(Frank sounds)

**Linda:** Yeah, it's just him.

**Sasha:** It's cool.

**Frank:** I paint ...

**Linda:** He also paints ...

**Sasha:** Oh, painting that way. That part I did not get ... now I understand.

**Linda:** He wears a hard hat and a paint brush, so those paintings are all ... (gesturing) that's Frank ... the one right behind you on the easel, they're all paintings he did ... and when he paints with that, he can only get this part of the canvas (gesturing), so he has to paint sideways and upside down to fill the canvas, so ... yeah.

**Frank:** Since high school ...

*Frank Moore and Sasha Cagen (video capture)*

**Linda:** That's when he started with the pointer? (Frank sounds) And the painting.

**Sasha:** Well, so this part's so ... I still kind of wonder at the whole history but I just have to say even if we come back to it, this part is so interesting to me, because you have so many obstacles to being creative that people can't even imagine and then people complain, oh I can't write or I can't make the time, and that part is just amazing to me, and I just wonder what is the impulse that says, I must do this?

(Frank sounds)

**Frank:** No choice.

**Sasha:** No choice, uh huh.

**Frank:** Like when I got my pointer, I wrote a piece about world government ... one-world socialism.

**Linda:** One-world socialism was the paper he wrote ... the first thing he did when he got the pointer.

(all laugh)

**Frank:** They wanted to t ...

**Linda:** ... take the pointer back?

(all laugh)

**Frank:** And I wrote a ...

**Linda:** Political column? ... This was all in high school ... and at one point he debated a G.I. that was in Vietnam in the local paper ... was it in your high school paper?

(Frank sounds)

**Linda:** And it was a very controversial thing to do because it was before there was much support to the anti-war movement, and ... Frank got a lot of pressure about being ... that he should be the perfect crip ... you know, he's the guy ... the smart kid ... and it was the first class of integrating disabled with regular, non-disabled kids.

**Sasha:** Hmmm.

**Linda:** And he was doing stuff like that.

**Sasha:** To not be a radical person, but be more ...

**Linda:** Yes.

**Frank:** I was ruining ...

**Linda:** They said that Frank was ruining it for those that would follow him.

**Sasha:** Hmmmm.

**Linda:** And he would reply, I thought the idea was to free ... was that the way you put it? (Frank sounds) To free the people.

**Sasha:** To be who you are.

**Linda:** Yes.

**Sasha:** Yeah, that's beautiful.

(Frank sounds)

**Linda:** So what, the community? So he met someone at the community, Debbie, and they ended up moving out of the community eventually, after a year, total.

**Frank:** After I danced ...

**Linda:** Oh, danced, at Carnegie Hall ... they had a band, the community had a band, and the lead guy, Michael, was the singer in the band, and Frank danced at Carnegie Hall when they played Carnegie Hall. Which was another thing that the people in the community ... (in a whisper) "You want to have Frank up on the stage dancing?" But Michael was, "Oh yes I do."

**Sasha:** The people from the community in Massachusetts had a band that performed at Carnegie Hall. And then how did you dance? What did it look like? Can you show us?

(laughter)

**Frank:** I am a dancer.

**Sasha:** Uh huh.

**Frank:** Look at Sunday ...

**Linda:** Oh, Sunday's performance, right, you can look at the performance that we did on Sunday, last Sunday, it's up on Vimeo, Frank's channel on Vimeo, and you can see him dance and sing.

**Sasha:** OK.

(Frank sounds)

**Frank:** B ...

**Linda:** It's the Bob Madigan Memorial Hootenanny and Séance.

**Frank:** Big ...

**Linda:** It was a big band. Yes, I don't even know how many ... 15, 20 ... something like that ... people in his band.

(Frank sounds)

**Frank:** And Saturday ...

**Linda:** Saturday, a week ago Saturday, Frank did a live concert via Skype, performance playing the piano here. And he sang and played chimes and played the piano ... it was a solo thing. And it was ... the woman who set it up was in Montreal, and so the audience was all in Montreal and they watched on Skype.

**Sasha:** Wow. And how does the singing work?

(lots of Frank sounds) (lots of laughter)

(lots of laughter and Frank sounds)

**Sasha:** There you go ... now I understand.

**Michael:** So is there anything worth being afraid of? I can't imagine you have stage fright. (laughs)

**Linda:** No.

**Frank:** Never.

(Michael laughs)

**Linda:** I don't know ... that story ... so, you moved out of ... they moved from the community.

**Frank:** Ma ...

**Linda:** They got married.

**Frank:** I don't believe in marriage, but ...

**Linda:** You guys did it at that point, I guess for various reasons ... (Frank sounds)

**Linda:** And then, I don't know, you moved ... they tried to do a couple things ... they tried living in California at some point, in this area, and going to school, and had all sorts of obstacles ... that was in the early '70s.

**Frank:** For two weeks.

**Linda:** They couldn't even get a place that would let them stay there. People were so put off by Frank ... so they ended up moving ... did you end up moving back to New Mexico at that point?

(Frank sounds and nods yes)

**Linda:** Because Frank knew Louise and knew people there, so they went back there, and lived in Albuquerque at some point and met Jo and Ray (Frank sounds), somewhere along there, separately, two ... Jo is a female and Ray is a male. They weren't together, but in the end the four of them were ... joined forces ...

**Frank:** I went to University of ...

**Linda:** New Mexico, right.

**Frank:** To get money.

**Linda:** Because as a student he can get money to live.

**Frank:** But I was looking for something to work with that people ...

**Linda:** People? No. That would bring ... you were looking for a way to work with people. (Frank sounds)

**Linda:** Frank had read a lot, because growing up, he wasn't always able to go to school, his father was in the military, so they lived all over the world. So, sometimes they were in countries that couldn't accommodate him so he would homeschool ... he read a lot a lot a lot. So, he had a lot of stuff as he calls in his back brain, just like, cookin', you know. What I know, is the one book, *Environmental Theatre* by Schechner, Richard Schechner, who is a teacher at NYU, or was. That kind of gave Frank some ideas because this theater group of Schechner's created ... they had theater without a stage, so that ... much the same way like what you came to ... where people were involved in the action, and what Frank noticed is that they inadvertently created community through their performances, but they weren't equipped to deal with that, because it wasn't a mindful thing, it wasn't what they wanted, and they were a little uncomfortable. And he thought, what if you applied all of that in a mindful way, **to** create community.

**Sasha:** Uh huh.

**Linda:** So, as he says, he ripped off Schechner's exercises. Of course, Schechner shows up at one of the first performances in New York. At some point they moved to New York City and, he kind of experimented with this form.

**Frank:** I started a drop-in workshop. (Frank sounds)

**Linda:** And there were things ... I think you had said something like the lack of commitment was an issue. You wanted something where people were more committed to it, than the drop-in thing.

**Sasha:** So, it is so interesting to me. I feel like the structure of this interview is that the story keeps going, but I'm going to interject with reflections.

**Linda:** Uh huh. (Frank sounds)

**Sasha:** Because I feel like I have done similar things in my life, but I haven't done it with a single purpose that this is my life. It's like I created community from a weird thing that we all do together, quirkyalone, or something like that. But I didn't have the idea that that was my career, because I always was also practical ... well, I have to earn money, right? So, I am just wondering, where does that come from to just say like, this is what I do, experimental stuff, and then ... like, are you concerned about money and survival?

(Frank sounds)

**Frank:** Money always comes.

(Michael laughs)

**Sasha:** Uh huh.

(Frank sounds)

**Linda:** I don't think it was about the art so much. For Frank I think it was always about people. So, he was just looking for a way to be with people in a community way, and that book gave him the idea of using art, and that particular form of art. It wasn't about the art, so much about form, it was ... it seemed like something he could use.

**Sasha:** Uh huh.

**Frank:** Intimacy.

**Linda:** He was looking for intimacy.

**Sasha:** Uh huh. So instead of looking for "the one", or something like that, this was the pursuit. Because people are looking for intimacy but they think they are looking for one person.

**Linda:** I think that the dissatisfaction with the level at which people interact, just generally, you know, like he would feel like he wanted to be deeper with people, and there wasn't any structure ...

**Sasha:** Structure ...

**Linda:** Structure in place, so he thought, I'm just going to create a structure.

(Frank sounds)

**Sasha:** Uh huh.

**Linda:** I'm going to create something where I can be with people the way I want to be with them. And then he followed where that evolved.

**Frank:** And people ...

**Linda:** Yeah, you know, that's the thing, Frank has always found that people are **there** when you approach them in that way ... it's like he never like ... he always has these high ... he addresses people as if they are going to be "right there" ... he never talks down to people.

**Sasha:** Right.

**Linda:** And like, over and over again, I see, they always are. You know, they always are. You think, oh my God, I can't believe he's saying that to that person, and then they'll be right there with him.

**Sasha:** Right.

**Linda:** So that was his experience. He would create these things, and people were always there.

**Sasha:** So it's like seeking the highest in people by just talking to them at the highest level.

**Linda:** By being that way yourself.

**Sasha:** Yeah.

(Frank sounds)

**Frank:** Demanding. (Frank sounds) Not ...

**Linda:** Right, yeah, well like when I met Frank ... the workshop ... that was one of the exercises, "demanding". We would do a weekly workshop.

**Sasha:** What's demanding?

**Linda:** Well, it would be like where ... the idea was, to have relationships that work, you have to not "settle". (Frank sounds) You have to demand what you need, and be willing to be what the other person needs you to be. To be willing to be demanded of. (Frank sounds) So he's saying it's not like this kind of thing. (bangs hand on table with hard stare) ... It's a more vulnerable, soft way.

**Sasha:** Uh huh.

(Frank sounds)

**Linda:** So, yeah, he used that in the workshops and then created a life from that.

**Frank:** And people even moved from Santa Fe ...

**Linda:** When you moved to New York, to be ... where Frank would be.

**Sasha:** Be part of this.

**Linda:** Yeah, yeah.

**Sasha:** Well, that was kind of another question I had was that on a very gross level there's like ... what's so compelling about you that people are willing to take off their clothes at one of these performances? Or, like on a bigger level, what's so compelling about you that people would move to New York to be part of this? So like, what is that?

**Linda:** Well, for me (laughing) 'cause I don't know, really ... I met Frank when I was working in a travel agency. I was a travel agent and he wheeled in and I thought, "Oh God, I hope this guy doesn't come up to me." He's in his motor chair clunking along. I had never talked to anybody that looked like Frank. Of course, he came right up to me. And he was asking about an airline ticket, and I was at the counter and I had to lean like this. (motions) And he could look down my shirt, and I never wore a bra. And he says, after we do the transaction, "You'd be great in this play I'm doing." And I go, "Oh, really?" (gesturing) (all laugh) There was no play. (laughing) But he was willing to create a play. But you know, the thing I think for me that was so compelling ... 'cause I quit my job weeks later to hang out with Frank ... but I think it was because ... like he would ... well there were two things. One was when I started talking to him, all of the surface stuff dropped away and I just saw the person that he was. So then that was a non-issue, immediately. And then the other thing was, just ... like he would show up to bring me out to lunch, during my work day, and stuff like that. (all laugh) I think what I got was a level of commitment and acceptance. I wasn't used to being around somebody that I felt really "got me", who really "saw me" in a way that didn't really quite ...

**Sasha:** Uh huh.

**Linda:** And that felt really good. It felt good. So I think perhaps that's what it is.

**Sasha:** Really seeing people.

**Linda:** Yeah. Seeing people and wanting to connect in a real genuine way.

**Sasha:** Right. To be part of them.

**Linda:** Whatever they kind of think, it seems that people respond to that.

**Sasha:** Yeah, that's what people want.

**Linda:** Yeah.

**Frank:** The workshop was not ...

**Linda:** ... really happening. I had been living here for a year and he had just moved to Berkeley not that long before. He was trying to get this workshop thing going and he had managed to get a free space in this seminary to do this workshop, and he needed people, but he couldn't get something going.

**Sasha:** Uh huh.

**Linda:** So that was the project that we did. I had come out here to study this "growth" thing, Fischer-Hoffman Process from Pennsylvania. I was a Fischer-Hoffman therapist. (Frank sounds) So he said, let's ... 'cause that was like what was happening. So he said what about if we rework this to have it fit more with what Frank's thing was. So that was our project. We reworked it and put posters up for that, to try and get this workshop thing going. (Frank sounds) We got one guy who answered the poster. He was a psychic teacher. And we had this office, so we sat in this office for a couple of hours talking to this guy to try to get him to sign up for this workshop. And in the end, he says, you know, Frank, I don't know about the workshop, but would you be willing to meet with me every week and I would pay you just to sit and talk like we did now.

(Frank laughs)

**Linda:** Frank being flexible said, sure! And that started a five, six year or more run of Frank doing relationship counseling. Because he went and told all of his students about his new guru. And they all wanted to meet with Frank. So Frank was ... people were paying him ... he was at this office eight, ten hours a day, two-hour sessions, getting paid to do relationship counseling. He ended up having several workshops at one time. Because people would eventually sign up to be in the workshop. He said, you know, if he wanted to be rich, he could have kept doing that.

**Sasha:** Right.

**Linda:** And made loads of money, but ... (Frank sounds)

**Frank:** Boring ...

**Linda:** It got boring.

**Sasha:** Right.

(Michael and Sasha laughing ...)

**Sasha:** Michael and I have talked about that before.

**Frank:** People have the same problems ...

**Michael:** Yeah.

**Linda:** But everybody thinks they're unique. And they don't like to be told they're not.

**Sasha:** Right, yeah.

**Michael:** Are they real problems, or not even real problems.

(all laugh)

**Frank:** I gave them what would work, but when it started working ... (Frank sounds)

**Linda:** They freaked out.

(laughing)

**Frank:** But ...

**Sasha:** Like, what started working?

**Linda:** Like, their lives ... their relationships.

**Sasha:** So they didn't want them to work.

(Frank sounds)

**Linda:** So it seemed.

**Frank:** But do you have that happen with you?

**Linda:** When you're working with people?

**Sasha:** Ummmm, yeah, it's a very interesting reflection. I'm new in my practice. I just started this year. So I don't have enough experience to say, but I can imagine ... I don't have a hard time believing it. Because people are afraid of success. Are afraid of having what they say they want. We're all accustomed to being how we are!

(Frank sounds)

**Frank:** They are fine during the shit phase.

(laughing)

**Frank:** But ... (Frank sounds)

**Linda:** When it all starts coming together and working, that's when they would freak out.

**Sasha:** And what do you mean by "freak out"?

(Frank sounds)

**Linda:** Well, usually they would undermine the relationship.

**Sasha:** Oh, they would sabotage ...

**Linda:** Yeah. Because it was right there. They could have just done ...

**Sasha:** Again, like they can't enjoy.

**Linda:** Yes.

**Frank:** Because then they would be responsible. (Frank sounds)

**Sasha:** Hmmmm, as opposed to placing the responsibility on the other person ...

**Linda:** Yeah, blaming, or whatever for what happens to them.

**Sasha:** Yeah, right. That seems to be the path in most spiritual coaching. All of that whole world is like a path toward full responsibility for your experience. Like, that seems to be, in a way, what it all boils down to.

**Linda:** Yeah. (Frank sounds) So we started doing plays. We did that show *The Outrageous Beauty Revue*, which was, kind of like a "hit".

**Frank:** The people who took my workshop. (Frank sounds)

**Linda:** Oh, started moving in ... yeah, so, what happened is that the people that ... we had a few workshops going ... things evolved. It's like, OK, so and so needs a job, so and so has a construction company. So Frank said to the guy who has the construction company, if you hire "bimbo girl", who's never picked up a hammer, you'll have somebody who's committed to you. She won't know what she's doing, but you can train her. So, that was an act of trust on his part. But, he ended up hiring all these people ... the people that needed jobs were people that were unskilled with this particular type of work. He became a millionaire, using that model of hiring people that he could trust and rely on.

**Frank:** I am ...

*Frank Moore and Sasha Cagen (video capture)*

**Linda:** Frank's good at making money for other people.

(everyone laughs)

**Linda:** We always have enough ... but ...

**Sasha:** Who was the guy?

**Linda:** He was one of the people that was in Frank's workshop. He was in the workshop, him and his wife. He was just starting up his construction company. It was a radical idea for him to hire these people.

**Sasha:** Uh huh, right, yeah!

**Linda:** They were all in their twenties ... they had never picked up a hammer and had no interest in that, but they needed work, so, OK. So, people started working for each other. There were clothes companies that we started. Successful. You know, just out of people playing, just being together. People started moving in with each other. You know, why don't we all get a house together? Why don't we rent a house together? So we ended up with several, I don't know, three or four houses of people. (Frank sounds)

**Frank:** So, at sessions ...

**Linda:** Frank would start bunching the sessions up. (Frank sounds) So instead of each person having a session, it would be everybody that lived together.

**Sasha:** In one of the relationship counseling things …

**Linda:** In the house.

**Sasha:** Right.

**Frank:** I made …

**Linda:** Oh, money? Right, because each person would still pay their amount of money, but they'd all be coming together.

**Sasha:** Yeah, well I think that groups are much more interesting than one on one, anyway. That's sort of one of my observations.

(Frank sounds)

**Sasha:** I don't really like the therapist/client or coach/client relationship. I like the group atmosphere where people get to be seen by a variety of people, and I think that that can be powerful.

**Linda:** Yes.

(Frank sounds)

**Frank:** The shows …

**Linda:** We did a bunch of stuff. We did plays. We did all sorts of thing, all sorts of things.

**Sasha:** Plus art with these people too, so it was like … these are the same group of people …

**Linda:** Yeah, Frank would come up with a play idea and it's not like anybody was an "actor". But we did one play that happened in a strip joint. It was about the dynamic of the three dancers in this club. And he based it on the lowest dive. 'Cause he was aware of the places on Broadway. So what he did, he had these three women that he cast in it, he got them jobs at this diveyest place on Broadway in San Francisco. And we would be there. They would do their set and then he would coach them. Because they were supposed to be their character. And he didn't have a script necessarily. He had a treatment. And they had to be their characters and interact with the audience, who were the people that came into this bar. So that's the kind of thing we did. But that led us to discovering the Mabuhay Gardens which was right on that same street. Because it got very boring sitting at these strip clubs, hour after hour after hour. (Frank sounds) We'd walk the streets looking for something to do and there was this punk club, so we went in there. And you know Frank in his usual way, saw the guy that was producing the shows there and went up to him and said can I do something here.

**Sasha:** Uh huh.

**Linda:** He had hit this playwright up for a play. This guy had a hit play in San Francisco, it was a big deal. And he lived in Berkeley. And Frank was always cruising the streets. And he went up to this guy and said I'd like to direct one of your plays. And this guy was kind of like, (changes voice and gestures) "OK, Frank, I'll give you a play." Very condescending, you know. And if you want me to change any of the stuff, we'll talk about it. (Frank sounds) Frank was, no, I'll just do it the way it's written. It was about a pre-Christian Irish queen and her concubine. It was called *MEB*. So Frank goes into this club, the punk club, and he says to this guy, Dirk, can I do this play here? So, you know, Dirk, on the other hand, didn't see a crip, he saw Frank. He goes, what do you got? So Frank tells him about this play and he says, sure. So we did this play for two weeks at the Mabuhay, after we finished the play about the strippers. Which then, nobody came to the play ... it was an early show ...

**Sasha:** The play about the strippers ... it was like an unofficial thing? Did the manager of the strip club know that it was happening?

**Linda:** Well, the play itself happened in Frank's theater. This was just rehearsal. (Frank sounds)

**Sasha:** Oh, I see.

**Linda:** Their job at this club was them learning their part. So, he got them the job. You know, you're going to learn how to be this stripper, by being a stripper.

**Sasha:** Uh huh.

**Linda:** So then we actually did the play at the storefront we had. And we fixed the place up like the dive. People would come in and we did the actual play at our storefront.

(Frank sounds)

**Linda:** So we ended up getting the Mabuhay Gardens, and we did this play (*MEB*), and nobody came. It was the early show. Dirk had this ... this is where all the punks played at 11 o'clock ... and he had this vision of this kind of Toulouse-Lautrec environment and we would be the artsy fartsy early show.

**Sasha:** Uh huh.

**Linda:** He just loved it. He loved the play, even though nobody was there.

**Sasha:** The owner of the Mabuhay?

**Linda:** He was the producer, Dirk, yeah.

**Sasha:** Oh, OK, yeah.

**Linda:** He loved it! And he said, keep it going. But we couldn't ... because Frank had dredged these people ... none of them thought of themselves as actors, and all had other things they were doing. But he said anything you ever want to do, you have a place. One of the people in the workshop, Diane, was a construction worker, but, who, liked the arts. She said to Frank, if I took a leave from work, could we do a project together? I'll come up with a few hundred dollars we can use to put it on. So he said, I always wanted to do a take-off on a beauty contest, but where instead of being "beauty", it would be "outrageous" ... who was the most outrageous. So, we arranged it with Dirk, and it was a one-time thing. We got contestants. Frank went around the Bay Area and got hundreds and hundreds and hundreds of dollars of prizes. It was unbelievable. He would come home with these gift certificates for these fancy restaurants, boutiques, hair salons ... (Frank sounds) record stores. But we couldn't find contestants that were outrageous. You know, not to what we wanted. So, eventually, he planted some of the people from the workshops as contestants, who were not eligible to win. But, he told the real contestants that he had plants, and he said, but you don't know who the plants are, so you have to be more outrageous than all the other contestants ...

**Sasha:** And what kind of outrageous ... looking or acting or ...

**Linda:** Breaking taboos, breaking ...

**Sasha:** An action that would be outrageous.

**Linda:** Yeah, edgy, you know, uncomfortable, pushing, pushing boundaries, real. Like a real outrageous, not just a fancy costume. But like, pushing through something.

**Sasha:** Uh huh.

**Linda:** So, we did this show but it was packed. There were hundreds of people there. We had never done anything for more than like five people.

**Sasha:** Uh huh.

**Linda:** And there were like rows of reporters. It was the second page of *The Examiner*. It was just like ...

**Sasha:** And this was in the '80s?

**Linda:** 1978, 1979 ... something like that.

**Linda:** So Dirk comes backstage during the show and says, announce that it's a weekly event.

(all laugh)

**Linda:** And Frank, being flexible, says OK. Even though we were midway through rehearsal on another play. He had rewritten *Lysistrata*, to bring it back to its original bawdiness. We never did that. So we did *The Outrageous Beauty Revue* for three and a half years, once or twice a week for that whole time. And that evolved into not getting contestants, but us ...

**Sasha:** Being outrageous.

**Linda:** We were the acts.

**Sasha:** So the lesson is to be flexible. That sounds like that's a big theme.

**Linda:** That's right.

**Sasha:** Just kind of following something.

**Linda:** Frank always says, he follows.

**Sasha:** I find that in my own life too. Things happen that you have no idea will be the things that pitch it.

(Frank sounds)

**Linda:** Yeah.

**Frank:** I need to not get in the way. (Frank sounds)

**Sasha:** Uh huh.

**Frank:** About everything we do. I did not plan to do that ... everything we have done, I did not plan to do.

**Sasha:** Uh huh.

**Frank:** Talk about lists.

(Sasha laughing)

**Sasha:** Perfect segue. Well, the whole planning thing is big, and lists and not having lists. I'm actually writing something now about ... I spent the year traveling in South America in 2010 and it was very much about exploring that idea of being unplanned. Because my life had been very planned, and very obsessive with lists and just sort of having goals and sticking to them, and almost being kind of mechanical ...

(Frank sounds)

**Sasha:** ... in getting things done. Which is very much the way of life, especially in this country.

(Frank sounds)

**Sasha:** So I was really interested in following the idea of an unplanned life. And what happens. And lists ... lists are what you want them to be. They can be ... you can be a slave to your lists, and feel like you have to follow that plan. But lists are also a jumping off point for desire and creativity. And it's a total openness to ... the root of lists is to lust.

(Frank sounds)

**Sasha:** The Middle English root is "to lust". So, it's about what do I want, ultimately. Like a way that you can trace the root of listing. So it's like, I actually went through a big journey in my listing of being very practical, to I only write things down I think I can do ...

(Frank sounds)

**Sasha:** ... to like writing just down everything, and appreciating that mystical part of lists that is like everything and anything, and you never know.

**Frank:** Then forgetting your ...

**Linda:** And then forgetting your list.

**Sasha:** Forgetting your list, yeah ...

(Frank sounds)

**Sasha:** Yeah, there can be that. Like, in a weird way you can write a list of so many things that seem impossible and forget about it and then go back six months or a year later and realize you did it all, and so ...

(Frank sounds)

**Sasha:** In some way, that might not be obvious, but you did it all.

**Frank:** It is like praying.

**Sasha:** Yeah, it's a prayer. It is, it's totally like a prayer. I have that line in something I wrote about lists, that it's a secular version of prayer.

(Frank sounds)

**Frank:** But you need to forget ...

**Linda:** ... once you pray for it/list it, then you need to forget it?

**Sasha:** Yeah, in some way, to not be too attached to it. But it's in your consciousness in some way. It's like rumbling ...

(Frank sounds)

**Frank:** Back brain.

**Sasha:** Umm, yeah, it could be like the back brain. Yeah. (pause) Yeah. There's like a superstition or something of like you don't want to be too attached to it. Like, oh, I have to have this. But it does feel like ... and I think that much more so writing versus typing. Like I think for Frank, there is no distinction. But I think like for me, when I handwrite, it has more of a mystical feel to it.

**Frank:** I don't do lists.

**Linda:** Right.

**Sasha:** You're not a lister?

**Linda:** He's not a lister.

**Frank:** That kind of list.

**Linda:** He would do lists of his all-time favorite rock 'n roll songs, and those kinds of lists. (Frank sounds) But not the kind of "to do" lists.

**Sasha:** Or things you want?

(Frank sounds)

**Linda:** Right, he doesn't do that.

**Frank:** Because that frames it. (Frank sounds) Opportunity.

**Linda:** It frames opportunity?

**Sasha:** Ummmm. You prefer that the opportunity is so vast and open without a list to frame it?

**Frank:** Yes.

**Sasha:** But it seems like writing the list is like setting the compass so that something can happen. How do you set the start point then?

(Frank sounds)

**Sasha:** What's the articulation?

**Frank:** Live!

(all laugh)

**Sasha:** No, you have to write it down first!

(all continue to laugh)

**Sasha:** You can't just live! No, it doesn't work that way! (laughing)

**Frank:** Although, when I did the four ...

**Linda:** Oh, the 48-hour ... right, that's right. Yeah ... (Frank sounds)

**Linda:** ... I guess it was in the late '70s Frank did this thing called the 48-hour process. And, he would tell somebody that if they stuck with him for 48 hours ... well, first he would have them make a list of what they want. But he said, not like a new car or something like that, but what you really want in your life.

**Sasha:** Uh huh.

**Linda:** There would be a $500 fee, and at the time that was a pretty good amount of money. And for 48 hours ... he said if you follow me for 48 hours, I'll put you in a position to have the things on your list.

**Sasha:** Uh huh.

**Frank:** But, first ...

**Linda:** You went through the list with them. They'd write the list and then Frank would have a session where he went through the list with them, to really boil it down ...

**Sasha:** I've done something extremely similar with the people in my coaching program/ study group, because one of the people is very into experience design and play. And you have to read this book, *Finite and Infinite Games*. It's all based on these principles. We would do something similar where we would do a 15-minute session to determine what kind of experience they wanted to have, and then they would leave the room for half an hour and we would create it for them. So, it wasn't a 48-hour thing but the principle was exactly the same.

**Linda:** Yeah.

**Frank:** It did work.

**Sasha:** So people ... what kind of things did they want?

(Frank sounds)

**Frank:** Every ...

**Linda:** Yeah, everybody was different and they all were ... wow, I don't know. (Frank sounds) There's so many ... Joe, Joe is an easy ...

(Frank sounds)

**Linda:** The one guy, he was into being enlightened. He wanted to be enlightened. To have that

*Sasha Cagen (video capture)*

kind of experience in his life. (Frank sounds) That's the thing that came to my mind ... he had a certain picture of himself as this very spiritual, enlightened kind of guy.

(Sasha laughs ... Frank sounds)

**Linda:** So what Frank would do is he would use the money ... he'd hire people, he'd plant people in the environment ... because we'd leave ... we had this storefront we used, but we'd leave the environment and go to restaurants, go to the movies, just do various things ...

**Sasha:** Yeah, similar. Our stuff had things like that too.

**Linda:** He would have people planted at different places ...

**Sasha:** Uh huh. So you would hire people, not just involve them as players ...

**Linda:** Yeah, 'cause we had this money ...

**Sasha:** So the money wasn't a fee, it was to facilitate the experience.

**Linda:** Yeah, it was a fee.

**Sasha:** It was a fee, and there was a budget.

**Linda:** And Frank used it, part of it ... was to hire people, so he had more possibilities.

**Sasha:** Uh huh.

**Frank:** I am never about money ...

**Linda:** Yeah.

**Sasha:** Uh huh.

**Linda:** So in the case of Joe, for the first eight hours or something ... we sat in the studio here and read ... was it *Steppenwolf*, or *Siddhartha*? (Frank sounds) *Siddhartha*. So Frank ... did Joe read it aloud or you have somebody read it? (Frank sounds) It was Joe reading it. Frank would keep interrupting him and drawing what was happening in the book into Joe's life (Frank sounds) so that his life was woven into this book. (Frank sounds) So by the end of these eight hours Joe was like ... he was completely blissed out ... this is it. You know, "I'm there" ... "This is what I wanted!"

(laughter)

**Linda:** Frank said great, let's go get something to eat. So, we go to the Jewish deli around the corner. It was filled with people. We get our food. And we're all sitting there eating and Frank takes longer to eat, so Joe was finished eating. So he said, why don't you just pick somebody that's here in the restaurant and go introduce yourself and sit with them while I finish eating. (Frank sounds) So, Frank knew the kind of person Joe would pick, so he hired this woman, and he told her how to dress (Sasha laughs) and he told her how to act, and Joe went right over to her.

(all laugh)

**Linda:** And sat down. So, then, when we're done Frank says, OK, now we're going, so he says goodbye to the woman and we are walking back and Joe just starts putting her down. Oh, he said, I was trying to explain to her what was going on, she just wasn't getting it. (Sasha laughs) As if like, her consciousness is so low, you know, she just couldn't conceive ... (Frank laughing) So, we go back to the space and I think you sent him into another room to meditate on what had happened. (Frank sounds) And while he was gone, Frank already arranged all of this, her name was Deborah, that after so much time had passed after we left, she was to show up at the door. So, she shows up while he's back meditating and ... we had this box, the size of a double bed that was padded with foam and had a lid and air holes. So, Frank and Deborah got in the box naked and put the lid on it. And then are directions to bring Joe back out. Was the lid open or closed? (Frank sounds) Closed. And he had to guess who you were in the box with?

**Frank:** And meditate ...

**Linda:** He had to meditate on the box, (Frank sounds) on who you were in the box with. So, at some point, we open the lid up, and Frank says to Joe, how did I do this? How did I get her to be in the box with me? (Frank sounds)

**Frank:** We were ...

**Linda:** Yeah, they were playing erotically. Deborah and he were playing erotically. Frank had made up that word eroplay, which you might have read in your research ...

**Sasha:** Uh huh.

**Linda:** So they were eroplaying, so, that's what Joe was looking at ... Frank and Deborah playing ... Frank says, so how did I do it? How did I get her to be here? (Frank sounds)

**Linda:** You picked her! (Frank sounds) Joe was like, "Well, you must have hired everybody in that restaurant."

**Sasha:** Mmmm.

**Linda:** "And then the one that I picked would get paid extra to come over here." So, Frank says, OK ...

**Frank:** I cracked up.

**Linda:** Yeah, Frank just started laughing. (laughter) So, at some point, we'd tell him, right? (Frank sounds) We'd tell him what happened ... Frank knew who he would pick and told her how to dress and act, and we paid her, and nobody else in the restaurant was involved in this in any way. "Do you believe that?" He said, "No it's impossible. It's impossible that you could have predicted who I would pick."

**Sasha:** Hmmmm.

**Frank:** I ...

**Linda:** ... cracked up again! (all laugh)

**Linda:** So eventually Frank said, OK, sure, I hired everybody ... if that is the thing that he would accept.

(Frank sounds)

**Linda:** And I think that's an example of ... where he did get what he wanted, but it was also kind of put in a position ...

**Frank:** We pushed.

**Sasha:** Uh huh, right, yeah.

(Frank sounds)

**Sasha:** You know, I really have to go to the bathroom.

**Linda:** Yeah, well, it's ... so how long have we been ... we're already kind of at the end ... this plays on our cable TV show and that's a certain length, so that's what we base the length of this on. (Frank sounds) So, should we wrap it up? (Frank sounds) Yeah. Tell everybody who you are.

**Sasha:** OK, my name is Sasha Cagen and I'm the author of *Quirkyalone* and *To-Do List*, and I'm a writer and a coach.

**Linda:** And your website.

**Sasha:** sashacagen.com, quirkyalone.net ... Google me, yeah.

**Frank:** Read ...

**Linda:** Sasha reviewed one of Frank's performances ...

**Sasha:** Yeah, it all began because I came to this show in December and wrote a blog post about it, and you guys saw it.

**Linda:** Yes.

**Sasha:** Yeah, it was very cool for me, I'll just say, because I felt like coming to your show was like returning to my roots in some way. Like, as I said, I have a history of doing this kind of stuff, but I also have my practical side. Like, I think it's kind of interesting that you guys developed all of this in the '70s, right, but I'm of a different generation so I've had ... I started with the riot grrrl, everything ... when I was 19, doing zines, going to punk shows, all of that. But then there's like, riot grrrl grows up and you have to ... well, you don't have to ... well, I have done conventional things too. I make money and have a "career" (quote unquote) but, there's a part of me that, the biggest part of me like so appreciates this kind of stuff that is totally authentic and real and free of fear, you know, 'cause I think that's where the juice is. So coming to that show was a nice touching in or tapping into that again because people who want to follow that path really need nourishment, or just to remember that it exists. (Frank sounds)

**Linda:** Yes. (Frank sounds) OK ...

**Frank:** Go ...

**Linda:** Go pee.

**Sasha:** Otherwise, you're going to have a problem here.

# Penny Arcade

Recorded March 8, 2009 on luver.com

......................................................................................................................

In Frank's own words, "Penny is funny, warm, sexy, erotic, kick-ass, political, subversive, plain talking, nude, up-lifting, real, wise, entertaining, committed, outsider, humane, community-building, rich history ... and a damn good artist!"

Penny had just finished a performance of her *BITCH! DYKE! FAGHAG! WHORE!* in San Francisco and was immediately taxied off to Berkeley by a couple of Frank's students. This was also the second session of the night for Frank who had just completed an hour and a half interview with another guest shortly before Penny arrived. When Frank announced the show, he said that they would be "comparing notes from our lifetimes of cultural subversion!"

Penny Arcade's transformative experimental performance work has been produced all over the world. Like Frank, her resume is rich good reading, and takes you on an amazing journey from leaving home at age 14 to "join the fabulously disenfranchised world of queers, junkies, whores, stars, deviants and geniuses", through Andy Warhol's Superstar Factory, into the European political theater of the 1970s, her art experiments and activism of the 1980s, prolific theatrical productions of the 1990s, and her growing international performance work since 2000. And like Frank, she (with Steve Zehentner) has produced a long-running public access TV show, planting seeds and exposing mainstream culture to the real art and history. This show, *Stemming The Tide of Cultural Amnesia, The Lower Eastside Biography Project*, actually featured the interview below, so it has been seen many times on both coasts.

This interview is "shop talk" between two legendary artists, and a primer for any artist just setting out on the road of art and the experimental life.

......................................................................................................................

**Linda:** (in mid-sentence) ... we play it as a repeat all night, so a new episode plays at like one in the morning, because we have like, almost 400 episodes.

**Penny:** Wow. That's crazy, I love it!

**Linda:** We've been doing it like ten years.

**Penny:** Yeah, and we've been doing ours about ten years. So, it's kind of interesting that we're on the same (gestures) ...

**Linda:** Yeah. Got into cable at the same time.

**Frank:** I just asked for a 2½ hour time slot.

**Linda:** Because they didn't have that as an option, but he said, I'd like to do 2½ hours and they said OK. But I think in Berkeley they don't have a lot of people that are doing shows. It's not like very competitive.

**Penny:** In New York it's really ... everything's a half hour. You know, maybe sometimes you could do an hour special, but I love it!

**Frank:** How do you fit life into a half hour?

**Penny:** Yeah, exactly! Total bullshit! But, one of the things that was the most fucking interesting thing was when I went to get that piece of pizza. And I had the books, right? So, I'm waiting for the pizza, and I started to read the NYU lecture [Frank's *Art Of A Shaman* - Ed.]. And I'm a fast reader. I'm the highest comprehensive reader in my ... when I was 12 years old in my age group in the state of Connecticut. So I'm reading and then my eyes fell on this whole ... you and I have to talk, of course a lot about the commodification of art, right? And I was talking with the boyz (Corey and Alexi) about ... I'm like totally an emerging arts fighter. I hate the whole concept of emerging arts, it drives me insane.

**Frank:** If art is not emerging, it is not art.

**Penny:** Yeah, but there's a big difference between suddenly saying, after a thousand years, where there were young artists who became old artists and now they have this ... the idea of emerging arts as a class of young people.

**Frank:** Yes.

**Penny:** This comes not from the art world. This comes from academia, because parents who are paying 250 fucking thousand dollars to educate their kids to be a performance artist, or a spoken word artist, or an experimental filmmaker, the same amount of money that it costs to educate somebody to be a lawyer (Frank sounds) or a surgeon. The parents want to be assured that there is an entry-level position for their kids. And this is terrible for young people because young artists, there's no two ways. Jack Smith said, you have to apprentice, it's the only way to learn how to make art! And not that people shouldn't also do their own thing, you know.

**Frank:** Or just do it for years.

**Penny:** Yeah, absolutely! But you have to be willing to be bad for twenty years in order to be good.

**Frank:** Yes.

**Penny:** I was talking to the boyz and I was saying what they've been doing with this emerging arts thing is creating this professionalization of art. And art is not a profession. Art is a vocation. And I was reading in your ...

**Linda:** *Art Of A Shaman*?

**Penny:** ... *Art Of A Shaman*. And I was reading this part where you were talking about what they did with performance, into making it into a certain amount of time. Many, many people said about my show ... I invite anybody, you know ... and they say, I didn't know it was going to be so long. (Linda laughing, Frank sounds) And that's not one of my long shows. (Frank sounds, Linda laughing)

**Frank:** Exactly! They think that 45 minutes is a long show.

**Penny:** Right.

**Frank:** And I do 48-hour performances! (Frank sounds)

*Frank Moore and Penny Arcade (video capture)*

**Penny:** Yeah, yeah, of course. That's because you're a master. You're a master. But it's so ... it's very empowering for me, because I was very, very tired. I was very sick the whole week. From the first night you came to the Thursday night you came, I was sick that whole week with very bad bronchitis. And I had hepatitis C a few years ago and I went on the interferon treatment and then I got an auto-immune illness called sarcoidosis that settled in my lungs. So it made me weak in my lungs. So when I get bronchitis, which I seem to get now every time I get a cold, I had no energy. So all those shows I'm doing with no energy, which is very hard, you know. And so I was worried about the length. You know what I mean, myself. I was going, fuck, I don't have the energy to ... like, usually the opening of the show when I introduce the dancers, that's like an assault. (Frank sounds)

**Frank:** Like a wrestling announcer!

**Penny:** Yeah, yeah, yeah, yeah!! Like a wrestling announcer, exactly! It's a very dynamic fighting, very aggressive, you know. And I didn't have quite that much energy, so I was like pushing it uphill all the way. It was very hard for me. So that night when I went to get the pizza then you gave me the book, I was looking at it. And then I read that thing about what they've done with performance. I think you and I are in agreement about a lot of things. For instance, I always say that performance only happens in the performance, right? It doesn't happen ... you don't rehearse performance art. You know what I mean, that's kind of (laughing and gestures) ...

**Frank:** Or the rehearsal is a performance!

**Penny:** Yes, absolutely! Perfect! No problem! So then when I was reading it and I fell on these lines where you were talking about how they've taken performance and tried to fit it into this kind of entertainment category, etc., and then if you don't do that, then you're sloppy or you're bad or you're unprofessional or whatever. And my eyes fell on that, and I'm like, oh my God, I was just getting seduced down this road. You know, getting twisted up and feeling bad about myself. And then the other thing was, and also, of course, the most exciting thing that I read at that moment was about how the show goes where the show's going to go. The performance goes where the performance is going to go. (Frank sounds)

**Frank:** You don't control it.

**Penny:** No, no, no! It has to go where it's going to go! And the thing is all my work is created improvisationally. And this show is the result of pretty much two years of straight improvisation. And then eventually it becomes kind of a set piece because it was ... my mind works a little like an old time word processor. I kind of scan, and then I cut and paste in my own head as I go along. I think this is something you understand.

**Frank:** Me too.

**Penny:** Yeah, yeah, yeah, yeah. I think, I was getting this. I was reading this shit and I was thinking maybe Frank Moore and I are the same person! (laughter)

**Frank:** Or mates.

**Penny:** Yes, yes, definitely, for sure. But we even possibly could be the same person! Why couldn't there be a sharing of almost persona, or something that we don't even know exactly what it is.

**Frank:** I could do your show.

**Penny:** Yeah, yeah, yeah, exactly. I could do yours! I love it!

**Linda:** He did that. There's a picture up there (gestures) of Frank dressed as Elvis Presley.

**Penny:** Oh yeah.

**Linda:** And he did that with an artist who was popular around here that called himself Extreme Elvis.

**Penny:** Oh yeah.

**Linda:** He was a big guy and he came out as the big Elvis. That was his outfit. And he'd end up naked real fast. Then he did the peeing and pooping on the audience stuff and just all this going out to the audience and trying to get them to be there with him. And they were mutually admiring each other. So he came up with the idea. He had this big date booked in a club in Oakland. He said, how about you be me? But we won't tell anybody. He didn't tell his band. He told one of his backup singers, that's all. And he played Frank in the audience.

**Penny:** Wow!

**Linda:** And so the backup singer wheels Frank in. And the place was packed. (Frank sounds) He's this hot act. And the band, because they know he's always pulling fast ones, they just kind of go along with it. Oh, OK! And Frank does the whole show as him.

**Penny:** You have video of that?

**Linda:** Oh yeah!

**Penny:** Wow, that sounds so fantastic!

**Frank:** Freaked the punks out.

**Linda:** Well, they started ... do you mean when the band had to come to your rescue? No.

**Mikee:** Gilman Street.

**Linda:** Oh wow! So what we did was, there's this little all-age punk club down the street, that's been around forever. And they were having this video festival and they contacted us out of the blue. We're not really involved with them. And said to Frank, could you submit something for us to play at this festival. So we had just done this show, and they needed like 15 minutes or something. So he said cut out the 15 minutes where the backup singer pees on me. So we play that. And they're these hardcore baby punks. And they freaked out. Why did they freak out? Because they thought that Frank was not there of his own free will. That he was being forced to be peed on and all this kind of stuff. Which Frank was not! That was the controversy!

**Penny:** It never ends. The political correctness never ends. Yeah, it's funny, because you're reminding me of ... a number of years ago, I guess it was around 1991, I got a call from Ron Delsener who is the big rock'n'roll promoter in New York City, from his office. And they said that this band ... now what the hell was the band's name ... I can't believe I'm not going to remember the name of the band ... the band is like, they're the superstars of industrial music ... Pig Head? Pig something. And it was like a guy from the Ministry, guys from out here, from the Ministry or whatever it's called ... it was a super hardcore industrial band. It was all the stars of all the different bands. Like a five-star band, they're the super band! And apparently they had requested me. So I go down there, and I'm talking to the guy on the phone from the office. And I said, you know, I don't think so. I said, the audience for this is like 16- to 24-year old guys. I said, I work with like ... you know at that time I was doing a lot of work on rape and sexual abuse and shit like this and I say, my work is about rape and sexual abuse. I said I have like six erotic dancer girls. And I went, and yeah! I think, yes, I should do this! (laughing) The guy's like, huh?! Well, I go there and I start doing this piece. And there's like, I don't know, 400 hardcore boys on the floor and I'm starting this piece and it was some piece about sex. It was a sexual piece. And the girls are grinding and dancing. (Frank sounds) And the boys just kept looking at the ground, you know. And then pretty soon it starts to look like oatmeal, like they're getting annoyed! They wouldn't look up, and it was bubbling like this (gestures). A guy at this point comes running up to me and goes, (screaming) we don't want to hear any more of your sex stories!!! I had the mic and I was like, oooohhh. Is it true what they say about hardcore boys? Is it true what they say about hardcore boys? And it became really, totally ... it was like really intense. And I was just going. And I just didn't stop. And I started talking about that there was a smell of new age order. Of the new world order was in the room. And I just kept going on and more and more. And they were like freaking out. (laughter) And I looked up and there was a guy who was the roadie for the band. And I yelled, I said, hey, how long do I have to perform to get paid? And the guy goes, 20 minutes. So I said, OK. I ended up on one of the amps in the front and I started talking to them, very quietly. And I said, well, Pig Face, that's the name of the band, well, I said, it's kind of a weird situation. I've got to perform for 20 minutes in order to get paid. I know you guys don't want to see me. And you don't want to hear anything that I'm doing. I said, even though Pig Face wants you to see me. That's why I'm here. And I went on. I did this whole long, very quietly emotional thing. And then I looked up and I said, how much time do I have left? He goes, you just did 20 minutes. And I went, bye! (laughter) And we all walked off the stage. And then I went upstairs and the guy from Pig Face, the main singer, he's this little English guy. He's quite famous, blonde guy. And I said, hey, your audience are assholes. And he goes, yeah, I know. And he's doing push-ups. I said, are you doing push-ups to be pumped when you go on stage? He's doing push-ups and he goes, no! It makes the acid come on faster! And then I watched him, and they were like ... their whole show was these young guys trying to get on stage and them beating them with their guitar and bass. It was like the mosh pit scene, you know. And then afterwards we were ... I was upstairs and all these guys kept coming over and going wow, you're way more hardcore than Pig Face! And you're more hardcore than anybody!

**Frank:** When I did *The Outrageous Beauty Revue*, we played ... my cast was ...

**Linda:** ... middle class people and they didn't quite get really what we were doing.

**Penny:** Yeah.

**Linda:** We were a community of people, had lived together for years.

**Frank:** This was in ...

**Linda:** ... the seventies, the mid-seventies. And so we're doing this show at the Mabuhay Gardens, which was the punk club. And we were the early show, for three and a half years, Saturday nights, sometimes another night.

**Frank:** I opened ...

**Linda:** ... Frank opened for all the punk bands. The show itself was kind of like ... the cast, it was just an extension of our lives. So they didn't really get how radical and subversive it was.

**Penny:** Right!

**Linda:** They thought it was just us kind of playing. You know, we'd go off on Saturday nights, we'd put make-up on ...

**Penny:** Right.

**Linda:** ... we'd play on the stage.

**Frank:** At a dive.

**Linda:** And it was a dive, of course.

**Penny:** Of course, of course.

**Linda:** So what is the point that they didn't ...

**Frank:** The punks would ...

**Linda:** Oh, well particularly, like certain bands, like Black Flag had a very heavy duty, hardcore audience. They'd all be there for the early show. And they'd throw things at our cast and they'd scream and yell. And the cast was like very uncomfortable and didn't quite get that that was OK. And so Frank had the idea of he would just park himself on the stage in the front corner, and he would just scream back at them. (Frank demonstrates screaming) So, the show would be going on and there's Frank doing that! (Frank continues screaming) Well, of course these hardcore guys are like (gestures mouth wide open dumbfounded). They don't know what to make of Frank! So, that would shut them up!

**Frank:** They were really tame kids.

**Penny:** Yeah. There's a lot of that. (all laughing) You're so brilliant, you know. Creating this (pointing to Frank's communication board). Such a good designer. I am very impressed. I was looking at your paintings in the other house [the Blue House - Ed.] and I see some here. Your paintings are really fucking phenomenal.

**Frank:** That is P-a ... (gesturing)

**Linda:** ... oh that's Patti Smith. Frank put that there for you (gestures to Patti Smith painting right behind them).

**Penny:** Oh yeah well, hmmmm (makes a face). (all laugh) Oh well!

**Linda:** Uh oh. Nice painting!

**Penny:** But I would say it has a real Patti thing going on there for sure.

**Linda:** Yeah. (Frank sounds)

**Penny:** No, but I think it's amazing, your paintings are amazing. (Frank sounds) Your paintings are completely amazing. Yeah.

**Linda:** Did you hear how he paints them? He can only ... he would wear a hard hat with a paint brush on it on his head.

**Penny:** Oh!

**Linda:** He could only paint that part of the canvas (gestures to lower portion of the canvas), so he'd have to paint it upside down and sideways to fill the whole canvas.

**Penny:** Right. So he could get the whole thing on there. Yeah. But I mean, isn't that amazing? Because you're so unlinear. Everything's coming from every direction. Inside out, upside down, around around.

**Linda:** Right.

**Penny:** And ... actually I was thinking about something about that ... um ... I can't remember what it is now, but it will come back, because it always does with me. (Frank giggles) But I was like very ... oh yeah! Also, I was saying to somebody the other day, because I went on your website and then I saw different things, right? And I was like, look at the fucking paintings! How the fuck does he paint?! Then I was over here in the house looking at the paintings and

*Frank Moore and Penny Arcade (video capture)*

I said to the boyz, yeah, that's crazy that he can paint like that! I said because when I hug him it's like hugging a dolphin! (Frank and Linda laugh) And I swam with the dolphins, so I know from where I speak! And also when you were in the audience and especially the first night, because you'd never seen me perform. Then you were just having the experience of the performance. And you're like me. You're a great audience! (Frank sounds) You know, a lot of performers are not great audience because they suck! (laughter)

**Frank:** Yes. I made it my business.

**Penny:** Yeah, yeah, yeah, of course. But it was so wonderful, especially the first night, because I'd never experienced you either. (Frank sounds) So we were experiencing each other for the first time. And I don't really think there's a difference between the audience and the performer (Frank sounds) at all, right? So what was really incredible, because it was your first experience of it so you were so vocal. (Frank sounds) And I know it was very powerful for me. And it was really powerful for the audience because people can speak. And they could make sounds that people understand. You were making these sounds that were so, not just emotive, but they were so eloquent. (Frank sounds) So we understood the very ... what's the word ... very specifically what you were feeling. We felt when you were expressing your isolation, when you were expressing your joy, when you were expressing your agreement, when you were expressing your pain, when you were expressing your understanding. That was like fucking far out, you know?! I was like really ... it was really intense. It was really an amazing contribution. And then when you came the second time ... because, of course, by then you were kind of more used to me, you know, just like I was more used to you. You can never have the first experience twice, right? That doesn't happen. But, when … I want to talk about the difference between the first time you came and my entering the stage because I just started playing "Creep" there, (Frank sounds) before I enter the stage, the Radiohead song. In 2006, in L.A. they asked me to do five performances for Outfest, for their Platinum Center. And I have never … *Bitch! Dyke! Faghag! Whore!* has never been presented at a gay festival, up until Outfest. And I was really angry, you know. So I didn't know I was angry. But when opening night came, I was in the audience with the dancers and they had these wooden floors, it's a place called Red Cat in L.A. It is part of Cal Arts. And the music's playing of the song, and I was like just wandering around the audience like looking pissed off and just like sullen and the song was playing and I start stomping my feet. (Frank sounds) And it became this very threatening and there was a guy who we brought from New York, Kevin Aviance, who's this black kind of dance music star who had just gotten beaten up within an inch of his life the month before. A terrible, terrible beating. He was fag bashed. They broke his jaw and all kinds of crazy shit. And I went to visit him in the hospital, and I thought well, he wasn't going to come to do the show in L.A. I mean he had a wired-shut jaw, and he was really fucked up. And I went to see him and I said, you know, of course I was so, I felt so bad, you know about what had happened to him. But I was saying to him, I was saying but this is also important because it's you, there was visibility. A lot! I mean it was on CNN and shit, you know. (Frank sounds) And I said I feel bad that you're not going to be able to be in the show. And he said, I'm in the show (says it as if her jaw is wired shut). (laughter) So, when we're in L.A. I stomp my foot and the stage was kind of a wooden hollow thing, so you really heard the sound. (Frank sounds) Then he started stomping his feet. And pretty soon, every, all the dancers were stomping and it was this very threatening, super threatening vibe. And we did it every night. So now we come here. We did five nights there, then a year later I did one performance at the Spiegel tent in New York, where, by the way, they took … it was a Tuesday night at 10:30pm where unbeknownst to me in the contract hidden, in fine print, which I didn't see, they took the first $4,000 that came in the door Tuesday night at 10:30pm! (Frank sounds) They did no publicity! No ads! I mean they … whatever their ad was, they maybe had me in their ad, but they wouldn't allow me to put postcards out in the venue for the month coming before my performance. So I just wanted to add that because it's such an attractive story! (Frank sounds) So we did one night, so we did "Creep" again. And I walked through the audience and I was of course in a rage about that. So then this time, Steve, I said, Steve, I said, he goes I think it's a good idea to use "Creep". And I said it has to be there now, now it has to be there. But I don't know what it's going to mean here. I don't know what it's going to mean here.

**Frank:** Most people did not know you were you.

**Linda:** When you first came out. (Frank sounds)

**Penny:** Yeah, yeah. No they didn't. And they were so mean to me too, a lot of them.

**Linda:** Wow. (Frank sounds)

**Penny:** A lot of the people were really mean to me. They wouldn't look at me.

**Linda:** Right.

**Penny:** Or they would be like ... (makes a rolling the eyes face) (Frank sounds)

**Frank:** Even after I gave you a ...

**Penny:** ... a hug.

**Frank:** Away.

**Linda:** ... after you gave her away.

**Penny:** You mean because I hugged you?

**Frank:** Yes!

**Penny:** Yeah, but I don't think they still knew but (Frank sounds) the thing is that in that moment I was coming down and kind of carrying this feeling of not ... it's not nice (Frank sounds) you know when you ... there's a big element of sacrifice in my work. I always have a sacrificial element.

**Frank:** Yes.

**Penny:** So you go ... and I'm a weird person because I'm a real person, you know?

**Frank:** Yes.

**Penny:** I'm not Patti Smith! (Frank sounds) Which isn't ... not to ... I think Patti's a great artist, but Patti's personhood, she hasn't been involved with that for a long time.

**Frank:** I freaked her out!

**Linda:** Frank freaked her out!

**Penny:** Oh, definitely! (laughter, Frank sounds)

**Linda:** She didn't know what to make of him.

**Penny:** No.

**Frank:** She asked ...

**Linda:** ... she asked for him to read her future as if this (gestures to Frank's letter board) was an Ouija board. She didn't even get that it was a communication device. (Frank sounds) And when he was still just relating to her and not doing her future, she got mad. (Frank sounds)

**Frank:** I said, no.

**Linda:** He said no, I won't read your future. (laughter)

**Penny:** Well the thing is, of course, because you are an intuitive being, even if you didn't have cerebral palsy you would still be an intuitive being. I mean, this is part of your nature, right?

**Linda:** Yes, yes.

**Penny:** But being an intuitive being in this package ...

**Frank:** Yes.

**Penny:** ... which immediately, this is what I always say to people ... people always want to say that my work is confrontational ... I always say: I don't agree with you. My work is not confrontational. I said people confront themselves so easily, you don't need ... no artist has to confront anybody because people are so busy confronting themselves! So ...

**Frank:** Yes. You don't know what pushes people.

**Penny:** Yeah, no, absolutely! I mean, for me, you are difficult. You are intense. (Frank sounds) Now I know you, you know, but the first day I didn't know. And none of us want to not know! (Frank giggles) Part of ... people don't want to not know how to be at ease in a situation. So you're in a conflict right away between being able to say, oh, I know how to deal with this! When I was in Australia (laughing) and there's a café called Piccolo. And it's like a totally, totally bohemian place. Very tiny, it maybe has like 15 or 20 seats. And it's open until 6 o'clock in the morning, and I always go there. (loud sound of Kittee the cat) And you are a cat! And there was this aboriginal guy in there, and I'm talking with the aboriginal guy. And he's drunk. And he's a poor aboriginal guy. But I'm like talking to him and but then he started to get sexual with me because I was talking with him. And then we started to have a physical fight. And then he got thrown out and I felt really bad because the whole situation was a kind of misunderstanding. And afterwards I was talking to somebody and I said, yeah, I said, I was there thinking, wow, aboriginal people like me! You know, I'm all proud, you know what I mean. (Frank sounds) So, you know, people are going to have their thing. I'm like, oh, I get along with Frank Moore. And he has cerebral palsy. But there is an element, I think, and I don't want to talk ... and I think it's a great portrait of Patti. To me it looks really, and I knew Patti very, very, very, very, very well at one point. She and I were very, very close friends at one point. And then Patti convinced me that I should leave New York and go to Europe 'cause she said, we're just slaves here, man, we're just slaves. And so I believed her and I went. (laughing) And I think that she did become what she really wanted to be which was a rock star. But I'm not ... I don't know how to say it without ... because I don't want to trash her, but I want to say, of course, she couldn't be in that space with you without a construct. And what the fuck does that mean that you're going to tell her fucking future?! (Frank sounds) That's retarded! That's being unwilling to ask a question. Like, OK, OK, you're here, what the fuck is this (gestures to Frank's letter board)? Not like I'm going to get all Tennessee Williams on you and make you like you're this figure, like in one of his plays where he always has some shamanistic, voodoo, black bone and a crow thing! But then, but that's what I think happens to people who believe their own publicity. (Frank sounds) So when I'm saying that for me, because I am a real person, because I have suffered a lot in my life, it doesn't take much for me to be ... like if I'm coming down the stairs and I'm looking at people, I am ambivalent about ... not about being a performer, because I know I'm an entertainer. I'm very clear on that. That that's what I do, I'm an entertainer. But I am ambivalent about taking the attention, of being the center of attention. I like it, but not so much. And I'm not really an exhibitionist, unlike you!

**Frank:** You are a conductor.

**Penny:** Yeah, I'm a conductor. And I'm a reformer. (Frank sounds) This just came up. I think you'd be very ... I want to send you the ... it hasn't come out yet but ... there's two essays on my work. And I think you would enjoy reading them. I want to share them with you. One guy is this guy, Ken Bernard, who's an amazing playwright of the ridiculous, but not camp. Like really dangerous shit. (Frank sounds) And I did his plays when I was just 17, 18, 19. The last one I did I was 20. With the Play-House of the Ridiculous. And he is 80 years old. Because of my background, the immigrant Italian peasant thing, it's really hard for me to ask anybody for anything. It's not in my culture, how I was raised. So I never would invite him or invite anybody to see my work. My whole relationship has been with the general public. So finally, in 2005, I invited him to come and see a performance that I was doing, it was a club work, I wasn't doing a full show. And then I asked him, because (unintelligible) was going to do this book on my work. I asked him, I wrote to him I said, look, I'd like you to see my work. And I sent him about seven or eight scripts. And I said, I don't expect you to write anything about me, but you did know me from when I was this very young performer. And if you felt like you had something to say. He wrote this amazing fucking essay without ever seeing any of the DVDs of the work. Which is important because what I write and how I stage it are very different. And he got it, totally got it! But one of the things he wrote about was about me as a reformer. And it was very interesting because I am a reformer. You're a reformer also!

**Frank:** Yes.

**Penny:** Because you see that things could be better. That we are limited. That we could be so much more. There's so much more, so much more to go, and have and be, etc. So when I'm coming down the stairs and these people are looking at me ... and the last night was the worst. Saturday night was the fucking worst because I'm coming down the stairs and hanging on (gestures hanging on a railing) and people are like this (acts like someone looking down, looking away). And some people smiled and were nice, but a lot of people weren't. By the time I get down to the floor I'm feeling like ... what am I doing? So, the first night this was happening, when I got down to you, by that time I was like, wow! I feel like I'm a creep, but Frank's a real creep! (Linda laughing) And that, when we embraced, (Frank sounds) in that communication between the two of us, because it is so easy for you because of your experience, to read the dynamic that was in the room.

**Frank:** Yes.

**Penny:** You automatically knew everything that I was doing. (Frank nodding his head yes) I didn't have to explain anything! (Frank sounds) Of course, right?! And then when I was going towards the stage, and then I kept looking back to you, and there was this very taut, the energy was very taut, (gestures and Frank shaking his head) it was like we had this (Frank sounds) elasticky thing.

**Frank:** Yes.

**Penny:** 'Cause it was ... we could ... I could move but then I was pulled back like this (gestures). And then without even ... and I didn't know anything about life at all, because I hadn't read the thing yet, and I hadn't gone on your website yet. And then I was having it all. (Frank sounds) And I have to tell you now I realized something I'm going to remember for a long time. When I was in seventh grade my life was really, really horrible. You heard some of it. Everybody said I was fucking everybody and plus I had a horrible home life. My father was in a mental hospital supposedly because he was going to drown me. And, of course, in a southern Italian family, it's not a buried memory because you can't have a buried memory in a southern Italian family. Because as soon as you're five years old they start screaming, (screams)

"And your father was going to drown you!" (laughter) And so, I had all of these things going on, plus all the insane tension and now I found out even more crazy stuff that I didn't know since my mother died. And I was acting out all of the time because I was like totally under, contents-under-pressure. So I went to seventh grade and this time ... in seventh grade I used to write all over my arms, all over my legs, I'd write all over myself. And I was totally persona non grata. And there was a boy with cerebral palsy. And he was mobile. He was mobile. And I would imitate him. And now I didn't remember, this is many years later. And at that time, I was saying to the boyz, I said, I didn't tell them that I imitated, I couldn't get myself up to that 'til now. But I was saying to the boyz that probably in ... now ... if it would be now, you would get oriented, the teachers would tell you about, here's this special needs kid, blah blah. Then, they didn't tell you anything! And he was always in the basement. In some special classes or something. And I almost never saw him. And I wouldn't imitate him in front of him. But I would do it to make everybody laugh 'cause I felt so fucking rotten. And now I'm thinking, fuck, this probably was this fucking brilliant fucking guy that I was completely even unaware of anything! You know what I mean?! (touches Frank and starts crying) (Frank sounds) I forgive myself, but still ... yeah, so anyway, then the second time when you came I got freaked out because you were on the other side of the room! (Frank sounds)

**Frank:** Yes!

**Linda:** Us too, really!

**Frank:** Because of the steps.

**Penny:** Right, right, right. But I didn't think of it, so I come in and I'm like, where the fuck's Frank?! (Frank sounds) What the fuck! And then I see you on the other side of the stage. (Frank sounds) And I was like, this is not good! (Frank sounds, Linda laughing) 'Cause I was already back in what we did the first time! I liked it!

**Frank:** Yes.

**Penny:** Fuck, I want that again! But of course, you know that you can never have the same thing again, right?! (Frank sounds) But that doesn't stop you from wanting it! (Frank sounds) Maybe not you!

**Frank:** Don't hold on.

**Penny:** I know, I gotcha. (laughing) I'm a fast assimilator. (laughter) And then, but then you're on the other side. So I said, fuck, OK, what am I going to do?! I'm going to do it different this time. So I went on the other ... I always go down the steps on the side that you were but I said, this isn't the same because I was going to get your back. But then I said, too bad, just go and do it. Just do what's in front of you. So I did it. Then when I came back, down, then a whole other thing happened. It was like very exciting. And I think that they videoed that night. I'm not 100% sure.

**Frank:** Yes.

**Linda:** Yeah, I think that's right.

**Penny:** Yeah. And then that was really interesting that it was also kind of like the inverse energistically of what happened the other, the first night. So it was kind of very ritualistic that you were there the first time and then the last time in this other place. That kind of algebra of alchemy. And I really loved it when I was going up on the stage and still maintaining this contact with you. And maybe, I might have thought that it might not have worked over such a distance. But I guess because we had already practiced with the shorter distance then it still was ...

**Frank:** Distance ...

**Penny:** ... doesn't exist, ha ha ha (Frank laughs) I jumped ya, I jumped ya!! I jumped ya!!! (Linda laughing) Yeah, exactly. That was fucking far out! Ask me some questions!

**Frank:** We are always the outsiders.

**Penny:** Yeah.

**Frank:** Of all the subcultures ...

**Linda:** That we get involved in.

**Frank:** We influence but they freak out.

**Penny:** (nods her head yes) Well, this is what I said to my dancers the other night that we had in the week since I had seen you. This big huge drama happened with the genderqueer kids who were coming to the show and I was talking about the trendiness around certain trans thing and nobody wants to be a lesbian anymore, and everybody wants to be a boy. The prestige that's in being a boy, blah, blah, blah. And while unbeknownst to me, Sunday night, this past Sunday night, I'm talking all this stuff and then I showed the video of my mother and this young man comes over to me and he says, listen, I think you're awesome, but I want to talk to you about the trans, your ideas about the trans men are ... I want to have a conversation with you about it. (Frank giggles) He was very nice and I was like, OK, but I wasn't talking about trans men. He goes back to his seat. I go on stage and I'm thinking, Penny, just do the show and do not veer off into this special-interest thing. (Frank sounds) But, no! (all laugh)

**Linda:** Didn't take your own advice.

**Penny:** No. So I start to talk to him and I said, I want to say to this person, this young man came up to me and said X, Y, Z, and I want to say this to him now. He stands up and I'm trying to say what I'm saying and he's saying stuff to me like, you don't know anything about trans men. And I said, I'm not talking about trans men. I've got this one peculiar problem that if I don't think we're talking about the same thing, I won't continue the conversation until we can get that we're both talking about the same thing! Oh my god! Well, he went to leave. And I said, you're going to fucking walk out? I said I just shown you this tremendous respect by stopping the whole show to answer and talk to you about this. I said, sit the fuck down. So he sat down but he still didn't like it and he ended up walking out. Then at the end of the night it turned out that all of my girl dancers were genderqueer-identified and either involved with trans men or very ... not partnering up ... or very involved! And they're all really upset, really upset. And I was trying to talk to them and they're all young. They're all like, you know, Nina's the oldest and she's like 35. So it was really interesting. And then I ... it was

*Penny Arcade (video capture)*

really hard for me because I'm very softhearted. I mean I'm very tough, absolutely, but I'm very, very, very softhearted. (Frank sounds) And it was hard for me to be in this situation with them. And at the same time what I wanted to say to them was like, I'm fucking twice your fucking goddamn fucking age. You're going to get in my face?! Don't get in my face! But then you can't say that to them 'cause I've learned. That's the kind of entitlement generation. And it's different from my generation which was the earning ... you earned the respect as opposed to you're entitled to respect.

**Linda:** Right.

**Penny:** But they don't understand that. So you can't even say that because it doesn't mean anything to them. They don't know what you're talking about.

**Linda:** Wow.

**Penny:** And also because empathy has been bred out of the culture. (Frank sounds) People have lost one of our great capacities, which is our ability to be empathetic. (Frank sounds) And to empathize. And to be able to empathize with you (gestures to Frank) or with you (gestures to Linda), or with you (gestures to Mikee). You say five sentences and then your empathy gets aroused and you start, you have the capacity to see it from your point of view (gestures to Frank). But that's gone! Anyways, I then, I was really physically sick also. That was the worst part. At my sickest. Very bad bronchitis. So no energy.

**Frank:** That is always ...

**Linda:** ... when these things happen.

**Penny:** Yeah, right. OK, cool. I'm with you. So anyways, I tried to talk to them. And I said, look, I'm going to investigate this. So I got into, I found this guy who's a pagan trans man in Massachusetts with an incredible analysis and he's disabled. But he's doing this wild shit and he's a shaman. I think maybe I got to send you his link. I'll send you the letters he wrote that were very great. I went back, then two more people were writing to me that were either trans identified or genderqueer-identified. And starting right away with you're a fucking, not you're a fucking racist, but it was disgusting to watch you describe your dancers by the color of their skin.

**Frank:** I don't even know what all of that means.

**Linda:** Those types. "Trans-identified". He doesn't know what that means.

**Penny:** The gender types. You don't know what that means? OK, so you know that there's a big movement now because it's 2009 where people can who have body dismorphia ...

**Frank:** Yes.

**Penny:** ... and then they can get sex-reassignment surgery.

**Frank:** Yes.

**Penny:** Well, then, there's also trans-identified, the genderqueer movement, do you know that?

**Frank:** No.

**Penny:** OK, so this is people who don't identify with the, what is that called, binary? Two, male/female culture. So they reject binary, that there is just two sexes. And they're gender fluid. So one day they're girlie, and one day they're not or whatever the fuck they are. (Frank sounds)

**Frank:** Like we all are.

**Penny:** Right. And this is ... (Frank loud sounds) exactly, but without it being institutionalized.

**Frank:** Yes.

**Penny:** Well, one of the things I was trying to explain is that in the '60s people fought and worked very hard for the idea that gender and genitalia were not connected. (Frank sounds)

**Frank:** Yes.

**Penny:** But now, of course, because it's forty years later, and these kids are young and they don't ... all the people died in the middle, from AIDS or from ODs of drugs. I mean a lot of alternative people are gone. There's not a lot of people in our age group, right? You're the same age as Patti, by the way! In case you didn't know. Everybody's five years older than me! You're 46?

**Linda:** No, he's 62 ...

**Penny:** No, no no, he was born in ...

**Linda:** Oh yeah, 6/25/46

**Penny:** He was born in '46.

**Linda:** Yeah.

**Penny:** I think Patti's either born ... she may be born in '45 because she's five years older than me. I'm born in '50. And you're four years older than me. Don't get too upstart! (laughter) So, a lot of people are gone in the middle generation.

**Frank:** Baby.

**Linda:** You're a baby, he said! (laughter)

**Penny:** I was just saying today to a guy who did my hair. Did you see my hair's a new color? (Frank sounds)

**Frank:** Yes.

**Penny:** Mr. Anthony was born in 1968 and I said as he was doing my hair today, I said, you were born in 1968, I said, shit, you were in a crib and I was doing LSD. I said you couldn't even get out of the crib, couldn't talk, I was doing LSD. I was eating pizza, you could only drink milk! (laughter) So that's what was going on with you. You were bigger than me. So anyways, what happened was I said, I entered into a dialogue, I'm sick and I'm writing these people, five, six emails a day! And they're still not coming. I'm writing them and saying first of all, I was in the original genderfuck thing, the Play-House of the Ridiculous. We started genderfuck. And then, don't say I'm racist because I got beaten up on the street from when I was twelve years old for being a nigger lover. So, don't even say that to me because you don't know what you're talking about. Because I live my politics with my body on the street not on a velour couch with six people who took the same Black Studies class as me. (laughter) And then when I went back to work, because I had two days off, Monday and Tuesday, everybody wanted to have a meeting. And I was like, OK, we'll have a short meeting, like a 15-minute meeting. (Frank sounds)

**Frank:** What is this democracy shit?

**Penny:** (laughing) Yeah!

**Frank:** I am the creator!

**Penny:** Yeah, yeah, but you know, I still understood, because it's still ... my big joke about it in the show is, and I might have said it the night you were there, there's a whole bunch of heterosexuals here who don't know what the fuck I'm talking about. There's a whole bunch of fags here who could fucking care less. And the end result is lesbians, genderqueer girls, and ex-girls who are now men, who care about this, it's not universal. So anyways I went in and I said to them, look, this is what I've been doing. I've been talking to all these people. I'm going to be more articulate, I wasn't articulate enough, have to give more history because people don't know what I'm talking about. And then I said, I almost started crying, but I didn't cry, but almost, and I just said, "All I know is I stick up for everybody and nobody ever fucking sticks up for me!" (Frank sounds)

**Frank:** Yes. I have the same experience.

**Penny:** Yes.

**Linda:** Frank is always talking about loyalty, being loyal.

**Penny:** Yeah, right! And steadfast! (Frank sounds) And steady. And also the reality is that you can't attain mastery if you don't fucking go through the journey to mastery. (Frank sounds) It's not like, and this is one of the things that's really missing, most young people because they're in a culture of being "experts", they're all "experts"! (Frank sounds) And I don't think ... I don't know if it was the night that you were there, I started ranting about be young! No? One night I just started ranting, you're young for such a short amount of time. And you're old for a really fucking long time, so fucking young up, man! (laughter) You know, be young! Stop with this ... and I understand that someone can be 29 and often people do feel older when they're around 29, 30. Because they feel like they've lived awhile right? Like fifteen years. Since they were 15 they were kind of conscious of being alive in the world. So they think, well, 15 years and they get tired. And they feel like they've really been through something.

**Frank:** Burnt out.

**Penny:** (laughing) Burnt out, exactly! (Frank sounds) You're so smart, exactly! So they have that feeling that they're older and then last night I made people mad because this person wrote to me, I'm 29 years old! Yeah, I said, 29, that's like 11. It's the same as 11. 29 years old is like eleven years old. And then somebody got mad at me about saying that. But I just think it's a message of hope.

**Frank:** They think they are special.

**Penny:** Yeah. People think they're special. Which is really problematic. (Frank sounds)

**Frank:** Because everybody goes through the same things.

**Penny:** Yeah. Well, yes and no, because in my show, *Bad Reputation*, I say there are women who have always been protected and women who have never been protected. And the idea that you can protect yourself is absurd, because protection implies that somebody else is looking out for you. When you're alone the most you can do is defend yourself. Defense and protection are not the same thing. So, you can have people ... if you don't have a rigorous inquiry in what it is to be alive, if you don't have, and not everybody does, not everybody does. We all have our nature. I happen to be a very altruistic person. That's my nature. I'm not like an especially great, nice person. I am compelled to be altruistic because it's my nature. It's not something that I struggle to develop in myself. Yet, I believe that ... I don't know if I believe, I should just say I feel that if you're alive that you have to ... that if you're awake and you're aware, then you're going to have an inquiry into what it is to be alive. Now I also do believe that there's only 10,000 people alive on the planet at any one time, as Ouspensky said, and I amended it to say there's only 10,000 alive on the planet at one time and 6,000 of them are aboriginals. (laughter) I'm a non-elitist and I'm a populist. So for many, many, many years I truly did believe that everybody was equally intelligent. And then I had to realize ...

**Frank:** In spite of all evidence.

**Penny:** (laughing) Yeah, right, to the contrary, right! But now as I'm saying this to you, I'm actually coming up with something. (Frank giggles) And that is that while all people do not share the same level of intelligence, all people do have the ability to have the same level of cognizance. Which of course is different from ...

**Frank:** If they are responsible.

**Penny:** You have to have some fucking modesty! You have to have some modesty and you have to have some ... what I don't like about the current youth culture is it kind of like wants to fool young people into thinking that they're all that. In my young time was also youth culture, right, the mid-'60s. But we didn't believe it. When they said, oh, the young people are the taste-makers, the young people are the ... we didn't believe it! That's the difference. When I was, like I said last night, nobody who's young is cool. When you're young the most you can do, is you try not to be uncool. So that cool people let you hang out with them. 'Cause you learn how to be cool. Nobody's just inherently cool. Because they're young and that's retarded. That's not possible. But I do believe that we all ... like I just was in Turkey in September. And I was in a lot of markets with these women who were coming down from the mountains and they're ... they don't even speak Turkish. They're so tribal. And I would be having these hour-long conversations with these people just with looking and body language, because they haven't lost the capacity to communicate that way. You can communicate with some quite deftness of emotion like you and I are doing right now. And that's a kind of cognizance that doesn't have to do ... it can be aided by intelligence, but the absolute ability ...

**Frank:** It is erotic.

**Penny:** Erotic? Oh, yeah, yeah, yeah, yeah, yeah, definitely. It's a property of Eros, absolutely, without a doubt. Yeah. But that's part of our, our guess our animal nature, no? (Frank sounds)

**Frank:** Yes.

**Penny:** Ask me a new question.

**Frank:** I ...

**Penny:** You can't throw Frank Moore.

**Frank:** I had a black hip-hop artist say he felt forced to be gay.

**Linda:** Oh yeah. This is the last time he was on the show, he said now what's cool is being gay and that he feels like it's not ... like now he's being treated as if being straight is not cool, it's not acceptable. He's feeling like there's a pressure on him to be gay.

**Penny:** That's interesting because the ending story of the story about the genderqueer thing and my dancers was that last night was left in the show and one of my dancers who was the most upset during this altercation last week, came up to me at the closing night party and very serious, and she told me that her lover and her friends came to the show last night and her friends had never seen her in her erotic dancer persona and they said to her that she looked really straight when she was dancing. And that she didn't look queer. And she ended up just sobbing and was being very upset after the show. (Frank sounds) I didn't see this, other people saw this. And then when she told me last night I was looking at her and I said well, that's full circle, isn't it? And she admitted that she often feels like she's being challenged that she's not queer enough. And this is counter-revolutionary and counter-evolutionary.

**Frank:** Yes.

**Penny:** And all of these kinds of identity politics ... the way identity politics hijacked what was going on in the sixties. 'Cause in the sixties I think we can safely say this: people that are our age, we were not racists, we were not homophobic, we were not misogynists because that was part of what we saw, that we called plastic or bad or ... we distanced ourselves, we were, even if we had no experience with homophobia, let's say, or with racism, we still decided to take it on, how do I say it, to just take it on something, that we did not agree with that.

**Frank:** Yes.

**Penny:** So I think for our generation things were moving along, moving along, moving along. That's why I say in the mid-seventies then the whole thing was hijacked by these people who came out of the closet and went on committees telling the rest of us who've never been in the closet, what we could ... and they actually hijacked the entire discourse. And along with a lot of other things, including feminism. These things were not allowed to go into the widest margins of society. In my show, *Bad Reputation*, I say, do you actually think it's because of men that feminism hasn't spread to the widest margins of society? No! It's because of women! And the same thing with the gay rights issue. In the mid-'70s it got hijacked in one way. And then after AIDS, AIDS was like, gave the same kind of sympathy to the gay world as 9/11 gave to America. And just like the way America squandered the goodwill of the world's people by going into Iraq and doing all of these criminal acts, the goodwill that came to the "gay world" because of AIDS was squandered because the so-called "gay community" instead of using this as a time to educate and include the public, they just turned it into a marketing strategy, and started selling people shit. And if you want to sell people shit, you've got to keep them in a small group. Quentin Crisp said, do you know Quentin Crisp?

**Frank:** Yes.

**Penny:** OK. Quentin Crisp, we did many shows together and at that time I was really an AIDS activist, I still am an AIDS activist, I guess, but at that time I was very busy with it, I was very, very angry. And Quentin would always disagree with activism. He just disagreed with it. And he said it didn't work. Of course, he's an Edwardian, so he's coming from a different time, right. But he said to me, and it was always very intense for me, he said, the so-called gay community says that it wants equality but what it wants is acknowledgment. 'Cause when you say you want equality you say I'm gay and people say, so what? But when you want acknowledgment, you're saying gay and people say, oh, do tell, what was it like for you! (Frank sounds) And so that's that thing about being special. And I've done a lot of stuff on this aspect and also these young people want to be special. Their genderqueer revolution is something that they think is totally new.

**Frank:** Yes.

**Penny:** The trans man, his name is Raven, from Massachusetts, wrote and said, look, in ten years these kids are not going to be "genderqueer". He said but maybe it will have softened up their opinions towards trans people, so that it will be easier for the future generations of people who really do have body dismorphia and who want to segue into different body types. And then what he was saying, which is quite interesting too because I think the lesbian view on it is protectionist. It's like, oh, here's these young kids and they're taking testosterone and they're cutting off their breasts and they're very young and what if they're just doing it to curry favor or to blah, blah, blah. And that was one of the things that made the guy mad, the trans man mad, because I was trying to explain to him what I was saying. I told him about Quentin Crisp and I going into a leather bar and Quentin Crisp said, (imitating Quentin Crisp) they look marvelous Miss Arcade, but it can't be true about all of them! What do you mean? And he said, when I was young if someone told me that there was a tavern in the town where the beautiful and the cool were gathered, I would have run all the way there. And I would have gone up to the largest and the leatheriest of them and I would have said, if you love me, kill the bartender! (laughter) He said, and they won't do it! They're standing there squeaking with leather, studded with steel and they're talking about the ballet!! So, there is this element of people who don't look, or they just want to look like something and they're really not like this. When I see people who are dressed super punk, young people in an elevator at the Chelsea Hotel.

**Frank:** They always are the ones who have the most inhibitions.

**Penny:** Ah-ha. It's true. You're right. You're absolutely correct.

**Linda:** We did a piece, "Erotic Play" for a number of years. Frank would go up to people and ask if he could do a video of them just being who they are. And he said the idea was to show sexy as just normal people as opposed to the like Playboy, Hollywood idea.

**Penny:** Right.

**Linda:** And so for three-and-a-half years we were videoing people like eight to ten hours a day, two hours at a time. And every single time, the people that, well we figured this out slowly, but the people that looked really interesting, and really hip, they were so not open. Then he'd get these secretaries from the Art Department or the History Department, they would come on their lunch break, and they would look so straight, and I'm thinking, oh right, Frank! Boom, clothes off, playing with the costumes, just being playful and open. No image to protect. They were just there to be with us and to have fun. It happened like that every time.

**Penny:** Yeah, I know, absolutely, it's true. It's really funny 'cause I go to certain events and because I have ties in the punk world, and there will be these young people, and I'll go, 'cause I just dress like whatever I'm dressing like. It could be anything. And then you'll be in the elevator with them and they'll be just looking at you and be just like (sighs and rolls her eyes).

**Linda:** (laughing) How uncool!

**Penny:** Yeah, how uncool. And then they find out that you're "somebody" and then they're like ... then they really feel like they're really superior to you. I've had a few conversations with people where I'm going, well if you're so fucking cool, why are you dressed the way I used to dress thirty years ago? Why don't you come up with something new? (Frank giggles) Because when I see you in your full punk regalia it looks like Elvis in 1976 to me. (laughter) It looks exactly the same! It doesn't look fresh. It looks like ... you look a little weird. But also the other thing is I do a lot, a lot, a lot of benefits. I've been doing them for quite a while for Mumia.

*Penny Arcade (video capture)*

And these people would come in full fucking heavy duty regalia with ten bucks worth of fucking wax in their hair and $250 Doc Martens shoes and then you ask them to throw a dollar in the box to get a bus to go to Philadelphia and they wouldn't do it! And I would flip out on them. I would always flip out on them, but it's true. That's very telling.

**Frank:** Want to hear a classic letter?

**Penny:** Yeah.

**Linda:** Is this Linda's letter? (Frank giggles) Oh, say what it is? So, when the group broke up that was doing the show at the Mabuhay Gardens, it was like thirty of us, and that all broke up. And in an effort to hook up with other people doing creative things, Frank came up with this idea, oh, I'll go to art school and get another Master's degree! He already had one Master's degree.

**Frank:** B-a ...

**Linda:** It was a bad idea. 'Cause we're thinking this is where all these creative people will be. So we go to the San Francisco Art Institute, and what department? We didn't care. So we picked video, because we thought that would be fun to know how to work video equipment and stuff. This was like in '80, '81, something like that.

**Penny:** Oh wow.

**Linda:** But the department was Performance/Video. And so we had been doing stuff for like

15 years and not knowing it was called Performance Art.

**Penny:** Right, right.

**Linda:** We were just doing stuff Frank would come up with.

**Frank:** O ...

**Linda:** *The Outrageous Beauty Revue*, was very ... got a lot of international press. So it was well known.

**Penny:** Yes, I know about that.

**Linda:** So we go to this school and nobody would talk to us, not even the teachers! (Frank sounds) We were just like, as if we were invisible.

**Penny:** Wow!

**Linda:** Two years! It was a two-year program. I mean I was ready to quit after a week! Frank was like this (gestures plowing ahead). It was rough. I would be spelling Frank's board and they would pretend it wasn't happening. And then the teachers! There was one class that was the graduate class where everybody goes to each other's performances and you talk about it. That's all the class is. Only one guy would come to Frank's performances. And they would pretend ... they wouldn't even talk about it. And so the very last semester they have this guest teacher, Linda Burnham, who was the founder and publisher of *High Performance* magazine, which because we didn't know anything about performance art, we didn't know the magazine, we didn't know to be impressed by anything. And she, of course, comes right up to Frank and wants to befriend him and know him, and she started coming over to our house and inviting all of her famous artist friends up from L.A. to meet Frank and puts him on the cover of the magazine. (Frank sounds) Well, we don't even still know to be impressed. Because we'd been getting a lot of publicity. But everybody ... but we knew by the way everybody was acting at school: how did he get on the cover?! So, Frank always said this was his revenge! So anyway, we have a friendly relationship with her. We would get together all the time after the school thing. Whenever we were in L.A. we'd get together. Whenever she was up here we'd get together. And she was very supportive of us and Frank and the work we did. Frank was always having run-ins with somebody, and she was always supportive of our end of it.

**Penny:** Right.

**Frank:** I was warning artists if they did not stop the P.C. (politically correct), someone like Meese ...

**Linda:** Meese, who was the Meese Commission on Pornography. It would open the door for somebody like that to come in and clamp down on everybody.

**Penny:** Yes, absolutely. Right.

**Linda:** If everybody didn't stop picking at each other.

**Penny:** Yes, yes right. Absolutely.

**Frank:** They were pissed ...

**Linda:** ... at you for talking like that. At the time it seemed like he was pulling it out of the air.

**Penny:** Right.

**Linda:** You know, there was no context.

**Penny:** Right. Yeah, but you're prescient.

**Linda:** Yes. So, she had not, she had come to one performance that we did in L.A.

**Frank:** Punk ...

**Linda:** Oh right, she came to that other thing too, the punk club, right. OK, but, she hadn't come to one of these five-hour things that Frank was doing. So finally we were both going to be in the same city, and she was real excited. We had gotten together with her for lunch and, I can't wait to finally, da da da da! So, she didn't come! And, you know, people always don't come.

**Penny:** Yeah, yeah, yeah, yeah.

**Linda:** But we get this ... this is the letter we get a few days later.

**Penny:** Read it! Read it!

**Linda:** This was July, 1989.

**Linda reads the letter:**

Dear Frank and Linda,

I was sorry to disappoint you by not showing up at your performance last weekend. I put myself in the ridiculous position of needing a ride and couldn't get anyone to bring me there.

The real problem, though, is that I was reluctant to go. I think you hit the nail on the head, Linda, when you said it seems to be hard to get people you know to participate. I think I was really afraid to be put in the position of interacting "erotically" in public with friends. I think I learned a lot about erotic play during the '70s, through performance, and it's not fear of the unknown. (Frank screams) It's just sort of abhorrent, the thought of facing decisions about that with friends and in front of friends and readers, etc. I'd rather carry out those experiments in other ways.

I've spoken with a lot of people in San Francisco about your problems there and the way they seem to feel is that your work is therapy, not art. By that they mean that it has a function as an interpersonal exploration (Frank giggles) but it doesn't address the concerns they are honestly interested in as part of the current art dialogue, (laughter) whether it be mainstream or "alternative". I explain that the fact that you have an audience means you are doing work that is valuable, but the general feeling is that even if you are an artist and it's art because you say it is, that doesn't mean everybody has to be interested in it or that curators and presenters are obliged to show it. (Frank giggles)

Most feel it doesn't belong in an art gallery but in your own studio or school, with you taking the responsibility yourself. I do agree that erotic play is not concurrent with what's being looked at in art, (laughter) and for many people ...

**Penny:** (shouts) What?!

**Linda continues reading:**

... such performance brings back awful memories of things tried in the '70s that proved to be embarrassing for all concerned. (Frank sounds) The only advantages you gain by showing in a gallery is exposure to their audience and a certain stamp of approval from the space itself. I don't think there's any reason to battle with them if they simply don't want your work in their space. Even if you have them on a technicality, you should just let it go.

I really love you both and feel you are to be congratulated for your courage and determination.

**Frank:** I hate it when they say they love me.

**Penny:** Yeah. Truly.

**Linda continues reading:**

The fact that you have a group of students now and are making something of a living from what you do is phenomenal. (Frank screams) That doesn't mean art presenters and editors are obliged to deal with it, especially if they already have.

**Penny:** You should get a fucking MacArthur [Grant - Ed.].

**Linda continues reading:**

It seems this is a time when you are going to have to carry the burden of presenting yourself in your own sphere, or in places you rent, and not try to force others to present you. I think that's the appropriate way for you to go, and, as you said, reduces the problems and disappointments. I know this is a little bit of a reversal on what I had said about the job of art spaces and about charges of "old-fashioned" and fear of nudity, but having examined my own feelings about coming to the piece in L.A., I have a little more insight into some of the reluctance you come up against. (Frank sounds)

The other thing that bothers people about dealing with you, Frank, is that they are very offended by the way you seem to use your handicap as a kind of force to get your way. In some ways it's interesting to consider that a physically disadvantaged person can actually grab power by using psychological force on others, (Frank yells) but in truth it's a bit unfair.

**Penny:** (screams) What?! This is psychotic! (laughter)

**Linda continues reading:**

You seem to have a compulsion not to take no for an answer under any circumstances, and to use as your weapon other people's reluctance to appear prejudiced. You might want to examine your methods and goals and consider whether your style constitutes undue force, and whether that is acceptable to you.

**Penny:** Undue force?! Slap her!! (laughter)

**Linda continues reading:**

A lot of people have said that it does, and force is unacceptable to most of us.

As far as our relationship goes, I would rather go on being your friend than your helper in the art world. I think my magazine and I have both given you a lot of help ...

**Frank:** I hate when they say that.

**Linda continues reading:**

... have given you a lot of help and would rather not be put on the spot anymore, so in the future, let's just relate as friends. I'd like to hear about your adventures, but I don't want to be involved in the process any more. It's just not interesting enough to me to deal with the struggle. It creates an awful lot of enemies somehow, and that has just as much to do with your attitude as it does with other people's. I am not a soldier, I am a mediator.

I know that this letter will make you want to fire off a rejoinder and shoot my letter full of holes, but that is really going to endanger our friendship. (laughter)

**Penny:** Whoa. This woman is fucked up! (laughter) So she wants to stop being involved with you as an art curator creature/power broker and just wants to be friends, but if you write her a letter telling her how you feel it's going to endanger your friendship!

**Linda:** Exactly.

**Penny:** You know, these people should all kill themselves. (laughter) That's my only response. I'm sorry, I want you to keep reading, but I just want to say that I have spent my entire career making people angry at me who have jobs in the Arts. And one of the things that used to make them really mad at me was I used to say publicly all the time, if you have a paying job in the Arts and you're not in service to artists, then you should kill yourself.

**Frank:** Yes.

**Penny:** That's the beginning and the end of it. You don't have to have more than five brain cells to understand that Frank has developed a tremendous vision in art, first of all under extraordinary circumstances that even somebody who was fully bodily able, blah, blah, blah, blah, blah ... didn't have a million fucking obstacles in their way! (Frank giggles) (laughter) But then, of course this letter was written in '89, now it's 2009, so we're already talking 20 years later, so when somebody consistently makes work over this amount of time ...

**Frank:** I was doing ...

**Linda:** ... he started in the late '60s, so he'd already been going 20 years by the time she wrote this letter.

**Penny:** I know, I understand that. The problem is that we have people like this who, number one, they haven't been doing it that long. (Frank sounds) See what I mean?

**Linda:** Right.

**Penny:** Like I always say, I'm not surprised that I have almost no reviews in America that are even on the level of a first-grade review ... a first grader could give a better review than most of the reviews that I get, because the people don't have the experience and the background to write about my work because my work is grounded in what I was doing in the '60s. And I always say, if you want to look at the work of a, what you call a "sixties artist", then you have to look at their work in the '80s and '90s. You don't look at their work in the sixties. If somebody is a 28-year-old artist right now in 2009, you don't look at their work in 2009, you look at their work in 2029! So what did somebody who is coming into a consciousness of art, right? This arc of development which doesn't exist. I've been talking a lot over the past few years, really calling for a secessionist movement, like the one that was in the 1890s in Vienna, which was the birth of modern art, which was when the artists in Vienna 1895-96 said to academia, we refuse to allow you to say what art is (Frank sounds), and by the way, whatever the fuck your name is ...

**Linda:** Linda.

**Penny:** ... there are six different things I could say at once, I'm so pissed off. (laughter) The reality is that, while academia is a reflection of the art world, it is not and never will be the art world. So anybody in that position, they are not artists. They're not the people making the work. And that is not ... (sighs) (laughter) It's like the people, pick up *Vogue Magazine*, I haven't read it for a while, but I can tell you that if we went to a library or something, and you took a *Vogue Magazine* from July '07, it would be talking about wearing boots, even in the summer time. And it would tell you to be wearing gray (Frank sounds) and that you should be ... it's fashion instead of style. Someone like Frank and yourself, you have developed your own vocabulary, your own language. (sighs) Someone like this does not have the right, at all to ... her letter is so stupid! (Frank giggles) It's so dumb, it's so sophomoric.

**Frank:** What in the fuck is the art dialogue?!

**Linda:** What in the fuck is the art dialogue, when she talks about the current art dialogue.

**Penny:** They're retarded. Honest to God, I'll tell you the truth. About almost ten years ago I started talking about appropriation. I used the word as a put down: oh, they're appropriating this, they're appropriating that. Do you remember Raiza Abdul? Do you know him?

**Linda:** Yeah.

**Penny:** Raiza Abdul. I'd go and see Raiza Abdul's work when he came to New York. And his work made me furious. Because he was the opposite of me. He was all surface and all imagery and there was no content. What he was doing, it didn't matter. And that was his work, and I think it's always important, it's a gift, when you can see somebody who does what you ... when you see an artist whose work is in opposition to what you believe in. That's a very powerful motivating force. It makes you really go, right. And it also brings out a lot in you.

And Raiza Abdul was that for me. And I would say all the time, oh nobody appropriates more images than Raiza Abdul except Madonna! (laughter) I go and I see a piece and, oh my god, that's from Visconti's The Devils and there's the burning book. There's not one original image here. So I talked about appropriation for a long time as a put down, oh this is appropriated, appropriated, appropriated. Oh, I don't want to see one more. Oh, it's like the Wooster group, it's like the junior high school version of the Wooster group doing Richard Foreman. I can't cope. And people would get very mad at me. But I would say, but the art world that I grew up in in the '60s in New York, because there was no money involved, the ability to talk about what you saw was very, was a currency in itself. And people didn't get mad at you when you could read something, and you'd say bop, bop, bop. There was like well what are you going to do, rocks are hard, water's wet, and bop, bop, bop. And then what happened was this academia took over. So after 100 years after the secessionist movement, academia took over again! This letter ... look, all I know is this, I've been performing professionally since 1967 and I'm going to be 59 years old. When I open up an envelope for my Social Security and it tells you how much you're going to get, mine says I'm going to get 280 bucks a month. So, what does that mean? That means that for forty whatever it is, 41 years, that not one not-for-profit venue that I worked in all of these years, not one of them ever threw a buck into my Social Security account. Yet every single one of them have Social Security, health insurance, 401K, paid vacation. Then they want to say to me or to another artist, oh, this is not really currently in the dialogue that we're having with art. (Frank sounds) Or, you know, we can't book you ever! Well, you know, what are you complaining about, you had your chance in the '80s. Whatever! I did a festival last year in New York ...

**Frank:** You talk to the same people ...

**Linda:** You talk to the same people that we talk to!

**Penny:** Right, 'cause they're the only ones that are there and they're all mostly full of shit. But the thing is, artists need ... see this is the thing that's pathetic! The thing that is pathetic is that ... I always say to young artists, there's nowhere to go. You're not going anywhere. There is no there there. There's no money, there's no career. (Frank sounds in agreement) It doesn't exist!

**Frank:** Yes.

**Penny:** One of my things about emerging arts is how dare these universities say to these students that there's a profession called Art when there is no profession. There's no profession! Because if there was a profession, and I'd been performing for 41 years, when I open up my Social Security I'm not getting $260, right! And I've been making ... not only have I been involved in five or six of the biggest movements since 1967, but I'm an adept. People like to see my work. They want to pay to see my work. The public has always wanted to see my work. They have always been in the way of the public getting to see my work.

**Frank:** Yes.

**Penny:** You know, it's all about access. They are gatekeepers.

**Frank:** Yes.

**Penny:** They provide or do not provide the access.

**Frank:** Yes!

**Penny:** So how are you going to have kids ...

**Frank:** Read "Mainstream Avant-garde".

**Penny:** Well, they're so retarded too. People talk about avant-garde, they talk about ... they use avant-garde as an adjective! Oh your work is so avant-garde! What the fuck does that mean?

**Linda:** This is a piece that Frank wrote in 1996. (Linda reads)

> I suppose this is a review of sorts. Two things evoke this review. First Martha Wilson of Franklin Furnace asked me to comment on the Furnace's plans. The second event was our going to a Karen Finley reading [which cost $3 as opposed to $30 for a Finley performance ... Which I could not afford].
>
> I have to start by saying I consider both Wilson and Finley powerful voices of the avant-garde. When other performance galleries were making artists create "acts" that would fit into "avant-garde" cabarets ... fit in terms of both time and fashionable subject matter ... Wilson at the Furnace was giving both artists and the art absolute freedom to perform magic ... until they shut the Furnace down for "fire violations". Karen and I were among the artists who enjoyed this freedom.
>
> In other reviews, I have likened Karen's poetry to Ginsberg's, and her performances to Lenny Bruce's in their intensity and laser commentary on the social injustices. Her poetry makes me cry. Her passions within her performances have transported me into very deep states of reality.
>
> So it is always tragic to see figures like these get sucked, seduced, absorbed, tricked, bribed into "the mainstream". It is tragic not only in personal terms for the individual artists, but in terms of the big picture. When an artist sets herself up as being an artist who goes beyond the normal frame, who tells the hard truths, who explores the unknown ... not to be hip, or controversial, or to be interesting ... but because that is how our tribal human being evolves, so it has to be done ... when that kind of artist then goes after money, personal fame, and/or glamour while still claiming to be doing avant-garde art, it is denying society the real evolutionary function of the real avant-garde. It tells people, audiences and artists alike, that the avant-garde is just a branch of the entertainment complex with the same rules, goals, reality as television, rock music, Hollywood, and sports. This is like telling people a can of Slim Fast is a balanced meal of real food. It is a lie. And the scary dangerous thing is artists are buying/selling this lie.
>
> Why am I on this rant? About a year or two ago, Wilson sent out a mass mailing in which she defended art [maybe to funders] as a profitable industry which pulls money, people, and jobs into cities. [True ... if you want to make a lot of money, buy property where artists live/create now to sell to the yuppies when they discover the area!] This logic is a very steep, slippery slope indeed. The first glaring danger of this commercialized logic is art, according to this logic, which is not profitable or sellable is not and cannot be successful worthwhile art! [Hey, ain't that the

American way?] I am sure Wilson does not believe this.

Although another mass mailing I received from her in November [I have been mulling it over until now] makes me wonder if she has fallen down that slope into believing the lie. Avant-garde art is art that tells the truth, explores the taboos, pushes the limits. Obviously this kind of art, if it is honest, cannot be focused outwardly. Historically, often "the people" [who are not the same thing as "the mainstream"] have identified with the avant-garde because it was telling the truth about their lives. The focus of the avant-garde should always be on telling the truth, not on popularity polls and bottom lines. The focus of the avant-garde has been, and should be, on doing art that is as "pure" as possible ... not on mass media entertainment of reaching as many people as possible by shaping "the product" to that goal.

In her letter, Martha refers to the avant-garde art as "once unpopular work ... formerly at the non-profit fringe" ... art that Franklin Furnace, according to the letter, has groomed for 20 years to get it ready for the mainstream ... and now "Franklin Furnace is in a position to lead the avant-garde into the mainstream ..." This hurts my head and heart. It is as if Martha does not see her own historical contribution of giving daring art a home. Instead, she tries to take credit for gravity and decay. The mainstream entertainment, by it sheer mass, has always sucked artists out of the fringe, the underground. That is just gravity. In reality, it takes a lot to enter, and to stay in, the underground. The underground is where the real freedom and the real ability to change society are to be found. This is why artists choose the underground instead of the mainstream. This is also why, when an artist is pulled into the mainstream, this freedom and ability decay. In my own career, I have worked very hard to stay in the underground ... this work has been hard precisely because some of the pieces have turned out to be "popular" [whatever that means!] ... attracting the mainstream sharks.

The mainstream has always tried to create a fake avant-garde with fake controversies, fake taboos, fake "hipness," etc. to give the marks a controlled fun-ride through a Disneyland to keep them away from the real edge of life. This is because the powers-that-be cannot control or exploit what is in the real avant-garde.

All of this is business as usual ... and doesn't scare me.

What does scare me is that someone like Martha bought into it and is becoming a producer of it! Her letter read like a bad *Saturday Night Live* skit. She is selling Franklin Furnace to get money to match a $100,000 N.E.A. Challenge grant. With this money, and by teaming up with the corporate and media America, Franklin Furnace will be a "content provider for new media" that sniffs out "emerging alternative artists". [Emerging from where to where? Alternative to what?]

**Penny:** That's my line: emerging from where to where?!

**Linda continues reading:**

These artists and their art must be suitable to be packaged as "alternative comedy

*Linda Mac, Frank Moore and Penny Arcade (video capture)*

[A.K.A. Performance art.]" The letter tells us this new alternative comedy will be "funny, yet provocative". There will be a half-hour TV show of this. Plus they will produce short pieces to be aired "through" *Saturday Night Live* [as if that show has been cutting edge, or even funny, in the past 15 years] and MTV [with its history of censorship!] Moreover they are seeking other ways of giving "audiences a glimpse of the avant-garde world" [whatever the hell that is!] "in an entertaining and easily consumable fashion" ... like avant-garde artist trading cards ... funded by Philip Morris companies!

**Frank:** I did not make this up!

**Linda continues reading:**

> The marketing phrase "alternative comedy [A.K.A. performance art]" is very damaging to performance art because it trivializes art. In fact it avoids "art" all together, selling "alternative comedy" as a weird, consumable form of entertainment which will give you a laugh for your buck. This is not what performance art is. Performance art is the performing/doing/experiencing the act of art. It is going on a physical journey into the unlimited realm of art. Sometimes this journey may be funny or entertaining. But these are not the true goals or rewards. The suggestion [promotion] that these are the rewards of art results in denying people, including the artists, the real full freeing experience of art.

All of this is selling the art, the artists, and the audience way short. I am not questioning Martha's personal commitment to the real avant-garde art. But realistically such art cannot exist in such an environment that she is envisioning. Moreover it is misunderstanding the new media such as the internet and zines. In these media, artists can relate to their audiences directly without middlemen, without compromises, without limiting concepts such as "mainstream" ... all for very little money ... so why sell out?

But this concept of "alternative comedy" is disturbing. I guess the Karen Finley reading was an example of alternative comedy. She read from her parody of Martha Stewart [why bother?] which she obviously wrote just to fulfill a book deal. The reading was empty shtick, a passionless exercise in cleverness with no content or message. The audience responded with reflex laughter, like a laugh track. The problem was Karen was trying to be an entertainer, a comedian. Karen is not a comedian or entertainer. That is not her function. Her function is to inspire, confront, transmute ... to tell the truth with passion. That is why people come to her. When she does not do that, the people are not fulfilled. When she ended her act, the people just sat there numb. Then I asked Karen (Frank shrieks) to read her very deep, very moving poem "Black Sheep" ... I just happened to have a copy of it with me. (Frank laughs) As she read it, magic, life, and power started flowing through her body and out into the audience, uplifting them. When she finished reading, people stood up and clapped ... because this was why they came.

Oh, by the way, do you consider yourself mainstream? Do you want to be?

**Penny:** When was that written in?

**Linda:** 1996.

**Penny:** Well, I mean the thing is that I don't know, one of the nights, I don't know if you were there, I say different stuff different nights, but one of the nights I said, "Any artist that thinks that they're successful because they're talented is deluded."

**Frank:** Yes.

**Penny:** Karen got a tremendous amount of access and Karen did a lot of good work, but all people stop developing at the point where they get the juice. That's reality. (Frank sounds) And the best thing that can happen to somebody is that they don't get any attention 'til they get over that desire for the approval. Not that it ever completely goes away, but when you have more loyalty to your work than you have to this other thing. And let's face it, that whole fucking art scene is a popularity contest! They can not handle ... they can't handle anybody original. They can't handle anybody with a point of view. They're terrified by ...

**Frank:** She always was freaked out because I was not ...

**Linda:** ... going after fame. It made her very uncomfortable. And she would want to, she'd want to get Frank to explain it to her. But, she ...

**Penny:** Yeah, but these people are pathetic!! (laughter) They're pathetic! And the thing is I have been ... this is one of the things that I identified so much with when I was reading the broadside of the NYU lecture because they hate me! They hate me! And then they especially hated me because I did get to do my work in Europe where a few really intelligent reviewers could really write about the work. I have been completely dismissed and my work has been completely scorned. And the fact that I created a lot of work was seen as a sign that ... they always had something to say either that I wasn't a "real artist"...

**Frank:** Like me.

**Penny:** ... or that I was ... they had a million things to say about me. I never have gotten a grant. I could never, like even in 1984 when I was 34, I couldn't get an Emerging Arts grant, because they said I wasn't an emerging artist because I was a Warhol superstar. Like I was 19 years old. I wasn't even doing my own work then. And then the N.E.A., people that worked for the N.E.A. told me for years that I needed to get to know the people on the panels (Frank sounds) because they really thought my work deserved to be funded, but the people on the panels had to know me! What does that mean?! What you mean they have to know me?! That's their job to go out and see who the artists are! Now, in New York, I did my work for 20 years at PS 122 always in a kind of opposition with Mark Russell.

**Linda:** He wouldn't book us, Mark Russell. He would send his flunkies to see Frank perform at Franklin Furnace ...

**Penny:** Oh, he's too scared, he would never!

**Linda:** But he wouldn't book us. And Frank talked to him for years, kind of negotiating something.

**Penny:** Yeah.

**Frank:** Except in Cleveland.

**Linda:** Yeah, the guy who booked for Scott somebody, I can't remember his name now. This was like in the '70s and '80s.

**Penny:** Scott at The Kitchen!

**Frank:** Yes.

**Penny:** He's the guy that said that my work had too much content! (laughter)

**Linda:** Well, he selected Frank to perform at the Cleveland Performance Art Festival, but he's the one, I think we told you that. He said I won't book him at my ... at The Kitchen ... because I'm personally uncomfortable with his work. Even though I think it's very important work and it should be seen. So he booked him in Cleveland because he wasn't going to be there when Frank performed.

**Penny:** Yeah, but see, I mean, I did a festival last year in New York called the Globesity Festival. That money was given to me by an Australian venture capitalist who had used fasting to control an autoimmune illness that he had and he wanted to do a film about fasting and he wanted to have a B role for the film which would have been ... he gave me a certain amount of money ... where artists would fast for ten days on juice. And then they would make a piece about over-consumption. And I had a panel called "Who is not for Profit, the Artist is not for Profit", and I called Martha from Franklin Furnace and put her on the panel and I did all this shit on the emerging arts because she's one of the people who was an architect of the emerging art thing! Her and Mark Russell, they were all over that. And now a lot of artists who are my age can't get booked in New York. Mark Russell does his Under The Radar Festival. You can't get booked in it. I have to send you a video of my show, *New York Values*, which is all about fragmentation. The show just falls apart through the whole show. (Frank giggles) And it's a show about failure. Naturally I say to the audience, I said, I ran into Karen Finley at a party and I told her I was doing a show about failure. And she said, you're not a failure, Penny! You're not a failure! You're not a failure! And (laughter) ...

**Frank:** But I want to be!

**Penny:** Yeah, well the thing is there's something called ... the Japanese have a concept which is called the nobility of failure. That if your heart is in the right place, and your mind is in the right place, and you fail, it is more powerful than winning.

**Frank:** Yes.

**Penny:** But I wanted to say about the avant-garde. In *New York Values*, I say that Gertrude Stein addressed Oxford University in 1917 and she said the avant-garde is in opposition to academia. As soon as academia accepts something, it is no longer avant-garde. Beginning, end of the story.

**Frank:** Yes.

**Penny:** And right now what's happened is a lot of these people, first of all they're destroying the audience because the audience ... see Mark Russell wouldn't book you because he thinks that people are not going to come to see a person with cerebral palsy in a wheelchair. He does not allow the audience, he will not allow that to happen. Like, OK, let's say only three people show up. He won't allow that to happen because he's concerned with his own failure. I just think it is something quite remarkable that in the sixties that would never have happened. There was an element ...

**Frank:** Even when I packed Franklin Furnace.

**Linda:** And Martha was telling him he should book Frank. She was telling him and Scott. And they still wouldn't do it.

**Penny:** Yeah. Well I think people ... look, there's a certain shock value that has always been in one corner of the performance art scene. Shock sells, you know. But besides that ... I just have a tremendous resentment towards these people as gatekeepers. The way *Bitch! Dyke! Faghag! Whore!* came about. I got to tell you this 'cause you'll laugh. Mark Russell booked me in 1985 because Ethel Eichelberger saw me perform and called Mark up and said I was a genius and you have to book her, she's a genius, before anybody else books her. So Mark ... Ethel apparently did a fantastic sales job on me and Mark was all excited. You know, a former Warhol superstar, blah, blah, blah. So I go there. He's offering me two weekends which in 1985 this might as well been a month or two months, because it was a one night stand, right. I go over and he starts asking me about the Factory. He goes, you know, I don't know anything about the Factory ... what was it like being at the Factory with Andy Warhol? (Frank sounds) And I said it was boring! (laughter)

**Frank:** Notice I never asked you about that.

**Penny:** Yeah, yeah, yeah. So he's asking me, I told him it was boring and then he started to get very defensive with me. When he started getting defensive, I started getting mad. (Frank giggles) Then he took away, he took one of the weekends off the table. (Frank sounds, laughter) So I went and did the performance, and it was four nights that were all improvised because all my original work was just improvisation, it was just performance, there was no ... I would have like five ideas ...

**Linda:** That's what Frank does.

**Penny:** ... and I'd go on stage with the ideas and make something from the ideas. So I put an ad in the paper, you know, a quarter-page ad. Because there were a lot of people who knew me as a performer when I was 17, 18, 19, 20. People don't usually forget the name Penny Arcade. I felt an obligation to have an audience. So we had like about 100 people every night, which was very unusual at that time. Like a full house would be like 40 people or something like that. And at the end of it I said to Mark, I said, well, I'd like to do this show again in the fall. And he goes, well, you've got to do a new show! (Frank sounds) I said, but it was completely improvised. (laughter) And he's like, yeah, you have to do a new show. Then I said to him, I said, did I get any press? And he said, press? You didn't get any press! I said, why not? And he said, people were very offended by your advertising! I was like, they're offended because I advertised?! And he goes, yes! That was '85, then '86, '87, '88, he never would book me. '89 there was a big financial crash and the whole thing with the N.E.A. started to happen. All of a sudden they weren't getting the money, there was no money. (Frank giggles) And it was August and he asked me to do August (Frank sounds) because Eric Bogosian was going on vacation. Because Eric Bogosian would do August to develop his work to do then in the bigger venues. I went and I did the show, also all improvised. And then that was '89. Then, in 1990, I called him up and said, hey, I'd like to work on some new material. He goes, we're completely booked up for two years. I said, wow, you're completely booked up for two years! And what happened was that in '86 Karen Finley had told me there was going to be a big benefit at PS 122, they had them all the time. And that she had been talking to Mark, and Karen at that time was a big fan of mine. (Frank giggles) And she told me that Mark said I was going to be on the benefit. So I ... I didn't hear anything. So I called him up and I said, Karen Finley told me that she was talking to you and that you were going to have me in the benefit. There's 60 people in this benefit! 60! He goes, well, Penny, we discussed having you on the benefit, but we decided against it! And I said, decided against it?! There's 60 people performing, there's no room for me?! (laughter) And he goes, well you know we've done things with you in the past. (Frank sounds) And I said, Mark, I hope that you're saying a novena to Saint Jude that I'm never going to be successful, 'cause I'm going to fuck with you. And he got all freaked out because he's middle class. I'm working class (laughter) and to me this is not a particularly big thing to ... I didn't understand that you can't say something like this to middle class people because they take offense. I was just trying to be direct. And I did not perform there again all those years. So then in '89 he had me there 'cause Annie Hamburger had booked me for her En Garde Arts Festival. And she had come ... I was performing in a venue called the Ballroom that was like where people like Peggy Lee and people like that would perform. And the guy was willing to have me there at 11 o'clock on Thursday nights because I would bring in an

*Frank Moore and Penny Arcade (video capture)*

audience. And Annie Hamburger came to see me there and she's like, I don't understand why you're performing here. And I said because nobody downtown will book me. And she goes, oh, you're just paranoid!

**Linda:** They always tell us that ... they always say we're paranoid when we say that!

**Penny:** No, I said, The Kitchen won't book me. I mean that guy Scott, I ran, after Mark wouldn't let me do the show again, I booked the place ... it's 100 seats above the 7A Café. I ran four days a week for four and a half months. So I called The Kitchen and I said, hi, I'm Penny Arcade and I want to invite you to see my work. And the guy says, well, actually I was there last weekend. I said, really! Silence! I go, oh, I think by your silence must mean you didn't like my show. He goes, it's not my cup of tea. He goes, but you were packed! And I said, yeah, I said, luckily, not everybody has the same taste as you apparently. (laughter) And then another guy who worked at The Kitchen, I was in something that was at The Kitchen, somebody else's work, and I was talking to the guy who was one of the co-people there. And I said, I was in the show, it was a total piece of shit, I said, this is such a piece of shit, but apparently it has no problem getting booked here. And the guy says yeah. And I said, well I called up Scott 'cause I would like to be booked here ... he went, Penny don't bother. He goes, your work has too much content for The Kitchen. And I was like, too much content?! And he goes, yeah, way too much content. And I was like, OK, that is really fascinating. So then in 1990 I called Mark and I said, I've some new stuff I'd like to work on. And he goes, oh we're completely booked for two years. Like, two years?! And he goes, yeah. And I said, oh, that's too bad I have a new show called *Bitch! Dyke! Faghag! Whore!*. It was completely made up. I just made it up in the moment. And he went, what?! And I said, yeah, *Bitch! Dyke! Faghag! Whore!.* And he goes, don't give it to anybody else! (Linda groans) And that's the secret history of where that came from. But the thing is, now I take it as a complete badge of honor because none of these people would really book me. I kept P.S. 122 open in 1992 for the summer they had no money to stay open. They had a 25th anniversary, they didn't even allow me, I was not ... they wanted me to be on the committee, on the committee, where they put your name on the committee. And I had spoken to Lucy Sexton. I wrote her a very long email from Australia. And I said, look, it's imperative that I perform at this benefit, the 25th anniversary. I've done twenty years of work there. I said, I know that I created a substantial part of your audience base. I find it hard to believe that there's no place for me to perform or present or introduce. And in the end it turned out that what they wanted me to do was be on the committee and that meant that I was supposed to sell five tickets for $250 each! (Frank & Linda groan) It was humiliating. And then that was where I got off the bus. It was very ... it's very interesting but I think that ... and I talk about this, 'cause I lecture at art schools, NYU, and I just tell the truth. The thing is that I will continue to make work because that's what I do. You will continue to make work because that is what you do. And all these people will fade away. They will fade away.

**Linda:** Right.

**Penny:** And as Quentin Crisp said to me, "Not to worry Miss Arcade. Time is kind to the non-conformist." And that's what you're up against. The great Jack Smith said, the art world thinks that it loves art but the art world hates art. And its only real response to real art is to destroy it. And the more tragedy that some person with a lot of essence has, the more they dangle that person in front of the public, because it increases the vampire thrill. And that's a reality. And there's a reason why in bohemia ... as a child in the sixth grade, a lot of the stories in my six grade reading book were by people who couldn't pay their rent 100 years before. O'Henry, Edgar Allen Poe, Guy de Maupassant. In *New York Values*, which is an autopsy on the death of bohemia, I question: Why is there always 100 years between the work of bohemia and being able to earn a living? And you will continue. You will ... people are looking for authenticity. Jack Smith said, people pay a lot of money to go to art school and then they find they're not being taught iota by iota how to make art. And then they find out that they're going to have to become apprentices. 'Cause that's the only way. I see people all the time that worked with me, shot video for me, whatever, they work with me for a year or something then they come and go, all my friends think you're a genius, but nobody can figure out why you're not getting a deal. (Frank sounds) And then they go and then they're going to do it.

**Frank:** We are ...

**Linda:** We are running out of time for the show, so we have to wrap it. So shall we say ... you are Penny Arcade!

**Penny:** I'm Penny Arcade, all day long and all night long. (laughter) This is Frank Moore all day long, all night long.

**Frank:** One of the best!

**Linda:** Penny is one of the best!

**Penny:** Thanks, one of the best! (laughter) We have so much in common. I found it very supportive and very something that holds you up, to read what you think. And I hope that you find it also equally supportive.

**Frank:** Yes.

**Penny:** And to hold you up to say, we're going to fucking survive. Because we have authenticity.

**Frank:** I have a funny story about The Kitchen ...

**Linda:** Oh yeah. So what are we doing? Are we saying goodnight to the audience now? OK. Goodnight!

**Penny:** Goodnight!

# Gerald Smith & Tracy James

## Slave Revolt Radio

Recorded July 1, 2001 on luver.com

Gerald Smith and Tracy James were co-hosts of the music, news and commentary program, Slave Revolt Radio, which was broadcast live on the infamous pirate radio station, Free Radio Berkeley, 104.1fm.

Gerald Smith is a former Black Panther, a political commentator and DJ on Berkeley Liberation Radio, which began as Free Radio Berkeley. Gerald also ran as a candidate for Treasurer of California with the Peace and Freedom Party in 2006.

Frank first met Gerald when his crew videotaped a political conference for LUVeR, Frank's internet station. Once he learned that Gerald did a show on Free Radio Berkeley, Frank asked if he could replay the show on LUVeR. Over the years Gerald hosted several different shows on LUVeR including Slave Revolt Radio, Radical Perspectives and a reggae music show, Grass Roots Revolution. He also was co-producer and co-host of several Shaman's Den shows, which included a panel on the Oscar Grant killing and a show about the Richmond Tent City protest with organizers and community leaders.

**Gerald:** Now there's problems, obviously, lack of resources, etc., etc., but very often our optimism is confirmed when it comes to these people that Tracy's talking about, these FOX idiots. Remember if you never watch that stuff, please don't start watching it! It's not even worth your criticism. But if you must, you can check them out and you'll see. I'll never forget when Tracy started talking about it I started ... just looking at the thing with the little child, what was his name?

**Tracy:** Which one?

**Gerald:** The little Cuban child.

**Tracy:** Oh, Elian. [Gonzalez - Ed.]

**Gerald:** That Elian thing. Oh my goodness! And what they did, you can count on it. You know, these kind of right-wing idiots will go too far, make fools of themselves, discredit themselves and alienate thinking people. And that's what they did. I was so happy! Because they were pumping it up. They were putting that stuff up every day! Going all Cuba this, Cuba that, Cuba, Cuba, Cuba. And it's so simple. A child's mother takes him, they die in transit, father wants the child to come back home. What's the big deal?! They just clown and make such idiots of themselves. I'm glad! I'm very happy that they made idiots of themselves. I could not have paid them to do a better job.

**Tracy:** But it would have been better if like ... you see part of the problem is, one, we have a very chauvinistic society where if issues aren't brought home to them, i.e. where they're feeling the pain, often when it's another nation, Yugoslavia, whatever, it's easy for them to just go off into another subject, even when the state and its little allies contradict themselves. So what I'm saying is is that FOX News is still a highly respected show amongst the American population. Where issues like this should have discredited, in a real thinking population, but the population has been somewhat Gumpified down to the point where ...

**Frank:** How?

**Linda:** How did that happen?

**Tracy:** Well it's happened on several fronts. One, you have a situation where, the history of this country has had dramatic dividing seeds on race, gender and special preference towards the ruling elite economically-advanced classes. And this has allowed them to exploit these issues and turn issues which should be relevant in the minds of many people across the spectrum of the working class, but it's dumbed them down. So now you have many right wingers who have made good movies, or documentaries like say on the Waco thing, and when I hear them talk in various milieus, they act as if this is the first time this has ever happened. The concept of the MOVE house. Because what often happens, the black people, it's like the canary and the mine, what they may do to us a decade, two decades earlier they often will do it to the masses of population down the road. But if you are so gripped up in your own little ideology and your own little caste, color, code and all of that, that you can't see that this was a class attack that was happening against the MOVE house, and then they've already got a precedent. Then they're able to smash and attack people who try to come out and argue against those, i.e. Mumia Abu-Jamal. But you're still blinded by the color thing. So then you end up aligning yourself with the state, the police, in their attack against Mumia and other dissenting voices. And then low and behold, boom, they're doing it to you and your neighborhood down the road.

**Gerald:** That's right. That's right.

**Tracy:** Well see, these type of things have helped polarize, demonize portions of the population, and Gumpified the population in a way that other countries that are industrialized could only be envious of. I'm talking about the ruling elite class. Because they would want the masses of their people as pacified and as confused and as materialistic, so easy tuned into things like sports so quick. But that's part of the whole Gumpification process. And also there hasn't been a strong enough working-class structure that could act independently, create its own independent news outlets. In other words, when Fred Douglass and them did basically what we are doing now back in the day, *The North Star* printing press, that was the voice of the abolitionist movement. But that should have continued on. That thing should have just continued on to the point where we continue to have a large ear of the masses of people, developed, conscious people speaking out of it to give an alternative to what's going on now. But with a lot of the set-backs that have happened, certain contradictions in the working-class structure on race and gender lines and stuff like that we don't have an independent, working-class voice that reaches the masses in the same way that you see in South Africa. So the working class, by and large, does not have a regular voice, independent voice that it can hear. This is what we're building for now. But this has had a devastating effect on the consciousness.

*Tracy James and Gerald Smith (video capture)*

**Gerald:** U-hmmm.

**Frank:** Even someone like me don't know what I should.

**Linda:** Even someone like you doesn't know what you should.

**Frank:** Like I just found out May Day ...

**Linda:** Oh, was based on the events that happened in the United States.

**Gerald:** U-hmmm.

**Linda:** We had this impression that it was something that happened like in Europe or somewhere else.

**Gerald:** Well, it gets celebrated in Europe today, but not in the United States!

**Linda:** Right.

**Gerald:** And by the way, just for the sake of our listeners. I want to make sure you get, and when I say get, I mean fully comprehend what Tracy's saying here. When we talk about Gumpification process, that's a word that we developed. What it actually is referring to is the film. There was a film called *Forrest Gump* about this poor fellow who went through all these experiences. But what the movie was really telling people is, it doesn't matter how smart you are. It doesn't matter how rich you are. If you're just a good boy. And you just go along in life, everything will work out for you in the end. And remember he got the shrimp ship and his buddy gave him a ... So that film was a real watershed in American culture. So, when we talk about Gumpification, that's what we're referring to. So people, understand the head-fixing that goes on. And boy, have we been fixed as a people!

**Frank:** We have a friend who thinks of himself as a liberal. He ...

**Linda:** ... well, he's very, very uncomfortable with what we do with LUVeR. Even though ... he has a lot of money, and we don't have any. So, for Frank's birthday he'll give us $100 for LUVeR. Yet, if we tell him about the content of the stuff we do, he gets really uncomfortable. And he'll make comments like, well of course you're having a hard time getting money! People don't want to hear the stuff you're talking about. And he's not kidding! He doesn't want to hear it. It makes him real uncomfortable. And he thinks he's like ... you know, he thinks he knows what's going on.

**Gerald:** Well he does, within a certain small circle. That's that atomization process that they put us through. They break us off into individuals, small cliques, families. And we don't really know what each other is doing. And this is the perfect situation for them. Because as we begin to come together, and we will, you can believe me. I don't know what the result is. I wouldn't dare to try to predict what the immediate result's going to be. But they're coming at us so hard right now, it's kind of ... you know ... that's why, once again, our historical optimism. It's not a dull-witted kind of just rah, rah, rah kind of stuff. They won't leave us alone. They're going to make you fight! They're going to make you fight! I was thinking about this poor woman in Idaho. I know I hope the listeners, if you read the papers you may have seen. They had a situation where the lady was arrested for child neglect, felony child neglect. And when she was arrested for child neglect ... her husband had died and she was arrested. And the kids decided they were not going to be split up and sent to a foster home. So these six children, they got their weapons out, they sicced their dogs on the sheriffs and they just said no you ain't taking us! The hell with y'all. Well, people should know, here's a follow-up for that story. According to the newspaper of record, this is *The New York Times,* the mother was freed in the Idaho case. What it was is the judge decided that they did not have sufficient evidence to charge this woman with felony neglect. It's true the house was not clean, that there were mice in the house, and even some maggots, which I think is rather tragic, is not good. Of course we don't want to have maggots where we live or with children there. That does not make her someone who does not love her damn children. This is madness! The way these child protective agency people go on and abuse their authority so much. It's terrible! Who can you trust? It's just good to see that she's out of jail. And I think that thing is going to take a positive ... you know what it really is about? They like to desensitize us to each other so that we don't sympathize. You're white, I'm not worried about what happens to you. Because 400 years ago your ancestors might have enslaved mine. Or you're from Mexico. What the hell you doing here taking my job?! Blah, blah, blah, blah. They got us going on like that. And it's very sad, but they do. But here's a situation where this woman deserved nothing but sympathy. Her husband ... they were living on a trust. They had to sell their house because they ran out of money because the husband died of a disease, like multiple sclerosis was it?

**Tracy:** Yeah.

**Gerald:** I forget exactly what, but he died. So, what's the answer?! It's very simple! The woman should have been placed on some sort, form of welfare and helped! And also, when people, your loved ones die, people get depressed and they go into phases where they don't clean up. You get in a funk, you don't do nothing, you know. They want to lock up people like this! What kind of country are we living in, y'all?! Come on! We can do better than this. We can do better than this.

**Tracy:** As far as some of the liberal contradictions, like you're talking about you guys' friend, part of that is like a fear factor.

**Gerald:** That's right.

**Tracy:** Because as far as people wanted to really know about these subjects, let's take the case where recently two reporters who got a contract with FOX News to do an exposé on Monsanto for FOX News. They did the report, they completed it. They found out very interesting information that not only every person would be interested in if they have a brain, because this is what they may be consuming! (Gerald giggles) Products from cattle, whether they're in the form of cheese, milk or just eating beef in particular. But especially mothers would be concerned about the effects of bovine growth hormones. And what other nations have found is that the insulin growth factor, when you put BGH into cows, the insulin growth factor proliferates in your bodies. And this is what proliferates cancer cells. Now this doesn't mean you will get cancer. It just increases your probability of getting cancer. So Monsanto found out about this report coming out by these two reporters. They knew they couldn't challenge it intellectually. So then they threatened FOX and then FOX comes to them and doesn't just say cut it or cut parts of it, but then they want them to out and out lie. So the reporters refused to do that.

**Gerald:** Good for them.

**Tracy:** They get fired. Then, they take FOX News to court and win in court. Now we did a thing, I call it "Ventures in Corporate Media Land". And that goes into segments where I know the masses of people would be interested in these topics, but the corporate media structure does not. And this is just not some bad conservatives conspiring, let's keep this thing from coming out. This is liberals also involved in it. Because both ideologies have an alignment and an agreement with the way the modes of corporate capital, financial institutions within this society should be run. And that is based off of a capitalist model. And things that expose the fact that we live in a society that puts capital finance over human life and human health contradict that. And they don't want that stuff out. So there are many liberals and many liberal mothers who would be absolutely thankful if they could have found out that information by these reporters. And that's what liberals like your friend know. That we would be taking them and saying, uh huh, see these are the contradictions in having this type of ideology that you have. And there's a fear factor amongst many liberals that they are going to lose their rank. That they'll be walking away from the Democratic Party, the lesser-of-two-evil concept and into a thing that has more alignment with humanity.

**Gerald:** There's also just cowardly, willful blindness plays a role too. You know, some people just would not be able to continue to support and publicize the illusions in this system if they constantly were being bombarded with basic truth or things like this biogenetic who'sits-name scared me to death. And I probably eat more of it than anybody else and don't even know it! They don't put the labels on the food!

**Frank:** In 1968 Vietnam was close to signing a peace treaty and Nixon ...

**Linda:** ... oh, the thing where Nixon approached them and said that if you don't sign, make this peace agreement now with the Democrats, that we'll offer you a better deal after the election. And they did that. And so Humphrey lost.

**Frank:** LBJ was b-u ...

**Linda:** ... and LBJ was bugging Nixon, so he knew about all this. So then the question was, well, why don't you just tell everybody what's going on? But there was that thing where everybody's kind of in it together.

**Gerald:** Yeah!

**Linda:** And so even though he was the one that was being screwed, he didn't tell anybody.

**Gerald:** A good point. You know, another example, just like that, very similar, is the Vice President Mr. Gore, who ran for president ...

**Linda:** Right, exactly!

**Gerald:** Clearly there was some very serious irregularities in the election processes. Not just Florida, but throughout the south. Turning people away from the polls, claiming that people had criminal records when, in fact, there was no fact that they had ever broken the law. It was bad. I found it personally very depressing, to be honest myself. But I noticed they sent Jesse Jackson out there and he went to Florida, they had a demonstration 50,000 people. That's a fairly large demonstration. It looks like there's something could have happened. And the Democratic Party made a political decision to pull him back! To pull Jackson out of that situation and, subsequently, Mr. Gore was shamefully, I think, I don't know the word, I don't want to say cooperative? Forgivefull? Or whatever. It's just that he did not want people to get hip to the system as a whole. He said, look, that's it. That's enough. It's getting out of hand. And it's better that even if I don't win, let's not have people opening their eyes to the nature of this situation here.

**Tracy:** He made a, I guess, logically, alignment with the system and the state. If you look at the fact that when some of the black people in black congress, or whatever they call themselves ...

**Gerald:** Black caucus.

**Tracy:** ... stood up and wanted some support either from him or some of the Senators because they needed one person to say OK, let's do an investigation. None of them did it. And then Gore gaveled them down.

**Gerald:** Not one!

**Tracy:** This is very similar to the Compromise Act in the 1800s when there was a deal made over some of the voting aspects against the Democrats and Republicans over OK we'll pull out of the South ...

*Tracy James (video capture)*

**Gerald:** Oh, the end of reconstruction, right.

**Tracy:** ... we'll pull our troops out of the South. Let you guys just wreak havoc on the negros. And then you go ahead and let our guy become president. So you have that type of consolidation in amongst the two factions of the bourgeois party and they end up defending the state.

**Frank:** Yes. We saw a movie about that period.

**Tracy:** Oh, OK.

**Gerald:** Was it *Freedom Road*?

**Linda:** Yeah. With Mohammad Ali.

**Gerald:** Excellent film! (Frank screeches) Do you know who wrote it?

**Linda:** No.

**Gerald:** Howard Fast. One of the guys who was blacklisted from Hollywood in the '50s during the McCarthy period. He wrote, there's actually a book called *Freedom Road*. And he wrote that book. A very, very good film. Our listeners, you know what, you can acquire that film at a video shop. Do yourself a favor, give yourself a little treat and check that out.

**Linda:** It's a long movie.

**Gerald:** Yeah, it's long ... but it's interesting and engaging.

**Linda:** I mean long in a good way. (all laugh)

**Gerald:** The industry standard is 90 minutes, man. You go 94 minutes you got to take them to court or something.

**Frank:** We ran a video about the vote scam.

**Linda:** Yeah. What was that guy's name that wrote that book?

**Frank:** It was five years before this election.

**Linda:** And he wrote this book, *Vote Scam*, which exposed everything. And they showed videos of him and his crew going into these voting places. And the people were just punching out the ballots and then sticking them in the thing. And they had it all on video tape and they're talking to the people, all these older women sitting there kind of smiling and punching the ballots.

**Gerald:** Oh, that's so sad.

**Frank:** Under Clinton.

**Gerald:** Oh yeah, oh yeah! You talking about Master Clinton.

**Linda:** Yeah.

**Gerald:** We call him Crime Bill Clinton. (laughter) That's what we like to call him.

**Frank:** That is why Gore couldn't do anything.

**Linda:** Because he's part of that whole thing.

**Gerald:** Guilty! Yeah! See old Frank is on that one, alright!

**Tracy:** They're more interested in defending their institution. They know their institutions are deceitful, are corrupt. They use those practices all the time. Look at the Supreme Court. You had one of these Supreme Court justices that, back in the day in the sixties, one of his roles was to fly down to Arizona and try to intimidate people from voting. Now, various activists have come forth and said that they had to set up an operation to stop these guys' actions from intimidating latin and black people from voting. Going up to them while they're in line. Do you have the right to vote? Are you documented? Are you this and that? And that's not when you're supposed to do these types of things.

**Gerald:** No!

**Tracy:** You had Supreme Court justices complain when they thought that Gore won saying, now I won't be able to retire from the bench because Gore's won. A Democrat has won. All of these contradictions. And in a civilized society with a civilized institution of information, i.e. media center that reaches the masses, these types of contradictions would have been explored. There would have been hearings. These people would have been called.

**Gerald:** Dealt with on some level!

**Tracy:** But see, they don't want to expose this. They don't want to develop this. They don't want to give an historical background on the longevity of this type of stuff. They don't want to bring in the authors like the one that you said because people then would start to draw the lines. Instead what they want to do is chase Clinton around and see ...

**Mikee:** James Collier.

**Linda:** They killed him.

**Gerald:** What?!

**Linda:** Shortly after this interview we saw, it was on a public access channel, that's where this tape was from. He took over a major Miami newspaper. He was from Miami. And he had plans on the big opening day of having these three stories that were going to expose the whole voting system in Miami ...

**Mikee:** The mafia corruption.

**Frank:** And expose Janet Reno.

**Linda:** And it was the day before it was supposed to go to press, he took deathly ill and died. It was like, boom, he just died. (Frank screeching) And so the paper never happened, the story never broke.

**Tracy:** That was convenient.

**Linda:** Yeah!

**Gerald:** But even when they do allow a certain amount of information to leak out about how rotten their politics are and how dishonorable they are as people, an example being the following: Mr. Clarence Thomas, who's a Supreme Court judge, should have and could have recused himself from the decision on the voting in Florida on the following basis. His wife is an employee for the Heritage Foundation! Now, I don't know, brothers and sisters, you may not have ever heard of the Heritage Foundation. I'm tempted to say don't even look them up, but I'll tell you what it is. It's an ultra right-wing think tank. They helped to produce the book, *The Bell Curve*, for instance. They're full, just infested with Nazis and they kind of do all these little right-wing intellectual projects, you know what I mean? And his wife works for them! In fact, her job was helping to coordinate the Republican vote.

**Tracy:** She's a consultant.

**Gerald:** A consultant, alright. Excuse me. But she was working with the Republicans.

**Tracy:** Oh, with them.

**Gerald:** Is this somebody that's neutral in an election? You're working and are getting paid to hustle votes. Come on, man! How dishonorable can you be? So clear! But where does a worker go that connects the dots on that issue? Where can he turn?

**Frank:** If it happens in Africa we would use it as an excuse to go in.

**Tracy:** And discount the election. (Frank sounds) Even when the elections are legit. Like when in Angola, Savimbi, the CIA asset, thug, henchman who, if you read the book, *In Search of*

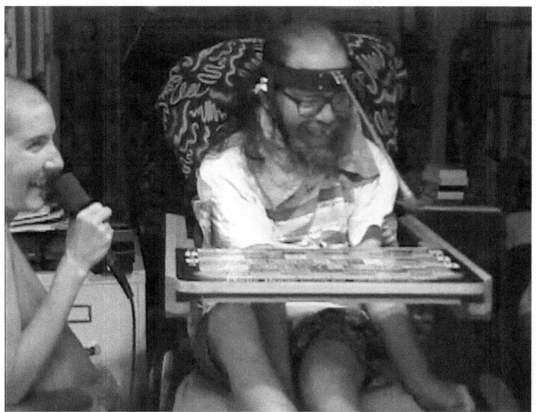

*Linda Mac and Frank Moore (video capture)*

*Enemies* by John Stockwell, goes into Savimbi and other people's role within the CIA. He was the high CIA ranking official who worked to destabilize Angola at the time. But when the Angolan government and people finally said to Savimbi, who was constantly raging a war against the population, OK, let's have an election. The U.N., other bodies, international bodies, came down, they had it. The U.N., other international bodies said it was a free and fair election. Savimbi lost. What do they do? They ignored it. Kept on with Savimbi. Savimbi goes back to war. Or you look at Haiti. Haiti had a person, Aristide who was running under Liberation Theology program which basically people should at least be able to live somewhat like human beings. So we'll have a minimum wage, we'll have a form of Social Security, child labor laws. Well, Nestlé's chocolate, Spaulding baseball, Mickey Mouse who were all over there exploiting the masses of people, were upset about this. But Aristide won. He got 67% of the vote. The candidate that the U.S. backed only got 13%. What was the U.S. response? Well they started to fund the CIA to help build an opposition group which in turn ended up being a group called FRAPH, a terrorist group led by Emmanuel Constant. So, Emmanuel Constant and this terrorist group end up performing a coup and running Aristide out of the country, making it then stable for the U.S. corporations to have their maximum exploitative regime and profit modes back in place. This is the way the U.S. empire works. Now when you have a situation leading back to the media system where Mickey Mouse, i.e. Disney owns ABC, well it's not too much of a surprise when you don't hear this type of information through those networks. So these are the types of contradictions that exist. And now Mickey Mouse owns hundreds of radio broadcasts throughout the country. So they pay off these politicians. The politicians change and sabotage the telecommunication laws and make it therefore even more possible to intensify the Gumpification process on the masses of working-class people throughout this country.

**Frank:** My friend, Jim Fallows, wrote a book about how journalists are now cozy with the government.

**Linda:** He wrote the book a bunch of years ago, didn't he?

**Frank:** Yes. He was the editor of *U.S. News and World Report.*

**Linda:** Yeah, he got a job, which was a big deal, that someone like him got this job. It didn't last long. They booted him pretty quick. Because he went in there and he was really thinking it shouldn't be that way.

**Tracy:** Right. Well we see that when you go against the grain or cross the line, i.e. like Gary Webb, that the punishment, who wrote, did the exposé on the Contra/CIA/L.A. crack connection, that the punishment is often swift and very vicious. And they want to set a tone for those who cross that line and start to act as if what they pretend the role of the reporter is supposed to be in this country is ... that it really is that. They will suffer vehemently. So we see that process going on. And as far as the way they help make the whole cozy relationship amongst other things, besides intimidation, is they give a lot of these little reporters extremely high salaries within the corporate structure. You know the Tom Brokaws and all of that. So they have a cozy relationship.

**Gerald:** Yeah, a big check!

**Tracy:** Because they do these speaking engagements, you know, for these governmental institutions and other things where they're paid lots of money. So they start to see that their role is not like a Daniel Ellsberg who released the Pentagon Papers. Because you'll be an outcast then. If you want to live "well" financially your role is basically to play the role that they have lined out for you. And many of them admit this. Barbara Walters, she does this little show amongst her other things, where she has this little regular TV show that comes on, and she ended up basically being a pitch woman for Campbell soups where she agreed that she would interweave a Campbell's theme within every show. (groaning and laughing) To the point where they would get the audience to say things like, yeah, this brings us back to the good old days when we would eat Campbell's soup. And then they go into a jingle of (sings) ummmmm ummmmm good.

**Gerald:** Shameless!

**Tracy:** There's this collaboration going on.

**Frank:** Ummmmm, I have space on my board. (points to empty space on his board)

**Linda:** Oh, you could put a little Campbell soup thing here! (laughter) Pick up some extra dough!

**Gerald:** Frank you need to quit your mess. The truth of the matter is that is why it is so important to support alternative media projects like this one, like Berkeley Liberation Radio, like all of ... this Indymedia trip that they got going. I've gotten some good information from them from time to time. You ain't got to worry. We ain't worried about being "out-castes" because we ain't ever been in castes!

**Linda:** That's right!

**Gerald:** So we know, you understand, what's going on. And it's important to us. And I'll tell you something else. Yeah, we don't get people throwing stuff at us or money or nothing like that, but everyday we get confirmations of what we're saying in the real world. So we know we're on the right track.

**Linda:** That's right.

**Gerald:** And eventually, it's a matter of time, they're going to keep on it and they mess with the electricity. Poor person ... you know people don't understand what an attack it is when they raise the price of things like gasoline and electricity. This ain't, you know, come on, this is not a third-world country, people walk around barefoot, they go to work and you know the sun is so nice just lay out there all night, sleep out under a palm tree or something. People freeze to death in America. They die! They gave it a name. What do they call that shit? Thermia ... some kind of thermia.

**Tracy:** Hypothermia.

**Gerald:** Yeah, hypothermia! Make it sound ... old people freezing to death! They've got to give it a fancy name so you don't have to say, they died because they didn't have no damned heat! Then you look at the situation with the electricity, it's just not realistic. It's one thing to conserve. And I think common sense is we should conserve. But workers, brothers and sisters, it's not you. It's not you! Don't believe it's you! (Frank sounds) There's plenty of electricity! And let me tell you something, there's no reason that they don't put solar cells on every single new house that's built. My friend in Concord builds houses ... has a house where he paid $25,000 to have this solar unit installed. But when you find out how it works, it's actually a very good idea. Because the electricity is generated through solar panels. Then what it does is it goes through some little device that tells PG&E how much electricity you generated. So all he pays ... he sells them electricity. His bill average: $2.

**Linda:** We actually looked into that at one point, because we thought, well we'll just take out a loan or something. And we were told it would be over $50,000 to do it on our house. And they told us that PG&E doesn't buy it. That if you ...

**Gerald:** They have to by law, the bastards. Somebody gave you bad information. If it was left to them, obviously, no, they would not. But there are actually laws in the books that protect your rights. If you have the money. $50,000!

**Tracy:** They try to discourage you and things like that.

**Linda:** Yeah!

**Tracy:** And when you look at ... to go on about the whole media aspect in connection with the energy and the chauvinism stuff I was referring to earlier, once again, the blueprint of what's going on in California was done in 1998 in Brazil.

**Gerald:** Oh yeah!

**Tracy:** Those same companies, Edison, all of little Bush's friends, were over in Brazil and they leveraged them through the whole IMF/World Bank structural adjustment process, but they were able to privatize it. Now Brazil ... the energy, up 500%. Rolling black-outs are a regular occurrence. So what happens when your information is isolated and it's based off of receiving it from a corporate structure that does not have your best will and intentions at heart. Well, you don't know about that.

**Gerald:** That's right.

**Tracy:** Then you're told this privatization rhetoric ... they'll make it more efficient and all of that rhetoric. You have these compromised politicians within the bourgeois structure who are just getting paid off and then they just sock it to you. This is the way the process works out.

**Frank:** Our friend Sandy.

**Linda:** She lives up in Northern California, right by the Oregon border and her little section has a co-op. They did it years ago. And none of their power prices went up at all. Yet, right down the street, everybody is paying.

**Tracy:** And that's where it gets to, it's not an issue of (Frank sounds) not enough energy.

**Gerald:** That's right.

**Tracy:** It's similar to the food situation. India is the second largest producer of food in the world. But it has millions of people who are starving. It's a distribution issue.

**Gerald:** That's right!

**Tracy:** That's the issue. That's the point. So the same thing as here. In L.A. they're paying 56% less than we are in the Bay Area because it's still under a municipal system. So right here, we're still in the same state. But see how the corporate media structure intentionally misinforms people because it says "California's energy crisis". And doesn't break down the fact that there's pockets within California ...

**Gerald:** Sacramento, Redwood City.

**Tracy:** L.A. ... That are within the state but are not going through the same process that we're going through. That's part of the Gumpification stuff that I was referring to earlier.

**Frank:** Or they don't tell us there are new technology that is about ...

**Linda:** ... about to become available. Frank was saying he had heard that there was new technology about to become available that would change the way we generate the electricity. And it was right at that point that all of this started happening.

**Frank:** It will be cheap enough for cities or even groups to ...

**Linda:** ... to have their own source of power/electricity.

**Frank:** That would decentralize ...

**Linda:** ... the energy, the electricity generation.

**Frank:** So they are in a rush to build more power plants ...

**Linda:** ... so they can say, well, we have all of these power plants, why invest in this other technology when we just built this other stuff?

**Gerald:** One more thing on this to show you possible responses and reasons to be optimistic: an American firm called Bechtel recently bought the water reclamation system in Venezuela. And so people in that country ... you start talking third world, you're talking about people making $2 to $3 a day ... started getting bills for $20 a month for water! They had a general strike. The whole country shut down. And they sent Bechtel back to where they belong. Well, no, not where they belong, but they sent them back on us. Back over here. And it just shows you ... well, also I must ... look, let's be really clear here, that was such a stupid thing for them to do. Those people backs already against the wall, they don't have no disposable income. So to do something like that, there's going to be civil war before people pay more money than they have, just for water! (Frank sounds) Just for water! Can you imagine if they fouled the atmosphere so bad we have to walk around with little oxygen tanks! Can you imagine having to buy that from them bastards?! They say, oops, wait a minute, we're going to raise the price on you! We're going to deregulate it, ha, ha, oh man!

**Frank:** If they do it gradually ...

**Linda:** Then people might go for it.

**Gerald:** Might swallow it. Well, they're going to have to fight. 'Cause I'll tell you what, some of us ain't going for that. That is just too much.

**Tracy:** There is a dichotomy that is happening. They definitely try these things strategically. On certain portions of populations they gradually raise rates, you know, put more and more pressure on. But one of the things that we're coming to now is that in many ways the earth is coming to a collapse mode. And see the earth has been gradually taking abuse, holes in the ozone, oceans' destruction, you have a crash in many of the fish species. The Black Sea has collapsed completely. The Mississippi has a dead zone in it that is growing rapidly.

**Gerald:** The chemicals are trapped or something?

**Tracy:** You have what is called Cancer Alley. And this is where all these pharmaceutical, the petrolchemical companies all along the coast of the Mississippi have been dumping all this toxic into the Mississippi for the longest. They pay off politicians so that they don't have proper regulations. Well, the earth can only take so much of that type of abuse before it starts to go into certain forms of collapsing. So what I'm saying is, I agree that of course you can ... it's like the old frog story: if you throw a frog in boiling hot water it will jump right out, but if you put it into water that's somewhat cool and then you just gradually turn up the heat, it will just sit in there and then it will burn to death. But see the thing is with the earth, what's happening with the earth is that we have many of the rivers where we get our water supply from, they're collapsing. We have major fish populations collapsing. We have ozone. In places like Chile they have ... they're in what they call an Orange Code, basically, where on certain days the population can only stay out in the sun with exposed skin for like 7 to 8 minutes before they can go back in. Well these type of things will have disastrous consequences on the world population. Say this happens in large farm lands, where people can't go out and harvest. Or if it starts destroying the food supply at its place! So these capitalists are playing a time bomb game. But what we must do is inform the population of the disaster that is already happening and more that are developing and head them off at the pass to stave off some of this almost genocidal type of episodes that can happen to large portions of the species population, not just the human population. But it's all interconnected. So the whole species apparatus within the world population.

**Gerald:** More bad news. I hate to say this and I'm not trying to frighten our listeners and people who ...

**Frank:** On another level kids are losing the ability to play.

**Linda:** Yeah, that's what we've been reading. We've been reading this stuff and reporting this stuff about all these studies showing that kids are losing the ability to play because of the way ... things like when people have kids now they don't give them any free time. Everything is scheduled. And the correlation between the ability to play and smart. And it's been found that people, children that play are smarter.

**Gerald:** People are over-managed.

**Linda:** Yeah.

**Tracy:** A part of the reason is that when you go out and play, say you're like nine years old, with other kids, you're setting up your own social structure with the kids. You're deciding, OK, if it's going to be a baseball game, where the bases are going to be, how the teams are going to be divided, who you're going to pick for whatever reason strategically ... I'll get him 'cause he's quick, I'll get her 'cause she's real strong, etc., etc., etc. But when you have all these parents controlling and manipulating, they're constructing the process of the kids' enjoyment.

**Linda:** Exactly.

**Tracy:** Thereby undermining a very important developmental and critical understanding of how to implement one's thoughts and theories into (Frank giggles) your immediate world.

**Linda:** Exactly!

**Frank:** Even three-year-olds.

**Linda:** They're even doing that with three-year-olds. (to Frank) The hygienist, is that what you're talking about? Frank's getting his teeth cleaned the other day and the woman cleaning his teeth is telling us about her three-year-old kid who likes to play and run and touch other kids. (Frank screeches) Well, the teacher got so alarmed she called in government people to look at this kid. And so the government people then tell the parents that it's not a problem now, but it's going to be. And they're scaring them. They're telling them the kid's going to have all these mental problems if they don't put the kid into play therapy. So this woman goes for it. She puts this three- now four-year-old kid into play therapy.

(Gerald groans)

**Linda:** So it's this big room of toys and the shrink is standing there, or the occupational therapist, with the parents, explaining to them everything the kids does, what that means and how that's right and how that's wrong and all this stuff.

**Gerald:** This is bullshit!

**Tracy:** See, that's a crime right there!

**Linda:** It is a crime!

**Gerald:** And it's also some jive-ass psychologist giving themselves some work!

**Tracy:** And also, that's where all that whole Ritalin and all of that poison ... also an aspect of creating a structure where the kid starts to conform early.

**Frank:** Yes.

**Tracy:** Because he gets or she gets used to established figures telling them how to think etc.

**Frank:** Don't think!

**Linda:** They're told: don't think.

**Tracy:** But like that goes into like recently there was a 15-year-old teenager. He was told that there was an assembly at his school and that everyone had to go because it was part of the whole school apparatus. But when he goes into the gymnasium, he sees it's a big Ronald McDonald fanfare thing where it's a whole recruitment thing for Ronald McDonald at his high school! (Frank sounds) And then they're having these mock things where you're going up for an interview. So they're already socializing kids. So then he decides he's going to go for the mock. So the person says, why do you want to work at McDonalds? And he says, I don't want to work at McDonalds. And he goes, you don't?! And he goes, no, because they feed people junk food that's not healthy for them. And they told Hindus that the french fries did not have any type of beef ingredients because Hindus don't eat beef product, and it turns out that it does. So right then what happens, the principal says alright, out, go to the office! He ends up going to the office. Then he's compelled to write an apology to McDonalds. (everyone groans) And then he's told to say an apology over the speaker, over the intercom, to his school about how he's a bad student, and so on and so forth. This is breaking the will and the spirit of a teenager so that he ...

**Gerald:** An intelligent little fucker!

**Tracy:** Right! Who had read the material. He had heard about Eric Schlosser's book, *Fast Food Nation*, and it turns out that in India right now there's mass protest.

**Gerald:** Yeah! Because they found out they did have beef in the grease!

**Tracy:** And they're forcing them ... actually they just want them to close it down right now. McDonald's ... Ronald's tap dancing around trying to work it out and stuff and spin words around like, oh, we didn't mean that, we really meant that ... this type of junk. But to get to the point, McDonalds has conceded that they do have beef product in their french fries, so the student was right. He has a critique and an argument which can be verified and backed up and that's what he's really being punished for!

**Gerald:** That's a shame.

**Frank:** 1984.

*Gerald Smith (video capture)*

**Linda:** It's right out of the book *1984*!

**Gerald:** Yeah, yeah, oh yeah!

**Tracy:** When you look at, like in Texas there was a high school that passed ... if you wanted to be an athlete you had to pass a urine test. If you wanted to be a cheerleader you had to pass a virgin test. A lot of the inner-city schools, you can't wear braids. (Frank screeches) You can't wear hair extensions. You can't color your hair. So all various forms of self-expression, which they come up with or deem something as being too independent to the outline that they want to subscribe to you, are being attacked. And you are being punished if you go outside of that. Coca-Cola had a thing where basically they bought off the school, bought off the principal and they said OK, look, we'll put a little ... we'll give you some money and buy a scoreboard but for that we want Coca-Cola machines. So the principal tap danced around and said OK, we'll do that. Then they had a Coke Day at the school (Linda laughing) where everyone was supposed to go running around cheering Coke.

**Gerald:** It's terrible! (Linda still laughing)

**Tracy:** So one independent-thinking student, you know, being a little smart ass, he wore a Pepsi t-shirt. (laughing) Boom!

**Gerald:** They put the SWAT team on him.

**Tracy:** He got suspended for a couple of days ...

**Gerald:** I'm sure he sued though!

**Tracy:** ... for that action. And once again, that goes back to that whole Gumpification, beat-down demoralization process. And it also gives insight to the role of the corporate media in how they choose what is important to cover and what is not important.

**Gerald:** That's right. I just wanted to share, look, a couple of things. What I was talking before, more bad news, because we were talking about the ... we had a little stream of consciousness going on, the ecology, and I just wanted to share this. And this is not no way-out radical ... this is on KQED. Where they say that the snowcap on the Sierra Nevada because of global warming is not going to maintain itself and then slowly melt away as spring approaches and then, you know, then finally the water just ... nature's a magnificent phenomena. It just ... nature's plan is sometimes just absolutely ... because what's going to happen now is when it rains it doesn't turn to snow. All the water's just going to come down at one time. So you're going to have flooding and drought. Because when all the water comes down at once, it's not slowly coming down through the course of the year. Later on in the year it's going to run out of water altogether. And that's not me! KQED, about as respectable? But, one more thing. He was talking about the kids. They did something like this in Oakland. I think we reported this on *Slave Revolt*. The youngsters ... similar thing in the black community. The youngsters were supposed to vote for who they wanted to be their commencement speaker. So the kids voted for Mumia Abu-Jamal. Now this idiot, the principal says, I want you to take some civic duty here. Let's come forward and participate (Frank shrieking) and all this old stuff. And they voted for Mumia. He said, well, wait a minute. (all laughing)

**Linda:** On second thought!

**Gerald:** So what he did, we didn't have enough Latinos offered on, so we're going to vote again. They voted again, (Frank shrieks) the little bastards voted for Mumia again! (all laughing) So now, it gets worse ... how do you justify that kind of stuff? He then asked some preacher to come to speak and the kids got to him and eventually Mumia's speech was actually played. But it's the disrespect that you teach young people. You want to know why kids may seem to be a little out of it, a little disrespectful, I can understand it. If that's the way they live it. And that's just on a big issue that got in the papers. Everyday they're disrespecting humanity like that in our schools.

**Tracy:** And this is a Kingfish process that principal's playing and that's why he's in that position. But when you look at that contradiction within, you have that going on and then about a month before you had the Merritt College situation where the students voted to honor Huey P. Newton and Bobby Seale, and then once again the administration went on the attack and tried to abort that. Now this is all in the same time that in West Oakland you had these night rider gestapo cops running around planting drugs, assassinating black people within the West Oakland community and then they're going to "wonder why" you have people trying to give respect to the very same type of people who came out and resisted what the police in West Oakland are being on trial for.

**Frank:** It just proves their war will not work. The kids are not buying it.

**Tracy:** That's why they're trying to train them now. And if you can wear them out and then if there's no real strong social movement ...

**Gerald:** That's the problem!

**Tracy:** ... no independent groups by the time they start to come of age, and then they start having families and other things then they'll just slide.

**Gerald:** Go along to get along.

**Tracy:** But if we do have these institutions and develop them like we plan on doing, and then there is a place for them to develop and hone in their skills, attach to different types of fighting class-combat entities, well then it's the world for the taking.

**Gerald:** That's right!

**Frank:** They tried it in the '50s.

**Gerald:** Explain what you mean by that.

**Frank:** The '30s were radical.

**Gerald:** OK.

**Frank:** The war ...

**Gerald:** World War II.

**Frank:** ... put a cap on that but it also liberated women who had to w ...

**Gerald:** Work.

**Frank:** ... so after the war they were very afraid it would get out of ...

**Gerald:** Control!

**Frank:** ... hand, so they focused on the communi ...

**Linda:** ... communication?

**Gerald:** No, Communist party!

**Frank:** ... yes, and ...

**Gerald:** McCarthyism!

**Frank:** Yes. And tried to push materialism. How great the kitchen could be.

**Gerald:** Ah-hah, um-hmm.

**Frank:** How great suburbia can be.

**Gerald:** Ah-hah, um-hmm.

**Frank:** How great cars are.

**Gerald:** Ah-hah, um-hmm.

**Frank:** Canned food.

**Gerald:** Ah-hah, um-hmm.

**Frank:** NASA. It did not work. The '60s followed.

**Gerald:** Right. Ah-hah, um-hmm. Actually, I would just substitute ... when you use the term materialism for what I would call conspicuous consumption.

**Frank:** Yes.

**Gerald:** Because there was a basis for that type of wealth. The United States came in the tail end of the war. The war started in '39. The United States waited 'til everybody cut everybody up, blew everybody up and then eased on in there and snatched all the goods. So the United States was producing 90% of the world's manufactured products right after the war for a period. Europe was devastated.

**Frank:** Yes.

**Gerald:** But that is the hope. The young people. 'Cause they said, y'all act the way we want y'all to act. Not! Y'all not going to listen to that devil negro Communist music. That shit didn't work there, boy. (Frank shrieking) Everybody likes seeing Elvis Presley shake his little money maker. (Frank shrieks) It's true. It's true. And that rock'n'roll took off. And not only the rock'n'roll as a civil rights movement was growing, a sense of the importance of black people being able to be involved in the production level of creating new music became a reality. And Barry Gordy started his Motown. And a few other labels got started that were quite successful and produced artists that will never be forgotten. So no, this shit didn't work! And mainly because they got bad musical taste.

**Frank:** Beats ...

**Linda:** ... and the Beats showed up (Frank sounds) and started talking about the stuff they talked about.

**Gerald:** Um-humm.

**Tracy:** Plus in capitalism you always have contradictions. (Frank sounds) There's always contradictions that explode out. So while it's running around the planet in the '50s and '60s talking about it's the great democracy, you had people like Robert Williams and Malcolm fighting for basic human rights and exposing to the world these type of contradictions. This shook up many young white people who had believed. And then, next thing they know they get thrust into this war called Vietnam. And many of them start to see all types of contradictions within that. And the role of U.S. as a so-called "liberator". Many of the people who had initially gone down to smash up Vietnam, this taking place right after World War II in 1945 when you had soldiers who went on like a little mutiny because right after World War II they were shipped to Vietnam. They're greeted by German soldiers who salute them on the docks of Hanoi, salute them and they're carrying French mercenaries. So many of these U.S. soldiers are like, what's going on?! (Frank sounds) And there was no such thing as two Vietnams then. There was no "divide and division" between North and South. The United States' role was to go back there and re-colonialize Vietnam. So these seeds start to permeate. And these contradictions were set right then. And they started to sprout and explode during the '50s and '60s. Well, many of the seeds that are being planted now and have been planted within the last ten years, they could be exploding five to ten years from now. Who knows what contradictions may explode out in areas like Iraq?! That may end up, if the process keeps going on, 5,000 kids keep dying, Saddam, the whole population is demonized as one big Saddam, the whole Israeli/Palestinian conflict, the contradictions keep exploding out. Who knows where those seeds may explode out ten years from now?! So this is how capitalism in the process of capital imperialist modes of operation plant seeds of contradictions that can have explosions that can be mind-blowing down the road.

**Gerald:** Um-hum.

**Frank:** And before we were on the air you were talking about they just gunned down ...

**Linda:** Tell us about that again because we weren't on the air for that.

**Gerald:** Oh OK. I was fortunate enough to go to Seattle in 1999 November, and I'll be very honest, at the time I went I knew very little about what it was about, what was going on ... but on the 18-hour ride up there, I guess I got a little bit of an education. (Frank sounds) And actually, Tracy was there too. So we got up there and there had been a real attempt to bring together the trade union bureaucracy, along with social reformers, environmentalists, to have a peaceful protest about the negative role that the World Trade Organization plays, mostly in other countries, and how they drive down the living standards in the Third World and people aren't blah blah blah blah blah. So I said, alright, let me see. But one little group of those youth, it wasn't little, probably 1,000 of them, probably more than 10,000 of them, had decided they were going to lock arms to prevent the WTO delegates from attending the meeting. And I don't think, to tell you the truth, that the big boys in Seattle took these youngsters seriously. (Frank sounds) But they actually did it! And when they did it, the whole thing just kind of came apart! All of the civility and the kind of just, you know, looks like things are going to run pretty smoothly ... it just came apart! Police started attacking people, tear-gassing people, it was just a mess! And we've seen several afterwards. On April 16th you had the World Bank thing. And all over the world there's been ... Quebec there's been actions ... and Barcelona ... and Czechoslovakia, Sweden, England ... there have been these globalization demonstrations. Now these nations that I'm describing now we would call, some people would call them First World (Frank sounds) or ... but let's call them "developed capitalist" ... not Czechoslovakia, but they're developed capitalist countries for the most part. But see who is it that really gets hurt by this World Bank stuff are the third world countries. Simple example, I'll try to keep this one brief because I just want to talk about the Papua New Guinea question. In Zambia, the World Bank comes in, they loan money to the government, they said, listen, you need money, but we ain't no bank, we ain't just going to give you this money! You have to reform! It may have changed the whole context and meaning of the word "reform". And what it meant to them is you have to close down the damn clinics, the free clinics that existed out in the rural areas, which they did! They closed them down. What was the immediate consequence of stuff like this? The story I read in a South African newspaper was about a child who contracted malaria. You can actually be treated for malaria if you get help soon enough. Well these people lived out in a rural area, they didn't have a lot of money, they didn't have a vehicle, thirty miles from town. When you're thirty miles from town, see, we don't think, thirty miles, hop in my little (Frank sounds) Volkswagen, I'll be there in 15 minutes! Well the problem is these people had to walk! But before they walked, they wanted

*Linda Mac and Frank Moore (video capture)*

to raise the funds. They had to go to their family, get the money together and then they got to walking. By the time they got the child to a doctor in the city, in Zambia, probably a month had taken place. You try walking thirty miles with a sick kid. I can see it taking a month! The child died! But here's the question. How much was the shot for malaria, how much did it cost? Well, they say three pence, and in American money that is six cents! That child died, and probably thousands of others, over six cents! This is very serious in the Third World. So they approached these people in New Guinea, Papua New Guinea, and they said, look, y'all don't know how to run no damned government. We know how to run government. So we're going to tell you how to run your business! You're going to have to privatize all of this stuff because this is nothing but corruption. And to be sure, there probably is some corruption. But the students, they understood the danger here, you see, to their economy, to their way of life, their culture, to the health of their people. So the students got to organizing and basically what they did was had a demonstration there against the World Bank and IMF like the other demonstrations that have occurred in other parts of the world that I discussed earlier. Only this time, you see, the little comprador bourgeois, they don't really produce very much. What they do is, they play the role of a middle man between imperialism and the oppressed colonial masses. That's more the actual social function that they play. They're not an organizing class like the early bourgeoisie that developed production. No! They want to pimp off of it. They want to get the foreign aid and then buy their little Mercedes. Anybody with a Mercedes in a country like that should be shot on the spot! (Frank sounds) On the spot! And I'm not against people having nice things. But you can only get a Mercedes in Africa and countries like New Guinea if you pimp it off of the people. 'Cause you sure didn't work for the damn money. So what happens is these young people, college students, are protesting, demanding that the World Bank stay out of their business, that their elected officials be allowed to decide what the national priorities are, etc. etc. And they were set upon, and shot by the army! And approximately sixty of them were shot. A number of them had to go to the hospital. And my understanding is, last time I ... you know I just read this stuff in the media ... three of them died! So we now have definite martyrs in the struggle against capitalist mobilization. It's a tragedy.

**Frank:** That will radicalize people fast if they hear about it.

**Gerald:** Oh lord, tell me! (Frank sounds) That's the problem. That's why I value programs like this one and all other independent attempts to try to get as much of the truth as we can to the American people. This is really tragic.

**Tracy:** And also it's a situation where, see the American population and the world populations, they know that if people just hear one little snippet on it or a sound bite or even hear it very descriptively one time, that's often not enough. It has to be repeated. And then people have to develop a more theorized way of looking at this and connecting it to other things. Because in many ways what's going on in New Guinea is similar to what has been going on throughout Latin America in the form of the Nikefication, you know, Nike, Levi Strauss and all of that. This is why they have a School of the Americas. This is why they send people like Manuel Noriega and Suarez, and all of these Latin American henchmen to learn the art of torture and all this training to suppress the population so that they can go back to their populations, suppress them, beat them down, make them docile and depleted and demoralized so that Nike and Levi Strauss and Kathie Gifford and all of them can come in and exploit them for 20 cents an hour. So once you have a situation that is set up like that, where you have these guys basically being operatives for financial capital. And they're armed by these institutions within the American capitalist system. They're financed through that. They get their payoff for playing their role. So that when corporations want to then say, OK, we haven't enough control over that part of the industry, we want to privatize more of it, we want to build unnecessary dams, etc., well, the population is already beaten down. And the World Bank and IMF can just slide on in and help in that whole privatization process. So this battle has been going on for a long time. The School of the Americas has existed for over fifty years now. They do this training right out of Georgia. And it's kind of hypocritical, oh it's kind of fascinating that when you name off Latin America's greatest henchmen and murderers ...

**Gerald:** ... they all went to the School of the Americas.

**Tracy:** And some of them, like Noriega, who is now in prison in the U.S., was one of the graduates from there. So this shows the contradictions but also the role of the U.S. and how it sets up mechanisms to penetrate and blast away on working populations throughout the world.

**Frank:** Am I a nigger?

**Linda:** Am I a nigger? You're asking if you are?

**Gerald:** You're about as close to one as I've seen! (laughter)

**Tracy:** Well, I mean if you put it like in a class aspect, the whole concept of the color class slave system, the concept of what that meant, and in the ruling classes, what being a nigger is, it means being dispossessed. Not being in power, not being able to control your standard of living, not being able to control your labor. Not being able to control, along with other people, the environment in which you live in. Well, in many ways what you see now taking place is the negrofication of America. (Frank sounds) This is why often in many countries like South Africa and stuff like that, many of the oppressed people, these Indians and so on and so forth, they did it! They just called themselves black. Because they see what that means in the class perspective.

**Gerald:** ... social sense right.

**Frank:** That is the key.

**Gerald:** Um-hmm. Race is definitely a social phenomena. It is not a biological phenomena. And it's probably one of the most important aspects for control in this society.

**Frank:** Like crip.

**Linda:** Like being a crip.

**Gerald:** Um-hmm.

**Frank:** When people think, oh, them poor black people, it is a shame how they are being treated. We should help them. It misses the point. We are niggers.

**Tracy:** Right! Well, what he's saying basically is like when you look at when they, in the name of a war on drugs, which of course basically means in reality a war on black, well, many blacks were realizing what was going on and one of their uses of attack on black people was what they called asset forfeitures. So they would charge your property, charge your home with a crime. You wouldn't be able to defend yourself. They'd take your home, make you homeless and stuff. Well, many people who were other shades, other complexions, didn't see themselves as being black, i.e. connected with that group of people. So what ended up happening is is that you may not think it, but the ruling class thinks it. (Frank sounds) So after a while the police started to get a certain portion of the money of these asset forfeitures.

**Gerald:** For their own organization.

**Tracy:** So this is how they were driving around in new cars and things of that nature. So quite naturally for them, they just didn't want to pick on just the "poor blacks".

**Gerald:** What are you going to get?!

**Tracy:** They wanted to get (Frank screeches) some of the more richer blacks and stuff. So they started going past the flatlands of East Oakland and West Oakland (Frank sounds) and into the Oakland hills to get the lighter-skinned negros, the lighter-skinned blacks, some of the people who call themselves different, i.e. white folks, and started to use asset forfeiture on them. You had situations where one guy who was fairly wealthy ... this one DEA agent said that he saw marijuana plants hanging from his tree and they used that as an excuse to then bust into his home. He hears people busting into his home, he goes to check it out. They end up shooting him down.

225

**Gerald:** In his house!

**Tracy:** It ended up turning out that the DEA actually wanted his house because of its worth. So they concocted this whole thing.

**Gerald:** And took the house, by the way, and was living in it!

**Tracy:** There were no marijuana plants, there was no anything like that whatsoever. And this guy did not call himself a nigger at the time. When he saw that gun pointed at him by the DEA agents he probably did realize that he was a nigger in the eyes of Sam just like Amadou Diallo did. Because it was basically the same type of situation. Death was headed towards his way. But this is how where many people may not see themselves as being connected ...

**Gerald:** Oh yeah!

**Tracy:** ... or the same as those other people down the way, but how you may perceive yourself in this world is often not the way that those in power see it.

**Gerald:** And it's subject to change!

**Frank:** And in five years you will be the target, so it ain't about helping those poor blacks.

**Tracy:** Well, like once again it just goes down to what Frank is basically saying that we have to realize that we're helping ourselves. And that there's a basic common thread in unity amongst us who are considered the rabble by this elite class that are here just to exploit us. Now they'll use various mechanisms to divide us but when you think about it the only reason why they would use those mechanisms to divide us is if they really think of us in that way. If you have a situation where they have intentionally blocked any effort whatsoever on treating all of the soldiers who have gotten the Gulf War Syndrome, and it's been over 70,000, then it's clear they look at all of them as niggers.

**Gerald:** Um-hmmm.

**Tracy:** You know, whether you're white ...

**Gerald:** We don't care about all their rhetoric, we're talking about how they're treating them. Asian, Latino (Frank sounds) ... to them, and Schwarzkopf included. What's his face, the negro that's up there ... ?

**Linda, Frank & Gerald:** Colin Powell.

**Tracy:** ... included, they all think of us as niggers, (Frank sounds) disposable. They served their purpose, they're used up, next batch come on in! That's the reality that needs to be understood.

**Gerald:** Um-hmmm.

**Frank:** Business schools ...

**Linda:** ... oh, business schools teach you that you're going to make all of your money from 20% of the people that you do business with. And so the other 80% you don't have to pay too much attention to.

**Tracy:** Or you don't have to value them as human beings.

**Frank:** Yes.

**Gerald:** That's the problem. That's the problem right there!

**Frank:** That is why they lock us up ...

**Linda:** ... oh, in jails ...

**Frank:** Kill us ...

**Gerald:** Um-hmmm.

**Frank:** ... ignore us. They think they would be better off with 80% out of circulation.

(Gerald giggles)

**Tracy:** Also it works as a mechanism of ... you know, when they're locking people up it's not just to "lock those people up". It's also to sterilize ...

**Gerald:** Intimidate.

**Tracy:** ... and alienate and terrify the population that is "not locked up". Because if they can sterilize you and intimidate you that way then you'll be in line not to rebel. You'll be scared. You'll be ready to conform to the policies that they lay out at hand even if it's dramatically against your interests. So, part of the whole process of the locking up and the terror campaigns that they use to assassinate portions of the population in brutal ways is basically to intimidate the population in general. When you look back at the lynching days, much of the lynching that went on ... look at how it often worked. They would get someone, they take pictures of them. They'd make sure that the corpse was left up there. They'd make postcards out of it. This was for other blacks to see. So it wasn't just the black who was killed, it was for the blacks who were living. Look, you'd better stay in check with our social order.

**Gerald:** These people do this and get away with it.

**Tracy:** And there won't be any repercussions ...

**Gerald:** That's right!

**Tracy:** ... on the mobs of us that do this terror campaign.

**Frank:** We ran the political prisoners ...

**Linda:** Oh, the Political Prisoners Conference.

**Frank:** What is dangerous about that was the love and the (Frank sounds) idealism and the softness. That would be extremely dangerous ...

**Linda:** ... if people saw that. If the general population saw that. Because you know, people, their picture of the people in jail (Frank sounds), and then you see something like that and these people are so kind and loving and idealistic. (Frank sounds)

**Tracy:** That's that whole, you know, they intentionally dehumanize prisoners in general.

**Frank:** Yes.

**Tracy:** And they want to tell you that they're monsters. Then they put out all of these little gung ho cop shows and movies and stuff like that (Frank sounds) to create these Hannibal Lecter-type characters and imagery within your mind. Have you terrified in your own community.

**Gerald:** In your own house!

**Tracy:** So many people who think they know a Mumia, have no idea of his passion, commitment and humanitarian nature as a human being. They have no idea. But what they do know is the imagery that these little henchmen portray Mumia as. And they use words, cop killer, former Black Panther, all these little words that already had negative connotations in their minds. So a Mumia to many people is not really that much different in their minds than just saying a Timothy McVeigh. So they want to strip you of ... and then they want to turn around, like in California, and if you want to go and interview a prisoner, so you can help develop and have that person develop his or her own character about themselves, you can no longer, as a reporter, pick a particular prisoner you want to go and converse with. It's random now. So they strip that away.

**Linda:** When did that happen?

**Gerald:** The last few years.

**Tracy:** Yeah. So they use it when they want. So if it's an articulate prisoner who is on death row, knowledgeable about death row, can break down some of the social conditionings about the death row system and structure within California in this country and connect it with other things that are going on, the old warden can say, oh no, you can't see him. You see, this is part of the dehumanization process.

**Frank:** Because their lie is very fragile.

**Gerald:** Oh yeah!

**Tracy:** No doubt about it.

**Gerald:** Oh yeah.

**Tracy:** And they know it's fragile and they're scared, they're scared to death. (Frank sounds)

**Gerald:** You see that's the one thing that kind of disturbs me about, oh people that say that they want to put up the ... they don't realize how weak our enemies actually are. (Frank sounds) Because they have very little going for them in terms of information, truth, you know, morality. Things like this matter to most people. (Frank sounds) They have to avoid, they don't want to engage. I'll never forget this. When the teachers decided to have the teach-in in the Oakland schools for Mumia, I want to be very honest with you and say, I said OK, that'd be good, get the children involved, enthusiastic in a certain sense, but I didn't think it was that big a deal. They made it a big deal! What they did was some cop had gotten killed and then they said to us, they said, well you don't think you should have this thing on a cop killer (Frank sounds) right after the funeral. Number one, Mumia Abu-Jamal is not a cop killer. He didn't kill nobody. In fact, and this is sad but true, we just got new information where a gentleman by the name of Arnold Beverly has come forward and admitted that he shot Faulkner. This is pure dynamite. A lot of people like to say to me, well why would he do it, why? Because people can't conceive of ever doing the right thing. (laughs) But let me tell you, people do have a conscience. Actually, this guy was in prison after Mumia was already put on death row. And he was in prison with MOVE prisoners. And just by observing their behavior under fire, he came to develop a lot of respect for what they stood for and he just said it'd been gnawing away at him for years and years. But nevertheless what matters to me is, I'm not a psychologist, I can't answer all questions of human motivation, but I do know they took him to the best lie detector test administer in the country and he passed that lie detector test. There's 80 pages of documentation explaining how the lie detector test works, blah, blah, blah ... why the guy, I think his name is Hont from Boise, Idaho, why he thinks that this is valid in this particular case. This is a whole new day. Media, they won't talk about this. They don't want this in the paper! Because then, you don't have to be a brain surgeon to see, well if they've got a guy that says he did it, and he passed a lie detector test, why is Mumia Abu-Jamal in prison at all? Let alone death row! And it's clear! They just don't have no intention of letting this man out. They want to kill him!

**Tracy:** And this is all political. And this is actually not the first time that someone has come forward about these type of murdering someone in the past. These Northwestern University students had uncovered a case about where someone had been in prison for like 18 years, wrongly convicted, on death row. And they ended up tracking down, these journalism students at this university, the person who did it. The person admitted it on video camera. They gave it to the various authorities. Then they let the person out who was in prison and went ahead and convicted the person who did admit it. My whole point is is that this is nothing new. Sometimes people over time, guilt, whatever, happens. But my point is that the authorities had accepted it before, when someone has admitted it. But see Mumia's situation is much more political. Because they had built a whole case on it.

**Gerald:** Of lies! Deceit!

**Tracy:** They had followed the whole program and had people testify and say these particular things to orchestrate Mumia's death. And that gets back to the heart of the issue of a political prisoner.

**Gerald:** They're all involved!

**Tracy:** Mumia's innocence in essence as a political prisoner is just a technicality. It's a technicality to overcome. A technicality to distort, to lie about, to deceive. Because at the end of the day, for them, Mumia must die. And this gets to the heart of the true morality and intentions of the state.

**Gerald:** Ummm, sick!

**Frank:** That has always been the case.

**Gerald:** Um-hmmmm.

**Tracy:** Well, when you look at part of the founding of this country, in the 1800s, mid-1800s, the capitalists plunged America into one of its vicious depressions. Various news reports came out, *Bismarck Tribune*, talking about the vicious and greedy bankers, railroad owners,

*Frank Moore and Tracy James (video capture)*

capitalists have plunged our nation into its worst depression. Our people are starving, etc. etc. But what was the response? The response was, now we have no choice. We must go into the Black Hills and break our treaty (Frank sounds) that we had with Red Cloud and plunge the Black Hills of its gold. Which is exactly what they did! So here they admit that it was the capitalists that caused all of this economic turmoil but the response was to turn their aggression on the original inhabitants of this country, and strip them of their rights and basically lives, and soon enough old Custer, old Armstrong himself, was leading an expedition into the Black Hills with Crazy Horse, Red Cloud, Two Moon, Touch The Clouds ... they're getting ready to make amends for that, which they did. But that's another story. But that shows you how the whole process of this country has always worked.

**Frank:** Why are they letting us do this?

**Tracy:** Well, first of all, they're not letting us do it! (Frank sounds) We're doing it in spite of many things that they have set up, especially against the whole guerilla pirate radio movement and stuff.

**Gerald:** Oh yeah!

**Tracy:** But also there's a situation where they are monitoring all of this. We get all types of information, and have information. And other things that we have done, we know that they monitor this. But there's also a thing where, they're experts at sabotage and things of that nature. They look for ways to create in-fighting. But also what they do is they don't want to "unnecessarily" create like a martyr situation where if they all of a sudden start to jump out, before the masses have really started to engage in the whole process. You can have people looking over at why are they so viciously attacking those institutions? All they're doing is this ...

**Gerald:** Sharing information.

**Tracy:** Yeah. They're doing it independently. They're not asking the government for "money". They're not asking for corporate hand-outs, so on and so forth. So, they know about what we're doing. They monitor what we're doing. And they have various consultants and people like that who tell them when is the best time to turn up the heat, when is not. So take the Independent Media Center. They've been watching them all along. They've monitored them. Now during certain episodes they said, OK, no, we ain't going for it. Like in L.A. That's where they drew the line when they were going to do that thing at the convention in L.A. (Frank sounds) They said, look, too many people are watching this stuff and they're growing pretty fast, so on and so forth. And this is revolving around a hot issue, the whole convention. And they're coming off the heels of some other successful events, so we're just going to whoride it and sabotage this whole thing. So they did shut that down at that moment. So they do pick their spots and stuff. And they'll be back for more before all is said and done.

**Gerald:** Uh-hmmmm. But, I think what's very important to realize ... see this is what they don't have absolute power over you! Oh man, I want our listeners to understand this. They can't control the way you think. Really, at the end of the day, it's your mind. Yes, they control the airwaves, the majority of the airwaves and stuff. But they can't stop you from talking to your family. They can't stop you from thinking and reading and sharing information with your fellow workers at work, the people you go to school with. At the end of the day they are in big trouble, and they know it! See, they don't want to talk about well what's wrong with those Russians, no, no! It was drilled into me as a child: the Communists, they don't have freedom of speech like we do in this great country! Except if you don't have no damn money, see?! That's right. And once again, I can not emphasize it enough, that is why shows like this matter! It is important that we begin to develop a support system for all independent media, to make sure ... because the corporate media is not ours. They're not our friends! They don't speak for us. They don't tell our stories. We must support and nurture independent media outlets if we are going to be able to effectively resist all of the attacks that they throwing at us, y'all.

**Tracy:** And part of our support system is a core part of our strength. This is what helps hold them at bay. I mean if you think about it, if you had Frederick Douglass running around in the 1800s with the *North Star* paper ... here's someone, a black person, a former slave ...

**Gerald:** Escaped slave at that!

**Tracy:** ... and he has a paper talking about the horrors of slavery and making strong analysis and pronouncements against the U.S. Government and its policy ... one would think, why didn't they just go ahead and shut him down and kill him? That's because he had strong support! He had a basis of support! That support, when it's based in truth, when it's based in conviction that's trying to uncover honestly the facts, it's like the sun! And when you're a vampire, which the capitalist state is, you don't want all that sunshine! (Frank sounds) Because you want to hide in the dark and do your little thing and hope that that one person or those entities that are out there are just walking around in the dark by themselves too. That they're not out in public. That they don't have a strong base of support. Because that base of support symbolizes the sun and that is what scares them away. They have to be much more cautious, I should say when you have that type of support around you.

**Gerald:** Uh-hmmm. And it is growing. We are getting support.

**Frank:** This show is almost three years old. LUVeR is almost …

**Mikee:** 2 ½.

**Linda:** It's 2 ½ years old.

**Frank:** … so people can do it.

**Gerald:** Uh-hmmm.

**Frank:** It don't take a lot of money. You don't need millions of listeners to make a difference.

**Gerald:** That's true.

**Tracy:** Right. Well, you also … it comes down to like your sense of priorities and stuff. And in many ways you can't base … if you're doing the type of stuff that we're doing … you can't base your type of (Frank sounds) values off of how the bourgeois bases it.

**Gerald:** That's right!

**Tracy:** Because for us it's not about money. It's not about being a millionaire and all of that type of stuff. But see if you have that type of concept and that's how you value "success", if that's how you value what is valuable …

**Gerald:** Uh-hmmm.

**Tracy:** … then you are caught up and cocooned within that system and in that mind-set and then they've got you beat because then they'll have you thinking, well OK, well, what we're doing is insignificant.

**Gerald:** That's right! Because there aren't millions of people listening.

**Frank:** That is their main weapon against us. (Frank sounds)

**Gerald:** Uh-hmmm, the mind game! (Frank sounds)

**Linda:** That's what we come up against, people saying, yeah but how many people are really listening to what you're doing!?

**Gerald:** Oh yeah …

**Tracy:** By the same thing, it's a process (Frank sounds), it's a process.

**Gerald:** That's right, it's growing.

**Tracy:** When Kantako first started the whole thing, there was just people within that little project who were listening to him. From there we started the thing at FRB (Free Radio Berkeley). We had an engineer, Steve Dunifer, who was technically advanced. He was able to create stronger transmitters. From that process we were able to get a larger portion of Berkeley and Oakland. From there it caught into the minds of other people (Frank sounds) who started making transmitters for other people throughout the country. We have two in Haiti, a couple in South Africa, East Timor.

**Gerald:** San Salvador.

**Tracy:** Was it important to the people, the Zapatistas, when we gave them one? Of course it was! Because they understood the value. Now, a few years back this wasn't even in our minds that it would expand that way. It starts off with an idea and a conviction (Frank sounds) that what you're doing is right and you believe in and that you too have something to say and contribute to this society and the way that you think has some value. Not based off of what they think but what you believe in, your understanding of the world.

**Frank:** Yes.

**Tracy:** From there, that helps set the seed and the foundation for what's to come.

**Frank:** That is power.

**Tracy:** Yeah, that's the true power (Frank sounds) of what we're trying ...

**Gerald:** The birth of our power.

**Tracy:** Right. It comes from a very organic and honest tradition of what ... Fred Douglass ... *Slave Revolt* comes from that tradition of the *North Star* tradition that Fred Douglass had built. Where he had escaped from slavery just like Harriet (Tubman). But that wasn't enough for him! He believed that true freedom was not just his freedom, but freedom for people who are locked within that type of system. (Frank sounds) So off of that idea he began to argue and develop and write and orchestrate a platform for that. And then it worked itself into the printing press and his publication known as the *North Star*. And at the end of the day, through his development and analysis, it ended up 200,000-plus black soldiers fighting in the Civil War which crushed chattel slavery. That was the end result of the idea that Fred Douglass had.

**Gerald:** And fought for!

**Frank:** If he thought in numbers ...

**Linda:** ... he would have never done what he did.

**Tracy:** "Oh, I'm overwhelmed ... "

**Linda:** ... nobody is really listening to what I'm saying (Frank squeals).

**Tracy:** "I'm just one escaped slave! This institution's been going on years." So on and so forth! But he developed an understanding. He developed his conviction. So who are we?! Here Frederick Douglass, an escaped slave, was able to make a fundamental role, change in advancement in the crushing the chattel slavery. And then here we are in the year 2001, we have no excuse, no excuse whatsoever but to say if Fred and Harriet and them can contribute in the crushing of chattel slavery then, that we can contribute to the crushing of this wage slave system. We're part of the same tradition, the same legacy, so and we have technology that can be used in a way that Fred could only dream of back then. So let's get to work!

**Gerald:** That's it! Having said that ...

**Linda:** ... Gerald's out of here! (laughter)

**Gerald:** We gotta cut ya off, man! That was it!

**Frank:** Glad you looked at me.

**Linda:** Well, we had a guest on a couple of weeks ago ... I won't say his name, right? But he does a show on LUVeR. And somebody that ... again we listen to his show and really like his show and the way he thought ... and then he came on the show and he was completely freaked by Frank. He would not look at Frank. Even though Frank was the one, like this, Frank is the one talking to him, he wouldn't look at Frank.

**Tracy:** Well, I don't know what he's talking about?! Because the horrible sight that I see is Bush! (laughter) These CEOs at PG&E and stuff, that's the horrible sight that I see around! So I don't know what this cat's problem is! (laughter)

**Gerald:** That's weak!

**Linda:** Yes.

**Gerald:** Frank is an inspiration in many ways. Just as Tracy said, if Frederick Douglass could do it, and I look at Frank and I say, goddammit, get up, get up, let's go! Keep fighting!

**Frank:** You can hear Tracy and Gerald ...

**Linda:** ... every week on LUVeR, *Slave Revolt*!

**Frank:** And Gerald ...

**Linda:** ... provides the stuff for *Radical Perspectives* which plays every week on LUVeR.

# Michael Peppe

Recorded May 22, 2005 on luver.com

Michael Peppe is an anti-performance artist, composer, vocal gymnast, and fixture of the San Francisco art scene. He is the creator of Behaviormusik, performance founded on the concept that "all possible behavior is musically composable".

Frank first met Michael in the late 1970s when they both performed at the infamous San Francisco punk club, the Mabuhay Gardens. When Frank's band, The Cherotic All-Stars, began performing in San Francisco in the early 2000s, Michael became a regular member of the band. He also participated and performed in many of Frank's other performances over the years including many Shaman's Den music jams.

**Linda:** And you're listening in the background to more tech ... tech, tech, tech. (Michael laughs) This is the Shaman's Den and tonight's guest is the Divus, Michael Peppe. And as Frank was just saying, Frank was ready 15 minutes before the program was scheduled to start ...

**Michael:** And so was the Divus!

**Linda:** ... and then, as Frank said, our guest, Michael Peppe, the Divus, demanded an entire new tech set-up! And you're still being able to share this with us. It continues.

(keyboard playing in the background, tech talk)

**Linda:** And this is the Shaman's Den on LUVeR.

(Linda does the introduction again, because of technical difficulties!)

**Frank:** I feel like I am in *Groundhog Day*.

**Linda:** The day just keeps repeating over and over. (laughing)

**Michael:** What kind of songs do groundhogs sing? (makes snorting sounds)

**Linda:** OK, now are we ready to begin the performance?

**Frank:** He has ordered me to not interrupt him.

(more tech stuff)

**Michael:** (in the background) Folks, it's not true! Although my mic isn't on now. I have not ordered anyone not to interrupt! (Linda laughing) By the time the intro is over, an hour and a half will have gone by and we'll be saying so long, so ... (Linda continues to laugh)

**Frank:** Which of us do you believe? (Linda still laughing)

**Linda:** Do you believe Frank, or do you believe Michael?!

**Michael:** Frank is the owner of production, the owner of the means of production. I'm just the employee trying to ...

**Linda:** ... trying to make a name for himself!

(Mikee trying to get Michael's mic to work)

**Linda:** The audience watches you moving your mouth, but they can't hear you say anything.

**Frank:** That is heaven!

**Linda:** His mic not working is heaven!

(Michael laughs)

**Linda:** Now our mics aren't working!

**Michael:** And mine is! As I was saying ... (loud feedback, all laughing)

**Michael:** Now none of us can hear anything. Folks, you think it's bad at home, how about us ... how do you think it is for us? Our eardrums don't work.

**Linda:** This is the first Shaman's Den that was all tech! All set-up!

**Michael:** I'm really ready to go! Now we have a mic going and there's no echo on it, that's good for me. Of course, we don't know if it was on tape.

**Linda:** I think it's on tape at this point. We're six minutes into tape.

**Michael:** So, are we good?

**Linda:** Can we begin? OK, without further ado, Michael Peppe.

(Michael does a musical performance for about forty minutes)

**Michael at end of performance:** That was verbatim Jim Jones from a tape transcribed off the radio. So in case you think I'm saying that as Michael Peppe, and trying to get you involved in a cult, but you send in your 50 cents, we'll give you some Kool-Aid, special Kool-Aid, and it'll solve all your problems, thank you. So, are we up to an hour yet? We must be up to an hour.

**Linda:** Are we switching now for conversation?

**Michael:** We may as well, I guess. I have some other, but have got to save some for next time.

**Linda:** Frank?

**Frank:** They may kick me off B-TV for this one ...

**Michael:** (laughing) Probably will. It's just a total performance, folks. We're not really feeding you Kool-Aid.

**Frank:** ... so there may not be a next time.

**Michael:** That's right! I'd better do the rest of it now. Get my end in while there's still a LUVeR on TV!

**Linda:** So, are you doing more?

*Michael Peppe (video capture)*

**Michael:** I don't know if I have it. I don't have too much more that's not going to get into really bad pop songs.

**Linda:** We don't mind bad pop songs!

**Frank:** I ...

**Linda:** Frank will sing along.

**Michael:** (laughing) Alright. So Frank, you want to sing along with this one? I think you might know this one.

(Michael starts singing "Alone Again, Naturally" and Frank sings along as they look at each other)

(Michael and Frank continue singing together: "Come Saturday Morning", "Stardust Memory", "Secret Agent Man" and an unidentifiable song segueing into a raucous "You and I" with both Michael and Frank singing at the top of their lungs accompanied by Michael's dissonant piano accompaniment)

**Michael:** OK, that's really it! I can't yell louder than that. That's gotta be an hour by now, I'm sure.

**Linda:** Close enough, Mikee said.

**Frank:** We could do the Plush Room. (Michael laughing)

**Linda:** Is that at the Fairmount? The two of you singing songs like that together. (laughter)

**Michael:** That's right! Let's do it! (laughing) We can do "Alfie", all the standards ... "Come Saturday Morning" ... I want to learn, I'm getting the music for another ... (starts singing "(Theme From) Valley of the Dolls") ... we could do Bacharach, "The Look of Love" ...

**Frank:** Jim Webb.

**Michael:** Who's that?

**Linda:** He's a songwriter ... "By The Time I Get To Phoenix".

**Frank:** "Up, Up, and Away"

**Michael:** Oh, I love that! (Michael starts singing it)

**Mikee:** "Galveston"

**Michael:** (Michael segues into singing "Windy") I love that one!

**Frank:** Association.

**Linda:** That's The Association.

**Michael:** Yeah, there you go, that's right! And then the one (starts singing "Along Comes Mary"). That's a great song.

**Linda:** That's The Association.

**Michael:** Do you have the music for that?

**Linda:** No, but we can get them online, though.

**Frank:** I saw ...

**Linda:** ... Frank saw The Association in concert.

**Frank:** At Disneyland, on graduation.

**Linda:** That was Frank's graduation from high school.

**Michael:** What, they played live for your high school class?!

**Linda:** The high school had their graduation at Disneyland ...

**Michael:** Oh, OK.

**Linda:** ... and The Association performed as part of it.

**Michael:** That's pretty cool. They're excellent! Of course our version wouldn't exactly match the record (Linda laughing), but you just don't put that on the tape that we send to the Plush Room. That would be great, though. And we show up in tuxes and do this stuff. (laughing) We take requests and then butcher the songs. (laughter) What's your favorite song, folks? And then totally dismantle it. (laughter continues)

**Frank:** We sing anything.

**Linda:** (laughing) We sing anything, folks!

**Michael:** Yeah, we sing anything! Just give it to us, we know it! And if we don't know it …

**Linda:** … we know it!

**Michael:** … we know it!

**Frank:** (laughing) Stump …

**Linda:** … stump the band! Play stump the band. (laughter continues)

**Michael:** And they won't be able to find anything we don't know. Every song will just start … (Michael plays banging, discordant music on the piano and then starts singing along to it the song "Cherish") (laughter) Just do all Association songs. (starts singing "Along Comes Mary")

**Frank:** We just saw them.

**Linda:** The Association on television.

**Michael:** Oh God!

**Linda:** It was a PBS special.

**Michael:** That must have been sad. Oh, I hate those. (Linda laughing)

**Mikee:** (from off camera ) Monterey Pop outtakes.

**Linda:** Oh, Monterey Pop outtakes, we saw that, right. But that's not what you were thinking of, you were thinking of that PBS thing?

(Frank sounds yeah)

**Michael:** Those things are sad. They're as old as I am. They should be ashamed to still be performing at that age.

**Linda:** (laughing) As you perform!

**Michael:** (laughing) Only I'm allowed.

**Frank:** Very white.

**Linda:** They were very white, The Association.

**Michael:** They were definitely white.

**Frank:** Even the Hawaiian dude …

**Linda:** … in The Association, was very white.

**Michael:** (laughing) Even the Hawaiian dude … Yeah, that was the last gasp of college vocal group, I think, The Association. That was after the Colby Five and all those college groups. But then there's the fabulous … (starts playing the piano discordantly and singing "MacArthur Park" loudly off key) We could do that one. I'd love to do that one … get back at it. (Michael starts singing "The Girl from Ipanema" while playing discordant chords on the piano) I could do the chords right, actually.

**Frank:** That may be below my standards. (Linda starts laughing)

**Michael:** Doesn't reach the high-level of quality that you demand, and that I demand in my material! (In a New York Mafia type voice) You know, you got to demand the real strong material if you're going to go up on a stage, really project yourself to the crowd. You know, you gotta have the high quality material. (Frank sounds) You can't just go on talent, kid. You can't go on just talent and looks, like me and Frank. You gotta have the material!

**Frank:** My cast of the *Outrageous Beauty Revue* never understood that. (Michael giggling)

**Linda:** That Frank did have standards.

**Michael:** (laughing) Yeah! I know! (in same New York Mafia-type voice) People, you know, they're not on the level that we're at on. (Linda laughing) They're not on the same level. They don't know that only a certain tiny group ... a bunch of material can be the Pâté de Foie Gras.

**Frank:** Then the punk bands ripped ...

**Linda:** ... ripped off our songs and started singing Sonny & Cher, and the various tunes that we had been singing. (Frank sounds)

**Michael:** Wait, did Sonny & Cher rip you off?!

**Linda:** No, the punk bands that played at the Mabuhay, and performed after our show would hear us doing these songs, then the next you know they're singing them in their act, recording them on their albums.

**Michael:** (laughing) Really? Hey, well then there's what's his name, Flea?

**Linda:** Yes.

**Michael:** Who was inspired by the *Outrageous Beauty Revue*.

**Linda:** Yes, he said it turned his art in a different direction.

**Michael:** Yeah!

**Frank:** The Dictators ...

**Linda:** ... do a pretty good version of "I Got You Babe" on one of their records.

(Michael starts singing "I Got You Babe")

**Linda:** They used to perform after us all of the time.

**Michael:** Well, then there's Kaos Kitty that does Nazi Sinatra.

**Linda:** Nancy Sinatra, "These Boots Are Made For Walking". We did that one!

**Frank:** Before it was hip.

**Linda:** It was definitively before it was hip to do those things, when we were doing them.

**Michael:** Oh yeah! 1981.

**Linda:** It was not hip at that point. It was actually 1978 when we started that show.

**Michael:** So Barry Manilow and Engelbert Humperdinck were still bad then. And they'll always be bad, anyway!

**Linda:** It certainly wasn't hip to be singing "Green Beret" at that point.

**Frank:** Then The STUPEDS.

**Linda:** They made a whole act out of singing those kinds of songs. Raoul and ...

**Michael:** They were great! I did the "Bohemian Rhapsody" with them. You know the Queen song? And he played the piano part from sight! He said, bring me the music. I went and got the music and he played it with no rehearsal! We just did it! And it was perfect, it was amazing!

**Frank:** They got their act from ... (giggles)

**Linda:** ... from the *Outrageous Beauty Revue*. (Frank sounds uh-huh)

**Michael:** They may have been there, probably were there.

**Linda:** Oh, they definitely were there.

**Michael:** Were they? Joshua and ...

**Linda:** Yeah, Rick and Ruby were part of The STUPEDS.

**Michael:** Right. They're still doing their thing.

**Frank:** Rick and Ruby even performed at the Blind Lemon.

**Michael:** What's that?

**Linda:** We had a club, briefly in the late 1970s, ahead of its time. There was no liquor and so it was an underage club on San Pablo in Berkeley. And because we were playing at the Mabuhay we knew all the big names that were performing, so we booked them at the Lemon. And Rick and Ruby was one of the acts.

**Frank:** The Mutants.

**Linda:** The Mutants performed at the Blind Lemon.

**Michael:** Oh man, they were great!

**Frank:** And I told ...

**Linda:** Frank told them to put their cigarettes out and they couldn't drink in the club.

**Michael:** (laughing) Oh really?!

**Linda:** And that was definitely before it was hip to tell people to put their cigarettes out and not drink!

**Michael:** Right! I remember Fritz Mutant and John Gullak did *Another Room Magazine*. I don't know what happened to all those folks. And Sally Mutant, Sue Mutant ... they should do an old timers PBS concert at 55, 60 years old.

*Linda Mac, Erika Shaver-Nelson, Michael Peppe, and Frank Moore (video capture)*

**Linda:** Get Dirk Dirksen to put it together.

**Michael:** Have all these grey mohawks. What about a grey mohawk? Maybe I'll have to start a trend and have a grey mohawk because you don't see grey mohawks too much.

**Frank:** You changed your hair color more (giggling) than Cher.

**Michael:** (laughing) Yeah! Well that's my goal.

**Linda:** (laughing) We watch all these old shows on B-TV now, and you're in a lot of them and you always have a different hair color.

**Michael:** (laughing) Oh yeah? Oh wow! Good! On your show?

**Linda:** Yeah, they replay this show now all night and it is called *The Best of Unlimited Possibilities* on B-TV, so it's *The Best of Unlimited Possibilities* every night, seven nights a week there's a different show.

**Michael:** Wow!

**Linda:** And so we pretty much get to watch the last six, seven years of this show and performances.

**Michael:** Amazing! That's good!

**Linda:** So, you're on it a lot.

**Michael:** Is this the same station?

**Linda:** Yes, Berkeley's public access channel 28.

**Michael:** But now it's every night?!

**Linda:** Yeah! This show, *Unlimited Possibilities* is on three nights a week, that's during the earlier part of the night. And then *The Best of Unlimited Possibilities* starts 1a.m., 1:30a.m., as late as 2:30a.m.

**Frank:** And *Deep Core Magic* ...

**Linda:** ... is another show we have on B-TV. We have three shows on B-TV.

**Michael:** Wow!

**Frank:** So ...

**Linda:** ... there are some nights when our shows run for six hours straight!

**Michael:** (laughing) That's good!

**Linda:** Monday night it starts at 10p.m. and goes six hours straight. A couple other nights it does that too.

**Michael:** World domination!!

**Frank:** I may be the most seen performance artist. (giggling)

**Michael:** (laughing) It's probably true! The Dr. Gene Scott of performance art. Remember, Dr. Gene was the only one that was always on 24 hours a day!

**Frank:** He still is on.

**Michael:** Yeah, incredibly. He's old now though, he looks bad. He doesn't have a long time. Back in the 1970s or early 1980s he was on there all the time, twenty-four hours. He wouldn't even say anything, it was true performance art. Just look at the camera.

**Frank:** He had a channel.

**Michael:** Yeah, he had the whole channel! Well, you guys, you're getting up to that. If you've got six hours out of 24 one day, anyway, you've just got to buy out the other time slots. (laughing) So you can have all Frank, all the time! And why not?!

**Frank:** That is LUVeR.

**Linda:** LUVeR is 24 hours, 7 days a week.

**Michael:** So you show tapes on that when you don't have a live webcast?

**Linda:** Music.

**Frank:** But most of our videos are on the website.

**Linda:** Yeah, most of ... a lot of our videos people can just watch for free on the website. The whole thing. So a lot of the performances we've done over the last however many years you can watch the entire thing on the website.

**Frank:** And there is always at least one person.

**Linda:** Yeah, there's always at least one person watching a video all the time, if you look and see. And often there's more than that.

**Michael:** That's good! World domination! World hypnosis, that's what we should strive for!

**Frank:** Funny, a lot of artists try ...

**Linda:** ... to get their stuff out there like that.

**Frank:** Reach ...

**Linda:** To reach the masses.

**Michael:** Yeah, right. (laughing) We're different. We're trying to attack the masses, so that's a difference. We're trying to confuse the masses, that's what we're trying to do. Confuse, appall and horrify them.

**Frank:** They are calling ...

**Linda:** We just got a phone call from someone at the station saying they got a call from a guy who was watching one of our programs (this was B-TV) and said, now, what's the story with Frank Moore? What's he doing?! What's it about?! (Michael giggling)

**Michael:** (giggling) They couldn't figure it out!

**Linda:** So they are trying to figure out what's going on. (giggling) And he was watching the show when he called.

**Michael:** (pretending to be the caller on the phone) What's up, man?! You're tripping me out, man. My brain hurts, man! That's good though.

**Frank:** I cannot leave the house ...

**Linda:** It's literally true. Frank doesn't leave the house very often, but every single time he does someone recognizes him from the show. And they're always excited. They get really joyfully excited. Like, we'll be walking along the BART to go get a train and we'll hear somebody going, "Hey, is that Frank Moore?!" Totally seriously! And, "Frank Moore is in the house!"

**Michael:** (laughing) In the house!

**Frank:** A lot of black ...

**Linda:** At least they're the people that most often tell us they watch, are the people that are black.

**Michael:** You give autographs and stuff?

**Linda:** He gives gleeful laughs.

**Frank:** They sometimes ask are you really doing it. (giggling)

**Michael:** I'm actually not! I'm a holographic projection of your mind. This station has taken control of your brain and we are merely projecting your own fantasies inside your mind. Please do not panic.

**Frank:** So, someone said I was just being selfish when I fought.

**Linda:** When Frank fought the censorship attempts at B-TV several years ago, someone said that he was just being selfish when he did that. That it was all about him.

**Michael:** Well, that's absurd! Every artist that gets censored wants to break the censorship and be free to express him or herself. That's not selfish. It's selfish to censor somebody.

**Frank:** And the censor is never censoring the artist, but it is really censoring the art.

**Michael:** Yeah, they censor the art and they censor the audience. That's the problem.

**Frank:** Exactly.

**Michael:** It's the audience's mind that is being censored, it's being denied the material. Well, as some of your viewers may not be aware, incredibly enough, when Frank Moore and company did a performance at a certain space, which shall forever remain nameless, they actually did, what was it, five performances of several hours each before deciding that they no longer wanted the video to be shown?! And that you couldn't watch the video, and that the present time had to be sucked into a vacuum of nothingness?

**Frank:** Oh well, so much for a segue. (Michael laughs)

**Linda:** (laughing) You were working on a nice, clean seamless segue into the topic. (Frank laughing)

**Michael:** (laughing) And he blew it! Not with Peppe you can't ...

**Linda:** There's no such thing as subtle.

**Michael:** There's no such thing, that's right! I'm channeling Shatner today! I don't have subtle.

**Frank:** I wanted to say, if they censor in Berkeley then that would have opened up censoring ...

**Linda:** ... public access channels around the country.

**Michael:** Oh yeah! I would think, because any town committee could always say, well they censored in Berkeley, so therefore it's nothing right-wing to censor it here in East Bumfuck.

**Frank:** Exactly. Which was why the ACLU ...

**Linda:** Got involved to represent what we were doing at B-TV, because they saw. That was the final thing. The last City Council meeting we attended, the ACLU attorney was there and spoke to the Council on our behalf, and it disappeared after that.

**Michael:** Oh! Good! Wow!

**Frank:** And they were ready to sue the city.

**Michael:** Oh good! See, when the lawyer gets into it then things get serious and then they stop. So, it's either the end or the beginning when the lawyer gets into it.

**Frank:** So I don't understand saying selfish in that situation.

**Linda:** Frank doesn't understand why someone would say that was selfish.

**Michael:** They don't understand what art is then. Because artists are by definition selfish, because they're expressing their selves. The expression has to come from an ego. It doesn't come out of nothing. It comes out of a human being. A human being has an ego. So censorship comes out of selfishness more, I would say, because you're trying to impose your view of what's right and wrong on people.

**Linda:** And the fact that the ACLU thought that it was something that was worth their getting involved in, you would think that would mean that they saw it as something beyond just about Frank and his work.

**Michael:** Yeah! Of course!

**Linda:** And so that's why Frank doesn't understand why one would say it's selfish.

**Frank:** But in the 1990s when the whole NEA thing was going on, a lot of artists said the artists who were targeted were just being selfish by doing art that was ruining the NEA for everybody.

**Michael:** Yeah. That's not true because the NEA I think already sucked for most people anyway. A lot of artists, a real, real, real, real lot of artists never got any money from the NEA anyway. I wasn't really so bummed out to see it go. It didn't do anything for me! It's just about bureaucracy, I think. Grants are good but they do encourage very ordinary work in that you have to put your work into a certain framework, a certain narrow definition, in order for it to appeal to the people that are making the decisions on the grants. It really has more to do with grantsmanship than it does artistic talent. So, I wasn't sorry to see it go, but I know there was a lot of hair pulling out at that time ... oh, the wonderful NEA is gone away, but I didn't care really. The fact that they censored Frank and others doesn't surprise me. Because grants censor by their very definition! Because all the people that they refuse to fund are essentially censored.

**Frank:** I did not ...

**Linda:** ... yeah, Frank had gotten one NEA grant at one point but that was it. That was just a fluke. An artist that we met, Paul McCarthy from L.A. ...

**Michael:** Oh yeah, I know him, he's amazing!

**Linda:** ... he had said, Frank, you'll get an NEA. Just fill out the paperwork. I tell you, you'll get it! So we got the form and filled it out. We didn't have to present anything. It was based on Frank's work up to that point. We had to just document what we had already done. We had a lot of pictures. And we just got it! It was $5,000, which for us that finances the art for years! That's a lot of money to us! But what we noticed was that toward the end of that year we started thinking in terms of, oh, the money is running out! And we thought, wait a minute, this is not good! And we decided at that point, that was the end of the grants for us! Because that wasn't good! We had been operating for how many years, 20 years, 10 years, 15 at that time, on nothing! And then you have one year of having money and you think you

*Michael Peppe (video capture)*

can't survive without it!

**Michael:** Yeah! You quit your job or whatever. That happened to me too. One of the few grants I got was about $5,000. It wasn't from the NEA. When you get it you think, whoa, I'll be able to live for years. And then a few months later it's gone and your life is exactly the same. And if you compare that with 30 years of performance, making art, it's nothing! That's why people get addicted to this pipeline from the NEA and it's totally artificial and it's only good for big organizations. Like if you're going to have the Los Angeles Festival or huge dance festivals and bureaucrats can make a lot of money off of grants. For every dollar the artist gets, bureaucrats get $5 probably. I suppose it's that way with private corporations too. So I never really thought much of grants. But some people are just really good at doing the paperwork and it just keeps coming! And if they're hip and trendy at the right time with the right material at the right time, then you can get on the pipeline.

**Frank:** But why need it?

**Michael:** Yeah! You only need it because you have to because you're poor, but at the same time since it's only a one-time payment, it's going to run out eventually anyway and you're going to be back to square zero. They're certainly not going to give you a living or something. And it'd probably be bad if they did for artists. So I just think of grants as being corporate by their nature. Like for theater groups that need $20 million ... but you go to see theater that's $20 million and it really sucks! It just becomes like a Las Vegas thing which happened! Now the Blue Men are playing Las Vegas. And all these art groups play ... like Cirque du Soleil.

I'm not putting down what they do, I've never been able to check it out because the tickets are always $25! I'm sure it's amazing but all the grant money goes to groups like that. A few groups like Cirque du Soleil ... really groups that are high tech, trendy, usually sexy in some sort of commercial way, and sell a lot of tickets so that they can do a lot of publicity for who the granting organization is, and they can all go to benefits together and the grantees can have a $100 dinner in their honor and blah, blah, blah, blah, blah. And it has nothing to do with individual art work.

**Frank:** mmmmmmmmmmm ...

**Michael:** We could all use $20 million a year I guess, but ...

**Frank:** No.

**Michael:** (laughing) But if you had it you would use it, probably. Would Frank Moore be better if he had $20 million?

**Frank:** No. No. No.

**Michael:** What, would you build a spaceship? What would you do? I might buy a fancy synthesizer, but would it be better than what I do, not necessarily.

**Frank:** Because look at what we do on no money!

**Michael:** I know! Exactly! Yeah, that's the way I look at it. You're free. You're doing what you want to do anyway.

**Frank:** Maybe buy a space.

**Linda:** And we'd have a place to perform.

**Michael:** I suppose, yeah. I remember George Coates bought a whole church. Now, I don't know if it made his work better or not, but I know that he started to charge 20, 30 bucks a pop. Maybe it made him more high tech, but was it better? I don't know.

**Frank:** He's on B-TV.

**Michael:** Well, there you go.

**Linda:** He puts on a news show.

**Frank:** He said no one watches B-TV.

**Michael:** Well that's a logical conundrum then if anyone's watching this. Because that means they don't exist. If no one is watching.

**Frank:** So the city needs to give B-TV more money because no one is watching.

**Linda:** That was his argument ... no one's watching B-TV so the city needs to give B-TV/BCM more money.

**Michael:** When artists start talking about grant money, then they start to get into these logical, circular insane logic.

**Frank:** Like would you put money into something that nobody was watching?

**Michael:** You wouldn't! People do that though. Then they have campaigns to increase participation on the part of the public. But that's the worst thing. Because then you're paying people to be involved and you don't want that. You want them to bring themselves to the table.

**Frank:** In reality, a lot of people watch B-TV. That is why the city should put more money into B-TV.

**Linda:** Because a lot of people do watch it!

**Michael:** Right! That would be a better argument, anyway.

**Frank:** Yes.

**Linda:** And it is true. We're constantly getting feedback.

**Michael:** You only need money if you really have a specific idea about something you want to do that can't be done without the money. Like, you need to blow up a railroad train or something. So you need explosive experts and insurance. But blowing up a railroad train is what Hollywood does, so they use a lot of money to make bullshit that has its head up its ass. So, why blow up a train?!

**Frank:** Oh! I thought you were talking about terrorists. (Michael laughs) And I was wondering why insurance?

**Michael:** (laughing) Terrorists need insurance too! (Linda laughing) In case he blows his hand off making a bomb, he's got to have that insurance. That's probably how they catch him is they check the insurance policies (Frank laughing) and you have a clause that says, "If you get your hand blown off at work, you get a whole lot of money." Yeah, see if you're blowing up a train, it is an act of terrorism, so why give those people money!? (Frank sounds) Here at the Homeland Security Department, we're looking out for you folks.

**Frank:** Segue ...

**Michael:** (laughing) Speaking of terrorism, we want to talk about lawyers. (laughter)

**Frank:** ... may not be possible (Linda laughing) ... to segue. (Michael laughing)

**Linda:** (repeats laughing) A segue may not be possible tonight!

**Frank:** I was waiting to ...

**Linda:** ... segue in with various topics we wanted to possibly deal with and talk about tonight.

**Frank:** But ...

**Linda:** It just ain't happening. You'll do all this fine work and you'll lay out a few key things that you think would normally lead in that direction (Michael laughing) and the next thing you know we're talking about insuring terrorists for blowing up a train!

**Mikee:** (off camera) We only have 20 minutes.

**Linda:** We only have 20 minutes left? Oh man, we better get to it or else it's a part one, part two, which is usually what happens with Michael Peppe!

**Michael:** I'm trying to follow the logic here. (laughing) Terrorism, lawyers, I get it!

**Linda:** Was there something you wanted me to read, Frank? Yes! We were doing a series of workshops at One Taste in San Francisco, an urban retreat center. And, in fact, regular viewers of this show were probably watching in January when we had as guests two people from One Taste. And when we described to them the series we had just lost at U.C. Berkeley ...

**Frank:** After I had the woman take off her bra.

**Linda:** Robert and Allyson from One Taste were the guests and they were all dolled up. And she had this beautiful, black, really revealing dress on but she had a beige-colored bra underneath it so you saw the bra. So early in the interview Frank pointed out the fact that you could see her bra and the dress would look a whole lot better without it, which led her to finally take the bra off right on camera and give it to Frank as a souvenir. (Michael laughs) And it's hanging in his studio right now.

**Frank:** So they knew what ...

**Linda:** ... Frank was like by the time we got to the part about telling them about the series we had at U.C. Berkeley that we had just lost.

**Frank:** And we talked about our two sex cults.

**Linda:** On the air ... them as a sex cult and us as a sex cult.

**Frank:** How we sex cults should stick together.

**Michael:** Sex cults should stick together. The sex cult that plays together stays together. Everyone knows that! Look at Scientology. No, they're not sexy, actually.

**Frank:** Exactly. Ever notice how sex cults are rarely sexy?

**Michael:** That's true, they usually aren't. Well, I don't know, I haven't been in a real one. But you hear about them and you read about them. A lot of times they're just concerned with diet and the right hair cut (Frank giggling) and having the right sneakers or Nikes or the right Kool-Aid.

**Frank:** Hence the bra!

**Michael:** Right! How can you have a sex cult with a bra on? (Frank sounds)

**Linda:** Especially a bra that you can see through the dress.

**Michael:** That's like a see-through shirt with an undershirt on! That's like wearing a white t-shirt with the top button gone. I guess, maybe it's nerd sex. But nerds aren't that sexy.

**Frank:** So I ...

**Linda:** ... when we told them about the series that we had done that we just lost, that we would tape every show and put it on our show on B-TV, they said, well, you should just do it at our space! And we'll do it for free just so it's just like what you did before. And that was how we got it going. And we did it five times.

**Frank:** But the first ...

**Linda:** It was first originally a performance series, then on New Year's Eve they got busted by the cops. They had a big party planned and the cops said they weren't licensed to have performances there.

**Frank:** Fifteen bucks a ticket.

**Linda:** For this New Year's Eve thing. So they called us they said, bad news. Because we were scheduled, our first thing was the early part of January. Bad news, we can't do performances any more. And so our series was gone. And then Frank said, how about if we do a workshop, if we call it a workshop? Because they did workshops. They said, that would be OK. So that's how it became a workshop series.

**Michael:** You can still videotape a workshop!

**Linda:** Everything else was exactly the same, it's just that we call it a workshop instead of calling it a performance. It did seem to have positive effects on people. People came in thinking they were coming to something that was participatory. Because people think of workshops as something you come to do. So that worked in our favor. It went very well.

**Frank:** And I have been doing workshops ...

**Linda:** ... for 30-plus years, so that wasn't a problem.

**Frank:** That was how I got started.

**Linda:** Doing workshops.

**Michael:** So what happened?

**Linda:** We met their attorney the first time we went there to check out the space. So he knew all about it. And he had actually attended one of them early on in the series. And then the fifth one that we did the attorney was also there, kind of hiding, and Frank pointed him out, (Michael laughs) drew attention to him. He said he was hoping to stay anonymous.

**Frank:** Brought him up to the front.

**Linda:** Shone the light on him.

**Michael:** That's good! Lawyers should have the light shone on them.

**Frank:** That may be one of the reasons ...

**Linda:** ... why we got booted.

**Frank:** And I really got ...

**Linda:** ... that first guy? When a workshop starts, whoever is there Frank would start talking to them. So this one guy was there and he started talking to the guy, he said well what do you do? He said, oh, I sell real estate to yuppies. Kind of condescending about the whole thing. He said but I really have worked at a non-profit, but I just recently stopped that and I do this now. Obviously his identity was the person that worked at this non-profit, but he doesn't do that anymore. Frank said, why do you work as a realtor now? He said, well, I need to pay the bills. So Frank said, oh, so you weren't paying the bills when you worked at the non-profit?

He said, well, yeah, I was paying the bills. Frank said, then why did you have to leave that to do the real estate thing? He said, well, I was barely paying the bills. Frank said, but you were paying the bills. (Michael laughing) He said, yeah, I was paying the bills. Frank said, then why did you do it? He said, I wanted to be able to do this workshop I'm leading on intimacy and how to get a girl. How to get an intimate relationship with a woman. Frank said, so you have a relationship? Where is your person? Are you here alone or do you have a person? Oh, I have lots of people that I'm in deep relationships with, they're just not in the country now. They're all traveling and in various places. (Michael starts laughing)

**Michael:** They've all left the country now (laughing), but they were here for a while. Now they're on the other side of the world.

**Frank:** So why should I take your workshop?

**Linda:** Frank said to him, why should I take your workshop?

**Frank:** Sell me! (Frank sounds)

**Michael:** Yeah!

**Linda:** And he did. He did a piss-poor job of it. He didn't sell him at all.

**Frank:** He said, well, I know what don't work.

**Linda:** They were his qualifications, that he knows what doesn't work in a relationship. (Michael starts laughing)

**Frank:** I said, so do most lonely guys ...

**Linda:** ... so do most lonely guys know what doesn't work in a relationship.

**Michael:** Right! That's why you're in the workshop, because you already know what doesn't work.

**Frank:** So why should I pay you?

**Michael:** (laughing) ... to find out what doesn't work, since you already know that?

**Linda:** (to Frank) And then there was the point where you asked him about you. How did you phrase that?

**Frank:** What do you get from me?

**Linda:** Frank said to him, what do you get from me? And he started talking about how Frank is unhappy and frustrated and saying all these kinds of things. (Frank sounds)

**Michael:** The guy ... really?!

**Linda:** Yeah. And Frank let him go, and let him go, and let him go and he would ask him questions and he would just keep going deeper and deeper and deeper and deeper into how miserable Frank was. And finally admitted that it all had to do with Frank's body, that's why he was isolated and miserable because of the way he looks. So Frank turned to Robert, who was a regular at the workshop, one of the people that ran the center and said, do I seem unhappy to you. And he said, you're one of the happiest people I've ever met!

**Michael:** (laughing) That's the impression that I always got! I mean, if you can tell happiness by someone's sense of humor anyway, Frank's always making jokes and seems to be having a good time. I wouldn't say that he was unhappy. No! Because I never feel unhappy when I come over! I don't feel unhappy at a Frank Moore show! If I did, I wouldn't be in the show! It's very depressing, you wouldn't!

**Frank:** Or come to my workshop.

**Linda:** You wouldn't come to his workshop if you thought he was unhappy.

**Michael:** (laughing) You see, that's why I secretly didn't come because I didn't want to be unhappy. No, I did come! You got my ... did you get my note, by the way?

**Linda:** Of course we did! Yeah!

**Michael:** I know you got my answering machine message, but you got the note?

**Linda:** Yeah, we got the note too. It's filed! (laughing)

**Michael:** (laughing) In the archive! Well, that's good!

**Linda:** (laughing) History will remember it! That you were there and you left a note!

**Michael:** (laughing) Thousands of years from now people will look back, oh, Peppe showed up late, again. Funny we have a note like this from this other space. No, Frank doesn't strike me as unhappy. Did it become clear that that guy was just projecting his own ... ?

**Linda:** Yes, I think so.

**Linda:** (to Frank) Don't you think it became clear that he was projecting? Yeah.

**Michael:** That's what happens when you let somebody go like that, they talk too much.

**Frank:** Which is why I think ...

**Linda:** ... Frank thinks that might be another reason we got booted. Because he was probably doing his workshop at One Taste.

**Michael:** Oooohhhh!

**Linda:** And there were people there that were thinking of taking his workshop and at the end of our workshop, when Frank said, are you still thinking of doing his workshop, he said, probably not.

**Michael:** Oh! (laughing) Right!

**Linda:** So there were two possible reasons why we lost the space.

**Frank:** But ...

**Linda:** But the other one, which is what they kind of gave as the excuse of why we lost the space, is because there was a woman who came in with the attorney. Frank would do this all the time, he would talk to people that were in the workshop, and have them come up and sit next to him and talk to him and read one of his poems or something. And in the course of that she had said she was having a bad day. And so he said you can have Erika rock you. And

*Frank Moore's letter board and pointer (video capture)*

so she went back, and they ended up doing ... which was coming from her ... an erotic dance together. And Frank made comments about, hey, and I only said to rock.

**Michael:** (laughing) Don't get all touchy feely here!

**Linda:** It wasn't that he was saying not to do it, but he was clarifying that that wasn't the thing that he had suggested. That that was something that she brought into it herself. And at a certain point when he looked up and realized that that was going on ... as is in all of the stuff ... there were many things going on at one time, so he sets them off to do that and then he's doing something else and then 20 minutes later suddenly he looks up and, oh, OK, well you guys should take your clothes off. Which they did at that point.

**Frank:** Could.

**Linda:** Right, he said you guys could take your clothes off. And then they did. At some point along the way she said that she noticed the camera for the first time.

**Michael:** Ah.

**Linda:** But you know our stuff, the camera is never hidden. We're always right out there.

**Michael:** The camera is always on and this is not the first one either anyway.

**Linda:** Right! But the camera at a certain point was moving around the space and she noticed it. But she kept doing what she was doing. And then at another point Frank had Erika and the woman go over to Mikee, whose back was out and he was just beached on the floor, to take his clothes off. And when she goes over to Mikee with Erika she starts freaking out. (laughter)

**Michael:** (laughing) She saw the camera?

**Linda:** She had seen the camera before, but that's the point that she starts freaking out.

**Michael:** I hope you kept the camera running, because that's when real art is happening.

**Frank:** Or she saw ...

**Linda:** It could be that she saw Mikee and freaked out! (all laughing)

**Michael:** (laughing) I've done that!

**Linda:** (laughing) And the thought of taking his clothes off.

**Michael:** (laughing) That freaks me out sometimes.

**Linda:** (laughing) When you think about it!

**Michael:** I wake up at night ... (makes "freaking out" sounds) Yeah, I have that nightmare.

**Linda:** So, at that point Mikee says, you have to talk to Frank. So she comes up to Frank and I, in the middle of the workshop, and starts telling us that.

**Frank:** And the lawyer!

**Michael:** This is brilliant comedy though!

**Linda:** And so we say, we're not going to stop the workshop to talk to you about that. We'll talk to you about it when the workshop is over. So she leaves and goes into the kitchen and stays there for the rest of the workshop. So the workshop goes on and ...

**Frank:** Hot!

**Linda:** And it was hot! Which they generally were, and this one was no exception. And when the workshop is over, everybody is feeling really good and really high and it's all wonderful, and then we get ambushed by her and the attorney. They just show up and they're in our face, and he's talking legal talk to us, you have to excise everything that has her in it from the tape before you play it anywhere!

**Michael:** That is absurd!

**Frank:** How?

**Linda:** Yeah!

**Frank:** So it was agreed that they would put a line ...

**Linda:** ... a line in their waiver. They started having people sign a waiver that week. That was the first week they did it. They had asked Frank about it two workshops before that. Frank said I don't want to have anything to do with it. If you want to do a waiver you can do a waiver. But my experience in the 30+ years I've been working is that it's better to leave all that out of it and just do the work. And I've never had a problem. But if you want to do a waiver, I'm not going to have anything to do with it.

**Michael:** Right!

**Linda:** So this fifth workshop, they had everybody sign a waiver when they came in. So the attorney said if you add a line to the waiver that tells people that they understand that they're going to be videotaped and then that's OK. So we said, we don't care what you did with the waiver, we're going to keep doing what we're doing.

**Michael:** Right!

**Linda:** So that was the way it was left. Two days later we get a phone message from Robert at One Taste saying that they've been talking with the attorney all weekend about what happened and he needs to talk to us. So we asked him by email if he would send it in an email because Frank doesn't really talk on the telephone.

**Frank:** Being a crip ...

**Linda:** ... comes in handy sometimes.

**Michael:** (laughing) Yeah! We all know Frank is faking anyway, so ... he doesn't fool anybody!

**Frank:** A lot.

**Linda:** Being a crip comes in handy a lot! So this what I have here (holds up sheets of paper), is his email to Frank, with Frank's responses intertwined in it.

**Michael:** Do I have a version of that?

**Linda:** Yes.

**Michael:** I brought it.

**Linda:** Do you want to read it?

**Linda:** (to Frank) Do you want Michael to read it?

**Michael:** I could do some of it. You could do one part, and I'll do the other part.

**Linda:** OK. Which part do you want to do? Do you want to be Frank or Robert?

**Michael:** (laughing) Well, Frank is the sexy one.

**Linda:** Frank has the best lines. (Frank giggles)

**Michael:** Frank has all the best part and it's sexier.

**Linda:** Well, since you're the guest you can be Frank if you want.

**Michael:** Good!

**Linda:** And I'll be Robert.

**Michael:** So you'll be the bourgeois geek (Frank giggles) lawyer-type guy for the people who don't follow their own ...

*Michael Peppe (video capture)*

**Frank:** Not the lawyer.

**Linda:** No, Robert isn't the lawyer. Robert is the guy that kind of runs One Taste and is the person that was the guest on the show the first time that was the one who invited us to do the series.

**Frank:** Who likes the workshop.

**Linda:** Robert was at every workshop we did and loved the workshop.

**Frank:** But will not stand up for it.

**Linda:** So you have the first line.

**Michael:** OK. So this is Frank talking. *Robert, I'll respond throughout your letter to you.*

**Linda:** *Hi Guys- First off, I enjoyed the workshop on Friday.* (This is Robert) *The energy it sent into me and the community has been VERY palpable. We've been on a big ride there.*

**Michael:** *Yes, it is very powerful how it is developing on all levels. But it is an on-going journey, more than a "ride." The word "ride" suggests a thrill ride which trivializes the journey of the workshop. I know you see the workshop deeper than a thrill ride. We are journeying outside the walls of fear, isolation, etc. I wouldn't be doing my job if I agreed to let those same walls limit, contain, undermine, that magic journey within the workshop. That would totally kill what is growing within the workshop. And I have not done that in 40 years of doing this in THE REAL WORLD. I don't plan to start now.*

**Linda:** *Personally, I felt dancing with Adam broached a lot of subjects with me that I'm slowly sorting through.*

**Michael:** *Yes, everyone got a lot out of it. And that liberation spreads out into the outside world through broadcasting it, through webcasting it, through writing about it, etc. It would be extremely sad to deny them this out of fear generated by a lawyer. According to him, what happened Friday night? What happened that didn't happen in the other 4 sessions, including the first one he was at? What are his "concerns"? What would jeopardize One Taste? How? You kindly offered me One Taste to do my performance/workshop after I described what I had done in my series at U.C.B. ... including videoing every session to play on LUVeR, B-TV, etc. This was during your first appearance on my SHAMAN'S DEN show. So you knew before you offered that we would be videotaping the sessions. You knew that videotaping was part of my art/work. We have videoed all 5 sessions with your full knowledge. So the below ultimatums are surreal!*

**Linda:** *Onto less fun things. I've been talking with our lawyer pretty extensively over the last few days. He is very concerned on a lot of levels about what happened on Friday night. His concerns, after talking about them, are valid in our book and we'd like to make some changes immediately. He says, and I agree, that not doing so puts One Taste in jeopardy.*

*(1) We cannot video tape the workshops anymore.*

**Michael:** *This would end my doing the workshop at ONE TASTE. This is your right of power. But it would be a shame. And I don't think that is your desire. It would be impossible to do the workshop without the freedom.*

**Linda:** *(2) We cannot have the past five workshops being broadcast on Berkeley public access television.*

**Michael:** *As you know, they've been playing on LUVeR and B-TV ... as have the two Shaman's Den shows you guys were on. You can't put the genie back in the bottle.* (Frank giggles) *The workshop is/was a public event of my work.*

**Linda:** *(3) We would like any mention of One Taste or any of our names taken off your website.*

**Michael:** *Why on earth would you want that? Rather insulting. But I don't hold that against you. Fear is irrational. But we have a history together.* (This is my favorite line out of the whole thing.) *I don't erase history.* (Frank giggling)

**Linda:** *(4) In future emails/promotions, please use only our first names and not our last names.* (Frank continues giggling)

**Michael:** *Again, why? No.* (Frank giggles) *And hey, how many good-looking ROBERTS are there at ONE TASTE?*

**Linda:** *(5) And, we would like the return of the 5 videotapes of the first five workshops so we can destroy them.*

**Michael:** *Those tapes are of my art/workshop and are property of Inter-Relations. One Taste has no right to them. RETURNING IS AN EXTREMELY STRANGE WORD to be using. But then so is "destroy" art and history. If I were you, I'd fire that lawyer ... or at least get a second opinion!*

**Linda:** *I am sorry it is going this way but in this era, it seems prudent. Regards, Robert*

**Michael:** *In Freedom, Frank Moore*

**Michael:** That was my favorite line: I don't erase history. You can't! Even if you ... for one thing, if you sent ...

**Linda:** We're at the end of the show.

**Michael:** Is it already over?

**Linda:** 2:20, we practically have like three minutes to fit it all on one show. Let Michael do a wrap. Go ahead, Michael. Wrap it up.

**Michael:** I just wanted to finish off with that, was the fact that sending the videotapes so he can destroy them ... you should have told him, if you like we can dub another copy of a video (laughter) and send you a tape and you can have yourself a little bonfire and go out and burn it if it gets your rocks off. But it's too late. Once you videotape something it's too late. It's out there, it's history, it happened and in fact it becomes more important to preserve it because of the fact that it got a reaction from people and the people are worried about it and they're wanting to censor it and they're wanting to destroy it. Obviously, why would they want to destroy it if it weren't something important? And something that is truly art! Which is what you get when something really matters. And people get upset and they get invested and their life changes and it has an impact on them. That's the kind of tape you're going to keep, forever, because it's a great art tape, because it shows people chickening out of their own philosophy, in some cases. Or standing up to their own philosophy, depending on the situation.

**Linda:** So, on that note ... very good! So that was/is Michael Peppe and this is the Shaman's Den, and we'll see you later!

(Michael and Frank start singing "Happy Trails". Linda joins in. Michael segues into singing theme song of *The Howdy Doody Show*)

**Linda:** (laughing) That's the next time around! OK, bye!

# Kevin Danaher

Recorded March 10, 2002 on luver.com

......................................................................................................................

When Frank ran for President, six years after this interview, he told a German journalist who was interested in doing a story on his campaign that he was thinking of Kevin Danaher for Secretary of State. This interview shows why! And you can see the seeds for many of Frank's presidential platforms in the alternative models discussed below. Kevin was reluctant to do a 2-plus hour interview ... and even when he agreed to be on the show, he still thought he wouldn't have enough to talk about, to fill the time. Frank has fun reminding him of this, two hours and eleven minutes into the conversation!

Kevin Danaher is well known as a co-founder of the human rights and social/economic/ environmental justice organization, Global Exchange. He also co-founded FairTradeUSA and the Green Festivals, which are the largest sustainability events in the country. Kevin has also authored and/or edited 13 books, and is currently a lecturer at San Francisco State University in the Department of Sociology.

In the wake of huge protests against the World Trade Organization, the International Monetary Fund, and the World Bank, followed by 9-11, their talk is a radical roller coaster ride through the issues of our time, seeming to touch on almost everything with a lot of humor and kicking ass, revealing the "combine". Frank's masterful interviewing throws those unexpected switches in the track, always taking their ride deeper!

......................................................................................................................

**Kevin:** They also set the voting machines, the ballot counting machines, in predominantly white counties. They were set in a way that if you put in a bad ballot, a spoiled ballot, it would kick it back at you and say, this is wrong, you got to vote again. In the predominantly black counties, they had it set so that the ballot would be accepted, it wouldn't be counted, and the voter wouldn't be told that it wasn't being counted. So, literally thousands of black voters, who were mostly going to vote either Nader or Gore, got eliminated from it, when you have a few hundred votes difference. Then there is the second piece. There were 170,000 ballots that weren't counted, because of the chads being dented, or one corner hanging off, whatever. The New York Times, Washington Post, Miami Herald, a whole bunch of media companies, formed a consortium. They went, they took the 170,000 ballots, and they did nine statistical tests on them. One, if the Florida Supreme Court's first decision had ruled, if the Florida Supreme Court's second decision, if Gore's strategy, if Bush's strategy. Nine different ways! Six of the nine gave it to Gore. Three of the nine gave it to Bush. And the way the media reported the story was, oh well, Bush won! Ah, excuse me, but my math tells me if six of nine say Gore won, and three of nine say Bush won, Bush ain't the president! And then he had to have the Supreme Court hand the presidency to him! So this is very sketchy stuff.

**Frank:** We aired a video on voting fraud.

**Kevin:** Yeah, it wasn't just Florida. Chicago and a lot of other places ...

**Linda:** This was before, the video that was done before this presidential election. It was a video on voter fraud.

**Frank:** Five years before this. In Florida.

**Linda:** They show his crew going into a room where there's all these little old ladies counting votes, and they are just like indiscriminately ... picking and choosing which goes where.

**Kevin:** Well, my wife, Medea Benjamin, she was running for the Green Party, running for the U.S. Senate against Diane Feinstein on the Green Party ticket. She went down there immediately, to mobilize people because the right wingers, the Republicans, had their people out in force, and they were intimidating the vote count, and stuff. And she went down and she said, is it only Republicans and Democrats who get to be in the counting room? I'm a Green Party candidate for the U.S. Senate. And they said, oh, I guess so. And she got in there, and she said you could see it was so half-assed, the way they were doing the whole thing! Here is the presidency of the most powerful country in the world, hanging in the balance, and there is all this jockeying and finagling going on. And then the presidency gets handed to this guy who doesn't read books! And the public is OK with that?! That really scares me. The scariest thing is that the public doesn't go out in the streets and rebel against it.

**Frank:** Why did not Gore do anything?

**Kevin:** Ah, that's a very good question. The Democratic party, not just Gore, but the Democratic party, what they did was, they took a legalistic strategy. They're all lawyers, so they said, oh, no, no. Let's stick to the courts. And it's this "don't rock the boat" kind of philosophy. If you go back and look at the photographs of the Republicans that were out in the hallway banging on the door, and doing all this pressure on the vote counting, the people have published these photographs and they can pick out and identify, this one is an aid to Republican congressman so and so. This one is a Republican staffer of senator so and so. They're all paid Republican staff people that were out there. It's like a goon squad putting pressure on the vote counters because they knew what was at stake, they didn't want Gore's votes to be counted. Not to mention the Palm Beach County ones, Jews for Buchanan! All these Jewish voters who supposedly voted for Buchanan?! Not likely! But the way the ballot was rigged, you had elderly people who would have voted for Gore and Nader, ended up being counted for Buchanan.

**Frank:** Was Gore just dumb?

**Kevin:** Dumb? Stupid! (laughter) I think it's a combination of both. I think there's a structural phenomena of guys who are inside the palace and they're part of the game. It's why the Clinton administration gave Jesse Jackson a job in the State Department as a roving diplomat. Because they'd rather ... you know there's this saying, better to have them on the inside pissing out than on the outside pissing in. And within those ruling circles, I saw this when I lived in Washington for five years, disagreement goes so far (Frank sounds), but questioning the system and real basic things, no! Then the criticism stops, if you want to have a career. And Gore was planning for the future, figuring, well, I can run again even if they screw me this time. I'm going to do well. He's very well paid. He can go out on the lecture circuit and get $50,000 - $60,000 for a speech. So they're playing that safety thing. And stay within the palace grounds.

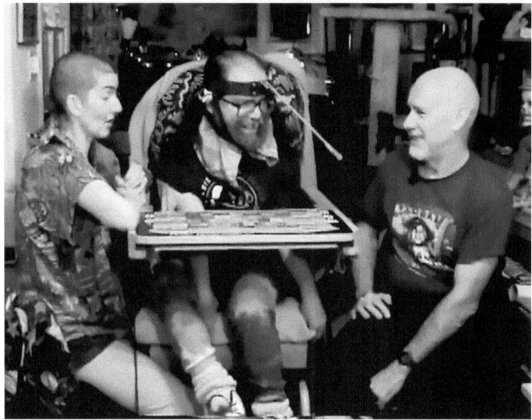

*Linda Mac, Frank Moore and Kevin Danaher (video capture)*

**Frank:** For genetic companies.

**Linda:** Oh, he's doing stuff for genetic companies, Gore. (Frank sounds)

**Kevin:** Well, you got to remember, that when the South Africa case came up, the South African government had affordable AIDS drugs that they could produce on their own. As does Brazil, India, a lot of third-world countries. What's being pushed for in the World Trade Organization is real strict limits on the ability of third-world countries to produce their own drugs. They want them to be bought from the big pharmaceutical companies. On Gore's staff, very high up on his staff, were people from the pharmaceutical industry. So, he was opposing, when he was vice president under Clinton, the right of South Africa and other third-world countries to produce their own generic drugs for AIDS and other things, when, of course, it's more affordable that way. And instead saying, no, we got to have global rules that will prevent them from doing that! So, you see, there's a very interesting thing going on here. When they're protecting the profits of big transnational corporations, that's patent rights and intellectual property rights. It's not called protectionism. (Frank sounds) When we try to protect workers or the environment, we're protectionists. Protect is a positive word. There's nothing negative about that word.

**Frank:** Who is the real global movement? Not them ...

**Kevin:** Well, what you got going on, I think, is, when they say in the press, globalization, they're talking about elite globalization, top-down globalization. The globalization of the big corporations, the World Bank, the IMF, the WTO. It's money values. There's another globalization, that we're doing in the global justice movement, in the environmental movement, coming up from the grass roots, saying, wait a minute, we're going to replace your money values and violence with life values and non-violence. And if you go out to a general public audience, I do this all the time, I say, which is sacred, commerce or life? Should you subordinate life to commerce, which is what the guys ruling the planet now say? Or should we subordinate commerce to life, human rights and the environment? Most people know the right answer to this! Once you answer that question, capitalism and the whole ideological underpinnings of the system, start to fall away like sand castles on the beach that get hit by a wave.

**Frank:** Yes.

**Kevin:** So, it's important, I think, when people use the term globalization, to say which globalization do you mean? Do you mean the top-down, elite, minority globalization of the bankers? Or the bottom-up people's globalization.

**Frank:** AKA imperialism.

**Kevin:** That's right, yeah. And this is what we've got to make people in this country understand in particular is the United States, we the people of the United States, the citizens who are supposed to rule over the government. We're the fourth branch of government that's supposed to rule over the other three. We have to make a transition in this country from being an empire, to being just another nation in a community of nations. What's going on right now, with the Bush administration, is this, you're with us or you're against us, take it or leave it, it's our way or the highway. And what it's doing ... just a few days ago I was in Amsterdam, meeting with a bunch of European groups. It's not playing well in Europe ... We're being laughed at. We're being mocked as a people, as a nation. People are saying, how could you possibly have somebody so stupid taking you in this unilateralist direction? "Get in behind us." You know, "we're going to kick ass in all these countries." It's not playing well. Even among the bourgeois elites in the corporate world in Europe, they're going whoa, wait a minute. You're going to screw up the whole game here. We had a pretty good thing going in terms of, redistributing global wealth toward us, and here you are, heavy handed, coming in, you got to follow us, or else! You could screw up the whole thing. And it's really scaring a lot of people. People up in pretty high power circles up in the top of the pyramid. So, people in the U.S. ... what we do at Global Exchange is we try to get people here in the U.S. to pay attention to what people outside are thinking. And what people outside are saying about us, because we have a lot to learn from that.

**Frank:** How did a punk like you (laughing) ...

**Kevin:** A New Jersey punk, yeah, I used to talk like this (with Jersey accent).

(laughter)

**Frank:** ... get into this?

**Kevin:** Ehhh, that's a good question! (laughter) Let's see, how far back do we go? (Frank screaming) My parents were not very well-schooled people. They were really poor. My dad worked his way up to being a bus driver. He was an illiterate Irish peasant. Never got a chance to go to school. My mom made it to the eighth grade. So for them, education and reading was important, because they'd been deprived of it. So, they really impressed on us, you got to get an education. You got to read, read, read. And my brother got a PhD and I got a PhD. And I think it was because of that sense of support and this notion that you can be anything you want to be. And then I turned 18, it was in 1968, right after the Tet Offensive when all of my buddies were coming back from Vietnam in bags with their heads blown off and their legs blown off! (Frank sounds)

**Frank:** Yes.

**Kevin:** And my government says, time for you now! And they try to draft me. And that really woke me up and that radicalized me. The first anti-war demonstration I went to in New York, we got attacked by the police. A buddy of mine got his skull cracked open by a night stick. Those kind of things really focus your attention. When your life is at stake, when you're physically threatened, all of a sudden that focuses your attention. So I started paying attention to the civil rights movement, the women's movement, the environmental movement, and that, reading books and traveling ... I started traveling to Puerto Rico, Northern Ireland, Southern Africa, Central America, and just listening to people. 'Cause my dad always impressed that on me. He would say, you can learn something from anybody! (Frank sounds) Don't look down at that wino laying in the gutter. You can learn something from him. And just paying attention to people. And asking them questions. And that gradually radicalized me. The reading books and traveling and listening to people, I think it will radicalize anybody, if you let yourself hear what's out there. If you really pay attention. If you do this (covers his eyes), then no.

**Frank:** Not tourism ...

**Linda:** Traveling, not tourism.

**Kevin:** One of the things that we do in Global Exchange is what we call, "Reality Tours", and this is like reverse Club Med. (Frank laughs) Get people off the beach, go out and meet real people. And we meet with ... we do probably about 60 trips a year. We do about 40 trips a year just to Cuba. And you take people to Cuba. Cuba's probably the country where the gap between what people think is there and what is really there, is the greatest of any country. They go there and they realize, oh, this place is not a hell. These are actually nice people. They're intelligent, they're literate, they're critical of their government, as all people should be. They're very fun loving, open, they want to be friends with us! Sure, they're critical of our government, we all should be! And we should be critical of all governments! And what we see in our tours is, when you take people to other countries, and you introduce them to real people at the grass roots, and they get to talk to them and hear their perspectives, the first thing they learn is not about that country, it's about here, it's about the United States. It's that they've been lied to. That our leaders in the media and the government have lied to us about what's out there. They want us to be fearful, ooooh, they, they, they're the enemy. No! They're like us! They are you and I dressed differently.

**Frank:** It is a shell game.

**Kevin:** A shell game, sure, yeah. If you think about the way magicians work, most magician stuff is misdirection. They're going like this (gestures), and the real trick is happening down here (gestures).

**Frank:** Yes.

**Kevin:** So they're putting out all this Super Bowl, World Series this, that and the other thing, all this flash bang, wiz bang, you gotta have Nike sneakers, you gotta have a Lexus car! Blah, blah, blah, blah, blah! Telling people that success as a human being is the quantity of things you own, rather than the quality of your relationships with people and the environment. And if you get people misdirected like that, you can pull all sorts of scams. But the proof that it's wrong and not the way to go is, if it were normal and natural for people to orient their lives around consuming commodities, you wouldn't need to hit us with thousands of commercial messages a day. You'd occasionally say, go shopping, oh yeah, and we'd all run to the mall! What's normal and natural is to focus on family, and community, and caring and love and togetherness and solidarity. And they have to bump us out of that normal, organic track into this treadmill: oh, I've got to go to the mall to get that new piece of garbage to put in the garage that I have to have a yard sale every week to get rid of the old crap, to make room for the new crap. And then you're on a treadmill working a job you don't enjoy to pay for it.

**Frank:** And make you think you don't have power.

**Kevin:** Power, yeah.

**Frank:** Unless you go through their channels.

**Kevin:** Sure, yeah. Over this way, folks! Get in line! Go right through this portal over here, and pay us your admission. (Frank sounds) It's like Disneyland. That's what our politics is. You know, it's like a Disneyland politics. It's not hands on, people controlling it. It's people relying on the people in power. We'll choose candidates for you, and you can have this rich, white, millionaire corporate trade lawyer, or you can have this rich, white, male corporate trade millionaire lawyer. Wait a minute! How about somebody different? How about somebody that is going to be critical of corporate power? And that's what I think we've got to get at. In our work at Global Exchange, we do a lot of work on the corporate takeover of government. Not just national government, but global government. The World Bank, the IMF, World Trade Organization. That's global government. It's secret global government. And even right wingers will agree, that if there's going to be global government, it shouldn't be secret, it should be out in the open. So these guys are really vulnerable. They've done a scam, they've done a little magician's game of hiding the truth from us, and we've got to reveal it to people, to empower them.

**Frank:** They are very fragile.

**Kevin:** Sure. If you think about this, they've already lost. At these protests that we do outside the World Bank and the International Monetary Fund, we put tens of thousands of people outside those institutions, so that they have to spend ... last, what was it, April 2000, they spent over 7 million dollars, just on police! Thousands of police out there, just for them to have a little weekend meeting! Now, what does it say, if my organization had to spend millions of dollars just to have a board meeting! (Frank sounds) What would that say about our credibility? We've been trying, there's a bunch of groups that have been trying to get the World Bank and the International Monetary Fund to debate us on TV. For eight months now, we've been begging and pleading to them, come on! They have thousands of PhD economists. We got the BBC and World Link TV to agree to a global broadcast. They'll foot the bill for the production cost. You think the World Bank and IMF will agree to it? No, they won't! So what are they afraid of? They say we don't know what we're talking about. If we don't know what we're talking about, blue hair, nose rings, a bunch of kids (laughter), then show us! Come kick our ass on TV! They won't do it! They're afraid of us!

**Frank:** They don't control World Link and BBC.

**Kevin:** Exactly! And what we're saying to them is, look, we'll have fair, neutral people (Frank screams) running the questioning. Then we'll just go at it!

**Frank:** Are you kidding?! (laughter)

**Kevin:** Well, no, what they want is, they want the kind of MacNeil/Lehrer softball throw it up ... in fact, in April 2000, when we did the big protest at the World Bank and the IMF, the *MacNeil/Lehrer Report* producers called us and said look, can you people put up two representatives of the protest movement to debate the World Bank and the IMF? We said, yeah, sure. Juliette Beck from Global Exchange and Vandana Shiva from, both very smart women said OK, fine, they'd go on there. The World Bank/IMF people would not appear on the same show. They said you have to have two shows, one for us, and one for the protesters. Well, what do you think we're going to pie you or something? What are you afraid of? (laughter) But they didn't want to be subjected to our questioning and criticism 'cause they know the TV commentators are going to play it nice because they're dependent on corporate advertising. So, you see that we've already won ... at the moral and ideological level we've won. They've got the guns and the money, yeah! And that's powerful. But we've got facts and moral authority and potentially the majority of people on the planet on our side. They're a small monocrop, we're biodiverse.

**Frank:** We had a very interesting talk with our son.

**Linda:** He's 27-28. He's politically active.

**Kevin:** Good, that means you did a good job raising him. (laughter)

**Linda:** We got nervous, in high school he got real straight.

**Kevin:** Well you always think ... I have two daughters. One is twenty-one and one is eleven. And you worry because if you push your politics too hard on them, they'll end up being Republican stockbrokers or something like that. So you've got to be careful!

**Frank:** In high school ...

**Linda:** ... he got real straight. He started gelling his hair, wearing logo clothes (Frank screeching).

**Kevin:** I think they do that just to scare us! (laughter) Watch, I'll freak my parents out!

**Linda:** Then he went to college in Santa Cruz. And then he started showing up with rings all over, piercings, long hair. (Frank screeching) Now he's very active in politics. But we said OK, so what do your friends think about what's ... is it going to take a revolution to make things different? How's it going to go?

**Kevin:** Well that's what it took for the United States to get its independence from King George. This country was founded on a revolution.

**Frank:** He said most want radical change.

**Linda:** Most of his friends want radical change.

**Frank:** But they think that would lower their quality of life substantially.

**Kevin:** Well, I lecture a lot on college campuses, and what these kids are being taught is, focus on job, focus on careers. So, if you say to them, and I do this, I say, OK, I want you to raise your hands. I'm going to give you two reasons for you being in college. First I say, to get a high-paying job. Ninety-some percent of the hands go up! Then I say, to find the meaning of life. And a few hands go up. Ahhhhhhhhhh wrong! Here is the one chance you have, outside the slipstream of funding and raising money, to figure out what life is about, and instead you focus on getting some stupid job. Make yourself a labor commodity to sell to some corporation.

**Frank:** This is kids who are radical.

**Linda:** So when he's talking to his friends, these are radical kids already that think that they want change, but the quality of life ...

**Kevin:** Well, if you look at the troops in this movement, the shutdown of the WTO up in Seattle. Yeah, it was trade unions and environmentalists, but the troops, the foot soldiers, were young people. The World Bank/IMF protest, the protests in Genoa, all these different protests around the world, it's the younger generation, which to me, at 51 years old, it's really good to see, that they're ready to take the baton from us. And we can play a facilitating role, and give advice and things like that, but they're ready to take charge of the movement. And I think that's a really good thing. I think we have to start handing it over to them and encourage them.

**Frank:** But, if they believe the lie ...

**Linda:** ... that radical change equals a substantial lowering of the quality of life.

**Kevin:** Well, this is why you got to help people get out of this individualistic framework, "me!" You need a "we" ideology, not a "me" ideology. What I say to them is, look, you can approach this as an individual, and think about your income, your little house, and your swimming pool and your minivan and that kind of stuff, things! Or you can think of yourself as playing a role in changing the course of history. After you die, on your death bed, don't you want to look back at your life, and not see a bunch of stuff, but look at the fact that you may have changed the course of human development and human society and have a lot of people saying, boy, the world's a better place for that person having been alive. Given that choice, most people are going to make the right choice. Our job as educators and activists is to create options and help them see their options. I think that's what empowerment is. Helping people see, look, you do have options! You may think you don't, but you do, no matter how hard you have been repressed, there's always options. You have choices, in terms of different directions. And that's our job as activists, is trying to create the visual of those options.

**Frank:** And think Nike shoes cost us 200 times what it costs to make them.

**Kevin:** Yeah. If you look at say a $100 pair of Nikes, there's about a dollar worth of labor. In terms of paying, I mean it's worth more than that, but that's what they're paid. The workers in Vietnam, for example. We just have a report that came out last year where when the first Nike campaign hit them with a lot of criticism, they made all these promises. So, we took all these promises and we went out. We hired researchers and then we went out and interviewed workers in these factories in different countries saying, what about this, what about the toxic glues, what about the work hours, what about the age of the workers, what about the pay. And showed they lied on all these things! There's a whole book. It's about a 120-page book that we have that shows they lied! And this is why people can't trust these companies. You can only trust them to make as much money as they possibly can. Make as much profits as they can. Pay their executives huge salaries! The guy, Phil Knight, he's the head of Nike, is worth about six billion with a "B", six billion dollars. What can you do with that money? The only thing you can do with that money is control other human beings. They could double the wages of their workers, and it would add like a dollar to a hundred dollar pair of shoes!

**Frank:** He makes in one hour …

**Kevin:** Yeah, in one hour what a worker makes in a year! Now, is that right? Because we look back now on things like slavery and everybody says, oh, that was wrong. Well, right now, there's slave conditions going on in a lot of places that are producing things that Americans use on a day-to-day basis. We just started a Fair Trade chocolate campaign. In West Africa, in Ghana and the Ivory Coast there is actual slavery going on on the cocoa plantations where the workers don't get paid anything! They're dragooned. They're young men that are actually, physically grabbed, stuck on these plantations and then they're forcibly kept on there. Now people who walk around, oh yeah, Valentine's Day … eating chocolate and not realizing there is slave labor in that! Now if we can look back fifty years and say, oh, what the Nazis did in the Holocaust that was terrible! How are we going to be judged thirty or forty years from now when people look back and say, you people didn't know! Why didn't you know? Why didn't you inform yourself? So what we're doing is taking the excuses away. We're putting the information out there on our website, globalexchange.org, and saying to people, look, it's a very easy thing to do. You go to See's candy, it's right there on the t-shirt, you go to See's candy, and you say, look, you're profiting, your company is profiting from these slave labor conditions. It means they're getting the cocoa really cheap. Their defense is just like Nike and these sweatshop companies was at first … they would say, we don't own those factories. And the chocolate companies say, we don't own those plantations. Yeah, but you profit from getting the stuff at a super low price because of the low wages that are paid. Or the no wages that are paid. So we, the consumer citizens here in the U.S., have to hold their feet to the fire and say, no, you're not going to get away with this.

**Frank:** And we get screwed too because we pay 200% more than it costs to produce them.

**Kevin:** Sure. That's where these huge corporate profits come from, right? Look at the way in which, during the California energy crisis, in a period where you had an 800 to 1000 percent increase in what we paid for electricity, our use of electricity only went up 4 percent! It wasn't the consumers that were at fault! Like, they kept saying, oh, it's you consumers, or it's the environmentalists are blocking the nuclear power plants. No! It was because these companies like Enron were just ... they pushed for deregulation first in the government. They got the deregulation. They raised the prices to whatever they felt they could get away with. They screwed us out of tens of billions of dollars. As soon as the Federal Energy Regulatory Commission instituted price caps, the California energy crisis stopped on that day! It was June twenty-something of 2001. Soon as they implemented those price caps, the whole thing ends. So we've got to re-regulate these industries.

**Frank:** Why don't people notice that? (Frank sounds)

**Kevin:** Well, you know, Socrates said, the unexamined life is not worth living. Malcolm X said, the examined life is painful. Is painful! To confront the truth. To think that, oooo, I might be wearing clothing or eating food that was produced through the exploitation of other people, destruction of nature. Yeah! But that's a fact of life in today's current global economy. And you're either going to put your head in the sand or you're going to get involved in changing it. John Madden, the football commentator, has a good maxim. He says there's three kinds of people in the world. The kind of people who make things happen, the kind of people who stand on the sidelines watching other people make things happen, and the kind of people who don't know what's happening! So you got to decide. Which of those three do you want to be? For me, it's easy. I know which one I want to be. It's not a sideline spectator sport.

**Frank:** And it is for no reason except for profit. There are technologies out there.

**Kevin:** Sure, sure. You look at wind energy, for example. The Bush administration, oil guys in the White House, they come up with an energy plan that says, oh no, we stick to burning fossil fuels, which is destroying our environment, causing global warming, build-up of greenhouse gasses, etc. And they say, oh, conservation and alternatives, yeah, that's nice if you want to do that as an individual, but not as a policy. Well, in fact, if you look at the price structure of wind energy, wind energy is now competitive with these other forms of energy. Countries like Denmark, a lot of our windmills here in California were manufactured in Denmark. There's a huge growth industry. Wind energy sales in the United States alone last year jumped 60%. There's a huge growth industry. If the federal government wanted to encourage that and put subsidies in that, the scientists tell us, three states, North Dakota, Oklahoma, Texas could provide the electricity. Just the wind energy could provide the electricity for the whole country. So the potential is huge!

**Frank:** But wind is hard to monopolize.

**Kevin:** Ah, that's it, see! (Frank sounds) Now watch, what's going to happen is, when the big oil companies, Exxon, Mobil, Chevron, etc., as they start to own more and more of the solar and wind energy companies, then we'll start to get it! So, ultimately this stuff is not about a technical fix. We always get people calling us at Global Exchange saying, amaranth, soy, solar power! You know the snake oil. As if there is something that we can rub on our head or put in our shoes and that's going to fix everything. It's political struggle is going to fix this. And the

269

political struggle that has to be aimed at separating corporations and the state. We established separation of church and state, now we need separation of corporations and the state. They've taken over our government.

**Frank:** Get rid of corporations.

**Kevin:** No institution ... it's a simple principle ... when they established this country, this principle of separation of corporation and the state, of church and state, was a simple idea. No one institution in society should dominate government. Government is supposed to be the tool of all the people and represent all the people. So why should corporations be able to dominate the government? With this money that they get through profit-making globally by exploiting workers in countries where people don't have freedom to form a trade union, or freedom to speak out. Notice how these guys, it's so hypocritical, you go back 10-15 years, they were all anti-communism. Now Bush is over there sucking up to the Chinese communist party. Oh, it's OK. Yeah, because Hewlett-Packard and Intel and all these U.S. companies are in China producing at very low wages, very low environmental regulations, and bringing this stuff back here. The United States imports more computer equipment and electronics from China than China buys from the United States. Because all these U.S. companies shut down their factories here, moved to China to produce it there and bring it back here.

**Frank:** The shell game.

**Kevin:** Sure, yeah. You can't allow people ... if the public ... if just I could do a brain dump of the stuff that I've learned from studying global economics, into the American voter, people would be out in the street, there'd be a rebellion! It's that they don't know. And I defy you, go through the 80 channels of TV or whatever it is, and you'll maybe find one or two that occasionally have something critical of corporate power. It's just not on!

**Frank:** LUVeR.

**Linda:** LUVeR has a lot of stuff that's critical of corporate power! (laughter)

**Kevin:** Right.

**Frank:** We are spoiled.

**Linda:** Yeah, right, well, we started LUVeR three years ago, and then the more and more we listened to LUVeR, the less we became able to watch TV.

**Kevin:** Sure. But think about the average person out there. I was just in North Carolina, in Elon, giving a talk at the university there. And you go around on the streets, and in the shopping malls and stuff and you just talk to regular people about what their concerns are, and what their analysis is, and you see that people have just been so propagandized. (Frank sounds) But think, Nike, just Nike alone, if you gave our movement, the global justice movement, not just Global Exchange, but all the groups, if you gave us just Nike's advertising budget for one year, it's a billion dollars, we'd kick ass! Because they are putting so much money into this misdirection of the public mind, and that's the bullseye issue is the public mind. If we reach the public mind with a life-values message against the money-values message, we win! If we don't reach the public mind, we lose. That's really what it's about is reaching the public mind and mobilizing people.

**Frank:** That is why they are scared of us.

**Kevin:** Right! It's why they have to mobilize the public airwaves. The public airwaves, radio and TV, belongs to us! We, the people own it. Our government, our quote, unquote, government gives it to these media corporations and they use it in a way that most people don't understand. Most people think that we're the consumers. We're doing the buying and what's being sold is the tires and the toothpaste in the ads. That's not the way it is. We are the product (Frank sounds) that's being sold to the corporate advertisers. It's why the cost of Super Bowl advertising goes way up, because the company, the media corporation is delivering millions more minds to the corporate advertisers, they can charge more. So, in fact, it's a form of slavery! We're being marketed and sold to these corporate advertisers. They don't care about our welfare. Whether we're good people or civilized. They just care about selling stuff! And making money! And that's it! And whether it's cars or whatever, they're just interested in increasing their profits. That's what drives the system.

**Frank:** One problem is radical groups buy into the money mass ...

**Linda:** Oh, thinking that they have to reach a lot of people, and it's not worth it if you're not going to reach a lot of people.

**Kevin:** One of the big problems in the movement that's now being dealt with and being solved, not completely, not quickly, but it's gradually being solved is, groups in the past, on the left, in the progressive movement would fight each other. Fight each other for funding, fight each other ideologically ... we have the correct line, you don't have the correct line. That's starting to go by the wayside. If you look at these big mass mobilizations like what happened in Seattle and Washington at the IMF/World Bank, etc., it's people realizing, OK, I might have my analysis, and I might have my particular issue, and I might have my way of approaching that. Maybe I'm into lobbying and you're into big demonstrations, and somebody else is into writing letters to Congress, whatever. We come together, we subordinate our egos, we subordinate our particular perspective into the bouquet, into this larger, biodiversity of a movement. That's what's going to ... it's like fingers in a fist. Each finger has its own specific function. Thumb might be better for hitch-hiking than a pinkie, but it's when they work together that you either get the power of the fist or the beauty of a piano playing or whatever. And that consciousness now is starting to spread throughout the movement. Let's get over the sectarianism and let's work together and let's come together and build a movement.

**Frank:** They come to us ...

**Linda:** Oh, we've had groups come to us to find out how to do an internet station, because they want to do that. And so, we tell them you can do it real cheap and we tell them how to do it. And what's happened, in a couple of the situations, is that they think that that's too rinky dink. They want to get thousands and thousands of dollars and do it bigger.

**Kevin:** If they can do it, that's great! I'd like to know!

**Linda:** But what happens is that they don't do it at all! And so we always say, just do it at this level, and then maybe you'll be able to go to a higher, bigger level.

**Kevin:** Well, it's like Global Exchange. People look at us, we've got forty-two staff people.

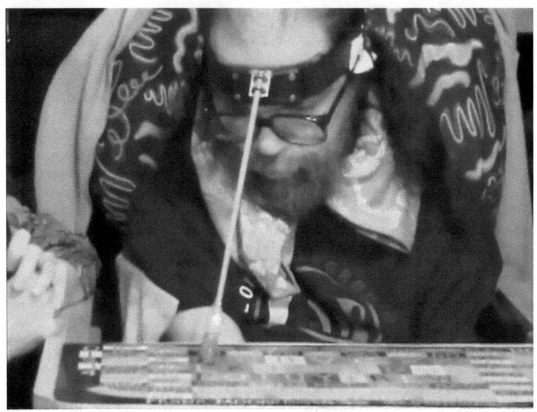

*Frank Moore (video capture)*

People say, "Wow, how'd you get to that size?!" Well, it took thirteen years! (Frank sounds) Gradually, slowly build, build, build and you add on pieces that can support themselves. The tours support themselves. The two stores we have support themselves. My books bring in royalties, not to me, but into the organization. When I get fees for speaking, that goes into the organization. "Reggae In The Park", we do events. And you get different streams of revenue, then you're not dependent on any one source.

**Frank:** We ...

**Linda:** That's what we do too.

**Kevin:** Yeah. There's a basic principle of organization and I think people should get hip to it, and that is, the more diverse the sources of funding, the more stability you have. It's like a centipede that has a hundred legs. You break one leg, no big deal. A lot of these NGOs are dependent on one or two foundations for the bulk of their money. (Frank sounds) If that foundation changes their direction, you're screwed. You go to a fiscal crisis. So if you diversify your funding base ... plus I think there's a consciousness. If everybody in the organization has the attitude of I have a responsibility, I have a fiscal responsibility to the organization, one, to minimize expenditures ... don't waste paper, you know, that kind of thing. Don't talk on the phone more than is necessary. (Frank sounds) And two, to maximize revenue coming in, then the organization will be stable. If people have this attitude of like, OK, you're the fund raiser, you raise the money and I'll spend it, you've set up now a ghettoization of the people who raise the money, and that's not healthy.

**Frank:** And don't focus on how many people you're reaching.

**Linda:** That's the other thing we find, that people get kind of obsessed that they're not reaching enough people.

**Kevin:** Yeah, well, there's different ways to reach people, too. For example, I do a lot of radio. Now radio is great because you can be laying in bed at home doing a phone interview and reach thousands of people on a Detroit radio station early in the morning or something like that. That's great. But, it's a thin hit because people are cooking, they're chopping up carrots, or driving in their car, they might be at work. It's not the same as an hour lecture where you've got them in one room to hit them with your message solid for an hour. Or having them read your book. There's different ways of reaching people.

**Frank:** Or a two hour conversation like this! (Frank sounds)

**Kevin:** Exactly, where you can get into stuff in detail! I do some radio shows where I'll say to the announcer, I'll say, well, what's your average sound bite. And some of these commercial stations, they'll say, try and keep your answers down to 30 or 40 seconds!

**Linda:** Wow! (Frank sounds)

**Kevin:** What are you going to say in terms of explaining the global economy in 30 or 40 seconds?! And then you just about get some momentum going, and it's a commercial! I got on one of these Fox News talk shows, Hannity & Colmes, where it's a fake liberal, he's really a right winger, and then a Nazi, a fascist. And that's their spectrum. (laughter) So, I'm in a studio out here in San Francisco, and you got these bright lights in your face. It's so bright, you can't even see the camera. And you've got a little speaker in your ear, where they're interrupting you before you finish your sentence! Going (makes squawking sounds and gestures) like this. And so my back-stage mind, my New Jersey street kid mind is saying, hey, listen moron, (laughter) if you were here face-to-face with me, you would not be talking this way to me. You'd be respectful and we'd have a conversation and you'd wait for me to finish and then you would start. But my front-stage mind has to say, no, no, no, you can't go there. You've got to be talking about, well, the terrorists who did September 11th we want to get them, but we want to get them smart. We don't want to get them stupid and kill innocent people. And these guys, you realize that they're not into debate (Frank sounds), they're not into discourse. They've got control of the microphone and they're just going to trash you if you disagree with them. (Frank sounds) Well, that shows they've lost! They can't stand up to a fair debate!

**Frank:** Yes. And I recently saw how many people ...

**Linda:** Oh, the statistics about how many viewers like, CNN actually has. And it wasn't that many!

**Kevin:** It's not that big, no. They define the public discourse, but they're not really reaching that many people.

**Frank:** I thought LUVeR reached a fraction of ...

**Linda:** Before you saw those stats you thought that LUVeR reached just a small fraction of the people ...

**Frank:** ... a fraction of a percentage, but we reach seven percent ...

**Linda:** ... of the amount of people that CNN reaches!

**Kevin:** Plus, it's not just the numerical quantity, it's the quality! (Frank sounds) I think, Chomsky has a great saying where he says, the dominant ideology in the United States in the public mind is a mile wide and an inch thick (Frank sounds). It's really thin! When you talk to people and you say, the free market, that's supposedly the dominant ideology ... *Business Week* did a survey, an opinion poll and they asked people, what do you think is the best kind of economy? When they described a free market economy, only four percent of the people they interviewed agreed with that! Most people, the overwhelming majority, 72% said, corporations have too much power, that there should be strict environmental regulations. People said they were willing to spend more money on a product if they knew it wasn't produced in sweatshop conditions. That's what's out there right under the surface. And that's why they have to do so much spending on all this propaganda and say, oh no, no, no, everything's fine, the market, leave it to the market, get the government out of the way. Because most people don't buy it!

**Frank:** LUVeR don't cost ...

**Linda:** It's like $300 or so a month. And then we have to pay ASCAP and BMI. But $300 a month!

**Kevin:** But now think. A very similar thing is going on in the movement in these mass mobilizations. I say to these World Bank guys, give us the same amount of money that you spend on your big meetings, (Frank sounds and laughter) give us that money for mobilizing our protest, we'll shut you down for good! We spend a fraction of what they spend!

**Frank:** Yes. They cannot compete with us.

**Kevin:** Yeah, we're much more efficient. And this is what I keep saying to people, when people say, oh, Kevin, you know, world hunger, how can you solve that? I say, wait, look at the numbers. The United Nations' Children Fund estimates that it would take about thirty billion dollars a year to eliminate malnutrition and starvation among children. OK, thirty billion, that sounds like a lot of money. That's what the U.S. Pentagon spends each year on maintaining the nuclear weapons stockpile to defend us against who? The Soviet Union isn't existing any more. You know, this is really not a huge amount of money when you look at shifting what we currently spend on stupidity. There's currently eight hundred billion dollars a year spent on military hardware. If you took that money, if we shut down all the national militaries ... and you got to shut them all down at the same time, you can't do one at a time, because they're all justifying their existence saying we're protecting you from those others. So, you say, OK, let's have a global campaign, we shut down all the militaries. Eight hundred billion dollars, you put that into health care and education and food and vaccines (Frank sounds) and stuff. All sorts of global problems (snaps his fingers) get dealt with really quick. There is enough money out there.

**Frank:** But no profit for anybody.

**Kevin:** Well, that's why we have to build a biiiiigggggg movement. (laughter) Because, and I think, if you look at it in these terms, if you put enough people out in the street, outside a building where policies are being made, you can influence any policy in the world. The Seattle protest at the end of '99 was the only time ever in history where a World Trade Ministers' conference got together and ended up in collapse. They didn't even issue a final communique, no final press conference, nothing! (Frank sounds) It collapsed! Because of our unity on the outside, created in-fighting on the inside and it fell apart, it disintegrated. And that should be our model: unite friends, divide adversaries! That's what all politics is about anyway at its core. So, we can do it, if we mobilize enough people. But, we've got to go out and reach people, educate them, make the movement attractive and seductive and bring in more people.

**Frank:** Funny, before 9/11 they were on the run.

**Kevin:** Yeah. If you go back, we had had a meeting in May of last year, a little over a year ago, May of 2001 in the AFL/CIO headquarters. And it was the AFL/CIO trade union leadership and everything ... the Nader right, left, all the way over to the anarchist community. And for three days we struggled around these global economic issues and we came up ... 'cause there had been a fracture from the Gore/Nader split, right, where the trade unions were largely backing Gore and we were all backing Nader, or at least most of us. And we mended that split and we came away from those three days of meetings and you know, it got testy at times, but we hung in there and used our communication skills and we got unity on three things: no fast track for Bush on trade negotiating authority; cancel the debt, no more structural adjustment, protest the World Bank and the IMF; and no new round of trade talks for the World Trade Organization. That's huge! So when September 11th happened, we were ready to shut down the World Bank/IMF meetings at the end of September. We were going to have about 100 thousand people out there, including trade unionists ready to do civil disobedience, it was going to be big! And September 11th came along and look at the way the people in power, Bush in particular, opportunistically jumped on it! It was like the Reichstag fire in Germany. Oh, everybody shut up now! You protesters are siding with the terrorists. There's more similarity between Bush and Bin Laden than between the protest movement and these terrorists! I always say to people, look, there's an oil millionaire who believes it's OK to kill innocent people because god is on his side, is that Bush or is that Bin Laden? These guys come out of the same damn mold. It's money values, god is on my side.

**Frank:** They were in business together.

**Kevin:** Sure, oh sure, yeah. Bush's father has had business dealings with the Bin Laden family, the Carlyle group that Bush's father is part of, they've been dealing with these guys making money. Cheney's company that he was head of, was making money doing business with Saddam Hussein in Iraq. Then they come out to the American people and say, oh, Saddam Hussein, terrible guy, we got to get him! Under the Reagan administration, from 1980 to 1988, the largest recipient of U.S. food-aid credits was Saddam Hussein in Iraq! People say, food-aid credits, what, they're not a poor country, they weren't starving back then, they are now because of the U.S. sanctions. There was a war that was fomented by the U.S. government between Iran and Iraq. Because you got to remember, Iran was run by the Shah who the U.S., the CIA put into power in 1953. They give the Shah, (means king, Shahanshah, king of kings actually) he rules for like twenty-five years. The U.S. government, Republicans, Democrats, they give him all these weapons, everything except nuclear weapons. Then in the late '70s he gets overthrown by Ayatollah Khomeini who says the U.S. is the devil. Uh oh, now you've got a problem. You've got a government that's got all these U.S. weapons and a guy who says the U.S. is the devil. What are you going to do? Well, the only neighboring country that could break the legs of Iran was Iraq. So the U.S. went to Iraq and said, look, we'll help you kick ass on Iran. And it was all sorts of military aid and food-aid credits and all this different stuff to help Saddam Hussein smash the Iranian economy. Then, once that's done by 1988, then they start thinking, OK, now how do we deal with Iraq? And they purposely set about getting Iraq, stupid Saddam Hussein, to invade Kuwait. They set him up for it. The Kuwaitis were slant drilling with Texas technology. Slant drilling into oil reserves that are under Iraqi territory. Kuwait was created as a piece of, the British did it, it was a piece of Iraq, that the British broke away as a way to block their access to the sea. So, they know that this guy is stupid and he's a power monger, etc. They lure him into invading Kuwait, and then it's, oh, hey, this guy's aggressive. Well, wait a minute, when the Israelis invaded Jordan and Egypt and took land away from Syria, invaded Lebanon, the United States government didn't say, oh, we've got to attack Israel to put them back in their cage and not have them invade. So you see this double standard that's out there. And really for that region, it's all about oil. If the major export of the Middle East were broccoli none of this stuff would be happening. It's about oil and the fact that this country's economy is addicted to oil. And if you go back and look at the history, at the same time that the U.S. government and the British government were imposing a monarchy in Saudi Arabia, the House of Al Saud, it's the only country named after a family. It's like United States of Rockefeller or something. They put in power this monarchy, no constitution, can women vote, women can't drive cars, OK? Not at all Democratic, very anti-Democratic, very right wing ideology, very conservative. At the same time they're doing that in the '30s and '40s, what's happening in the United States? In the United States, General Motors and a whole bunch of other automobile-related companies: rubber, glass, tire, petroleum, etc., They form a consortium. They go around the United States and they buy up about three dozen mass transit systems, light rail vehicle systems, like the J-Church in San Francisco.

**Frank:** Here in Berkeley.

**Kevin:** Los Angeles had the largest mass transit system in the world. It was a light rail vehicle system. And this consortium systematically destroyed those systems, replaced them with cars and highways, running on internal combustion engines, burning petroleum. They were taken to court! They were proven guilty! They were convicted of a criminal conspiracy to destroy the U.S. mass transit systems. They were fined $5000. (slaps his hand) Eeeewww. So you see the double standard. The rich, oh, don't do it again. (slaps his hand again) The poor, shoot that kid in the back, (gestures shooting motion) he just robbed a liquor store. Three strikes you're out. You stole a pizza, you stole a bicycle. Tough luck! If we had three strikes you're out for corporate crime, (Frank sounds) and, let's say we said, three felonies for a corporation, no more government contracts, every major Pentagon contract would be crossed off the list, just like that. Because they've already done more than three felonies.

**Frank:** Five hundred thousand died a year from tobacco. Three thousand died in 9/11. (Frank sounds)

**Kevin:** Yeah, now, this is not to say ... I don't want anybody to think that I'm not appalled by what the people who did September 11<sup>th</sup> did. It's wrong, it can't be justified. (Frank sounds) No violence against innocent people can be justified. That same day that three thousand or four thousand people were killed in the United States, there were between thirty thousand and forty thousand children who died from the effects of hunger, and hunger-related diseases that are totally curable! There's plenty of food in the world. We have millions of children dying each year from gastroenteritis, diarrhea. It comes from bad water. Billions of people in the world are drinking bad water that's killing them and killing their children. The cure, quote/unquote, is clean water with a little bit of sugar and salt in it. We're talking pennies! There's kids dying from measles! We wouldn't allow our kids to die from measles because the vaccine is like a few cents. So when you have children dying for lack of a few cents, you got to say something's wrong! Right now, in Africa, each year there are more children dying from AIDS than died in Nazi Germany during the entire German holocaust against the Jews, and gypsies and homosexuals. And yet Americans are there, rah rah our military in Afghanistan flying Apache and attack helicopters that are named ... Blackhawk helicopters named after the Native American groups who we did genocide against. If the German military named their attack helicopters the Jew and the Gypsy and the Homo, (Frank sounds) what would we think?! We'd think, god, they're sick. And most Americans don't even think about this. It doesn't even enter their consciousness. So we have this huge project in front of us. Can we get people to wake up and pay attention to what the hell is going on? Because we will get judged. History will judge us. And I'm afraid it's going to judge us negatively if we don't get our act together soon.

**Frank:** Dumbsfeld (Rumsfeld) said killing Afghans on our side is col...

**Kevin:** Collateral damage, yeah. Well, think about this. Osama Bin Laden says it's OK to kill these Americans because they're infidels, non-believers. The Pentagon says it's OK for us to kill innocent civilians in Afghanistan because they're collateral damage. There's no justification for killing innocent people. (Frank sounds) We started a program at Global Exchange, a victim's fund: a fund for the victims of U.S. bombing in Afghanistan. A little edgy in-your-face humanitarianism. We got on CNN, *The Today Show*, Fox, all this kind of stuff. Our website got up to ninety-five thousand hits a day from penetrating the corporate media. Because people understand it's wrong to hurt innocent people. If somebody in my neighborhood commits a crime and you come in and burn down the whole neighborhood, everybody knows that's wrong. So my wife and three other staffers from Global Exchange, we go over, and my older daughter went too with a video camera, and they taped interviews with people like, and I'll just give you one case ... Twelve-year-old girl, the U.S. bomb hit their house, killed the mother, the father went crazy. This twelve-year-old girl is now responsible for raising five younger brothers and sisters. I have an eleven and a half-year-old girl. A twelve-year-old girl is not going to raise five younger kids. That's just not going to happen! At least not in the way children should be raised. There's no way that twelve-year-old girl's going to raise enough money. Is the U.S. government going to go in and make it right for all these victims of family members who were killed and had their homes and lives destroyed? That's up to us as citizens! We've got to push this.

**Frank:** Never did before.

**Kevin:** Yeah, well, one of the things we're talking about is, OK, we've got this victims' fund for the victims of U.S. bombing in Afghanistan. What about the victims of U.S. war in El Salvador and Nicaragua and Guatemala and Honduras? There's famine going on right now in Central America in a part of the world that has good soil, good rain, talented people and a lot of sunshine. There shouldn't be any famine! There shouldn't even be any hunger! But it's an exporter of calories. They're growing coffee, tea, cocoa, cotton, beef for Wendy's and McDonald's. They're growing stuff for us instead of for their own people. And that's basic to the global economy.

**Frank:** Yes. I had ...

**Linda continues:** We've had two ... we had the people that started the company Planet Organics, which delivers organic food. And then we had a woman that started Full Belly Farm, who does community-supported agriculture.

**Kevin:** One of the things that I'm working on right now at Global Exchange is a green economy project. And we're going to do a green economy festival. Get the organic, the solar, the wind energy, the community-supported agriculture, the environmental groups ... get everybody together in a huge place in the concourse, where KPFA does their crafts fair. And get people together and say, look, we're an alternative system. Whether you're talking about energy or transport or healthcare or housing or food. There is an alternative way to do it that's respectful of human rights and respectful of mother nature. We can do it a different way.

**Frank:** They don't quite get ...

**Linda continues:** Well in both cases it seemed that they didn't quite get that it wasn't OK to have people producing stuff outside of our country to send to our country.

**Kevin:** Well, it's not necessary. Do you really need grapes out of season? (Frank sounds) From Chile? You know, you don't really need that.

**Linda:** Right! (Frank sounds) But that was like ... we were frustrated because they didn't seem to get ... they were thinking, well, their customers need some strawberries in the winter.

**Kevin:** Yeah. Well it's one thing if you grow them in a hot house! But flying them in from Chile, that's something else again.

**Frank:** They don't get that means ...

**Linda continues:** The people that live where these farms are, aren't getting their food.

**Kevin:** This is why we do the reality tours! If you take people down to Central America. And you take people out to two different kinds of coffee growing farms (Frank giggles). One is a coffee plantation that was done by corporations. About thirty years ago they re-engineered the coffee bean to survive outside of shade trees, out in the open sun. The shade trees, though, historically provided the biodiversity that kept down the pest infestations. When you go to open sun coffee, you got to throw a lot of chemicals on it to kill the bugs, and diseases, whatever. Poisons the soil. Poisons the water. Poisons the workers! You'll see kids bathing in a 50 gallon drum that used to hold chemicals. That drum wasn't cleaned out and washed out. The instructions are in English! So, they can't even read it. Now you go ... then you take people over to a Fair Trade coffee co-op that's shade tree production, organic production. The farmers are getting paid $1.26 a pound for their beans. The free market price is about 45 cents and the farmers aren't even getting that. They're getting maybe 25 or 30 cents. The 45 cents is going to the guy with the truck, who can go out and get it from them, right? And the farmers don't own a truck so they don't have that power to take it to the market. The Fair Trade coops on the other hand, there's 550,000 small farmers, grouped into the Fair Trade movement, with groups like Global Exchange, Transfair USA in Oakland here in the global north that are pressuring the coffee companies to sell the Fair Trade stuff and it cuts into their profits because they got to pay more for it and they have to pay 10 cents a pound for the license that says Fair Trade Certified. But it's us using our political muscle and our organizing educational skills, mobilize customers, put pressure on the company and say, you're going to spend this extra money and we'll guarantee it gets to the producers. And we can go to your customers and say, hey, if it means an extra penny or two per cup in that $1.50 cup of coffee, and we guarantee you it gets to the poor farmer, will you pay that extra penny or two? Most customers are going to say yes! (Frank sounds) And that's the achilles' heel of these companies. We can educate and mobilize their customers.

**Frank:** A no brainer.

**Kevin:** That's right. And that's what we say to these companies when we meet with them. We say, now look, there's two ways we can do this. We can do it the nasty, conflict way where we do demonstrations out in front of your place and drive down your profits and make you look bad. And then, in a year or two, when you go along with us and do what we want you to anyway and look like you just did it because of the pressure. Or, you can get out in front of the curve right now and look real good and do the right thing, do the smart thing. And if you get enough people inside that company to see that light bulb and go, hmmmmm, yeah, that makes sense. What we do is, when we do a corporate campaign, we buy stock in the company. So that we can go into the shareholders' meeting. We can do a demonstration outside, but we can also go in to the shareholders' meeting. And we get up and we say, look, do you want to lose money? Do you want the value of your stock going down? Do you want to lose profits like Nike and the Gap? The Gap right now, we've had a campaign for a couple years and a big lawsuit against them because of their sweatshop conditions. Just yesterday in the paper shows their profits and revenues are tanking. Now, we can't prove that we made that happen but they can't prove that we didn't make it happen.

**Frank:** They always work in the dark behind doors.

**Kevin:** Yeah, sure. The whole system is based on secrecy because the structure of the corporation is a hierarchy. It's not internally democratic. And its impact out there in the world is not democratic. Just like the World Bank, the International Monetary Fund, the World Trade Organization. They're hierarchies. It's like a military: the person at the top can fire people down here, totally get away with this. It's not a democratic process. And their relationship to our governments is one by domination by money values. So it's neither internally democratic and it's not democratic in terms of its relations with government. So of course it has to operate in secret. The World Bank and the IMF, which we pay for with our tax money, documents are secret. When they do these negotiations around debt agreements, they only make public the documents after the agreement is signed, so the people in Argentina or whatever the debtor country is, they can't intervene in the process, because you don't know what the negotiations are.

**Frank:** Like B-TV.

**Linda continues:** The same thing. The cable access channel, they do the same thing, where they do it where nobody knows about it.

**Kevin:** Behind closed doors. (Frank sounds) Sure, well, that's why you'll see these organizations schedule meetings on weird days. The fact that we have elections on a Tuesday! How about having elections on a holiday or a weekend?! Make it a day off! People have to go to work! So, of course a lot of people don't vote. I'm not making excuses here, but of course, a certain percentage of people, they get up in the morning, they got to rush to work, the end of the day they're tired from working ... ahhhhh, I'm too tired to go vote. And then you get half the population not voting, even in presidential elections. And in local elections you get maybe 70 or 80 percent don't vote! So, what's all this stuff about America's a democracy, when most people are sort of asleep at the switch. They're not even participating in the process.

**Frank:** But if you shine a light on them ... (Frank sounds)

**Kevin:** Well, they don't like that of course, it's like a rat. Rats don't like lights shining on them too. But that's ... I think that's the role of educators and activists, is to open things up and say, wait a minute, let's look at what's really going on here. Let's not live in Never Never Land and believe what feels comfortable to believe. Let's look at the truth. The truth will set us free. But the truth is painful. The truth is scary. You know, you can really get freaked out by looking at the truth. When I started traveling in Africa, and seeing children die right in front of my face, right in my arms, because of things like calorie deficiency, protein deficiency, measles, things that shouldn't even occur, that does something to you. And the first stage is to just freak out and cry. But then, after you work through that, you get really angry and you say, OK, if I'm going to channel this rage into something productive other than just going nuts, I have to find out what's the source of this? There's a story about two women who are walking along a river and they see a kid drowning. And a woman dives in, saves the kid, the kid's OK, they return the kid to their family. They walk a little further, there's another kid drowning! Same woman swims out, saves the kid, the kid's OK, they return to the family. They walk a little further, a third kid's drowning! Woman swims out there, same woman. As she's coming back with the kid, the other woman takes off running along the bank. And the one in the water says, where are you going? And she says, I'm going to get the bastard who's throwing these kids in the water. If you don't get at the source of the problem, you end up getting compassion fatigue. And in fact, in the aid industry, this is a term, compassion fatigue, 'cause they're constantly intervening to feed starving people without raising the question, wait, in a world of abundant food, (Frank sounds) why should there even be one hungry person?! There's no reason for it. There is no defensible reason for it.

**Frank:** And each and every person can do something.

**Kevin:** Yeah, and that's what it requires, it requires acting. If you think about, if we're walking down the street and there's a house on fire, and you say to me, Kevin, look, there's a kid in an upstairs window screaming for help. That house is on fire! And I say to you, well, I don't really know much about fire, I'm going to go to the library and get a book about combustion ... you're going to assume I'm morally bankrupt, and you're going to be right. And the thing to do is to call for help, call 911, break down the door, to do something! Well, the planet is on fire in that sense and the children are screaming at that window on a global level. And that's why the people in power keep doing this to us, (gestures putting blinders on his eyes) saying, oh no, no, it's OK, don't worry about that. Leave it to the experts. We'll take care of it. While the environmental crisis gets worse, every biological system is in the state of collapse and the inequality crisis gets worse. And then that means that in order to ignore that, the moral/spiritual crisis gets worse. Because people, instead of dealing with it, and paying attention to what's really going on, they're doing this, (gestures looking away and blocking their vision) they're doing the misdirection and saying, well, it's not really that bad. Well, it's the fault of the poor, they have too many kids. Blame the victim. (Frank sounds) There's a million different excuses, but that stuff will be judged historically as a cop out, because that's what it is, it's a cop out. So, our job is to make it easier for people to take that first step. That's why at Global Exchange we do Fair Trade coffee. It's very easy to go in a store, and instead of buying plantation coffee that destroys the environment and hurts people, you buy Fair Trade coffee that's a different system. OK, that's the first step. Or, our stores, we get people who come in our stores and they'll see, like a pencil box that was made in Haiti. And it's nice, it's colorful, it's cute. And then you can say, do you know about Haiti? Do you know what's going on there? (Frank gestures towards an item we got at the Global Exchange store) Yeah, the metal work, they do great metal work. And you can say, OK, this is the first step. You did the easy step. Now would you like a little information about what's going on in the world? And if you can get them to take step after step, the longest journey begins with that first step. So, we're trying to reach out. We produce stuff for radicals, but we're mainly focused on reaching mainstream audiences with that first step. Don't you want to understand the world and get involved in changing it?

**Frank:** I wrote a letter to the editor.

**Linda:** This was about the B-TV thing? Yeah, yeah.

**Frank:** That ...

**Linda:** That was all it took to start everything changing. He just sat down one afternoon, wrote this letter. Just looked up all the addresses to the letters to the editor. It took us a few hours.

**Kevin:** And sometimes you don't know the impact you're having.

**Frank:** Yes, always!

**Kevin:** I was just down in Porto Alegre. Fifty thousand people came to Porto Alegre. And I'm friends ... actually one of the organizers, is a Global Exchange person who's based in Brazil, and I said to him, you have to be incredibly happy about what you've done here because there is no way you can even predict all the cross-pollination that's going to go on because you've got grassroots activists from 130 countries. From the global north, the global south, women's activists, environmental activists, people struggling on water, against the World Bank, all

*Kevin Danaher (video capture)*

these different issues, they come together, they start strategizing. There's all sorts of chemistry that comes out of that. And new movements get started. We started the coalition on Enron, to make sure that something happens in terms of a structural critique. Because Congress is going to do this, oh, it's just one bad company, a few individuals, sweep it under the rug kind of thing. And we want to make sure that it gets out there to the public. Like, no, this is just the tip of the iceberg. This is a structural, systemic problem. So all sorts of stuff comes out of that, and you might not know! I've had times where I've done a radio show that I thought, oh, probably nobody's listening. And then you get a letter from a woman out in Montana who, she says, I'm out here with three kids on my own, struggling to keep this farm going and I heard you on the radio and it was like I felt part of a global movement, and it gave me hope.

**Frank:** Years later.

**Linda:** That happens to us all of the time. Years later somebody will call us or email us or something and say, coming to that event you did changed the course of my life.

**Kevin:** And even if somebody, let's say God came down and told me, none of this stuff you're doing is going ... I'd still want to do it!

**Linda:** Right.

**Kevin:** Because it's the right thing to do. As opposed to copping out or being part of the problem. We used to say in the '60s, you're either part of the solution, or you're part of the problem. There's no middle sideline, etc. You've got to get involved in it. And to not choose, is to choose. You're making a choice when you say, oh, I'm not going to get involved. That's a choice.

**Frank:** Like that labor song, "Which side are you on?"

**Kevin:** Which side are you on? Yeah. Pick a side. Because if you think you don't have to pick a side, you're fooling yourself. And see, one of the problems with this country is there's so much affluence, there's so much stuff. You could almost live off the garbage. Some people do. Not that it's a fun lifestyle. But you go to other countries, you go to really poor countries, people are struggling just to survive, just to get their kids to reach adulthood. The life expectancy in Afghanistan is about 40 years! That's just not right. The Soviet Union, I was just in Europe at a conference in Amsterdam, and a buddy of mine, who lives in Moscow, says that the average life expectancy of the average Russian male has declined over ten years, since capitalism came to Russia. So, it's like, yeah, you've got some millionaires. You've got this elite class that's doing very well, smoking cigars, drinking champagne, but the bulk of the population has had the rug pulled out from under them, the safety net has been pulled away, and they actually now have a regular occurrence where the temperature drops in Moscow and people die out on the streets. And he says, a lot of it, it's not just homelessness, it's drunkenness. It's people who are so despairing and hopeless that they go out, they get drunk, they fall asleep on the sidewalk and they freeze overnight. That's a really serious crisis that everybody needs to get freaked out by and say, wait a minute, something's seriously wrong when people are just dying by the side of the road. If we read that happening in history 500 years ago, we'd say, oh, what barbarism. Well, that's happening now, right now, today! It's our responsibility to do something about it.

**Frank:** In S.F.

**Kevin:** Oh, we've got homeless people right outside our office at 16th and Mission. People who are living out on the streets, strung out on drugs, sleeping on the streets, sleeping in doorways. Does the mayor ever walk through that neighborhood? The only time the mayor comes through that neighborhood, you know when he's coming through the neighborhood because about 20 or 30 minutes before he comes, the street sweepers come through, the police come through to clear out the prostitutes and the drug dealers. And then Willie [Brown - Ed.] Brown) comes through with his entourage. And I think if you have a system set up where the people who make mass transportation policy never ride the bus, and the people who make energy policy don't pump their own gas, and the people who make housing policy live in mansions and gated communities, of course you're going to have screwed-up policy! That makes sense! If you've got somebody making mass transit policy, you don't pay ... in San Francisco they pay the guy who runs MUNI about $140,000 a year and a car! They give him a car! Give him a pass! Have him ride his own bus, so he knows what the conditions are!

**Frank:** Why ain't the bus free?

**Kevin:** Yeah. (Frank sounds) If mass transit were free, and going across the bridge was $10 per car, you'd see people switch right away. But obviously, the power of the auto industry has something to do with that. What you see in Washington is, the Transportation Department is colonized by the auto industry. The Environmental Protection Agency gets colonized by the chemical companies, the big polluters. They understand that if there is government that could possibly be a tool of the people for regulating them, they have to get in there and control those agencies and make sure that they're defanged and that they can't be an effective instrument for we, the people. And that's why we're pushing this separation of corporations and the state. Until we take government back for the people, and that people have this consciousness. Notice what the right wing did. The neo-liberal conservatives did a very brilliant thing. In all their propaganda, one of the themes that was suffused throughout all of the specific stuff was, get government out of the way. Government's bad. Get government out of the way. Government is us! (Frank sounds) If government is bad, that's our fault and it's our responsibility to fix it. So what we've got to do is do a counter-message of say, no, wait a minute. We are the citizens. We are supposed to rule. Government is supposed to be our property. It's not supposed to be privatized and taken over by the corporations. It's supposed to be our tool to defend us against these powerful money types. And that consciousness should suffuse all of our work in the corporate accountability movement, the global economy movement, the environmental movement.

**Frank:** That is just the first step. We will not be safe until the corporations are broken up.

**Kevin:** Yeah. And what's going on is, you have a two-prong movement going on. The corporate accountability movement, anti-corporate globalization movement is doing the frontal assault on the corporations saying, look at the damage they do to the environment. Look at the damage they do to human rights. That's the outside the castle, like this (gestures). Then there's the alternative economy movement that's coming around the other side, saying to people, look, not only is your boat on fire but we're building an alternative boat here. And I think you got to do both. Screaming your boat's on fire, if you only do that, at a certain point people are going to say, hey, I agree with you Nike sucks. What shoes do I buy? If the movement had created a Fair Trade sneaker, (Frank sounds) during the anti-Nike campaign, we could have sold tons of sneakers! We could have made a lot of money. So the movement now is developing enterprise skills and saying, look, it's not that money is evil, it's the love of money that's the root of all evil, and that's actually out of the bible, Timothy 6:10. So, when you're dealing with your Christian friends … (laughter) we use it at demonstrations outside the World Bank: (chants) the love of money is the root of all evil (Frank sounds) with drummers! And the bankers hear that, they've read the Bible, they go, eh, yeah, that's out of the Bible. So we're building enterprise skills to say, we can create goods and services without exploiting people, and without exploiting the environment. And the profits you make, 'cause you got to make a surplus or you go out of business, you put it back into the movement. That's all, simple. You don't make profits so that I can have ten BMWs and a cocaine habit! That's not what it's supposed to be about. These guys that are worth billions of dollars, are they really happy? Yeah, they sleep on a good mattress, but are they really happy when there's a lot of people around the world who are miserable because of them? I don't think so.

**Frank:** I am pushing maximum income.

**Linda:** Frank likes the idea of maximum income.

**Kevin:** One of the ideas that I've been pushing is we need … if you look at the development of any national economy, at a certain stage in the development of a national economy, you get a minimum wage for that economy. All the industrialized countries have it. And in fact, a lot of countries have much better than the U.S. In Denmark it's $14 an hour. (Frank sounds) $14 an hour right?! It would be great here! But you get a living-wage movement here, both living wage domestically and living wage for farm workers. So, what I say is, look, if we're going to have a global economy, let's have a global minimum wage. And you can figure out what that is. You can go into any economy, see what does it cost for a kilo of beans? A kilo of rice? What does it cost to live? So let's just say, for the sake of argument, that we had a $10,000 minimum wage, that's a floor underneath everybody. That sounds low, but for most people that would be a huge increase. (Frank sounds) A lot of people live on $200-$300 a year. But if we're going to have a global minimum wage, let's also have a maximum wage. (Frank sounds) And let's say you set it at 10 million dollars. That's huge! That allows all this movement, 'cause they say, oh I've got to have incentive. Hey, if you need more than 10 million dollars to live, (Frank sounds) you've got a big drug habit, baby! (laughter) So, these guys would fight like hell. And I want to see them get up in public or get up in the well of Congress and say, oh no, we can't restrict income to 10 million a year! The American people are going to say, what?! (Frank screaming) What?! What kind of drug are you taking?! So, reason and rationality is on our side in this. And we need to use it and get out there and stick it up their nose.

**Frank:** That is why the standard of living will not drop ...

**Linda:** ... like our kid's friends think.

**Kevin:** Well, if you look at what's going on in the U.S., I'm actually working on a book that is mostly charts and graphs of the U.S. economy, you go back to the 1970s. It was Nixon that started implementing these free market policies. Let the corporations move the factories out of the country. Don't charge them taxes when they bring the products back in. This is why we have more computer equipment coming in from China than China buys from the United States, etc., etc., 'cause they started back in the '70s loosening the controls on capital. Let them go anywhere they want, do anything they want, and we get these free trade agreements, so-called, like NAFTA, now the World Trade Organization. And if you look at the data, and I have like probably around forty or fifty charts and graphs. And what it shows is, the average wages for the average worker go down. The relationship of the average worker's pay to the corporate CEO's pay keeps getting bigger and bigger disparity. The inequality among families between the richest 20% and the rest of the population gets more extreme. The inequality between whites and blacks does not improve over forty years, in terms of the average wealth. The ownership of business assets gets more and more concentrated. You do a pie chart: the little piece of the pie chart, it's what's owned by 90% of the businesses. And the big piece of the pie chart is what's owned by 10% of the businesses. And just all along the economy you see the government going bankrupt. Our federal government now is seven trillion with a "T", seven trillion dollars in debt! The interest payments on that federal debt, last year, 2001, was 400 billion dollars! That's bigger than the Pentagon. Where's that money going? That's interest, not principle, interest paid to banks, insurance companies, corporations. And a lot of them are Japanese banks, British insurance companies. It's money leaving the United States. So these guys have gutted the U.S. economy. They've created more inequality. They've bankrupted our government. The balance of payments' deficit is going like this (gestures down) for over 25 years now. We can't go on! The reason we've been allowed to get away with this by the rest of the world, is because we're the biggest dog on the block! We're the biggest economy! And there's a lot of foreign investors who are willing to invest in U.S. Treasury bills, that is, U.S. government debt. But if the U.S. dollar starts to go down, and all currencies eventually go down, they don't all just stay up there forever, if the U.S. dollar starts to go down, all bets are off. This economy could unravel like a 1930's-style depression in a matter of weeks. And it would really be the kaka hitting the fan. And unfortunately, I don't want people to wait for that kind of crisis for them to wake up. I would rather people look at the information now and say, look, we're headed at a brick wall at 80 miles an hour, the guys driving the car are talking about what cd to play. We should be hitting the brakes and turning the wheel. We're gonna crash. It's just a question of how soon is it going to come. And can we prepare ourselves and change these policies? So we need to re-regulate the economy. We need to emphasize life values, worker rights and the environment over money rights of the corporations. And we've got to get them out of power. We need campaign finance reform, full public funding of campaigns. We need to end corporate lobbying and corporate welfare. All of that! We need a constitutional firewall. We need a constitutional amendment that says a corporation is not a human being. I want to see them get up in Congress and say, no, a corporation is a human being! Aaaa, you can't argue that. So we've got them by the short hairs if we get out there and do the organizing.

**Frank:** Have the CEOs be responsible for what the corporation does.

**Kevin:** OK, there's two ways of looking at this. One is a structural analysis and the other is an instrumental analysis. The structure analysis says, look, if I were the CEO of a corporation, I would be forced to maximize profits, because if I don't, I'm going to lose my job, the board of directors is going to take me out. That is structural, it's built into the genetic code of the system: maximize profits. The danger of that is that a thousand-year-old redwood tree is not a gift of the creator or gift of mother nature, it's $300,000 worth of lumber. A fish swimming has no value until you kill it and turn it into a marketable commodity. That's built into the system. The only thing in nature that has that same kind of drive, that kind of on switch with no off switch is a malignant tumor, a metastasizing cancer cell, it will grow, grow, grow, grow, grow. That's all it knows is growth. And that's what the capitalist economy does. Well, think what a cancer, a metastasizing tumor, does to its biological host, the body. It kills it. What is capitalism doing to the planet, the biological host? It's killing it! That's at the structural system level. Then there's the instrumental analysis that says, let's look at the individual behavior of these particular people. Who is Bush beholden to? Who are these corporate executives that are making these decisions? They could make different decisions. They could decide to speed up going away from internal combustion engines that burn fossil fuels, dead dinosaurs that are destroying our climate, to solar and hydrogen cells is what they are going to go for. It's fuel cells where it's run on hydrogen. The only exhaust that comes out of a fuel cell vehicle is water, is pure water. You can drink it right out of the exhaust. There are already buses in places like Greenland and Canada that are running on fuel cells! This technology exists now, it just needs the investment made in it. And that's where we've got to hold these people responsible that are making bad decisions.

**Frank:** They are repressing that technology.

**Kevin:** Sure. Yeah. You can find cases throughout history. There was a lubricant, an engine lubricant, that was invented decades ago, that was a far superior lubricant than anything that was out there on the market. And literally, one can of it would have replaced four or five cans of the old stuff. But they held it off the market because they wanted to be able to sell all the old junk that they had before they brought this on the market. If you look at the way big corporations work, they don't compete anymore like in the old days when this ideology of oh, competitiveness is going to cause them to come up with the best products and that causes (Frank sounds) advancement of civilization. What they do is a thing called price leadership. Instead of competing and saying, OK, I'm going to lower my price under him and I'll get more customers, they do this thing called price leadership where Ford will announce that they're raising their price a certain level. If General Motors and the others don't go along with it pretty soon, Ford will retract that increase. They do not compete in terms of price. They compete in terms of advertising and stuff like that. But they understood, particularly in these monopolized sectors, they understood a long time ago, hey, we don't want to cut each other's throats, we want to make as much money, bilk as much money out of the public as we can. So there's a collaboration. Now, technically it's illegal, it's against anti-trust legislation for them to formally sit down and say, OK, let's do this, and to strategize. So they have to develop mechanisms like price leadership, or one of ... another one of the things they did do and Enron was doing this, it's a thing called transfer pricing. You've got a multinational corporation that's operating in 10 or 15 countries. On your books you manipulate your pricing within the company. You've got a part coming from this country, a part coming from that country. You manipulate your pricing on your books, so you show a loss in countries like the U.S. that have the high tax rate, and you show your profits in the countries that have low taxes or no taxes. And in fact, that process of transfer pricing is so basic to these big transnational corporations, there's a whole journal, it costs thousands a year to subscribe to it, but they sent me a sample copy (Frank sounds) because I subscribe to *Business Week* and stuff, they think I'm an executive. They send me this thing. It's a whole journal on how to manipulate international tax differences among countries so that you can pay no taxes. Enron in the last five years, four of those five years, paid no taxes to the federal government. Excuse me! You're making billions of dollars, you're one of the biggest companies in the country and you're not paying taxes?! So what you find is multi-billion dollar companies, big transnational corporations that pay less taxes than Joe Blow truck driver. Not just less percentage-wise of their income, but less as an American, as a quantity!! It's unbelievable, but they get away with it. In fact, there's a good book called, *America, Who Really Pays The Taxes?* by Barlett and Steele, these two reporters who ... it's actually a very interesting book. I never thought the IRS code would be interesting to read about. But these guys take it apart and they show there's two tax systems. There's one for the rich, and there's one for the rest of us. And I had a friend once, years ago, who is a tax attorney. And she said the only millionaires who pay taxes are the ones who are too stupid to hire a good tax attorney. Because there's enough loop holes out there, that you can get away without paying taxes. Whereas the average working class person, and in fact, the IRS for years had a conscious policy of auditing working-class and middle-class people more scrupulously than the rich because they knew the rich would fight it out and had lawyers, whereas working-class people were intimidated by the IRS and they'll pay up real quick. So you get a quicker return on your pressure. It's amazing. But it is a system and it is understandable.

**Frank:** Funny, I have been talking about what I call the c ...

**Linda:** ... the combine? Back when I met Frank in 1975, he was talking about this combine plot. (Frank sounds) And it was like ... "One Flew Over The Cuckoo's Nest", the Ken Kesey book, he talks about how everybody's kind of wired. And so it's like when you do something, you get this shot and so that's what keeps everybody in line. And Frank was saying, well that system exists so we're all kind of in that system. And people would look at him like, hello?!

**Kevin:** There's a great film that people don't know about called *Harrison Bergeron*. It's based on a Kurt Vonnegut short story. You won't find this film around because it's very subversive. It's exactly this. It's set in the future, but it looks like the 1950s and everybody's kind of happy and the soda shop and all. But everybody wears these electrodes on their head. And when somebody gets out of line, the secret government, everybody thinks there is no government, they can zap you and dumb you down, and nobody is supposed to be really smart. (Frank sounds) So it's this kid, Harrison Bergeron, and he's acing all of his tests in school and he's really smart and all, and they keep turning up the amplitude on his thing (Frank sounds) and they can't dumb him down so they say, OK, we're going to have to give you an operation. We're going to do a lobotomy. We're going to take out your frontal lobes. And the doctor says, OK, the operation is tomorrow. Here's an address, there's a party there tonight. Go and have yourself a good time, you know, there's girls there and stuff, before you get this operation. Because after you have the operation, you're a vegetable. So he goes to this thing, and it's not a party, it's a recruitment center for the government where they're skimming off talent from the population, but keeping the government secret. And he gets recruited into the government. He sees what's going on and he gets really appalled by it and then he launches this rebellion. He leads this rebellion. It's a great story! And it's totally appropriate to the way ... and TV plays a big role. Everybody like eeeaaaaaaaaaaaaaaaaaaaaaa ... watches TV and gets zoned out, right, on this mush! And it's very interesting to me that it's like a story within a story, that you can't find this video, *Harrison Bergeron*, in any of the Blockbusters, or any of that kind of stuff, because it sort of holds the conceptual key to what's actually going on in our society. Very dangerous stuff.

**Frank:** Now ...

**Linda:** ...Well, as the years went on, people started to know what he was talking about. Now everybody talks about it!

**Kevin:** Sure. Look at Enron! This Enron scandal, it's all there! You can actually see it in the corporate press. You just read the details.

**Frank:** After every guest ...

**Linda:** ... Every guest that Frank has on this show ends up talking about the same thing, which is this.

**Kevin:** What's the source, the power structure?

**Frank:** No matter what their thing is.

**Linda:** If they're a farmer, if they're a musician, they're a poet.

**Kevin:** Let's trace it back to what's really the core of the problem here? (Frank sounds) And it's about who controls, who makes the decisions? The fact that it's not Democratic. And I'm not saying that if there were popular democracy and there was great citizen involvement that that automatically solves problems, but without that, we don't know what people are actually thinking. If you never get a chance to sit at the table and make your contribution, we don't know what your perspective is. And there's a huge section of the world's population, the majority, who are excluded from a seat at the table. So what the movement is doing is, it's saying, look, when these big decisions get made, there's two basic questions: who's sitting at the table, is it a mono-crop of just the millionaires or is it the biodiversity of the human family, the human bouquet? Little Richard, the rock'n'roll singer says, all the races are God's bouquet. I like that idea. The second question being raised by the global justice movement is, what are the values? What are the values guiding that decision-making process? Is it money? Make profits for corporations? Or is it meet all social needs and save the environment? Those latter values, those life values are going to win! They're going to win 'cause nature bats last, nature's the home team, always! No exceptions to that! Human beings are one species here for a short blip of geological time and we have this opportunity to either get in tune with nature and flow with it like surfers do, or to try and put wind in a box, you know, and try and make right angles out of everything. This is crazy! It was an experiment that shot its wad, it's now at the end of the paradigm. And I think humanity's emerging from its adolescence into adulthood.

**Frank:** Yes. I am having Fritjof Capra.

**Linda:** Fritjof Capra is coming on the show.

**Kevin:** Oh, Fritjof's great. His book, "The Web of Life", is one of the few books I've read twice, 'cause it was just so good. And he shows, look, there was this paradigm that dominated our thinking: very mechanical, rigid, control nature, make money, industry, workers are there to just be drones. That whole paradigm. And now we're making a transition into a life-values paradigm out of that money-values paradigm. And in any transition you can see it ... I gave a talk to the League of Women Voters the other night and their document on global economy and trade, you can see one leg of it, one piece was still back in the 1970s: free market, oh free trade. But then the newer part that was written more recently was about saving the environment, and about workers' rights and human rights. And you can see they're sort of torn. And there's this contradiction, it's like somebody riding two horses. So, people have this sense of transition and shift and what we need to do is say, that's OK, go with it. Let's make the shift. Let's go to life values, let's subordinate commerce to life instead of the other way around. It will be a much better world. It will be a happier world. It will be a world without starving children and without clear cut forests.

**Frank:** When Helms targeted artists, he used sex but who he targeted were artists who were political, who used eroticism to ...

**Kevin:** To control people.

**Linda continues:** Well, they used eroticism to make political statements, the artists that Helms targeted. And so what he did was he focused on the sex and acted like the other part of it wasn't going on.

**Kevin:** And there's two ways to use sex. The way that the corporations use sex to sell stuff, to get you to buy stuff you don't really need. I always like those things like a naked woman selling like snow tires. What do snow tires have to do with a woman in a bikini?!

**Linda:** Whenever we see stuff like that, Frank says, "And I get shit!"

**Kevin:** Yeah, whereas we're using sex as a liberatory, something that opens up possibilities, not restricts people's possibilities.

**Frank:** Yes! That is the real reason ...

**Linda:** That the artists were targeted was for that, their political subversiveness.

**Kevin:** Yeah, using sex the right way! Instead of the commercial way! Eww, no that's bad.

**Frank:** They were gay or women or me! (Frank giggling)

**Linda:** Frank was one of them. Either gay, women or disabled.

**Kevin:** Troublemakers. (everybody laughs)

**Linda:** Troublemakers!

**Kevin:** Yeah, right! You rocked the boat! (Frank screeching) Somebody's gonna come along and smack you in the head! But see, I see that as a sign of success.

**Linda:** Yeah, us too!

**Kevin:** Whenever we get repression come down on us, that's a sign that you're doing the right thing. It's like hitting a nerve at the dentist. Ow! Oh, you know you're on target.

**Frank:** I did ...

**Linda:** ... see it as a sign of success. A lot of the other artists got bummed out and burnt out and said that it's keeping them away from their art. And Frank said, hey! (Frank sounds)

**Kevin:** Gandhi had a great saying where he said, first they ignore you, then they denounce you, then they repress you and then we win. So, we're at the repression stage, so next is we win! I tell this to young people out when we're getting tear-gassed at the World Bank and things like that is that, no, no, no. This is not a sign of their power. This is a sign of our power and their weakness.

**Frank:** Yes.

**Kevin:** That they have to resort to this. If they were really powerful, they'd come out to the public. They'd say, here are our views. Here are our beliefs and values, and here are our policies. And everybody would say, oh, wow, that's brilliant, we'll follow you. But, that's not the way it is. They've got to come out and shoot people, tear-gas you, beat you over the head, try and corral us like sheep or goats. No! That's not a sign of power. That's a sign of weakness. (Frank sounds)

**Frank:** Yes, yes.

**Kevin:** So we actually are winning, we are making progress in the struggle.

**Frank:** And they could not do anything to me.

**Linda:** Well, when that investigation was going on, because Frank didn't get any money from the government. He just kind of always like … whatever money we had, that's the money that went into the art. None of the clubs that got money from the government, except for one, ever booked Frank, because he was a troublemaker. So, he had nothing to lose. So he could just kind of like go with it and use it as an opportunity to reach more people.

**Kevin:** Yeah. It's like in our organization, we don't get government money or corporate money. OK, that means we get less money, and we have to be more frugal and our salaries are low and we've got used equipment but it means what are they going to do to threaten us (Frank screeches)? And we've had times where, for example, the government hassled us around our trips to Cuba. And said, ah, you know, this is against the law, and blah blah. And we're going to come down hard on you. And our attitude was, bring it on! You want to try and do it, OK, fine. If you think you're going to intimidate us … and intimidation only works if there is somebody willing to be intimidated. Otherwise it doesn't work.

**Frank:** Yes.

**Kevin:** So that's really important for people to understand. It's actually a sign of victory when they try to intimidate you.

**Frank:** I am always ready to dance. (laughter)

**Kevin:** Yeah, yeah, you got to be ready. (laughter) You never know when the opportunity is going to present itself, so you got to be ready!

**Linda:** I always say, "Frank they don't know how much fun you're having over this." (laughter)

**Frank:** I predicted Helms ten years before but I did not think I was important enough…

**Linda:** To be one of the ones. For ten years before that Frank was telling artists, he said everybody's trying to censor each other. The women are trying to censor this group, the gays are trying to censor this group. And he predicted that there's going to be a Helms that comes in and just kind of takes advantage of that.

**Kevin:** Divide and rule!

**Linda:** Yeah.

**Kevin:** They're great at that. And we need to learn from that. Unite friends, divide adversaries. We can't let them divide us.

**Linda:** Yes (Frank sounds).

**Kevin:** I've seen this happen in movements. It's very destructive, where people start fighting amongst themselves. We can't have circular firing squads. We need to be clear on who the enemy is. And that's why this earlier analysis of, this structural analysis, what's the source of these problems? Let's look at who's up on top, who's pulling these strings? Let's focus on them and taking their power away. Let's not fight with other people who are down here with us, who have very little power. That's what they want us to do. And I think the model they use is what they do in the prisons: you get the black prisoners, the white prisoners, the Latino prisoners fighting each other, they're not going to unite against the warden and the administration. Well they do that in the larger society as well, and we can't let them run that game on us because it's a scam!

**Frank:** Shell game.

**Kevin:** Yeah, yeah. It's the same old thing of like, eh, keep people confused, keep them distracted. And that's what we've got to focus on, is getting people centered and paying attention to what's really going on.

**Frank:** And it is not Helms either.

**Kevin:** Not just one person?

**Frank:** It was the liberals.

**Kevin:** Yeah, well, it's like people saying, if only Gore had been elected instead of Bush. Well, I think if you look at Gore's statements, he would have been bombing Afghanistan as well. These guys are part ... it's like there's two factions within the corporate elite. One is a little bit more sensitive to labor issues and the environment, and the other is just full out, go get 'em, kick their ass. But it's still corporate power. They are still beholden to corporations running our society. So until we get somebody like Nader or somebody who's actually critical of corporate power, we're not going to get at the real source of these problems.

**Frank:** Helms is the bad cop in bad cop/good cop.

**Kevin:** Bad cop/good cop, yeah. One person slaps the hell out of you (Frank sounds) and then the other one says, hey, come on. So that's the way the elections are done. You get the Republicans, you get eight years of Reagan, aaagghh god that was depressing. (Frank sounds) Oh, yeah, well OK, you know, we'll give you Bill Clinton for awhile then oh, OK. Well in fact, if you look at the eight years of Bill Clinton, it was eight more years of the Reagan/ Bush right-wingization of the country! Who destroyed the welfare system? It was Clinton! It wasn't Republicans. It was Clinton, the liberal Democrat. So, I think if you look at it actually, historically, right wingers like Nixon, Nixon was the one who did détente with the Russians and the Chinese communists. Because his right wing has cooled out. He can move a little bit to the left. A liberal like Clinton, his left wing has cooled out, he can move to the right and implement right-wing policies that otherwise would have been resisted if it was a right winger doing it. So they're constantly playing this tough cop/nice cop game on us.

**Frank:** Hey, at least you still have welfare.

**Kevin:** Yeah, but like three million people have been purged off the rolls. And there's been some studies done of the women that were forced off. What kind of jobs do they have? And they're the most menial, dead-end, no-career kind of jobs.

**Frank:** But, just think if the bad cops ...

**Linda:** ... had, it would have been worse!

**Kevin:** Yeah, yeah. They could wipe it out totally and ...

**Linda:** But he's saying that's the way they justify it. They'll say it like that. Well, it's bad, what Clinton did was bad, but it could have been worse, if it was Bush ...

**Kevin:** This is the scraps off the table approach.

**Linda:** Yes.

**Kevin:** It's like, OK, I hit you five times, and that hurt, but I could have hit you ten times. Well, how about you hit me no times, OK?! How about if we rule, not through repression, but through dialogue and understanding.

**Frank:** Freedom is not something that is given.

**Kevin:** It's taken.

**Frank:** Yes.

**Kevin:** Yeah, you only get freedom by standing up and demanding it and taking it. It doesn't get given. If you look at all the major advancements in our civilization in terms of women getting the right to vote, the end of slavery, the forty-hour work week, social security, unemployment insurance, that was stuff that was a result of mass struggles. Of people going out in the street and fighting for it. People got killed. The women who pushed for voting rights got spat on, they had stuff thrown at them, they were called names, they were trashed. Didn't stop them! And the ones that started that movement died before they saw it come to fruition. That didn't stop them from doing good work. So I think the consciousness we need right now is the consciousness of, let's say the masons who laid the first layer of the Great Wall of China, or those cathedrals in Europe that took 300-400 years to build. You know that you're not going to see the end result of your work, but you do really solid work because there's going to be a lot of weight come on it. So, we alive right now are responsible for laying the foundations of the future Democratic global economy with no starving children, no military, no clear-cut forests. That will happen! The question is, is it going to take 150 years of disaster happen first before we wake up? Or are we going to get out there and do the education and mobilizing to get people to do it before we actually have to have massive disasters even worse than today and head it off before it hits? Because it is coming! You see it in the biological collapse of all these different environmental systems: the ground water, the ozone layer, ocean levels rising, severe weather events, etc. It just goes on and on. The signs are clear.

**Frank:** Genetic engineering.

**Kevin:** Yeah, they could be unleashing already stuff that we don't know. They're doing a massive experiment with us as the guinea pigs.

**Frank:** It makes atomic bombs look ...

**Kevin:** Mild in comparison. Well, there's another case. The government is now preparing a mountain in Nevada, Yucca Mountain, spending billions and billions of dollars of our tax money. Free market?! Oh, wait a minute, free market means you don't want the government involved in economy. (Frank sounds) They're using the taxpayers' billions of dollars to build this storage facility so that the nuclear waste from "privately-owned energy companies" can be stored in Yucca Mountain, Nevada, at taxpayers' expense. And it's going to get stored for hundreds of thousands of years and not leak out into the environment? I doubt it! So they're doing this massive experiment and whether you look at that, whether you look at chemical intensive agriculture, the bioengineering that's going on, they are messing with us, they're

*Linda Mac, Frank Moore and Kevin Danaher (video capture)*

messing with our planet, the commons, the human commons. And they have no right! That's ours! It's our property!

**Frank:** I keep asking why, because they live on this planet.

**Kevin:** Yeah, but see, they think that they're buffered. And they think they're different from us. It's an elitist consciousness. When I lived in Washington, the thing that shocked me the most was, I would wear a nice suit with a nice attaché case to penetrate and you know, to do interviews and to see what I could find in terms of documents and stuff. And you would hear things on elevators where it made you realize they think that it's OK for them to make decisions over our lives for us, as if we're little children. Oh, the ignorant masses! Eh, no! That's OK, don't think of me as some ant that you can step on or push aside. The notion of democracy, it comes from two Greek roots: *demo* which means "people", and *crat,* which means "rule". "People rule." We're supposed to be a republic. Republic comes from two Latin words: *res* meaning "thing" and *publica* meaning "of the people". So a Democratic republic is a double referent to "the people are supposed to rule"! Do the people rule? The people don't rule! So you've got this promise of democracy on the one hand, and then the actual fact is it doesn't fulfill the promise. That's our job as citizens, to make that happen.

**Frank:** Amy Goodman got into their party.

**Linda:** Did you hear that? She got into one of the parties …

**Kevin:** She's great at doing that.

**Linda:** And she got actually into a conversation with a guy that she was recording the whole time, before he started to realize maybe she wasn't one of the elite there at the party.

**Kevin:** She did that with Chevron. She got one of their people in Nigeria to admit that Chevron provided the helicopters to take in a group of police in Nigeria that are called the "Kill and Go", because they come in and they kill and then they go. Chevron provided the helicopters to fly them into a demonstration, a protest against Chevron facilities in Nigeria where they kill people, and then split, these military police. And Chevron provided the helicopters. And she got this guy to admit it on tape. And of course afterwards there was this huge hullabaloo. We actually had a meeting with Chevron executives. It was their PR department over in San Francisco before they moved out of San Francisco. And it was very interesting to see. They brought in five of their people and we had five people representing different organizations: Global Exchange, CBE, different community environment groups, etc. And they had to so tightly control this meeting and so tightly control what was portrayed, that at certain times, when certain members of their group would start to say something, their ice queen, the woman that was running their show, would cut them off and say, no, no, no, wait. We're not going to say it. And they wouldn't allow us to ask questions. And at one point I naively asked like a follow-up question to what one of these guys said and she cut me off and said, we said no questions! And it's like, wait a minute, you're totally controlling the situation and you're not allowing any questions. We weren't taping it or filming it or anything. But even just for the possibility of the truth coming out to the five of us sitting there, they even brought in a judge to supposedly "mediate" the meeting. And it wasn't like we were negotiating, it was just a conversation. And this judge then kept intervening and stopping the normal flow of dialogue. And you realize that if you can't allow a normal human conversation, the most basic connector between human beings to just run its course, you're pretty uptight! (Frank sounds) And there's something you're hiding, obviously. It was very shocking, even to me, and I expected it to be bad.

**Frank:** You thought two hours would be too long. (Kevin laughs)

**Linda:** It's been over two hours. (laughter)

**Kevin:** Touché, touché. Point well taken! (Frank sounds) I underestimated my own bull-shitting capabilities! (all laughing) But see, I'm used to doing more commercial radio where it's like these short time sessions.

**Frank:** You were trained.

**Kevin:** Well, it's a pattern. There's a group called the Mainstream Media Project up in Northern California, and they get me on mainstream radio. So if I'm doing a Christian radio or a right wing ... I did a thing in Louisiana, it was a network of thirteen stations. But it's this (snaps fingers) compressed and very tight, hostile interviewers. Somebody else on there in the studio who's hostile to you. So, one, there's a lot of tension. And you know, I have my bibles out. (laughter, Frank sounds) You know, I've got all my materials out and stuff. And you're ready for anything they might throw at you. Because what you get is, you get guys who will call and say this guy Danaher sounds like a Communist, but I agree with him this World Bank/

IMF, they're bad institutions. So you find out there's a real mixed ideology out there, where people, yeah they've been brainwashed with all this stuff, but if you come to them with the facts of how these institutions actually operate, you can penetrate that helmet and get inside there and say, wait a minute now, you've been told this, but let's look at what's really going on here. And that's particularly rewarding, when you reach people who otherwise you would think, oh there's no chance that we're going to convince them. And you get them to open up their mind a little bit, that's really rewarding! And I think that's what this is about, we have to mainstream this struggle and mainstream the message. 'Cause we're the ones that are putting out the truth. The clowns that are putting out all the Nike commercials and all, that's a load of garbage. And I think a lot of people know it!

**Frank:** Which is why I do two-hour interviews.

**Kevin:** So you can get into the depth of the issues, yeah, and really explore stuff, yeah.

**Frank:** And expand the frame.

**Linda:** The interview frame.

**Kevin:** Yeah. If you look at, there's stuff on TV, it's all so compressed. The news is snapshots. It's a bunch of snapshots: a plane crash, a train wreck, a murder, a rape and then a puppy story and the weather and sports. It's guns and puppies, basically. There's violence and then there's little kitty cat puppy story at the end. That doesn't tell anybody anything about understanding reality in order to change it.

**Frank:** But on my show they have to watch two hours ...

**Linda:** To get the nude people! (laughter)

**Kevin:** To get the good stuff! (laughter) It's a brilliant strategy! (laughter continues) Brilliant!

**Frank:** Funny, but the complainers do watch those two hours ...

**Linda:** ... to get to the stuff that they can complain about!

**Kevin:** Yeah! They probably tape and then edit out the political stuff (laughter) and then complain about the nudity. Yeah, it's like, I like the model of the right-wing minister who sits on the anti-pornography commission, who gets to look at it all and enjoy it, and denounce it! It's the best of both worlds! So what I say to people is if you're living in a rich country like the United States and you're not working to change the inequality in the world, you're like that minister. You're benefiting from the inequality in the world, but you're saying, oh yes, I'm against inequality. But you're not really doing anything about it. So it's like the definition of hypocrisy. It makes hypocrisy have a bad name. So we need to walk our talk sort of!

**Linda:** OK! So on come the nude girls, huh?! (laughter)

**Kevin:** Thanks for having me on. I appreciate it!

**Frank:** Not really.

**Linda:** Yeah, I know. Not really.

**Frank:** Because ...

**Linda:** ... it's too late. We've gone through our 2½ hours, (Kevin laughs) so we only have time for the closing song. Well, maybe next week.

**Kevin:** There's always next week.

**Frank:** Tune in next week.

**Linda:** So, it's been Kevin Danaher, Global Exchange. www.globalexchange.org.

**Frank:** I want your mate on sometime.

**Kevin:** Medea. Yeah, when she's in the country! I want her in my bedroom once in awhile, (laughter) that's what I want. She's on the road more than she's at home. I'll tell her. Yeah, she's great.

**Frank:** How does that work?

**Kevin:** What we do is tag-team parenting. I go away, she's at home. I come home, she goes away and I'm the parent. So our daughter has alternating single parents, but she's very well adjusted.

**Linda:** And what about you two? How often are you two in the same place? (Frank sounds)

**Kevin:** Well, what it means is, when you are together, you really appreciate each other and you make the most out of the time you do have together. I say in the past six weeks, we've been together maybe three or four days, three or four nights that we've spent together.

**Linda:** Wow!

**Kevin:** Because our travel ... she was in Afghanistan, I went to Brazil, I came back, she went away. I went to Amsterdam, she went to Vancouver.

**Linda:** And how many years has it been like that?

**Kevin:** Ah, let's see, '84, so that's what, 18 years that we've been together. We met, we had one date and (snaps his fingers) we moved in together and that was it. It was love at first sight, and we've been together ever since. Very faithful to each other. It's one of those very lucky ...

**Frank:** Both are radical.

**Kevin:** Yeah. And one of the ways it's a great relationship is we both write. And if your mate, if your loved one says this second paragraph is jive, get rid of it, you know, get rid of it! It's the best editing you can get. Because you trust that person. They have your best interest at heart. So we've really benefited from each other's editing skills. In bed a lot of times, hey, read this! Hey, put it aside, take your clothes off. (laughter) But very productive in more ways than one.

**Frank:** I even want your kid. (Frank sounds)

**Kevin:** OK, I'll ask her. That's a tougher one. She's kind of quiet. I don't know how she'd do in an interview.

**Frank:** How is it being raised by two radicals?

**Kevin:** Well, our older daughter is at UCLA, she's finishing up at UCLA. She's doing fine.

And wants to do international rights work. And our eleven-year-old wants to be the first woman President of the United States. (laughs) I don't know where she got that from?! Maybe from my wife, but ... she's pretty serious. She won second place in a contest the other night, a talent contest. She recited the preamble to the constitution in one breath! That was her act! (laughs) She came in second place.

**Frank:** Don't she know the President is not where the power is?

**Kevin:** Well, she's eleven so she sees that as the most powerful position and that's what she wants to do. She once said, well, I think I'll be President and then I'll be Governor. And we said, well, usually people do it the other way around and be Governor first. And then she said, oh, OK so then I'll do it that way. (laughter) So she has a sort of casual approach toward power positions so, we'll see if she keeps at it as she gets older. But it's the gumption that's the good thing. She's got big goals for herself so that's good.

**Linda:** OK. Oh, and before we close, Frank's new theme song: "Totalitarian State" by Buster Poindexter.

**Frank:** I lost ...

**Linda:** (continues off mic) ... Frank's theme song for a year was "Fuck the War". He had this Irish singer/songwriter come on the show ... (fades out)

# John the Baker

Recorded on March 25, 2007 on luver.com

........................................................................................................................

Trained as a vegan baker, John the Baker is a singer, songwriter, punk musician and member of the band, Instant Asshole. Other bands that John has played with include John the Baker & Slimy Penis Breath and JTB & The Banned.

Frank first met John in 1998 in Wilmington, North Carolina at the WE Fest, an independent music festival that both Frank and John had been invited to perform at. After seeing John's powerful solo set, Frank, Linda, Mikee and John spent a couple hours talking together on the sidewalk in front of the club. They have all been friends ever since then.

John and Frank co-produced the cable TV series, *Going Deep to the Core at Ramen with Frank Moore*, at Burnt Ramen, an illegal, underground, all-ages punk club in one of the most dangerous parts of Richmond, California. John was also a member of Frank's Cherotic All-Star Band that performed regularly in the Bay Area from 1994 to 2012.

........................................................................................................................

**Frank:** I told Alexi not to saw during when you sang tonight.

**John:** What, are they working right now?!

(Frank laughs and screeches)

**Linda:** No, they're not. He's being a wise guy. (Frank continues laughing)

**John:** (laughing) Well, thanks, Frank! Thanks a lot man! That's good consideration, I really appreciate that.

**Frank:** Not like at Ramen.

**John:** Ohhhhhh!

**Linda:** It's a reference.

**John:** Jesus Christ!

(all laughing)

**John:** It's time for a song, I think! (laughing)

(all continue to laugh)

**John:** Is it 10 o'clock yet?

**Linda:** It's going to be a loooooong two hours, starting out there!

**John:** Thanks, Frank.

(Frank laughs and screeches)

**John:** Will you start the damn thing!!

**Linda:** It's already going.

**John:** Oh, it is?!

**Linda:** Yes!

**John:** OK, that's cool. Because I had a little bit of a hard night last night at the end. The show was great, all in all … awesome. And then today was a tense day. And somehow … there's people at the house, I wasn't sure who my friends are. Finally they all left and I said "I gotta go" to Joanne and she said, "Well, Frank's your friend, huh?" I'm like, "Yeah, Frank's my friend." So when we're talking and we started laughing just now, that made me feel great. You teased me but that's 'cause you're my friend, dude.

(Frank starts spelling out and John interrupts)

**John:** Now he's going to say, "No, it's because I'm pissed!"

**Frank:** Longtime friend.

**John:** Yep.

**Frank:** They see you in the opening …

**Linda:** Right, of this show, every week, on B-TV. On B-TV it's called *Unlimited Possibilities* and you're part of the opener.

**John:** Oh, awesome. Well, I meant to say, "Fuck you, people" then! Stop staring at my privates!

(laughter)

**John:** You see him take a double take?! Oh, it's awesome!

**Frank:** Ooooh?!

**John:** "Are your privates in the intro?! Oh, I missed it!"

(laughter)

**John:** Oh, you make me feel good, Frank! I swear. East Bay Ray showed up at the show last night.

**Linda:** Who's that?

(Frank laughs and screeches)

**Linda:** See you can't impress us, we don't know who anybody is.

**John:** Frank knows!

**Linda:** No, he said he doesn't!

**John:** East Bay Ray, guitar player for the Dead Kennedys. We opened up for them many times. And, you know, I don't like him. I don't like him! (looking at the camera) The dude stole the Dead Kennedys' music off Alternative Tentacles and put it on Manifesto Records, Evan Cohen's record label, scum of the earth, fuck you! Really pissed me off. I did not want to see that guy at my show, so … Yeah, I'm sorry. (all laugh) I'll try to be a nice guy for the

*Frank Moore and John The Baker (video capture)*

rest of the show, OK?

(all laughing)

**Frank:** Oh!

**John:** Frank is speechless! How often is Frank speechless, huh?! (laughing)

**Linda:** It's more like, "Where do I go with this ... here, here, here, here, here?"

**Frank:** I am just waiting for you to settle down.

**John:** Yeah, I'm having a hard time settling down. I had a hard day, so .... I was thinking, oh man, I'm not really in a great space for an interview. I've been actually just sitting still for the last six hours waiting for people to leave the house, and emotions are deep and you know like when you're just anxious and nervous?

**Frank:** That is ...

**John:** ... a good time for an interview.

**Frank:** Yes.

**John:** That's what I thought. You know, remember when I first met you and I ran away from the show? I said I was too scared to face those things.

**Frank:** Why did you run away?

**John:** I was afraid to go deeper, I think.

**Frank:** How so?

**John:** I felt vulnerable. I felt Frank was going to do something to me or something. I didn't know what the Cave was. I didn't know what you did in there.

**Frank:** Even the jam ...

**Linda:** You were afraid to go to.

**John:** Yeah! I didn't go. I drove 350 miles away and then came back. (laughing)

**Linda:** Wow!

**John:** 350 miles to the other end of the state and back.

**Frank:** I am flattered.

**John:** Well, as you know, then I wrote you a letter and said that I did that. But I said that I want to go deeper. So that's kind of what happened today. I'm like, "Geez, I'm really not in a good space for a normal interview. But this wasn't going to be a normal interview." (laughter, and Frank sounds) But I thought, this is a good place for me to talk about things because that's what we do here.

**Frank:** Yes.

**John:** I don't need to get a peppy answer. I don't need to be "on it" and say the right thing. I can tell you what I'm going through.

**Frank:** Boring.

**Linda:** The peppy answer.

**John:** Yeah.

**Linda:** (to Frank) Is that what you mean, the peppy answers are boring?

**John:** No, he means, you're being really boring!

**Linda:** No, that's not what he means! We've had plenty of peppy answer people and they're the worst shows. (Frank sounds)

**John:** Well, I'm good at that too. And sometimes it's appropriate. What I've learned is I have to let my guard down and be vulnerable around Frank.

**Frank:** On tapes.

**Linda:** Oh, they have tapes. Their replies are like they're playing tapes. It's all rote.

**John:** (starts talking rote tape-like) I'm the guy arrested for the lyrical content of my song in 1994. Went to jail and then proved my case on constitutional in court and then sued the town of Woodstock for $20,000 ... I won an outright settlement for $20,000 and made a record and went on tour. (laughs)

**Frank:** We flew to North Carolina, drove to Wilmington ...

302

**Linda:** Right, from Raleigh.

**Frank:** Just got ...

**Linda:** We just pulled in in time for the first show, and you were the first person we saw. We were just straight out of the car, dropped our stuff at the hotel, came right to the place, and that was you. You were performing.

**Frank:** Solo.

**John:** Yeah, it was solo. My band couldn't get out of bed. They were all junkies. And I'm like anti-heroin totally. Almost straight edge. It was not the greatest situation. They were great musicians and we made great music together, but I don't want to be around that shit.

**Frank:** Then we talked on the sidewalk.

**John:** Yeah, on the street for two hours. Friends ever since!

**Linda:** That's right.

**John:** Well, except I missed your gig. (laughing) I became friends after that, really, when I was willing to ... we were friends on the street, I had respect, I dug it. We enjoyed talking to each other. I don't deny that, but ... yeah, flattered, you should be flattered ... I was scared! I was scared ... I was like, oh God, I don't need to be there! (laughing)

**Frank:** Of what?

**Linda:** Scared of what?

**John:** Now as I look, I'm sure it's myself, my inner truth. But certainly not dude in the wheelchair. Not going to kick my ass or anything! (laughing) Can't verbally berate me hardly, you know what I mean?! Come on, I can walk away! Jesus Christ, what would I be afraid of, I don't know!

**Frank:** Well ...

**Linda:** ... the verbally berate part!

**John:** Here we go! (laughter) He's going to unleash it! But you know what I mean, I don't mean it disrespectfully.

**Frank:** And kick your ass.

**Linda:** (to Frank) You could do that too. (laughing)

**John:** You kicked my ass at Ramen the other night. You totally threw a leg out at me and almost tripped me. (laughter) Frank, I'm pissed! Yeah, got a good kick in. How'd it feel? (laughter) A violent society, I swear to God. Even the hippies are on a rampage.

**Frank:** It hurt.

**Linda:** (to Frank) It hurt your foot. (laughter)

**John:** Well, don't do that again! "Does this hurt?" "Does this hurt?" (laughter)

**Frank:** But why did not ...

**Linda:** Is this about John being afraid to come to the North Carolina thing? Why didn't he want to?

**Frank:** I am trying to understand why people ...

**Linda:** ... are afraid.

**John:** Trying to understand why people avoid it. Yeah, well, you want my ... for myself?

**Linda:** Give us some insight from your experience.

**John:** I think I was intimidated. I was nervous that I was going to be in a sexually inappropriate scenario and that I wouldn't be able to avoid or something or then maybe I would be cheating on my girlfriend even or ... I didn't know my boundaries well enough, I think, probably to be able to ...

**Frank:** This is the jam ...

**Linda:** Frank is asking are you referring to the jam when you say that.

**John:** Whatever it is you did down there.

**Linda:** We did two.

**John:** I have no idea.

**Linda:** You didn't know. You weren't breaking them down as two separate things.

**John:** No!! I was just avoiding it. (laughing)

**Frank:** Did you know ...

**Linda:** ... that one was a jam and that the other one was called "The Cave"?

**John:** No! I don't think so. I didn't know they were different. 'Cause there was a jam at the Cave too. Outside the Cave.

**Linda:** There were a couple of musicians jamming, right.

**John:** So that really inspired me. Because I dig that kind of shit. For myself, I try to do that for people too. I'm like, wow! You pushed me to my boundaries! You pushed me to my edge! And I was like, wow, the dude pushed me to my edge. That's cool! And then most people run away from that, and they never come back, you know what I mean? But, I didn't! I said, oh, I want to push that edge further on. I want to know this guy, because the dude pushed me to my edge!? How the fuck did that happen?!

**Frank:** Even before the performances.

**John:** Before I ever saw you perform. Yeah. It was just us talking on the street, and I was like, fuck that shit! Maybe you described it. I don't know. I don't know why I bugged out exactly. It was like eight years ago, nine years ago now, right? I'm not totally certain why or how but I know it happened. I know I drove 350 miles one day and came back the next. (laughing)

**Frank:** Toronto.

**Linda:** Oh, that weekend. We performed in Toronto and not very many people came. And then the guy booked us again because there was such a buzz after we performed. He said, everybody's writing about it, everybody's talking about it. You're the hot thing, so I want to get you back here. And he said you have so much power that all of the artists in Toronto have gone out of town for the weekend.

**John:** Yeah, that's amazing.

**Linda:** He was pretty blown out by that. He said, these were all people that were just saying how great ... they heard about Frank's performance and they dadadada.

**John:** I wanted to learn! I wanted to know what your chutzpah was that got me to do that. Got me nervous. 'Cause that's what I like to do. I like to make people nervous. And then all of a sudden I'm running away from it. I said, that's not cool. That's why I wrote you a letter. I said, I fucked up. I should have been there and this is why and we became pen pals. And then a year and a half later I came out here pretty much. And we just kept going from there. I think it's a unique situation. I've now seen you for the last eight, nine years perform to nobody and I still support you. I think it's great. I like that people can't come. (laughter) I think it's super cool! I don't want those fucking people coming to my show either.

**Frank:** Last show ...

**Linda:** What was the last show?

**John:** The Darlings!

**Linda:** Ooooooh! (Frank sounds)

**John:** Oh, I can't say that on the air, can I? (laughter) The Dickend Darlings? Whoops!

**Linda:** The Deadend Darlings.

**John:** Oh right. Not the Dickend.

**Frank:** Yes, you can.

**Linda:** Say their name. Because we didn't say we weren't going to say their name!

**Frank:** But I call them "The Brats".

**John:** That's more of a compliment I think to them. What fags, I swear to God! (laughing) And is it a minor only in the drinking sense? Not in the legal sense, right?

**Linda:** It was under 18.

**John:** Oh, I thought the person was 19.

**Linda:** But he wasn't there! The under-18 one left! He wasn't there! And we told him he could leave. Because when they said he had to go to high school the next day, we said, how old is he?! He's under 18. We said, yes, he should go. And that's when Frank said, is anybody else under 18. And they said no. So the one who wrote to us, sounded like it was the parent of the under-18 one. That person wasn't even there.

**John:** I think it was a 19-year-old person they were talking about. Maybe I'm wrong! Whatever.

**Linda:** But certainly the ones that stayed were ... they seemed like they might have been in their twenties. We don't know.

**John:** Yeah, they were.

**Linda:** They didn't seem like they were kids!

**John:** You can take the redneck out of Stockton ... (laughter)

**Frank:** Tracy.

**Linda:** They're from Tracy.

**John:** They were playing in Stockton. I saw a flier for it, so I thought they were from there. Tracy, Stockton, tomatoes, tomatoes ...

**Frank:** Embarrassing.

**John:** Yeah, how embarrassing. (laughing) That's the dynamic, though, dude. That's the same dynamic, man. It's not different than me. I'm not dissing you guys, because I went through it too. You all should come to your senses though, because Frank's a fucking genius! The shit that he is throwing out there is important for artists. It's challenging. It's something that helps us grow, so that we can create better art. You know, you want to be stale, fucking keep your normalcy! I'm here. (laughter)

**Frank:** I should have ripped their clothes off and had ...

**John:** ... my way with them. (laughter)

**Frank:** Then they would ...

**Linda:** ... have something to complain about, or freak about.

**John:** Yeah.

(Pause)

**John:** Basically, that's probably what their fears are. That you would do that. (Frank sounds) That's probably what my fears were. That there was going to be some kind of ... you hold me down or ... (everyone except John laughs) ... No, for real! I wouldn't be able to control the boundaries is what I was afraid of. And I'm sure they were freaking out that you were going to touch them inappropriately or ... and today I know you much better, but I also know myself better, because of it. You guys are nothing but respectful! (Frank sounds) I've never felt pushed too far at all. Even though I push myself and you give me a place to do that, you've never had your way with me, ripped off my clothes and had your way with me. And that is really cool, man.

**Frank:** Which is one of the keys to doing what we do.

**John:** What, that you don't rip people's clothes off?

**Linda:** The respect, yeah. The respecting.

**John:** I know, it's awesome. But I think people's imaginations run wild, and they don't know what the possibilities are. And the possibilities are unlimited!

**Frank:** That is great art.

**John:** That is great art, I agree, man! That is great art because you're ... like if you look at a painting, (points to one of Mikee's large drawings) that painting there that this man did has meaning to him but the possibilities are endless for me. I look at it and it's like, my imagination can go wild. That's great art. That's what you're saying, right?

**Frank:** Yes.

**John:** That's the way I see your performance, too. I can never take it all in at one sitting. Like when we're performing it or when I'm in the room while you're doing your thing if I'm just doing sound, or whatever. I tell people too, "Watch it online! Or just take a snapshot of one second of the performance! Just a snapshot, and look at the artistic quality there. The blending of color and the low resolution online that makes it mold and blend together. Fuck, you cannot deny it! You cannot deny its beauty and its strength as great art!" So. People are just weak. Most people are fucking narrow ... now I'm pissy.

**Frank:** And I don't do it.

**Linda:** Frank doesn't do that, he doesn't create the stuff you described. He's not the one that does that.

**John:** It's bigger ...

**Linda:** ... it's bigger than him.

**John:** It's bigger than the sum of its parts. And that's great art, too. Exactly. So I gained a lot of respect over the years, and appreciation and a lot of wisdom from interacting with you. Most all people, as you know, go, "What are you doing with that guy?!" (laughter) Wankers!

**Frank:** I get that about you. (laughter)

**John:** Probably true, I'm sure. I know. (Frank sounds)

**Frank:** Like Dirk said (Frank sounds) don't hang out with Fluff Grrl.

**Linda:** That's what he told us after he emceed the Balazo thing. And Fluff Grrl was the first band that played, so he introed them. And then when we talked to him on the phone afterwards ...

**Frank:** And Bob had ...

**Linda:** Is it like snuff movies on the background?

**John:** Yeah.

**Linda:** Playing while they were performing. And then we were talking to Dirk about the fact that Balazo wouldn't even let us rent the space anymore. And he said, have you ever considered that it's who you hang out with? He said, because people know you by who you hang out with. And maybe you shouldn't be booking people like Fluff Grrl at your shows. Obviously, we didn't go for that! (Frank sounds)

**John:** Of course not! Because it's about family. (Frank sounds) It's about connections. It's about friends. And Bob [Madigan - Ed.] is family.

**Linda:** Yeah, absolutely.

**John:** I don't give a fuck, Bob is the man. Bob extended himself to me, (Frank sounds) through you. And then introduced me to Boom and Scott Alcoholocaust. And introduced me to the San Francisco underground, a New Yorker who came out here and knew nobody. And those are my best friends because of it. Frank, Bob and Boom. Fuck the rest of you all! (laughter)

**Frank:** He is the most dependable.

**Linda:** Bob is one of the most dependable people we know. (Frank sounds)

**John:** He is.

**Linda:** It's amazing.

**John:** People have no clue. That's the way I see it. I say, Frank is my first strand of community in California, why I'm here. (Frank sounds) Why does Frank get to be performing at Burnt Ramen? Because he's going to be the last one standing too. And the strength that I gain from working with Frank at Burnt Ramen, or outside of it, is what fuels the ability for other people to appreciate that space too. Why am I still working with Frank? Because Frank is the one. Frank is the number one, the first one that extended himself to me as a friend. Not Gilman Street! Those fucking people closed their door on me when I came to town. Frank opened his heart. And I'll never deny that. I'll never turn my back on that. And assholes that are opportunists that just want to fucking get over for a day ... you don't get to play there. You suck it, OK?! Frank's the man. If I'm not working with Frank, I'm not working there. So, that's why Frank gets to perform at Burnt Ramen.

**Frank:** We all are about community.

**John:** Yeah!

**Frank:** The other stuff is an excuse for the community.

**John:** Right, right, right. Like building it or draining it or building it or stealing from it.

**Linda:** We use the art and we use the music as an excuse to build community.

**John:** As an excuse to build community?

**Linda:** Yeah. It's like the cover.

**John:** I see what you mean.

**Linda:** But it's really about the community.

**John:** Exactly.

**Frank:** Con.

**Linda:** It's a con. The art and the music is the con to build community. (Frank sounds)

**John:** Or the tool. I don't think it's a con. Your music isn't dishonest.

**Linda:** He always calls things "cons". (laughter) He called his painting a con. Everything he's done in his life ... relationship counseling was a con. He always calls them cons.

**John:** I know what you're saying. You and your family has fed me when I had nothing. There'd be no fucking, oooh, the Burnt Ramen. Who cares?! It's not the building, it's the people. It's always the people.

**Frank:** Yes.

**John:** The first year I was poor and hungry. Had no friends except for Frank and y'all brought me food every week, organic produce to the baker. (Frank sounds) You know, kept me going. That's why the first strand and will always be the last strand standing. (Frank sounds) Kick me one more time, though! (laughter)

**Linda:** And it's all on camera, always.

**Frank:** Funny, people think I don't know how to do ...

**Linda:** ... how to do it "successfully". People think Frank doesn't know how to put a band together and draw a big audience. And they don't get that he knows how to do it and that's not what he wants.

**John:** That's right. I know.

**Frank:** I have been doing this for ...

**Linda:** ... thirty-five years or so, forty, I don't know.

**Frank:** The people who think I don't know how to do it ...

**Linda:** ... have all come and gone, and Frank's still doing it.

**John:** Those are the opportunists, right? That want to cling on and ...

**Linda:** They want fame.

**John:** For a minute they think that Frank has the key, and then they go, oh, Frank doesn't have the key, I'm going to move on, right?

**Linda:** Why isn't he famous yet?

**Frank:** Karen Finley.

**Linda:** Karen Finley, one of our favorite stories.

**John:** Yeah, I know that story.

**Frank:** Freaked out.

**Linda:** She just didn't get it. She said, I don't know anybody who's as good as you. Your paintings are amazing, your performances are amazing, you're one of my favorite performance artists. Why aren't you famous?! Let me take your paintings. Let me get you in galleries. Let me get you in museums. Frank was like, yeah, yeah, alright. (laughing) She never did anything anyway. But she just freaked out. It made her very uncomfortable that we were at this level on purpose. She didn't get it.

*John The Baker (video capture)*

**John:** You have to compromise to do that. That's the key.

**Linda:** To do what? To get famous?

**John:** Right. Successful. You have to be able to ... you got to be commercial. You have to play the game. Who the fuck wants to do that?

**Frank:** I had a crip ...

**Linda:** ... Oh, Bethany. She was a guest a couple weeks ago. She's a tiny person, real sexy outfit and just was taking her bar exam. She moved here recently from Florida. The thing that broke things open for her in Florida was she took a risk and she put on this event that had to do with sexuality. And she got all this publicity for it.

**Frank:** She brought in a midget porn star.

**Linda:** And she got all this publicity and she thought, that's the way I'm going to change the world. I'm going to use sex and my legal skills. And then she ended up coming to San Francisco from that experience directly and working on sexuality, taking some sexuality classes. She teaches at U.C. San Francisco, as she's taking her bar exam. She spends the whole interview talking about how she needs to sell out, basically. And that that's the only way, everybody says the same thing ... I have to sell out to get in a position where I can make the changes that I want to make. And Frank was trying to point out to her that the risk was what got her to the position she's in now. And why wouldn't she just see that that worked and keep taking risks? She said, "I am drawing my lines. I'm setting my limits. Everybody does that.

You do that!" He said, "But I don't do it based on some external thing".

**John:** Right. Based on the way you feel, or your intuition, but not based on what society wants or what you perceive society would respond to.

**Linda:** Yes. Which is exactly what she's saying she's basing it on.

**John:** Well, she wants to be successful in that world. That's not what we want to do.

**Frank:** She said she wanted to be nude.

**Linda:** Yeah, she was the one that brought up nude! We never brought it up! (Frank sounds) She said, she wants to be nude, but she can't be nude because of her grand plan, on camera.

**John:** So yeah, weird.

**Linda:** "If you have an event that's not being videotaped or taking pictures, I want to come and be nude. But I can't be nude because of my grand plan. Everything I've worked for." And she really didn't want to talk about it. She got very uncomfortable, and started throwing around stuff like, "We crips should stick together!" As if, why are you giving me a hard time?!

**John:** You never stuck together with crips, dude. (all laughing) Remember you told me they were always trying to get you to be the poster child, and you're like, I ain't no poster child!

**Linda:** Yeah.

**John:** I'm not going to pretend to be this or that or a victim. Right? I'm listening! (laughs)

**Frank:** I love your basement.

**John:** You mean the basement I grew up in and turned Burnt Ramen to be like?

**Frank:** Yes!

**John:** Yeah, you listen too. (laughter) Thanks, Frank. That's way cool, man.

**Frank:** But they don't know that story.

**Linda:** Tell them about your basement.

**John:** When I was a little kid I had brothers that were older than me ... seven years older and nine years older. It's a tape recorded question. (laughter) In the basement we could do whatever we wanted. My parents let us ... we could just go down there and ... My older brothers who are musicians, I was just a little kid ... there was a piano down there and my brother when he was twelve turned garbage cans upside down and turned them into drums. The next year my parents bought him a drum set. My brothers, see, they didn't get along very good, their whole lives. They're two years apart. But when they became twelve and ten, thirteen and eleven, they started to play music together. It was the only time they ever really ... that's when they started to get along. They had a new way to communicate. And in the basement anything could go. You could do anything. My brothers grew up there. They did drugs there. They painted on the walls. There was a big "Are you experienced?" It was the late '60s, early '70s, as they were growing up. My brother had little blocks of wood up on the wall with day-glow paint underneath that said "pot" underneath one, "lsd" under one. (laughing)

The day-glow paint dripped down the wall. There was incense burning. Things like that. We would put on shows for like my parents and stuff, and I would be the go-go dancer. And we got an old refrigerator box and we cut out the front. Go-go dancer, see? Connection!!

**Linda:** (laughing) I'd love to see that!

**John:** There's home movies. We've got home movies. I should get them. I'll talk to my dad. I'm going to see him soon. See if he's got them. I remember there being blue Christmas lights around the box that I would dance in when I was around four. (laughter) And then they grew up. When my oldest brother was fifteen was when Woodstock happened, 1969. And he changed his name to Jimi, because his name is James, you know, Jimi. He spelled it like Jimi Hendrix. Stopped playing the drums and became a guitar player after Woodstock. And so then it was my turn. And I grew up down there too in the basement. There's a phone down there, you write phone numbers on the wall, there was like a million phone numbers. We would call girls down there. Prank phone calls. I had a great stereo. And I had the biggest record collection in the neighborhood. And all the kids from the neighborhood would come down there. And we smoked pot down there, and did acid, experimented with alcohol, drugs and stuff and girls, and parties. So, that was where music was born for me, in my life. And also where we learned that music was important. Like we learned to communicate as a family, because we didn't do very good with words. (laughs) We weren't able to really relate the same way. (Frank sounds) It's kind of sad, but it's true, and it's also a good thing, too, because now we do have music and that does bind us. So, I take that where I go. And I try to create the basement where I go. And Burnt Ramen is a version of the basement I grew up in in New York.

**Frank:** Slaughterhouse.

**Linda:** Slaughterhouse was another version.

**John:** Slaughterhouse is another type of basement. I always look for the basement-type things: cement floor, musty, moldy, (laughter) and the ability to be free! To be able to paint on the walls, be able to graffiti, be able to make out, be able to drink, party, rock out. Musicians, to me, musicians need a place of freedom. A place where they can just let it all hang out. Where they don't have to worry about, oh, you know, I can't wear my hat backwards, or I can't play without my shirt on, or I can't fart. So many rules in most venues. So I was trying to make a place that was free form.

**Frank:** Basically, caves.

**John:** Yeah, like a cave. I like the basement because it's cool during the day. And I can stay in there and I can work and get stuff done. I don't have to go outside in the heat. It's like a cave! That's why we are together. We are very similar.

**Linda:** Frank likes caves too. Frank's always got a version of a cave in everything he does.

**John:** It's pretty cool. It's a protective ... it's a shamanic thing. It's a shamanic place. That's where we relate.

**Frank:** Not everyday reality.

**Linda:** Not the everyday reality.

**John:** Right. It's a place you can go to escape the everyday reality and create the now reality that you want to, whatever it is.

**Frank:** What The Brats did not get.

**John:** Yeah, they didn't get it, but, you know what, they got some of it! They were there! They were in there! What happened was, they went home and the parents definitely did not get it!

**Frank:** They were infected.

**John:** Yeah, I think so. That's my long term hope for a lot of things.

**Linda:** Always. That's the way we look it.

**John:** I plant seeds. I do my thing. And hopefully it ripples (Frank sounds), whatever. I live a symbolic life. I live in a way that I hopefully affects other people. And that's my hope. (laughs) Otherwise, I don't know if it's true, but whatever! That's the way I live. It keeps me going.

**Frank:** Us too.

**Linda:** That's the way we see it too. Yeah.

**Frank:** And why years later people ...

**Linda:** ... will tell you something that shows that that is actually true.

**John:** I agree. I've gotten numerous feedback. Especially around the basement scenario. Kids are like, "I grew up there!" "Just like when I was fifteen. Just like when my older brother was fifteen. It's so cool!" (Frank sounds) And they ... how old was I? When I was like twenty-four, my mom got cancer. And my dad, who grew up in Minnesota near the Mayo Clinic, decided to move my mom back to Minnesota so she could be at the Mayo Clinic, which is a good cancer hospital, the best probably in the world. So, I stayed behind with my wife at the time. And we sold their house for them. But my friends, who grew up in the basement, all were like, "You can't sell the house! What about the basement?!" (laughter) And I'm like, "I know, but ..." "You should buy the house, John! You should buy it!" But I know that wasn't my thing. Maybe this is the first time I really learned that it really is the people, it's not the place.

**Linda:** Right.

**John:** And it probably is. The basement got shut down at my house too. (laughs)

**Frank:** You can ...

**Linda:** ... create the basement wherever you go.

**John:** Yeah.

**Frank:** Anywhere.

**John:** That's what I try to teach too. (Frank sounds) Make it happen.

**Frank:** At U.C. Berkeley ...

**Linda:** ... when we did the last series, or either series, right. We created that in the classroom for however many hours every two weeks.

**John:** Yeah, it doesn't matter, you can do it in a classroom.

**Linda:** And the janitors got it.

**John:** Yeah.

**Linda:** They would start hanging out, and they would start feeling.

**John:** They knew the magic was going.

**Linda:** They could feel it. And they were just like, "We're going to make sure you guys are OK."

**John:** Yeah. They protected the space?

**Linda:** Yeah.

**Frank:** And it built.

**Linda:** In that case because it was a regular thing. It just kept building, people kept coming back, then more people would come.

**John:** I think that is a key to where you build the cave or the basement, where you put the cave or the basement, is that you can do it consistently. At least weekly, is the way I like to do it.

**Frank:** Yes.

**John:** It does, it builds. It creates a momentum and people come back and then you can really develop a following, if you have consistency. I mean, not following, a community.

**Linda:** Yes.

**John:** If you are consistent, because then people from different realities can come on the same night. And they end up there and they get to meet each other and bond ...

**Linda:** And see that it's all the same thing. Have that experience.

**John:** Really! Amazing! That's what happened at Burnt Ramen! Fifteen, twenty different types of scenes started to come to shows they would never go to. And meet people and go, "Wow, they're really doing the same thing, huh?"

**Frank:** Exactly.

**John:** "I kind of really like that! I never liked that kind of music. I really dig that."

**Frank:** That is how LUVeR works too.

**Linda:** Yeah, gathering different kinds of people together, community.

**John:** And consistently. You're daily, so that's a very strong routine. And it really, really helps. People can return to it after going back and reflecting and then coming back in with new perspectives. But if you do it once a month, or once every couple of months, it's harder.

**Frank:** B-TV.

**Linda:** Same thing with B-TV. We've been on there for years now.

**John:** Yep!

**Linda:** All the time.

**Frank:** And mix everything ...

**Linda:** We mix everything together on the shows. So, for this show, you'll have like us now, then you'll have like a politician, and then you'll have a bluegrass band, it's all mixed together, but it's all the same thing because it's us.

**John:** That's also what we did at Burnt Ramen, it was multi-genre. And it wasn't like, OK, every Wednesday is going to be Blues. (laughter) It was whatever it was! And it came in a random fashion.

**Linda:** Right. That's important.

**John:** And not everything had to flow through me, as well. The way I booked the stuff at Burnt Ramen especially, and Slaughterhouse too, is I empowered individuals to book their own show. So I didn't have to pick the bands! I didn't have to like every band. It didn't matter.

**Frank:** LUVeR.

**Linda:** That's LUVeR.

**John:** Yeah, it is LUVeR!

**Linda:** We play everything.

**John:** "Send it to us, we'll put it in there!" (laughing)

**Linda:** Yes, that's what happens. (laughing)

**John:** I like that. People get to make their own choices and decisions of what they like.

**Frank:** And then Skip ...

**John:** Skiffington!

**Linda:** Oh! They just sent us a DVD, those two guys. We should give John a copy of that DVD.

**John:** That would be awesome.

**Linda:** It's really ... they're doing this because of us. That's why they're making a video of the two of them playing. And they're so great. They're so pure, they're so into it. It's the two of them in a garage or a basement with all their guitars and speakers and stuff and a mic. And they're so into it. They're really rockin' and they're together, they're one thing, together, these two guys.

**John:** That's awesome.

**Frank:** Because of the cave we have.

**John:** Because of the community we have, the cave we have.

**Linda:** The cave, the community that we have.

**John:** Yeah! They have an audience to them. They're like, "We are a part of something. We need to express as well." Right?

**Linda:** Right. Because I think they're in a vacuum where they are. And all of a sudden, here we are and we're like, "Great!" We're giving their stuff out. We're playing it on LUVeR. We sent them the CD of when you used their stuff to mix it.

**John:** When I mixed all of their stuff in between, that was fun.

**Linda:** Yeah. So all of a sudden they belong.

**John:** Yeah!

**Frank:** It is dangerous.

**Linda:** What we're doing.

**John:** It is dangerous, that's right. Hopefully, it's dangerous. (laughter) Well, it's one of the things that repels people, the danger aspect. I think people are like, "Whoa, dangerous, what am I going to do?! I better get out of here! I might expand my consciousness."

**Frank:** They pin it to the nudity.

**John:** Yeah, they go, "But it's the nudity, that's why I don't want to do it. That's disgusting!" (laughing)

**Frank:** But, that ain't what it is.

**Linda:** But that ain't what it is.

**John:** No way, that ain't what it is. Of course not! (laughing and Frank sounds) No, it's the burning pubes. (laughter) That's what it was last night. Bob [Madigan of Fluff Grrl - Ed.] burned his pubes and everybody goes, "He's burning pubes out there!" I'm like, I love that part! (laughing) I love it when it stinks like death. (laughter) I made a post online, at this Myspace profile. I don't know why, there's this girl and she made a post about something and she was from Detroit. I wrote back on her comments page, I said, not a Cum Dumpster but a total Instant Asshole. (laughing) You know, Detroit, Bob's band was called Cum Dumpster, pretty famous in 1981 in Detroit. I don't know, if she was older, I thought maybe she would get it. (laughing) I haven't heard back from her, she probably deleted it immediately! Oh, danger! (laughing) Not a Cum Dumpster. I thought that was polite. (laughing)

**Frank:** You were showing your age (Frank giggling).

**Linda:** Oh, you're showing your age now by knowing that band from '81.

**John:** Yeah. Well, I didn't know about them until '99. (laughter) But, [Jello - Ed.] Biafra did, I guess. Biafra thought they were a good band. At least that's what Bob said. (laughing)

**Frank:** She may be younger.

**Linda:** She may be younger and not get the reference.

**John:** Yeah, she might. Whatever. I don't care. I thought it was funny. I have a bizarre sense of humor and most people don't get it, but whatever.

**Frank:** How does Bob grow … ?

**Linda:** … enough pubes. (laughter)

**John:** I know! I don't know! (laughter) It's one of the reasons why it's important that he's not allowed to play too many gigs. (laughter)

**Linda:** Well, then he works on his head!

**John:** He couldn't be dangerous if he got all those gigs. Because then he couldn't burn his pubes at every one of them. You see what I'm saying? I don't know. (laughing) Yeah, I've seen him do his hair.

**Frank:** He tries …

**Linda:** Yeah, especially when we were doing shows with him all the time and there was a couple-year period when we were always doing shows together.

**John:** Yeah, I remember.

**Linda:** And he obsessed on burning my pubes. That's all he wanted to do! And he tried to talk to me about it before and after the show. And he'd come up during the show with his lighter and he'd be following me around trying to burn my pubes. (laughing)

**John:** When we came here on tour in 1999, we did stuff with you guys. Bob shaved my singer's cooch (laughing) in Barney's bathroom. (laughter) So he loves doing that.

**Linda:** He's into it!

**John:** He likes tickling the hairs down there. (laughter)

**Frank:** Did you see my picture?

**Linda:** Oh, did you see the art Frank did for Bob, "A Pussy for Bob"?

**John:** Yeah, it was awesome.

**Linda:** Yeah, you saw the actual art, not just the t-shirt?

**John:** Yeah. You sent me it.

**Linda:** Oh, we sent it to you online?

**John:** Yeah.

**Frank:** He …

**Linda:** … he finally got it. He kept saying it looked like a cheese sandwich to him. He kept calling us and saying it looks like a cheese sandwich!

**John:** Oh, he couldn't see it.

**Linda:** As if we're going to explain it to him. We would just laugh when he would say it's a cheese sandwich. And then finally, recently he said, "OK!"

**John:** Good impression. (laughter)

**Linda:** She's pulling the underpants aside, and she's got her fingers ... and he describes the whole thing.

**John:** He finally could see it!

**Linda:** And we said, right, he got it!

**John:** He cared. He really wanted to hear it, he wanted to see it.

**Linda:** Yeah, he wanted to figure it out.

**John:** That's what makes Bob a great guy! And the rest of ya, losers! Adults don't listen!

**Frank:** He took months.

**Linda:** It probably took a month. And I bet he looked at it a lot.

**John:** That's a long time of trying. (laughter) Yeah. And that's really important. That's a really important thing you're describing because what I find in music is 15, 16-year-old kids, they need it. They listen. They listen like it's life or death! It is life or death for them. They need to know what other people have learned and how other people have grown. They're hungry for it, thirsty for it. You get to be 20, 25, you get into a job, you want to get married, you get into regular routines. You end up listening to the music you liked when you were 15. (Frank sounds) And they stop listening, they stop caring. They stop wanting to know other people's perspectives and wanting to create and expand their own perspectives. It's boring. You know, adults suck!

**Frank:** Again, that is why LUVeR ...

**Linda:** ... is the way it is, to challenge that.

**Frank:** Mix.

**Linda:** The mix of the music, to challenge that.

**John:** It forces you into a listening space. You can't space out and listen to a whole genre for an hour. It's like jarring, right?! When ... this is going to be great ... when you're listening to Distopia and then Pacer comes on. (laughter)

**Linda:** How about Sonny & Cher and classical music?

**John:** They go hand in hand. (laughter) Yeah, that's the dynamic. And no disrespect to any North Carolina band that might have the name Pacer. (laughter) That's an old WE Fest '98 reference.

**Frank:** When we first started, people complained about ...

**John:** ... the Mix, the way it was ...

**Linda:** When we first started.

**John:** I remember. Now they herald it I bet, too.

**Frank:** Black ...

**Linda:** Yeah, people would say you're playing nigger music because we play a lot of black people (giggling).

**John:** Jesus Christ!

**Linda:** They came into the chat to say that! (laughing) We had a guy who came into the chat to say that.

**John:** He really wanted you to know. (laughing)

**Frank:** They were listening to good music ...

**Linda:** ... then all of a sudden something comes on that they really don't like a lot, it pisses them off.

**John:** Yeah. (Frank gleeful sounds)

**John:** (laughing) It makes him happy! (laughing and pointing to Frank) (laughter) Numero uno thorn in the side.

**Frank:** That is art! (Frank gleeful sounds)

**John:** That's right! It throws you for a loop. Knocks you off your normalcy.

**Frank:** Not business.

**Linda:** It's not business, it's art.

**John:** Right, separate, I see it. (Frank sounds) Right, because if you're a business then you try to define your market and cater to them. Jesus! Who needs that ... more of that ... who needs more of that?!

**Frank:** Whereas when people complain about something, I ...

**John:** (laughing) Do it more! (laughter)

**Frank:** When we see people (giggling) shutting LUVeR off when the news comes on, we add more news. (laughter)

**John:** Give them what they don't want, dude! Keep giving them what they don't want! (laughter) With a name like Smuckers it has to be good. (Frank sounds) What was that *Saturday Night Live* skit, with a name like Vaginal Itch, it has to be good! (laughter)

**Frank:** But who is on cellphones?

**Linda:** Right, what internet station is being played on cellphones?

**John:** LUVeR! (laughter)

**Linda:** Without compromise!

**John:** Oh yeah, that's right!

**Linda:** We did it exactly the way we wanted it.

**John:** Not on mine.

**Frank:** Not yet.

**Linda:** Well, apparently they have some master plan and by July it will be able to be played on every Java-enabled cellphone.

**John:** Very cool.

**Frank:** Funny, I am not into getting mass ...

**Linda:** Right, we're not into getting mass listeners.

**Frank:** But ...

**Linda:** ... it's like everything else we do, things just come to us by just doing what we do and not going for it. And it's the way we want it.

**John:** This is the difference between the Bethany approach and the Frank approach.

**Linda:** Right, exactly!

**John:** Is that you are going to do The Mix with different songs every fucking song and people don't like it at first. And then five years later, it's what people are craving! (Frank sounds)

**Linda:** Yeah! (laughing) It's like a fad!

**John:** But you never compromised. You never changed. Maybe it won't ever be huge mainstream or whatever. Bob Fluff Grrl has done the same performance since 1980. (laughter) And he's not going to change! He's going to burn his pubes. (Frank sounds) And then, who knows, maybe one day, it will be the "Marilyn Manson" type will be burning his pubes or whatever. Maybe that will be the big thing.

**Frank:** He did go a period when he tried. (giggling)

**Linda:** Is this after Kimos, after our Kimos thing?

(Frank sounds yes)

**Linda:** Well he tried to do things with clothes on and stuff to get gigs. Nobody would book him. (imitating Bob) Nobody's booking Fluff Grrl! Nobody's booking Frank Moore! They won't even talk to me about it!

**John:** I remember that. After we did those three series at Kimos? Those three shows, remember those, with those nice posters? It was like on holidays.

**Linda:** Yeah! We were the holiday band.

**John:** It wasn't a good draw.

**Linda:** It was when Boom lost Kimos, that's when it all changed.

**John:** Yeah.

*John The Baker (video capture)*

**Linda:** And he got the other spot ...

**Mikee:** The Cherry Lounge.

**Linda:** The Cherry Lounge, and they didn't want us and they didn't want nudity, and Bob started wearing clothes, so he could keep playing there. That's when it all happened.

**Frank:** Obviously he ...

**Linda:** ... has taken his clothes off again. (laughing) He's played that out.

**John:** He's a really bright guy. He's a really intelligent man, so I'm sure he saw his errors of his ways that way, too. You can't keep a down man good. (Frank sounds) He's awesome. I don't want him to wear clothes and not burn his pubes! (Frank sounds) I want him to be repulsive! I want him to be the shock guy that he is, man. He is fierce. (Frank sounds) And honestly Bob, if you are listening, I do get concerned for your health and your longevity as a human. Because you have the most endurance as an alcoholic than anybody I know. But I do care about you and don't want you to die from alcohol or drugs or a bad car accident or something. So I do want you to take care of yourself. I don't want you to stop taking your clothes off and burning your pubes, ever! [Bob Madigan died of liver failure at the age of 47 in 2012 - Ed.]

**Frank:** Hey, he may outlive all of us.

**Linda:** Bob may. He is that kind of guy!

**John:** I know! Actually, Joanne, her best friend, I don't know why he got ... something happened and he was pissed off, depressed, he was going to kill himself in Santa Barbara, and he jumped off a cliff, that students fall off all the time and die! And he just bounced off and didn't break a bone or anything. (laughter) That's what happens, you know, that drunk gets in a car accident and they don't get hurt! They just get tossed around.

**Frank:** That is exactly why I don't jump off cliffs. (John laughs) I want to be sure.

**Linda:** If you try to kill yourself, you want to be sure it's really going to work. (laughter)

**John:** He was pretty sure. (laughter) I guess you can't be really sure, that's the thing. It's really hard to kill living things. Have you noticed? Have you tried to kill things? They don't want to die! (laughing) It's really hard to kill something, I've found. You can beat it. You can just keep beating it, mash it and step on it.

**Frank:** Will you read my poem, "That Goddamn Weed of Life"?

**Linda:** He is asking if you'd read it now aloud.

**John:** Oh sure! (John starts reading)


THAT GODDAMN WEED OF LIFE

by Frank Moore

11/28/02


That goddamn weed of life,

Green, yellow, purple,

cracking through the blacktop

in the park.

We don't own it.

We own all life.

All life is our property...

Except weeds!


After the riots,

We put all living greens,

All living color,

Behind tall black iron fences.

Lovers, babies can't lay on the grass,

No dreamers stretched out in fresh smells,

Looking up into the fluffy clouds of possibilities

Ever changing.


All of that was too dangerous.

Now we separate flesh

From life colors.

Now, walk or roll on blacktop,

Squint thru black bars

At grass, trees, flowers...

All at a safe distance...

Sit straight up on benches

With hard arms of separation,

Preventing love-making,

Sleeping...

Showing any tender pleasure.


All of that

Is kept in a safe distance

In the past

In this zoo,

In this gas chamber

Of a park...


All at a safe distance

Under control

Under lock and key...

Except for this goddamn weed of life

RIGHT THERE!

We sprayed it with poison,

Ripped it out,

Crushed it...

But it keeps coming back!

Doesn't it know?

We own all life now.

It's our personal property now.

We own the building blocks,

The dna keys of life...

Under our patents and copyrights.

We own the water.

We own the seeds.

We own the monopoly on life,

Hijacking evolution itself

Into the goal of profit.

We who sit in first class,

In box seats,

Behind oak doors,

Not to be seen.

WEEDS! WEEDS! WEEDS!

80 percent of all humans,

and of all life

are useless weeds,

to be ultimately destroyed

by all means necessary...

and in the meantime

to be contained within warehouses,

keep them moving from warehouse

to warehouse,

nomads without space

on blacktop

without water wells,

rain barrels,

farms of independence,

or music of a free soul.


We own the rights to all imagination

And dreams.

We hold all the cards!


So why is this goddamn weed

Cracking the blacktop?!

How come this single weed

is spreading unprocessed life

all around?


And the cracks

In the blacktop

Are spreading!


**John:** Awesome!

(laughter)

**Linda:** Woooo. That was great! (Frank sounds) That was a good reading. (laughter)

**John:** Want to smoke some weed? What's the greenhouse effect? I don't know, it's something to do with hydroponics I think. That's one of the recorded answers I use a lot. It's one of my song lyrics! You don't remember?! (giggling)

**Frank:** Yes. Is that a segue to you playing a song?

**John:** Yeah! This is a good time.

**Linda:** Alright!

**Linda:** He lost his mic!

**Frank:** Some pro!

**Linda:** Some professional!

**John:** You wouldn't invite me if I was a real pro! (Frank sounds)

**John:** (while tuning his guitar) So last night at the show we did with Womentors and Angry Samoans at Bottom of the Hill, there was this kid up front (Frank sounds, "Yeah") and he was going, every time in between songs, "Play Crack Baby! Crack Baby!" That's not one of our songs. It's my old band's song. But it's a song that me and Frank have done together before, so. What do you think? Want to do that song again? Do you want to sing?

**Frank:** Yes.

**Linda:** Frank can do it, yes. I'll hold the mic in front of you, I think that's easier. I'll follow you around as you move.

*(John and Frank sing "Crack Baby" and John plays the guitar)*

*(John performs another song)*

**John:** Something else I'd like to do. Another song that's not by me. It's a guy named Jay Silverman. I learned this song from my brother and I think it's really funny. I sung it for many years. And back in the early days, like in the mid '80s when I used to go to the Anarchist Coffee Houses in Santa Cruz and San Francisco, I got kicked off stage for this one. (laughs) And it's not for really for any righteous or good reasons. It's pretty much a bad sexist song. (laughing) So, I thought Frank might like it! (laughing)

**Frank:** If they were anarchists ...

**Linda:** ... why should they have a problem with it?

**John:** Well, I think the PC revolution was happening and a lot of people were really unconscious when they said these things.

**Frank:** REAL anarchists!

**Linda:** REAL anarchists.

**John:** Well, you know, I don't think ... the musicians, they didn't care. They thought it was funny too. But it is, it's a pig song. It's a song pretty much written by a chauvinist pig, but it's funny as hell. It's called "Drunk and Crazy". You can sing along. (laughter) And sometimes it's just appropriate.

*(John performs the song. Frank sings along.)*

**John:** So, you know, that's what happens. Twenty-five years ago or twenty years ago I got thrown off stage for that song. Here, at this particular venue, I get applauds for that song and actual belly laughs happened.

**Frank:** What is un-PC about that song?! (laughter)

**John:** That's what I'm talking about. The times change. I kept playing that song for twenty-five years even though they kicked me off stage, and now they love it!

*Linda Mac, Frank Moore and John The Baker (video capture)*

**Frank:** He got his ...

**John:** Yeah, he got his ass beat, huh?

**Linda:** Yeah!

**John:** That's right. I don't know why ... it was just ... (quoting from song) "I was about to put that cake in the oven" ...

**Frank:** They didn't hear Country Porn.

**John:** This is pre-. This is really early.

**Linda:** Country Porn, the band.

**John:** Oh, I didn't know there was a band called Country Porn.

**Linda:** Yeah. (giving song titles) "Cum Stains on my Pillow Where Your Sweet Head Used to Be".

**John:** Ahhhhh!

**Linda:** (giving another song title) "Dry Humping in the Back of a '55 Ford".

**John:** Ahhhhh! Cool!

**Mikee:** "Cum Unto the Lord"

**Frank:** Where I got my start.

**Linda:** That's where Frank got his start. Because we used to go to see them, they played locally. And the guy, Chinga Chavin, another Cancer, loved us, and he'd always put the mic down for Frank to sing along with him on all these songs. And that was the beginning of Frank's singing thing.

**John:** What's his name?

**Linda:** Chinga Chavin.

**Frank:** Huge cult following.

**Linda:** They were very popular around here. This was in the 1970s.

**Frank:** Penthouse …

**Linda:** … was their financial backer. Then they had the Beaverettes, a couple of women that were the backup singers, topless. Very formative for Frank! (laughing)

**Frank:** Great …

**Linda:** … they had incredible musicians. The band was top of the line, tight. And the songs were really good. And he wrote all the songs.

**Frank:** But …

**Linda:** … he had all this popularity, now it's time to go straight and go for the "real" thing. Just disappeared. Moved to New York, did a straight album, *Jet Lag* which wasn't very good, and disappeared.

**John:** Bethany, take note!

**Frank:** We should go to the Anarchists Event and sing …

**Mikee:** … sing some of those songs!

**John:** They don't tell me where their shows are anymore! (Frank shrieks) I'm teasing. No, those people really, in general are really awesome. I met some great singer/songwriters like Mark Levy. Mark Levy lives in Felton, on the top of the mountain by Santa Cruz.

**Linda:** We play him on LUVeR.

**John:** He's one of the coolest guys. One of the best singer/songwriters leftist folkie I've ever met. Great friend of mine from the '80s. If you're ever … if anybody sees Mark Levy, knows Mark Levy, tell him John the Baker says "Hi". He, unlike most people, dug "Fist Fuck the Pope"! He got behind it. He's cool. There's a strong folk network and when I wrote that in New York other folkies sent word back to him, because he was a friend of mine, and he heard of my song and he corresponded with me and said, "I really dig that shit!" Because Mark was a really subversive guy, but he was such a talented guitar player I can't cover his songs. He's too good. Even though they're really simple … oh, I've got one I can do. He used to say, this is the only two-chord song he ever wrote because the issue was just that simple. I won't remember all of the words but, it's a sing-along. And he would always get people to sing along with him. You'll figure it out.

*John performs the song, "Every Sperm Does Not Deserve a Name". Frank sings along.*

**John:** He's awesome, right? Isn't that great? The only two chord song Mark Levy ever wrote. Mark Levy, Darryl Cherney, another big influence for me. I love those guys.

**John:** He does this other one that I can't play because he's too good. It's called, you'll love it, it's called, "Take Off Your Clothes To Those You Oppose". He told me, he said, "John, I've been trying to write a song about the Arab/Israeli problems." This is like 1988 or so. He says, I haven't been able to do it. He's a Jew, he's Jewish. It's an important issue to him so he didn't want to just write a shitty song, so he's waiting and waiting. Then one day he read in the paper, it said, the headline was something like, Jews sunbathe, Arabs retreat. (laughter) The scenario was in the article was the front lines, the Arabs were posted on the front line with their machine guns, and about 100 feet away or 100 yards away was a nude beach! And there's Jews out there nude sunbathing. And so the Arab in charge, the General, or whatever said, let's move back so you can't see the naked women! (laughter) So they moved the frontline back 100 yards! And so he got this idea, he said, "Take off your clothes to those you oppose. Be well exposed to foes and strike a pose!" (laughter) "The sight of muff will be enough to halt the tough." (laughter) And he goes on and on. He's such a master! Ask him to sing that!

**Frank:** I tried.

**Linda:** Oh, we tried to get him on the Shaman's Den. That's why I know his name. What happened?

(Frank giggles)

**Linda:** He didn't respond.

**John:** I don't know. I'll talk to him. I want to see him. He is really great. When Judi Bari and Darryl Cherney got blown up in the car, the Earth Firsters in 1990, during the Redwood Summer organizing, Mark worked for me in San Jose, and we worked for Campaign California. I was the manager and he was a telephone fund raiser. I think he's a little older than me. At least he had more experience than me. When that happened, I was like "Wow!" That was the first time I really realized that I could get killed for the work I did. Like I was a pretty intense activist at the time. And I was like, "Wow." The Combine could really focus on me and knock me out! You know what I mean? Like what they tried to do to Darryl and Judi. And I remember Mark saying that for him it was Brian Wilson, when Brian Wilson's legs got cut off at the Concord Naval Weapons Station. That was the first time he felt like he could get killed for the work he did. I don't know, that's just something I remember about the guy.

**Frank:** Being a crip has some advantages.

**Linda:** People would be less inclined to physically hurt somebody like Frank.

**Frank:** They don't ...

**John:** I don't think that's necessarily true, but, I think they'd take you out if they felt ... I mean, they tried to take you out right? Jesse Helms targeted you already, you know what I mean, back in that day. It's the same kind of thing. Whether or not it's a killing machine or it's a propaganda machine, they're still trying to take you out. You're scary Frank! I'd kill you if I was the man. (laughter)

**Frank:** Why don't they?

**Linda:** Why don't they, Frank wonders?

**John:** Why don't they kill you or me?

**Linda:** Him. He wants to know what you think of why they don't kill him.

**John:** I don't know. I imagine it's because we're not that much of a threat to them at this point, but I'm sure we get watched. And we're tapped. And if things are changing, if tides turn, they're going to have their finger on our pulse. But, one of the reasons I live so obscure is to avoid that.

**Frank:** Your middle name is "the". (laughter)

**Linda:** That's being obscure. (laughing)

**John:** It's true, I changed my name ... actually I use my moniker mainly to protect, initially to protect my family who are more mainstream musicians and they were young kids at the time. I was really fucking shit up. I wanted them to be able to make their own mistakes and live their own lives and not have it be clouded by shit that I did. Now they've been through their own processes a lot and they're men and they're pros, professional musicians in and out of big bands and touring the world, so it's not as taboo for me to use my real name in that regard. And I'd say I'm probably less subversive today than I was in 1985.

**Frank:** How so?

**John:** I'm not really necessarily an organizer of major protests. I'm not always getting arrested out in front of corporations, like I was there for a time. I was really on the front lines in that regard. Targeted my action towards different ... well, actually, what happened with me is that, in '92, I went back to Arizona to meet with my shaman because I was confused and I felt like I needed some guidance. So I went and she said you need to do a vision quest, a winter vision quest. So it was January, and I went out into the desert and I did a vision quest, and I came back and she said I needed to, based on my vision, I needed to ... first she said, I want you to write an essay on the difference between a community organizer and an activist. And I go, aren't they the same thing?! (Frank sounds) No! And it took me a long time. I was really pissed off, because I really wanted fucking clarity! I wanted her to say, bedink, bedank, bedunk! Not like set me into a process. (laughter) And it really set me into a process!

**Frank:** We shamans never are clear.

**John:** Well, I wanted it to be a little easier. It took me a long time. But then when I got back to where I lived ...

**Frank:** Or always are clear.

**John:** Exactly! It's one or the other with you guys. So I lived in a geodesic dome in upstate New York with a wood stove and a solar panel, but it collapsed while I was gone, in the month that I was in Arizona, it had collapsed under the weight of the snow. So I got back and the director of the community that I was living at came down with pneumonia. So I moved into another space and I started working full time in the office. And I kept things going. And at the time they said I saved the community in a way because she couldn't work and she did everything. Her old man is a really great author and a psychologist but she's the backbone. She did a lot of the work. And for about six months I kept that thing going until she was better able to do her work. That's when I started to see that there's a difference between community organizing and activism. That activism was more of a lashing out. Was like a trying to push something away. Whereas community organizing is a way to hold everything and a way to bring people in. And it took many, many years after that though to really incorporate that and to realize that I was on a different path now. (Frank sounds) I didn't need to get arrested in front of United Technologies Corporation in San Jose. I didn't need to do that. What I needed to do was to build a strong community that got so big and so strong that I didn't even see that or need to be around that. It's like we're too powerful to be affected by that in a way ... is what I'm trying to do.

**Frank:** Create alternatives.

**John:** Exactly! And that's become my focus. And I think that is more threatening. (Frank sounds yes) And ultimately I think The Man will see it as more threatening too if it does ripple and become a dominant force. Right now, all it does is save a thousand or a couple of hundred kids from the mundane perspective that society scripts for them and it gives them a way to view life and reality in a different way. Which hopefully will set more seeds in their lives and then more seeds from the people that they influence and then it will be neither after ... it's going to be my grandchildren or ...

**Frank:** Activism is linear.

**John:** Yeah! Oh, you can totally see that.

**Frank:** Community building is non-linear.

**John:** That's how I even described it. I said activist (gestures straight line) and community building (completes a circle with his arms). It's another perspective. And that's the lessons that I learned. And I haven't done another vision quest since. I'm still working those lessons. Sometimes they're lifelong. I don't even know. When I'm confused again, I'll go and seek new vision. (laughing) But I'm still working this out and still ... That's what Burnt Ramen is. That's what I do in the basement.

**Frank:** Yes. Did you watch that video *In My Own Language*?

**Mikee:** It's a YouTube video that Frank sent out.

**John:** I don't have sound, so I don't end up watching a lot of videos.

**Linda:** Oh, it was amazing! It's an autistic woman.

**Frank:** The first part is just her doing (moves his head from side to side, imitating autistic behavior) ...

**Linda:** Autistic type behavior. What you think of as autistic type behavior.

**Frank:** Then she starts speaking via a computer voice.

**Linda:** It is her typing and then you hear a voice that's generated saying what she's typing.

**John:** That's like a translator for her own language?

**Linda:** She's communicating to us by typing it out, but it's coming out as a regular voice so we can hear what she's saying.

**John:** That's cool.

**Frank:** And ...

**Linda:** Well, she's incredibly articulate! She really starts kicking ass about the values that people put on different types of communication. "And now that I'm talking to you like this, now you're paying attention to me? Now you think I know what I'm doing? But if I don't do that, you think I have less value than you?" And she just kicks ass!

**John:** (to Frank) You can relate to that, dude! (laughing)

**Linda:** Well, we felt that we were as guilty as anybody else! It wasn't like we didn't feel ... obviously we didn't look down on autistic people, we thought there was value, but we didn't really ... we assumed that an autistic person wasn't thinking in such a clear way as she was communicating.

**John:** Yeah.

**Frank:** Everything she did was for a reason.

**Linda:** All the movements and things that she does, she's saying are for reasons. (laughing) You're just not hip to it is basically what she's saying. Just because you don't get it, you think there's no value in it.

**John:** Don't point at me! (laughter) That's cool. That's really important work. Maybe sometimes dogs will talk like that and animals.

**Frank:** Destroyed everything!

**Linda:** The way she was talking, it destroyed everything ... all the pictures. (Frank sounds)

**Frank:** That is punk really.

**John:** That's really punk! Yeah!

(Frank sounds)

**Linda:** That's a wrap!

**John:** Thanks for having me. Always a pleasure joining my favorite person. (laughter)

# APPENDIX 1

# Platform For Frank Moore's Presidency 2008  *I GET RESULTS!*

I'll do away with welfare and social security. Instead, every American will receive a minimum income of $1,000 a month. This amount will be tied to the cost of living and will not be taxable.

We will have universal prenatal-to-the-grave health care and universal free education with equal access.

I'll do away with all tax deductions for over $12,000 income. Instead, there will be a flat tax of 10% on annual income of less than one million dollars for an individual and less than five million dollars for a corporation. But the flat tax will jump to 75% on annual income exceeding these limits.

I'll cut the military budget by at least half.

Public mass transit will be free, 24/7, and reliable.

All patents and copyrights will expire in 20 years. Inventions, products, etc. which are developed with governmental money and/or public institutions can not be patented.

All businesses selling their products in the U.S. will have to certify that their products were manufactured in accordance with this country's labor, wage, environmental, and safety laws … that they meet or exceed these … no matter where they were produced.

Each city and each "media market" will have at least two public access channels on radio, broadcast television, cable, AND satellite!

Election day will be a paid holiday.

I will push for complete public funding for all political campaigns and the banning of political contributions and the use of personal wealth in political campaigns.

The President should have a line veto. But the Congress can over-turn this line veto by a simple majority. Also, bills should be limited to 5 pages in length and/or limited to one subject.

An individual taxpayer will be able to direct her taxes to what functions she wants to support. But corporate taxpayers should not have this option.

Every corporation should come up for a renewal every 25 years, at which time it must prove that it has been operating in the public interest. If it fails to do this, it loses its right to exist.

Corporations that have existed before this policy will have 10 years before they will have to prove they are worthy.

Government should leave marriage to churches. Instead, any two or more adults who have been living together for at least 2 years should be able to register as a "family".

• • •

The end of hunger, poverty, and discrimination in this nation will be my main focus domestically. This will also shape my foreign policy.

The minimum income and the minimum/livable wage, linked to the cost of living, will rise every time the congress members vote themselves a pay raise … will rise by the same percentage of their raise.

Education should be federally funded, based on the number of students, adjusted to special needs of each student, in each school district. But schools should be locally controlled. The equal access of education for every student will be insured by the federal government.

I will call for a major rebuilding of America. We will repair our school buildings and will build needed new schools. I will encourage a society of small villages connected by mass transit. Within these small villages, people could walk or bike to work, to school, to shopping, to entertainment, etc. Mass transit will combine these small villages within 15 miles radius into dynamic communities. Living in these villages will end gridlock traffic, will cut greenhouse gasses, will cut stress and isolation. Housing for all incomes will be included equally in each village.

We will encourage electric cars, fast trains, clean sustainable decentralized energy generators. I would shut down all nuclear generators.

I will destroy 10 percent of our nuclear weapons each year to reverse the nuclear arms race.

We will stop giving/selling arms to other countries. All private arms sales should be illegal.

Now my policies are pro-business. The universal education system will provide business with a superior, flexible work force. The minimum income and the universal health care will remove the business's burden of providing health insurance and pensions to workers. In reality, this relief will be much more than any tax cut could give. Moreover, the minimum income will make the starting and maintaining a small business much easier. This is also true for small family farms. The minimum income will encourage independent invention and artistic pursuit, on which true progress depends.

• • •

The primary function of the government should be the protection of the health, the civil and human rights, the freedoms, and the general welfare of the people … instead of the protection and the promotion of corporate profits and interests. The government should exist to serve the people, and not to make a profit on the services to the people. My administration will be governed by these basic principles.

I will bring the troops home from Iraq immediately. Moreover, I will change this country's self-image from that of THE SUPER POWER/WORLD LEADER to that of a member of the global community.

Prisons should be only for violent or otherwise dangerous criminals. Prisons should be a part of the health and educational system and should include drug rehab programs. This should also be true for the new creative in-community programs for non-violent criminals for paying-back, rehab, and education sentencing. These programs will be more effective and much less expensive and harmful to the community on every level than the current human warehouse system. Flexibility of sentencing should be returned to judges. I will ban the death penalty.

The use of drugs should be legalized and taxed. Pot and spirits should be sold over-the-counter to adults only. Tobacco and other addictive drugs should be sold by prescription only. Free drug rehab programs should be readily available.

All of the opt-out schemes should be illegal. If a corporation wants to sell your information, it first should directly and clearly get your permission. Before this happens, all such information is a part of your privacy, not the property of a corporation.

The selling/buying of debt should be illegal. Moreover, there should be a maximum interest rate of 10 percent on the original principle over the lifetime of a loan.

I will forgive the loans to the so-called third-world countries over the original principle.

We will use half of the money we will save by cutting the military budget to pay down the national debt. I will reduce the pollution caused by obscene corporate profits.

I will also reduce the federal government while raising services to the people by getting rid of welfare, social security, the so-called war on drugs, etc., and by the cuts in the military, the IRS, prisons, etc.

THIS PLATFORM OF MINE GIVES YOU AN OUTLINE OF WHAT WE WILL DO TOGETHER, OF WHAT I SEE THIS COUNTRY AND THE WORLD BECOMING ... IT IS DEFINITELY POSSIBLE, IF WE ARE WILLING. YEP, IT IS RADICAL. BUT IT JUST MAKES SENSE! DOESN'T IT?

-- Frank Moore

# APPENDIX 2

# Complete list of Frank Moore's Shaman's Den on FAKE Radio, LUVeR and Post-LUVeR

## FAKE Radio

### 1998

| | |
|---|---|
| 08/23/98 | Chris Roberts, software engineer and co-founder of FAKE Radio |
| 08/31/98 | Fred Hatt, artist, dancer, photographer |
| 10/11/98 | Don Jelinek, Berkeley Mayoral Candidate |
| 10/18/98 | Lee Williams, poet |
| 11/15/98 | Louise Scott, a wise woman, cultural pioneer, midwife, international bag lady |

### 1999

| | |
|---|---|
| 01/10/99 | Barb Golden, musician, artist, performer |
| 01/17/99 | Attaboy, poet, publisher, performer |

## LUVeR

### 1999

| | |
|---|---|
| 02/21/99 | Annie Sprinkle, performance artist, author, ex-porn star |
| 02/28/99 | Word-Music Continuum, musical group |
| 03/07/99 | Attaboy, poet, publisher, performer |
| 03/14/99 | Giovanni Moro and Teresa Cochran, musical jam and conversation |
| 04/04/99 | Chris Cortese, Joanna, Bob Madigan (Fluff Grrl) from Pervertidora Records, San Francisco |
| 04/18/99 | Laurence Lasky, poet, Alphabeat Press |
| 04/25/99 | Jethro Jeremiah Band |
| 05/02/99 | Walter Funk, musician and Colin Manning, filmmaker, animator, painter |
| 05/09/99 | Suran Song in Stag, rock band from New Jersey |
| 05/16/99 | Jesse Beagle, poet, musician, performer |
| 05/23/99 | Sez Giulian, singer/songwriter |
| 06/13/99 | Lee Gerstmann, poet |
| 06/27/99 | Colin Manning, filmmaker, animator, painter and Zoeie Smart |
| 07/04/99 | Raindog, poet, musician and Marshall Astor, musician from Southern California |
| 07/11/99 | David Steinberg, photographer |
| 07/18/99 | Giovanni Moro and Teresa Cochran, musical jam |
| 07/25/99 | Dixi Cohn, poet |
| 08/01/99 | S.K. Thoth, musician, performance artist |

| | |
|---|---|
| 08/08/99 | Beatriz Flores, KPFA staff |
| 08/22/99 | Dale Jensen, poet, publisher |
| 09/05/99 | Seth Hebert of Dufus, musician from New York |
| 09/19/99 | Small press publishers D. Michael McNamara (*)ism()* from Seattle, Washington, Lindsay Wilson (*unwound*) from Laramie, Wyoming, and Kelly Dessaint (*phony lid*) from Los Angeles |
| 10/10/99 | tHE rESONANCE iMAGE pROGRAM, experimental music group |
| 10/17/99 | Walter Funk, musician |
| 10/24/99 | Attaboy and Ben Burke, poets, performers |
| 11/14/99 | Bill Mandel, broadcast journalist, left-wing political activist, author, Soviet analyzer |
| 11/28/99 | Paul Kealoha, Media Center of the East Bay |
| 12/05/99 | Leroy Moore, poet |

## 2000

| | |
|---|---|
| 01/09/00 | Frank Shawl, dancer, choreographer |
| 01/16/00 | Barb Golden, musician, artist, performer |
| 01/23/00 | Diane Parker, author |
| 02/13/00 | Joe Bryak, author, leftist, child of the '60s |
| 02/20/00 | Rebecca Kaplan, politician |
| 02/27/00 | Philip Gelb, musician |
| 03/05/00 | Eileen Kaufman, wife of Beat poet, Bob Kaufman and Jesse Beagle, poet, musician |
| 03/12/00 | Les Radke, teacher, activist |
| 03/13/00 | Paul Krassner, founder, editor, contributor to *The Realist*, founding member of the Yippies, author, comedian, member of Ken Kesey's Merry Pranksters from Southern California |
| 03/19/00 | Mary Davis, Berkeley icon and activist |
| 03/26/00 | The Slow Poisoners, rock band |
| 04/09/00 | Kerwin Kay, author |
| 04/23/00 | Marie Kazalia, poet, author and Kelly Dessaint, author, small press publisher |
| 04/30/00 | Andy Goldfarb, musician, singer, songwriter, illustrator, author |
| 05/14/00 | Charles T., musician |
| 05/28/00 | Musical jam with Walter Funk, Giovanni Moro, Teresa Cochran, John the Baker, Corey Nicholl and Frank Moore |
| 06/04/00 | Barb Golden, musician, artist, performer |
| 06/18/00 | Big Willie, musician |
| 06/25/00 | Tony Ryan, photographer from Tasmania, Australia |
| 07/02/00 | Audio Terrorist, rock band |
| 07/16/00 | Stoney Burke, street performer and actor |
| 07/23/00 | Dan Mattson, San Francisco Bay Area Indymedia |
| 07/30/00 | Lori Surfer, filmmaker, musician |
| 08/06/00 | Erik Core, punk musician |
| 08/13/00 | Denise Demise Dunne and Damon Malloy, San Francisco punk scene |
| 08/20/00 | Gerald Smith, activist, former Black Panther, Green Party candidate |

| | |
|---|---|
| 08/27/00 | Paul Griffin, pirate radio DJ |
| 09/10/00 | WRP Diana, community builder and massage therapist |
| 09/17/00 | Sharon, "The Hidden Revolution" |
| 09/24/00 | Dustin Prestridge, poet, artist |
| 10/08/00 | Larry-bob, small press publisher |
| 10/15/00 | Bern, singer/songwriter |
| 11/19/00 | Pauline Oliveros, composer and accordionist who is a central figure in the development of experimental and post-war electronic art music, and jam with Frank Moore and Teresa Cochran |
| 11/26/00 | Audio Terrorist, rock band |
| 12/03/00 | Left Out Lamont, rock band |
| 12/17/00 | Lori B., singer/songwriter |

## 2001

| | |
|---|---|
| 01/07/01 | John Good, M.D., our family doctor |
| 01/21/01 | Faun Fables, band |
| 01/28/01 | Jill Nagle, author |
| 02/11/01 | Manta, rock band |
| 02/18/01 | Katy Bell and M.I. Blue, DaDa Fest organizers |
| 02/25/01 | Andy and Aaron, Thrush T.V. |
| 03/11/01 | Stephen Kent, didgeridoo performer, percussionist, composer and recording artist, and jam with Frank Moore, vocals |
| 03/18/01 | Barb Golden, musician, artist, performer |
| 03/25/01 | Kirk Lumpkin, poet, activist, musician |
| 04/01/01 | Tony Seymour, poet |
| 04/08/01 | NSR Productions: Bryan Birchard and Camile |
| 04/22/01 | David Johnson, San Quentin Six and Elder Freeman, Black Panther |
| 05/20/01 | P. D. Scott, poet, author, political activist |
| 05/27/01 | Elliot Lessing, videographer, performer |
| 06/03/01 | Steve Zeltzer, labor activist |
| 06/10/01 | Peter Weiss, singer |
| 06/17/01 | Chemystry Set, rock band |
| 07/01/01 | Tracy James and Gerald Smith, radio hosts "Slave Revolt Radio" |
| 07/08/01 | John Seabury, artist, musician |
| 07/15/01 | Jam with Kalib, Annaka, Alex, Teresa, Pixie and Frank |
| 07/22/01 | Mike Boner and Aimee, performance artists |
| 07/29/01 | Matt Armstrong and Dominic, Superpig and Gsharp Studio |
| 08/05/01 | David Johnson and Sundiata Willie Tate, San Quentin Six and Elder Freeman, Black Panther |
| 09/09/01 | William Florian and Christina Sophia, tantradance.com |
| 09/16/01 | Swan Childress, Art Healer |
| 09/30/01 | Discord Aggregate, experimental artists/musicians |
| 10/07/01 | Stevanne Auerbach, PhD, "Dr. Toy" |
| 10/14/01 | Larry Bearg and Lorene Reed, founders Planet Organics |
| 10/28/01 | Richard Edmondson and DJ Deek, S.F. Liberation Radio |

| | |
|---|---|
| 11/04/01 | Sue Supriano, "Steppin' Out of Babylon" producer and host |
| 11/11/01 | Miri Hunter Haruach, PhD, musician |
| 11/18/01 | eXtreme Elvis, artist, performer |
| 12/09/01 | Christian Lunch aka Xtian, punk musician |

## 2002

| | |
|---|---|
| 01/06/02 | Cindy Lubar Bishop, writer, vocalist and Neil |
| 01/20/02 | Michael Peppe as Sol Divus, musician/performance artist |
| 02/03/02 | Ron Jones, performance artist |
| 02/10/02 | Blake More, poet |
| 02/17/02 | Kara Herold, Grrly Show, filmmaker |
| 02/24/02 | Andrew Goldfarb-Poisoner!, musician, writer, artist with Tom Neely, bass player |
| 03/03/02 | Judith Redmond, Full Belly Farm |
| 03/10/02 | Kevin Danaher, co-founder Global Exchange, author and anti-globalization activist |
| 03/31/02 | Koala Bear Moore, Frank's son |
| 05/05/02 | Dr. Suzy Block, sexologist, author, filmmaker, therapist, cable TV talk show host, cultural commentator from Los Angeles |
| 05/19/02 | All-Star Jam with Kalib, Pixie, Gio, Alex, Teresa, Frank |
| 05/26/02 | Kalib and Pixie's "Wedding" |
| 05/26/02 | Kriss Worthington, Berkeley City Council Member |
| 06/02/02 | Clint Marsh, Wonderella with Andy Goldfarb, author |
| 08/04/02 | Shelley Doty, musician, singer/songwriter |
| 08/11/02 | Marie Kazalia, poet, writer |
| 08/18/02 | Tallulah Bankheist, hooker activist |
| 08/25/02 | Formerly The No No's, rock band |
| 09/08/02 | Jen! Neuber, student activist, recently returned from Palestine |
| 09/14/02 | Visitations, band |
| 09/29/02 | Cuir Bleu, band |
| 10/20/02 | Vicente Balvanera, Argentina Labor Activist |
| 10/27/02 | All-Star Jam with Russell Kline, Kalib Duarte, Stephen Jones (Red Martian), John the Baker, Xtian, LX Rudis, Teresa Cochran and Frank Moore (piano) |
| 11/03/02 | Aaron Loeb, Planet Moon Studios and Kathy Roberts |
| 11/17/02 | Alison Chokwadi Fletcher, poet |
| 12/01/02 | Mel Gordon, UC Berkeley Professor, Theater, Dance and Performance Studies |
| 12/08/02 | Carl Bryant, union organizer, letter carrier and public access TV producer |
| 12/15/02 | Joe Monday, Berkeley Liberation Radio DJ |
| 12/22/02 | LX Rudis, musician |
| 12/25/02 | eXtreme Elvis and Frank xmas special w/Jordana, Xtian and Dea |

## 2003

| | |
|---|---|
| 01/12/03 | Kathy Stuart, author, historian |
| 01/19/03 | Kellia Ramares, R.I.S.E. |
| 01/26/03 | Star Jewel Smith, getunderground.com |

| | |
|---|---|
| 02/02/03 | Francine Manuel, physical therapist |
| 02/09/03 | Tom Odegard, poet |
| 02/23/03 | Attaboy, poet, publisher, toy designer, performer and Annie Owens, artist |
| 03/02/03 | Cindy Cohn, Legal Director, Electronic Frontier Foundation |
| 03/09/03 | All-Star Jam with Dr. Oblivious, Nate Scott, Kirsten Rose, Teresa Cochran, Frank Moore, Chris Miller and Lena Strayhorn the jaw harp queen |
| 03/30/03 | Ruby Pearl and Steve DiAngelo, owners of Sacred Profanities Gallery |
| 04/20/03 | The Leeches, punk band from the U.K. |
| 04/27/03 | She Mob, rock band |
| 05/04/03 | "Peace Jam" with Dr. Oblivious, Nate Scott, Kirsten Rose, Michael Peppe, Kalib Duarte, Pixie, Kitty and Frank Moore |
| 05/18/03 | Irina Rivkin, Rose St. House of Music with Rebecca Crump, musician |
| 05/25/03 | Shroomy Shroom, rock band |
| 06/22/03 | Carol Brouillet, creator of the Deception Dollar and activist, with Abel Ashes |
| 06/29/03 | Simon Harris, Organic Consumers Association |
| 07/06/03 | "Peace Jam #2" with Michael Peppe, Andy Goldfarb and Frank Moore |
| 07/27/03 | Normal, poet and Charlotte from New York State, with Dr. O., Kirsten Rose and Frank Moore background jamming |
| 08/03/03 | Debby Goldsberry, Berkeley Patients Group |
| 08/17/03 | Michael Peppe, musician, performance artist |
| 08/31/03 | Slow Poisoners, rock band |
| 09/07/03 | Lee Callister, Videowest TV producer |
| 09/11/03 | Amy X Neuburg, composer, vocalist, and electronic musician |
| 09/28/03 | Dietmar Lorenz, "Green" architect |
| 10/12/03 | "Peace Jam #3" with Frank Moore, Kirsten Rose, Erika Shaver-Nelson, Dr. O., LX Rudis, John the Baker |
| 10/19/03 | Alden Bryant, co-founder of New Energy Movement, godfather of the United Nations Global Climate Stabilization Treaties |
| 10/26/03 | Bill Beasley, Civil Rights and Gay Activist, a founder of the Gay Pride Celebration in San Francisco |
| 10/29/03 | "Chaos Love Play Jam" with Stephen Jones, Carlos, Sky, Michael Peppe, LX Rudis, Kirsten Rose, Erika Shaver-Nelson and Frank Moore |
| 11/02/03 | Kene-J and Psyko Myko, hip-hop artists |
| 11/17/03 | Soul, DJ Berkeley Liberation Radio |
| 11/30/03 | Global Culture, hip-hop group |
| 12/14/03 | LX Rudis xmas special |

## 2004

| | |
|---|---|
| 01/04/04 | Winston Tong, actor/playwright, visual artist, puppeteer, and singer/songwriter and jam with LX Rudis, Walter Funk, Winston Tong, Kirsten Rose and Frank Moore |
| 01/11/04 | Wendy-O Matik, freelance writer, poet, performance and spoken word artist, and radical love activist |
| 01/18/04 | Pucca Pangenitor, musician |
| 01/25/04 | Dr. Richard Kerbavaz, Frank's ear, nose and throat doctor |

| | |
|---|---|
| 02/01/04 | Jack Hirschman, poet and social activist |
| 02/08/04 | Suzanne Joi, owner of It's Her Business and Code Pink Activist |
| 02/29/04 | "What Should the Left Do?" Tracy James, LUVeR DJ, "Slave Revolt Radio" |
| 03/07/04 | Ignacio Chapela, U.C. Berkeley professor, microbial ecologist and mycologist and Deborah Garcia, director/producer "The Future of Food", Lily Films |
| 03/14/04 | Michael Parenti, political scientist, historian, and cultural critic |
| 04/25/04 | Agneta Falk-Hirschman, poet/painter |
| 05/23/04 | Jesse Townley, Berkeley City Council candidate, punk musician, radio DJ |
| 05/30/04 | Half Past Gone, rock band |
| 06/03/04 | Leni Stern, singer/guitarist from New York |
| 06/13/04 | Moby Theobold, B-TV producer/host |
| 07/11/04 | Dirty Dave Sanchez, DJ Rampage Radio, KUSF and Misti |
| 07/18/04 | Kirk Lumpkin, poet, activist, musician |
| 07/26/04 | Pamela Madison, Director, Women's Sexuality Center, Santa Barbara, California |
| 08/01/04 | Paul Goettlich, activist, the health and socioeconomic effects of technology - plastics, pesticides, genetic engineering, nuclear radiation, and so on |
| 08/08/04 | Cuir Bleu, rock band |
| 08/15/04 | Marco Berti, artist |
| 08/29/04 | Pattie Lockard, singer |
| 09/12/04 | Jesse Townley, Berkeley City Council candidate, punk musician, radio DJ |
| 09/15/04 | Dr. Oblivious, musician, activist. RNC protest and more |
| 09/19/04 | Tomas Michaud, New World Flamenco Jazz Guitarist |
| 10/03/04 | Audrey Auld, singer/songwriter and Mezz |
| 10/07/04 | Jessica Burks, singer/songwriter from Iowa |
| 10/10/04 | Dr. Oblivious, part 2, musician, activist. RNC protest and more |
| 10/24/04 | Good for Cows, rock band |
| 11/14/04 | Robert Kandell and Allyson Wyenn, One Taste Urban Retreat Center |
| 11/21/04 | Helen Von Mott, wrestler |
| 11/28/04 | Santa Frank and Erika the Elf, holiday show |
| 12/12/04 | All-Star Jam with Dr. O, Dr. Gruve, Michael Peppe, Andy Poisoner!, Erika Shaver-Nelson, Goeff Walker, Keith Adams, Frank Moore |

## 2005

| | |
|---|---|
| 01/09/05 | Tanya Fermin, singer |
| 01/16/05 | Lori B, singer/songwriter |
| 01/30/05 | +Dog+ jam with Steve and Bobby, with Frank Moore and Erika Shaver-Nelson |
| 02/06/05 | The Slow Poisoner!, singer/songwriter |
| 02/13/05 | Sue Supriano, "Steppin' Out of Babylon" producer and host |
| 03/06/05 | Chris Odell, "Why is public access underused?" Producer of the TV show, *That Last Show Sucked* |
| 03/13/05 | Nicole Daedone and Robert Kandell, One Taste Urban Retreat Center |
| 03/27/05 | "Easter Killing Jam" with Dr. O, Dr. Gruve, Carly, Frank Moore and Erika Shaver-Nelson |
| 03/28/05 | John Sinclair, poet, writer, and political activist from Amsterdam |

| | |
|---|---|
| 05/15/05 | Chris Odell, "Chris asks Frank Moore questions that all his friends want to know the answers to." Producer of TV show *That Last Show Sucked* |
| 05/22/05 | Michael Peppe, musician, performance artist |
| 05/29/05 | Leuren Moret, geoscientist, activist |
| 06/11/05 | Barbara Tedlock, cultural anthropologist, shamanic healer and diviner, author of *The Woman in the Shaman's Body: Reclaiming the Feminine in Religion and Medicine* and Dennis Tedlock, Anthropology Professor, New York State |
| 06/12/05 | Will Psoma, Orange Sunshine Superman |
| 06/19/05 | Jam with John The Baker, Lob, Erika Shaver-Nelson and Frank Moore |
| 06/25/05 | Brian Bonz and the Fort Green District, rock band from Brooklyn, New York |
| 06/26/05 | Shelley Doty, musician, singer/songwriter |
| 07/10/05 | Gerald Smith, radio host, activist, former Black Panther |
| 07/17/05 | Aimee Allison, Conscientious Objector in the Persian Gulf War and Oakland City Council Member |
| 08/21/05 | Kriss Worthington, Berkeley City Council Member |
| 08/28/05 | Russell Shuttleworth, aka Dr. Gruve, Anthropologist, LUVeR DJ |
| 09/04/05 | The Duct Tape Mafia, punk band |
| 09/18/05 | Shelley Doty X-Tet, band |
| 09/25/05 | "The Blues Chaos Jam" with Tomek Von Schachtmayer, Dr. Gruve, Michael Peppe, Erika Shaver-Nelson and Frank Moore |
| 10/02/05 | Psycho Myko, hip-hop artist, producer |
| 10/09/05 | Lob, Part 1, Instagon Director, Thee Instagon Foundation, artist, poet, musician |
| 11/12/05 | Janet Bates and Instruments of Change, folk band |
| 11/13/05 | Julie Tan and Julene Jones, musicians |
| 11/20/05 | Urban Monks, rock band |
| 12/04/05 | Carl Bryant, union organizer, letter carrier and public access TV host/producer |
| 12/11/05 | Phil Johnson/Roadside Attraction, musician |
| 12/18/05 | Lob, Part 2, Instagon Director, Thee Instagon Foundation, artist, poet, musician |

## 2006

| | |
|---|---|
| 01/22/06 | Happy Turtle, band |
| 01/29/06 | Fiyawata, hip-hop band |
| 02/12/06 | "Sexy Jelly Jam", with Frank Moore, Erika Shaver-Nelson, Dr. Gruve, Michael Peppe, Tomek Von Schacter, Shiloh Callisonn and Walter Funk |
| 02/19/06 | Kriss Worthington, Berkeley City Council Member and Jesse Townley, activist, musician, past City Council Candidate, "Passion Politics" effecting change via the local level |
| 02/26/06 | Ron Jones, performance artist |
| 03/09/06 | Pamela Walker, artist, actress, author |
| 03/19/06 | Daniel Lippencott, "Splintered Tree" |
| 04/02/06 | Javier Prato, video maker from Los Angeles |
| 04/30/06 | O.N.E., hip-hop artist |

| | |
|---|---|
| 05/11/06 | Russell Shuttleworth's Class: "Critical Perspectives on Disability and Sexuality" |
| 05/21/06 | Tha Archivez aka Kene-J, hip-hop artist |
| 05/26/06 | Big Fellas, rock band from La Jolla, California |
| 05/28/06 | Drats!!!, rock band from Oregon |
| 06/11/06 | Organic Flood, rock band from Grass Valley, California |
| 07/09/06 | Bell the Cat, rock band from Forestville, California |
| 07/30/06 | John Sinclair, from Amsterdam, poet, writer, and political activist, with Jim Epstein |
| 08/06/06 | Christopher Robin, poet, zine publisher from Santa Cruz, California |
| 08/12/06 | Steve Messina and Dave Diamond of Blow Up Hollywood with Chris Messina, rock band from New York |
| 08/13/06 | Stefan Rosenzweig, attorney |
| 08/20/06 | Jack Hirschman and Agneta Falk, poets |
| 08/26/06 | Two Loons for Tea, rock band from Seattle, Washington |
| 08/27/06 | Jesse Townley, "Passion Politics, pt.2" |
| 09/25/06 | Traciana Graves, singer with Erik Nielsen and Dave, musicians from New York |
| 10/05/06 | Angelique, singer from Southern California |
| 10/08/06 | Billy Armi, actor, screenwriter |
| 10/15/06 | Latent Anxiety, musician from South America |
| 10/22/06 | Walter Groditski of comedy doo-wop duo Chaston and Groditski |
| 11/05/06 | Esmerelda Strange, one woman band |
| 11/19/06 | Ann Cohen, musician, poet, artist, wife of Allen Cohen, founder and editor of *The San Francisco Oracle* |
| 11/26/06 | Year of the Wildcat, rock band |
| 12/12/06 | Sandy Myers-Kepler, CEO of Global-ID Consulting from Fairfield, Iowa |

## 2007

| | |
|---|---|
| 01/07/07 | "Lessons from Richmond's Tent City" with Gerald Smith, Freddie Jackson, Wilma Miller, Rev. Andre Shumake, Albert Lee, Jubrieel Ahkile |
| 01/11/07 | Dog Swan, TV show host, musician, artist |
| 01/14/07 | G Smooth, hip-hop artist, musician with Gerald Smith and Deandre Brown |
| 02/25/07 | Stephen Emanuel, from Southern California and the "Legs Wide Open Jam" with Frank Moore, Stephen Emanuel and Erika Shaver-Nelson |
| 03/04/07 | Pamela Holm, aka DJ Pixie, Pirate Cat Radio |
| 03/11/07 | Bethany Stevens, disability culture nerd, sexologist with Leroy Moore, poet |
| 03/18/07 | Marilyn Bagshaw, photographer |
| 03/25/07 | John the Baker, musician, activist |
| 04/03/07 | Eddie Williams and Gerald Smith, "The S.F. 8" |
| 04/06/07 | Kristi Martel, musician, singer/songwriter |
| 04/15/07 | Eva Sweeney, author of *Queers on Wheels: The essential guide for the physically disabled GLBTQ community* |
| 04/22/07 | Shannon Flattery and Bob Ellison, *Touchable Stories* |
| 05/06/07 | House Jam with Tomek Von Schachtmayer, Erika Shaver-Nelson, Frank Moore |
| 05/10/07 | Russell Shuttleworth's Class: "Critical Perspectives on Disability and Sexuality" |

| | |
|---|---|
| 05/13/07 | Kriss Worthington, Berkeley City Council Member |
| 05/20/07 | The Julia Lau Band |
| 05/27/07 | Sara Wingate Gray, the Itinerant Poetry Librarian from the United Kingdom |
| 07/11/07 | Pete Holly, musician from Boise, Idaho |
| 07/22/07 | Lindell Reeves, blues musician |
| 07/29/07 | Koz and friends, variety show |
| 08/05/07 | Mr. Lucky, entertainer |
| 08/12/07 | "Surreal Hot Pepper Jam" with Frank Moore, Erika Shaver-Nelson, Tomek Von Schachtmayer and Kay Griffin |
| 08/19/07 | Dr. Richard Kerbavaz, Frank's ear, nose and throat doctor |
| 08/24/07 | Delmark Goldfarb, blues musician from Portland, Oregon with Kate |
| 08/26/07 | Carl Bryant, postal worker, social activist, grills Frank on his presidential platforms |
| 08/29/07 | East Bay Politix, Sinista Z and Ras Ceylon, hip-hop artists, with Gerald Smith |
| 09/03/07 | Cosmic Starfish, singer/songwriter from Los Angeles |
| 10/14/07 | Shelley Doty, musician |
| 11/04/07 | Tha Archivez, aka Kene-J, hip-hop artist |
| 11/18/07 | David Steinberg, photographer from Santa Cruz with Pleasure |
| 12/02/07 | Amber Gaia, singer/songwriter |
| 12/16/07 | LX Rudis Holiday Special, music |

## 2008

| | |
|---|---|
| 01/13/08 | +Dog+ from Los Angeles, Night Nurse from Sacramento, plus jam with all including Frank Moore and Erika Shaver-Nelson |
| 01/27/08 | Carol Swann and Vitali Kononov, Moving On Center |
| 02/10/08 | Bert Glick, poet |
| 03/02/08 | Larry Rodriguez recording session, music jam with Frank Moore and Erika Shaver-Nelson |
| 03/30/08 | Adnan Marquez-Borbon, musician, plus jam with Frank Moore |
| 04/06/08 | Art Lessing, Flower Vato and Erin Hamster, musicians from Sacramento |
| 04/13/08 | Richard Winger, Ballot Access |
| 05/02/08 | Richard Kerbavaz, "How to Reform the Healthcare System" |
| 05/11/08 | Steve McCutcheon with Gerald Smith, the Hidden History of the Black Panthers |
| 05/18/08 | Kristi Martel, singer/songwriter with Kim Leadford from Rhode Island |
| 06/04/08 | Russell Shuttleworth's "Sexuality in Illness and Disability" online class, University of Sydney, Australia. |
| 06/22/08 | Lee Gerstmann, poet |
| 06/27/08 | Phog Masheeen with Bill, music, plus jam with Frank Moore |
| 06/29/08 | Ericka Huggins, Professor of Women's Studies, poet, writer, former Black Panther Party leader, former director of the Oakland Community School formed by the Black Panthers, on the occasion of the Oakland Community School Anniversary |
| 07/13/08 | Cosmic Starfish, singer/songwriter from Los Angeles |
| 07/20/08 | +Dog+, featuring Steve Davis, Eddie, Hailey Heckler, Andrew Surber, Lob, |

|          | Tate, Frank Moore, Erika Shaver-Nelson, and Jen Wilson |
|----------|--------|
| 07/27/08 | Kevin Ohnsman, Global Peace Foundation |
| 08/10/08 | Hot Sex Jam with Larry Rodriquez (Flower Vato), Dan Quillan (Art Lessing), Troy Mighty (Dead Western), Walter Funk, Erika Shaver-Nelson, Jen Wilson, Frank Moore |
| 09/08/08 | Joe Deninzon and Stratospheerius, jazz/rock band from New York |
| 09/14/08 | Dorado, rock band from Portland, Oregon |
| 09/15/08 | The Visitations, rock band from Athens, Georgia |
| 10/26/08 | Sticks and Stones, rock band from San Francisco |
| 11/02/08 | David Gans, musician, DJ, writer |
| 11/09/08 | Tha Archivez aka Kene-J, hip-hop artist |
| 11/16/08 | Phog Masheeen Jam with Phog Masheeen from Los Angeles, Erika Shaver-Nelson, Jen Wilson and Frank Moore |

## 2009

| 01/11/09 | Bell the Cat, rock band from Forestville, California |
|----------|--------|
| 02/08/09 | Francine Manuel, physical therapist |
| 02/15/09 | Tha Archivez, hip-hop artist |
| 03/01/09 | Corsica, rock band from San Francisco |
| 03/08/09 | Marjorie Swann Edwin, a founding member of the Committee for Nonviolent Action (CNVA), a radical pacifist organization formed in 1957 to resist the U.S. government's program of nuclear weapons testing |
| 03/08/09 | Penny Arcade, performance artist from New York |
| 04/05/09 | The Simple Things, band |
| 04/12/09 | Marjorie Swann Edwin, a founding member of the Committee for Nonviolent Action |
| 06/21/09 | Ava Bird, poet from Los Angeles |
| 07/19/09 | Steve Taylor-Ramirez, folk musician |
| 07/31/09 | Carl Bryant, "The Battle for Public Access" |
| 08/02/09 | Judy Gumbo Albert, an original member of the 1960s countercultural anti-war group known as the Yippies, author |
| 08/08/09 | Magick Orchids, band from Los Angeles |
| 08/16/09 | Shelley Doty, musician |
| 08/19/09 | Imra, band from Portland, Oregon |
| 09/13/09 | Jonathan Krop, graphic designer and Barb |
| 09/16/09 | The Oscar Grant Panel with Gerald Smith |
| 09/21/09 | Seth Faergolzia of Dufus, musician from New York |
| 09/29/09 | Alyssa Lee and Galin_dog aka Guillermo Galindo, POW POW Action Art Festival organizers, San Francisco |
| 10/04/09 | Nellie Wilson, founder, Sacred Touch School |
| 10/11/09 | Beltaine's Fire, hip-hop band |
| 10/12/09 | The Family Curse, band from Seattle, Washington |
| 11/01/09 | boatclub, rock band |
| 11/08/09 | Kevin Becketti, Jawbone Press |
| 11/17/09 | Tracy Rosenberg, Media Alliance |

11/29/09    Richie Unterberger, journalist and author, *White Light, White Heat: The Velvet Underground Day-By-Day*

12/06/09    Jhon Thumb, musician

## 2010

01/17/10    Persephone's Bees, band plus Jonathan Krop and Barb Orr

02/14/10    Max Good and Nathan Wollman, filmmakers, Vigilante Film

03/09/10    Roger Sussman, Sussman Communications from Bellingham, Washington and John the Baker

04/11/10    "Hot Chocolate Fudge Jam" with Tomek Von Schachtmayer, Travis Munn, Marz Estes, Tha Archivez, Frank Moore and Erika Shaver-Nelson

05/02/10    Tha Archivez and Phatboy, hip-hop artists

## 2011

02/06/11    Philip Huang, performance artist

03/07/11    Kyra Rice, dancer, performance artist

04/13/11    Todd Clouser's A Love Electric, jazz/rock band from Mexico City

05/22/11    The Golden Path, musical trio

06/19/11    Deborah Crooks, singer/songwriter with Kwame Copeland, guitarist

08/16/11    Monte Mar, rock band from Los Angeles

10/02/11    The Golden Path, rock band

11/25/11    Toni Ivashkov, performance artist, and Pollenland, band from Los Angeles

## 2012

01/29/12    A Winter's Morning, band from Seattle, Washington

03/18/12    Sasha Cagen, author and Michael

# Post-LUVeR

## 2012

04/30/12    La Fleur Fatale, rock band from Sweden

06/10/12    Katie Clover Band

06/17/12    Black Angel, rock band

07/29/12    The Raven, author and her son, D-Way, radio show co-hosts

08/19/12    Tha Archivez, hip-hop artist

10/14/12    Ann Cohen, musician, poet, artist, wife of Allen Cohen, *The San Francisco Oracle*

11/25/12    Natty and Dany, fuckforforest.com, from Norway

12/16/12    Djin Aquarian, member of Brotherhood of the Source and Ryan Marchamp, musicians from Mount Shasta

## 2013

05/19/13    "Hot Marshmallow Jam" with Tomek Von Schachtmayer, Tha Archivez, Erika Shaver-Nelson and Frank Moore

# About Frank Moore

Frank Moore was an American performance artist, shaman, teacher, poet, essayist, painter, musician, and internet/television personality who experimented in art, performance, ritual, and shamanistic teaching from the late 1960s until his death in 2013 in Berkeley, California.

Moore is perhaps most well known as one of the NEA-funded artists targeted by Jesse Helms and the GAO (General Accounting Office) in the early 1990s for doing art that was labeled "obscene". Frank Moore was featured in the 1988 cult film Mondo New York, which chronicled the leading performance artists of that period. He is well known for long (5–48 hours) ritualistic performances with audience participation, nudity, and eroticism. But he has also become well known for his influential writings on performance, art, life, and cultural subversion, for his historic influence on the San Francisco Bay Area music and performance scene, and more recently for his performance/video archive on Vimeo.com that has been viewed by over 15 million people worldwide.

Moore coined the word, "eroplay" to describe physical play between adults released from the linear goals of sex and orgasm. He explored this, and similar concepts in performance and ritual as a way for people to connect on a deep human level with each other beyond the social and cultural expectations and limitations, and as a way to melt isolation between people.

Moore has been an underground counter-culture hero and artistic inspiration for decades. He was born with cerebral palsy, could not walk or talk, and wrote books, directed plays, directed, acted in and edited films, regularly gave poetry readings, played piano, sang in ensemble music jams, and continued to lead bands in hard core punk clubs up and down the west coast until his death. He also produced a large collection of original oil and digital paintings that have been shown across the United States and in Canada. Moore communicated using a laser-pointer and a board of letters, numbers, and commonly used words.

Performance artist Annie Sprinkle considers Moore one of her teachers, and Moore performed with a host of performance and punk figures of the underground since the 1970s like Barbara Smith, Linda Sibio, The Feederz, and Dirk Dirksen - The Pope of Punk.

Frank Moore first came to be known in the 1970s as the creator of the popular cabaret show, *The Outrageous Beauty Revue*. In the 1980s he became one of the United States' foremost performance artists. In 1992 he was voted Best Performance Artist by the *San Francisco Bay Guardian*. In the early 1990s he was targeted by Senator Jesse Helms. From 1991 to 1999 Frank Moore published and edited the acclaimed underground zine, *The Cherotic (r)Evolutionary*.

In addition to his books, *Cherotic Magic*, *Art of a Shaman*, *Chapped Lap*, *Skin Passion* and numerous other self-published pieces, Frank Moore was widely published in various art and other periodicals. In artist Pamela Kay Walker's book, *Moving Over the Edge*, Moore is one of the artists featured as having "greatly impacted me and many people through their artistic expression and their lives."

Frank Moore's award-winning video works have shown throughout the U.S. and Canada, and in 2001 Moore began producing shows for Berkeley's public access channel, Berkeley Community Media, Channel 28. His shows continue to play several times each week.

In 2011, Frank launched his online performance and video retrospective on Vimeo. At the same time, he created the EROART group featuring videos by eroart artists from all over the world.

Frank Moore's Web of All Possibilities, www.eroplay.com, features a growing archive of his audio, video, visual and written work, as well as the work of other artists. He founded Love Underground Visionary Revolution (LUVeR) in 1999, a webstation combining live streaming and on-demand libraries of audio and video programming, described by Moore as a "non-corporate, d.i.y., totally uncensored, noncommercial, nonprofit internet-only communal collective with 24-hour 'live' programming (by amazing people) with 'no-limits' content." LUVeR ran until 2012.

In 2006, Moore announced his candidacy for the 2008 election for President of the United States. He became a qualified write-in candidate in 25 states. His campaign was responsible for reforming the write-in candidate qualifications and procedures in many states. His platform videos are available on YouTube.

Moore also hosted his regular internet show, "Frank Moore's Shaman's Den". Moore described it as a show that "will arouse, inspire, move, threaten you, not with sound bites, but with a two-hour (usually longer) feast of live streaming video. You might get an in-studio concert of bands from around the world ... or poetry reading ... or an in-depth conversation about politics, art, music, and LIFE with extremely dangerous people! But then you may see beautiful women naked dancing erotically. You never know, because you are in The Shaman's Den with Frank Moore." Video and audio archives of all of these Shaman's Den shows are available online.

Frank Moore performed regularly in the San Francisco Bay Area up until his death.

His students and the people influenced by his life/work continue his vision.

# Frank Moore Online

**Frank Moore's Web Of All Possibilities**
http://www.eroplay.com

**The Shaman's Cave**
Performance archives, writings, articles and more
http://www.eroplay.com/Cave/shaman.html

**Frank Moore's Shaman's Den Archives**
Includes an archive of this online show
http://www.eroplay.com/underground/shamansden.html

**Books by Frank Moore**
http://www.eroplay.com/books

**Vimeo.com**
Online video and performance retrospective
http://www.vimeo.com/frankmoore

**Vimeo.com - EROART**
A group created by Frank on Vimeo.com for EROART
http://www.vimeo.com/groups/eroart

**Vimeo.com - Eroplay Featured Artists**
http://www.vimeo.com/eroplay

**Frank Moore's Painting Gallery**
http://www.eroplay.com/Cave/painting-slideshow/paintings.html

**The Cherotic (r)Evolutionary**
http://www.eroplay.com/contents.html

**2008 Presidential Campaign Platform Videos**
http://www.youtube.com/user/frankmooreforprez08/videos

**Frank Moore on Wikipedia**
http://en.wikipedia.org/wiki/Frank_Moore_(performance_artist)

*Frank Moore, 2008. Photo by Michael LaBash.*